In The Eye
of the
Hurricane

The Inside Story of a Disciple's Journey

Devakant

Acknowledgements

Special Thanks to RajRishi
for the encouragement since the beginning
to write it all down.

I wish to thank Ma Prem Chanchal
for her constant support and timely wisdom
and encouragement along the way.

Thanks also to Juan and Monica
for their joyful support, and putting it in perspective,
with constant laughter throughout all the process.

Dedication

Dedicated to Beloved Osho, having visited this
planet for a brief time, who touched my soul
and opened my heart and mind to unthinkable
mysteries; and to the community of thousands
of fellow travelers who travelled with Him for
awhile on an unimaginable journey,
and continue on their way to infinity.

PROLOGUE

We are what we think…
All that we are arises with our thoughts…
by our thoughts we make the world…

Gautama the Buddha, c. 500 BC

Dear Reader: These following stories, happened to me as 'factually' as I have written them. All of my perceptions are purely my own, subject to my own predilections, particularly those involving the relationship that I have had with that mysterious and multi-dimensional being that is now called 'Osho'. These stories are my 'dreams', although experienced in my waking life, in the manner that we human beings commonly agree on a certain dualistic framework in which to dream collectively. That framework involves up-down, left-right, yes-no, now-then, black/white…through this we interact, in a very limited but manageably comfortable way, with the unspeakable infinity that surrounds us, and which can be utterly terrifying in its un-fathomability to our minds which crave security and a sense of control. Through this mental framework made of words, we make our passage on this mysterious earth a little more manageable. The light photons striking the retinas of my eyes and the sound waves entering my ears passed through the filter system of my own memories, becoming the images in my brain; certainly they are colored by my own colors, and the same dramas which have unfolded perhaps look different when viewed from a different point of view, as numerous and different as there are people on this vast earth. I do not dispute that. Certainly there are people with more interesting stories, and can tell them far better than I. But, this is my story, as I have experienced it. I hope it can in some small way be of use to you in your journey of return to the infinite.

Devakant
October 1, 2018
Pucon, Chile

CHAPTER 1

First Turnings

All Beings are from the very beginning Buddhas

Hakuin Zen-ji, c. 1850

The Void needs no reliance; Mahamudra rests on naught.
Without making an effort, but remaining natural,
One can break the yoke, thus gaining liberation.

Tilopa-Song of Mahamudra, c.1200 A.D.

As I begin this tale, I am living in a small house on the south coast of Japan. Softly the waves strike the shore today, a dull and constant murmuring, just over the stone sea-wall at the edge of the little garden outside my painting place, on the edge of this long and empty beach. The sea is a grey green quietude, which disappears into the ashen sky before becoming a horizon. The 5 boats offshore sit bobbing gently in a half circle, just in front of my perch on the lonely stretch of sand, punctuated only by the cries of the sea-eagles which gather and swoop through-out the day. They are the masters of the air in this small fishing village on the southeast coast of Japan.

In the small boats 30 yards away, they only show themselves occasionally, one slim female figure pulling at an anchor rope, another coming up for air after long minutes, yet another disappearing with a flash of fins like a dolphin or humpback whale. They are the 'Ama-san', the women of the sea, 'umi-no-onna'. Diving in the stretches of water slightly darkened by the reef below, they rise to the surface with sea urchins in their hands, and pop them in the floating baskets they keep on the water's surface.

I've seen their pictures in Tokyo, in the old book shops: Centuries-old Hokusai woodblock prints of dripping women half-naked with knives in their mouths, sea-creatures half-disguised in human form, a baby on their hip, chained to the sea for the duration of their time on this earth. But, here, bobbing just a few yards in front of me on this whispering sea, the picture takes on a new dimension. They wear black wetsuits now, the hair is cropped short, and they use rubber fins, but not much else is changed. They spend more time under the water than in the air, and I suppose the world they see is as good or better than the one I walk in each day: No cars, no neon Pachinko★ parlors

Women of the Sea...the."Ama-san".. on the south coast of Japan

or crowded subways...just the silent water and the undulating seaweed, the constant play of light and darkness, shadow and form amidst the rocks, revealing the small prizes for which they dive all day, purple spiny creatures, looking not very edible. But on the sale of this they manage to maintain their lives, through the centuries , wars, earthquakes, fires, tsunamis, revolutions, evolution, atom-bombs, and the changes of relentless time that have marked the life on these islands.

My journey begins with a day 57 years ago....

It was 7:45 in the morning; a beautiful sunny day, with the sky a clear blue, and the shining white mountains all around in the distance. Back then almost all the days were beautiful and sunny, as it was Southern California before all the cars came. The air was filled on that day, and every day in the winter, with the perfume of orange blossoms, which saturated one's senses with an overpowering feeling of delight and joy. The skies, as I remember them at that time, were always blue; Really blue! It wasn't the kind of white pale blueness with brown near the horizon that is seen today on 'clear' days, but rather a deep cerulean blue disappearing into nearly indigo straight overhead. It overwhelmed my mind with its depth and I would stand and stare straight upward until I would loose my balance and fall over, as 6-year-old boys are sometimes prone to do.

I was walking to school, and my young mind was elated to be walking to school, which I found to be rather fun and full of surprises. It was a lot more interesting than being alone at home, that's for sure. I can remember the sound of my lunch pail covered with astronaut photos jiggling in my hand as I crossed the street about 50 yards from my house. It was a normal day in January, 1961.

Then, with no warning, and for no apparent reason, 'IT' happened! Suddenly, in the middle of the street, the VOID happened to me. Suddenly, I was not this little kid happily walking to the 1st grade of school, nor was I the boy who had all the experiences and memories and dreams of home and school and friends and toys. Even my name, my body, my thoughts, all were suddenly so far away, as if they belonged to someone else, like a film-projector had been suddenly switched off, and there was only pitch black darkness. Silence: The GAP. There was no 'me'; there was not even 'NO me': No-one being, no-one not being; JUST being. ISNESS. How to describe it? There was no sense of time, or light, or form. But IT continued for most of the morning.

"I" somehow walked to school, took my place in the class, acted like all the other kids and answered roll call, but all of it was happening so far away, to somebody else. Slowly, somehow, without me doing anything about it or saying anything, everything returned to "normal", I never mentioned it to anyone. But it stayed deep inside me, a strange secret which I could not decipher.

Allow me, dear reader, to rewind the clock three months, to the first day of organized education in my young life. It had been memorable. I was in a Catholic school, in Riverside, California. The nuns who ran the school were very serious-looking in their long black 'habits', jet-black long dresses, with big white cardboard ovals in front, covering their chests, and a kind of white frame and tight band around their faces. It made them look a little bit like aliens, which was probably the intended effect. Definitely they weren't supposed to be motherly-types or glamorous-looking women. They were 'Franciscans', which was a lineage of people who claimed to adhere to the teachings of a very kindly and sincere person named St. Francis who lived 8 centuries before the beginning of this story, in a place called Italy. He used to talk to birds and wolves and basically loved everybody. That was about as far as one can get from some of those nuns that I knew. Some were Irish, some German, some Mexican, short and fiery and energetic, and some were sincere and kind and I presume well-intentioned, having chosen a life that in their minds was 'in service to God'. But some, actually quite a few of them, were rather dried up and bitter: amongst that select group were some who were quite adept at psychologically and physically terrorising little children.

Although they weren't 'bad people' as such, whatever that may be, I'm sure they had their good moments, but there were a few notorious 'big meanies' amongst them. One was the principal of the school, Sister Doretta. The very name would send shivers down the spines of young boys caught on the wrong side of the law, of which laws there were so many, it was nearly impossible to not be on the wrong side of it. This was one case in point, the very first day of school in September.

My home town Riverside sits on the edge of the great desert of California, where some of the hottest surface temperatures on planet earth have been recorded. September is a bit like being an egg in a frying pan on a cast-iron stove in Death Valley: Namely, its hot, about 120 degrees Fahrenheit some days. We had to wear uniforms, with ties, and 'real' shoes instead of sneakers, which was a kind of imprisonment for my 6-year old feet which were used to being free all year long in that desert climate. That day, was designated 'hot-dog day'. It was the day when there were hotdogs for lunch, a major event in our school. To keep the hot dogs from rotting before they got cooked, there was a kind of cooler with dry-ice in it; frozen carbon dioxide, which for little kids is a strange and mysterious substance, resembling ice, but instead of melting, it turns into smoke. So, some of the older kids got a hold of this and were tossing it around in fun at each other. When Sister Doretta found out about it, all hell broke loose. Suddenly our little school resembled Auschwitz, Stalag 17, or a Soviet Gulag. At 1 o'clock in the afternoon under the full heat of the blazing sun, 115 degrees in the shade, we were forced to line up outside the classroom in perfect order, and stand there, and stand there, and stand there, as the black-robed nuns patrolled the lines with sticks. There were 400 children in straight lines, the sun casting no shadows, coming straight down. An hour passed, maybe two. Little kids were dropping to the ground, face down in the dirt, passed out, unconscious. If you moved or slouched, one of the nuns would be prowling along the lines and would whack you with a pointer, a long hard wooden rod that really was not fun to get hit with. This memorable occasion was my introduction to organized education, and the message was clear: "Do what we want, whether or not we tell you what it is first…or, you're in BIG TROUBLE! We have total control over you."

In that school that I went to, the history books started with Adam and Eve, mentioned Columbus, Cortez, Vasco da Gama and ended with Harry Truman and a few phrases amounting to God bless America, making perfect sense, watertight and seamless. All is in its place, and the steady hum of life rolls on unimpeded in the pristine world of the "Truman Show". That's how life was in Southern California in the 1950s, all seemed perfectly in place, no dead bodies, nobody terribly sick, nothing too ugly, nothing too amazing. It was middle-class monotony all in pastel colors, every house a slight variation of the one next to it, every lawn well kept, every car running perfectly, old people disappear in cleansed aging homes hidden away somewhere, the streets are wide and the streetlights always functioning, between the shopping mall, the Macdonalds, the gas station, The 7-11, the Bank, and the occasional yearly journey to Disneyland, 20 miles away. Disneyland itself was a mythical dreamworld which took on monumental proportions in my young mind, something like 'heaven' or 'paradise'. In fact, I think I got it a little confused in my dreams, and I believed for a good while that Disneyland was where you go when you die if you are good.

As I was in a so-called religious school, the history lessons which were driven into us were not actually 'factual' about my demographic or genetic origins. They followed more the 'origin of the propaganda' that was being downloaded into me, the history of the religious ideas, without calling them such, as they were considered to be the unquestionable truth.

That being the case, my education continued along the lines of the Bible, a book which was apparently written by God, or in other words, The Creator of the Universe. Never knowing actually what was 'God', still I fervently tried to believe in this invisible entity of whom everyone was assuring me had written the Book, which eventually I realized was not the story of the universe but was the history of the Jewish religion and then, the Catholic Christian one. Apparently this same entity named 'God', started everything off all of a sudden, then within a week he had made everything in the universe, except humans. So he made a guy named Adam, and then a bit later from one of Adams bones, he made a woman named Eve, and from them came everybody else, although they only had two sons, one of which killed the other. So, it wasn't really clear where everybody else came from after that, as there was just Adam, Eve, and one son.

The original couple had a happy life in a paradise, until they ate an apple that they were told not to eat, by God; they had been convinced to do so by a talking snake that had been a slightly earlier creation of this same God, but God didn't like this snake anymore and they were now enemies, although God had made him and all the aspects of the whole universe that he lived in. After eating this said apple, the original couple had to put clothes on and leave paradise and go to work. So, it seemed a little out-of-control, the whole thing to me, like things didn't really unfold the way this God envisioned, even though he had made everything, knew everything, and could see everything, and he was perfect. But through the course of the first 3 or 4 years of my schooling, a direct line of authority was drawn from God, via Adam, Abraham, Moses, the Jewish kings, Jesus Christ, European civilization, and then, in rapid order, the Founding Fathers of The United States, Abraham Lincoln, and Harry Truman.

This story being downloaded into me continued in a similar seamless way regarding current politics; As for world problems, I heard about 'World Wars', usually won by the Marines; They were dramatic events, full of heroism, and we always win. There had been, so far, 2 of these mega-tragic events, and now it seems we were 'waiting' for the third one, in the hope that perhaps it can be avoided, or at least delayed. The Japanese and the Germans were bad some years ago, now they are o.k. and the Russians are bad. We always win these terrible wars because, actually, God is on our side. God is that aforementioned entity with a long beard up in heaven who made Adam and Eve, and since then watches everybody and keeps track of all the bad things you do, to see whether or not you can go to heaven when you die, which is the nicest place you can imagine, or, if you are a creep, you go to hell, where it's very hot, and unpleasant, even hotter than Riverside. And here on earth, those nasty wars, well, they are terrible, but thank the Good Lord that we win them! But although he used to talk to people in the beginning, it seems God hasn't really spoken to anybody in a few thousand years.

Something of this didn't quite sit right with me. I often thought, "If God is really on our side, and he says, 'Thou shalt not kill', then why do those wars happen, and we have to kill? If he set up the whole universe, Why do bad things happen? If he made up all the rules and everything, and made the garden of Eden, with the apple-tree, and the apple, and the snake, and Adam and Eve, he set up the whole show, so how come his son had to get nailed on a cross to fulfill the rules in the books that he wrote, because someone ate an apple? After all, those books are 'the word of God'; that means that He wrote them. If He made all the rules, that's a funny way to set it up", I thought.

It's like making a monopoly game in which you make the dice, and the dice-board, and the minds of all the people playing, so you know everything; you know what the dice are going to say when they stop rolling, yet if somebody rolls the dice, your son gets nailed up on a cross and has to be dead for 3 days, then he comes back for awhile and disappears in heaven for a couple of thousand years. But He's going to come back again, and everybody who didn't do what he said will burn in hell for eternity, and the people who aren't Catholics will end up in 'Limbo', a kind of Twilight Zone where it isn't bad and it isn't good, and there is no way out. (This place called 'Limbo' seemed a lot like Riverside to me.)

Well, after this download of information into my young and innocent bio-computer continued for many years, my mind, having trustfully, passively, and willingly consumed the greater part of this 'educational material' in bulk format, naturally and quietly reached a moment in which it simply rejected the sum total of it wholesale around the age of 15. It was a kind of mental indigestion. Seeing the idiocy of all my schoolteachers and all the accepted authorities being completely wrong and out-of-touch with the obvious manifestations of 'reality' evident everywhere, and they obviously had a dysfunctional vision about nearly everything, I realized all this information did not reflect a true working idea of our present collective situation, which seemed to me to be more and more a mess. And thus, I began to critically question and doubt everybody, everything and anything which I thought I 'knew', and seek ways and means to root out these false ideas from my psychological operating system. It was the beginning of a lengthy process. Thus I began a process of absorption of ideas which were more acceptable to my reasoning mind and feeling nature. It took the next 20 years of Yoga, Transcendental Meditation, Dynamic Meditation, Zazen, several hundred therapy sessions, encounter groups, re-birthings, acupuncture, color-puncture, Reiki and Bio-energetic sessions to wipe this entire mess in my brain data banks relatively clean, and start over again 'from scratch'. That is, so to say, I stopped subscribing to the ideas which were given to me before I had the capacity to resist them, and I began to doubt everything I had learned from books and authorities. I slowly started to perceive, think and form new opinions with no fixed idea beforehand as to what is real and what is unreal anymore. The only criteria which seemed valid to me to accept or reject new ideas is what I could actually see with my own eyes or feel with my senses, including that quiet and internal feeling of 'agreement' which arises in the center of the chest when words that ring with truth are spoken. I trusted nothing, I doubted everything, and I felt as if I were floating on a small melting ice floe in the middle of the ocean of lies, grasping at any messages in bottles passing by to slake my incessant thirst for information.

I slowly started to find here and there bits of information from more 'reliable' sources , that is, those not officially endorsed from my local indoctrination center, called 'the Catholic Church' or the State Board of Education. I sought and found obscure books from Ancient Chinese mystics, hermits in the woods of early America, archaic Russian novelists and Tibetan mystics, Mexican shamans and Indian ascetics; I began searching like a wanderer in the desert blindly seeking water. I had no idea who or where these beings came from or how they came to know what they knew, but I could feel when they were speaking the truth, as opposed to all the empty words which had already been pumped into me and no longer held any meaning for me.

Consider it as a brief preamble to my story, in locating myself as a sentient being, like billions of other travelers on this vast sea of infinity, we need an address to locate ourselves at a certain place and time, which makes our journey across the void seem a little less unfathomable and slightly more comfortable for a brief moment. All history is mythological; it is partial explanations which serve to give us a temporary identity in a time, place, society, and structural framework in which to live and act. None of it is absolute truth. It is a working and ever-evolving 'theorem'. The myths I was given while my young mouth was open like a little bird needing nourishment, were particularly toxic and designed to provoke an attitude of victimhood, confusion, and a life of 'filling up the void with even greater emptiness', that is, materialism and unchecked consumerism. I prefer to give myself another evolving myth, one that somewhat acknowledges and respects the tremendous and constant efforts made by 'ALL THAT IS' to constantly create and perfect ever more with each moment of continuous creation, this divine tiny blue speck of a planet in the infinite ocean of existence.

One fine sunny day in the middle of winter, my consciousness, being, or essence, that which I call 'myself', found itself in a little and nearly helpless human body being cared for by other bigger humans, until the day when I would be deposited in a 'school' to receive the download of a large quantity of information generally assumed to be the 'story of my origins'.

'By chance', I was born and grew up in the place called 'America'. It is called that supposedly because of random events of which nobody quite agrees upon. According to the 'official story' told in my history book, It seems that 500 years ago, a certain Italian mapmaker who had never set foot on a sailing ship and had thus never seen the landmass he was now drawing on the newly expanded communally accepted view of THE

WORLD, needed a name for this newly 'discovered' landmass. As the story goes, having a burst of inspiration, and being Italian, he named it after himself, namely, 'Amerigo'.

But actually, that particular landmass hadn't actually been 'discovered' by this European mapmaker, as we might normally think of that word 'discovery'. Rather, it was at that time in the process of being rather aggressively invaded, conquered and subjugated by the people who chose to think of it as a 'discovery' rather than a robbery and pillage. Coincidentally, these were the same people who printed and emphatically promoted this same 'Bible' that was given to me in my childhood. As for the 'discovery of America', it was like 'discovering' a new car in your neighbor's driveway, shooting him, and putting the car in your garage; and then taking over his house and making his kids work for you for the rest of their lives. But because he doesn't go to the same indoctrination-center, that is, 'church', that you do, it's 'o.k.' to do that. Also, he is a different color, much darker than you, and he doesn't speak your language, so, he obviously isn't really human and doesn't need the car, according to your priest, your friends, family, and relations and colleagues at work.

In fact, the aforementioned continent newly 'discovered' by these ever-more-greedy-and-cruel Europeans with their Bibles, was already named long before their arrival on those sandy shores, AMARAKA, a word surprisingly similar to 'America'. This Amaraka is in Quechua, the pre-Colombian maternal language of the Andes, which means: 'The place where reins the Lord of the Sky' , or, in another way of saying it, 'The Land of the Immortals'. The Legends which have been preserved orally for several thousand years in that very place by the people who have been continuously living there since time immemorial before these Europeans came, has it that the name was given many thousands of years ago, by survivors of the cataclysm of Mu, a great continent and advanced civilization which existed long before the last ice ages covering the planet, which sank into the

Pacific Ocean, leaving its traces as the volcanos distributed here and there in Polynesia and Indonesia, and the inexplicable stone pyramids, huge statues and sunken temples hundreds of feet under water found throughout that part of the world and subsequently ignored by a century or two of 'modern archaeologists', who just don't know where to file the information, as it would destroy all their doctoral papers, scholastic funding, and foregone conclusions, ...not to mention, their Bibles.

For 500 years there continued unabated the European subjugation and plundering and destruction of the nature and humanity of this continent AMARAKA, now slightly changed to 'America'. Eventually a large social collective was formed by the descendants of these Europeans, and it was called 'The USA', which would become the dominant player on the world stage throughout the entirety of my brief lifetime, mostly because it had a particular knack at making large quantities of guns, cannons, ships, airplanes and missiles, the various implements used in the most recent mass events of pathological reciprocal destruction, commonly known as 'wars'. I landed there, in that social collective, as a tiny drop in the vast wave of human embryos which arrived in the country of the USA from 'The Source of Everything' after the cataclysmic episode of collective insanity and reciprocal destruction formally known as 'World War II'.

Almost every young male alive at that time in that country was involved in that catastrophe in one way or another. This country, the USA, was commonly thought of as 'the Winner' of that collective cataclysmic insanity. After 4 years of hell or relentless boredom, the entire generation of young men of that country having been shipped here and there all over the world to kill and maim others of their kind from different countries, were all sent home to where they came from on the continent of North America and they joined with female others of similar age, most of which were also involved in producing destructive materials for that collective insanity or bandaging the wounds of those who were injured in the fray. These newly found eager genetic mating partners, wishing to forget the violent events of the last 4 years of madness as quickly as possible, formed themselves into small separated social units, called 'nuclear families', doing what is generally referred to as 'procreation' as quickly and thoroughly and repetitively as possible, thus bringing forth rather rapidly a large new generation, numbering in the many millions, of similar beings, known commonly as the 'Baby Boom'. This 'Boom' was a wave of new human beings on the North American continent of which I am a part, and I say this as neither good nor bad, simply a fact.

The particular place in America where I was born was named, 'California-the-Golden-State'. At some moment in the dim past of my very early childhood, probably before the age of 3, I found myself with the distinct idea reinforced by every adult person who would speak to me, and they did that rather forcefully with their rather large faces stuck very close to mine, actually overshadowing the view of the sky from my now rather confining baby-stroller, that I was particularly blessed to be living in what was the best place in the world, and the best part of that best place, Southern California. Much like the intellectuals of the Middle Ages saw their cosmos/universe as revolving around a flat earth with them in the very middle of it, so I saw the universe itself radiating outward from the center of Los Angeles, as the best of all places in the best of all times, and everyone everywhere else in the world was basically looking at my homeland enviously. It took 15 years of breathing the increasingly brown and smoggy air of my homeland and walking the endlessly multiplying hot asphalt parking lots and shopping malls, to look around the corners of that movie screen, and see that perhaps 'things weren't exactly as I thought'.

(Note:* 'Pachinko' is a form of mild gambling in Japan; it resembles slot machines, and it takes place in huge salons found all over the country, each one of plastic and neon with hundreds of such machines inside, each one of them in use almost all the time, by someone not wanting to go home right away. The name comes from the sound the machines make when one puts in a coin in that distinctively Japanese form of onomatopeia; it resembles 'Pa-Chin-Ko'.)

CHAPTER 2

Second Turnings

O lord, from the unreal, lead me to the real.
From darkness, lead me to light,
from Death, lead me to Eternal Life....

from the Upanishads

My father was a pillar, a rock, an angry rock, but a very sincere man who did his best. His father was a taciturn Sicilian peasant who arrived in America in 1907 from Palermo with 12 dollars in his pocket to start a new life in a new world. He worked 7 years in brickyards to send back the money for the boat ticket for his wife, my grandmother, to come from Sicily. He found his way to California where the climate and the work was the same as that he had left behind, to work in the orange groves, and at home he was a somewhat taciturn and much respected patriarch. My father was one of 8 children, 6 of whom were male and my dad the youngest of them. The need to constantly defend himself amidst all those bigger brothers must have made him strong, and he was a football star and remarkable athlete in high school. He got to the No. 1 ranked-college in the country on a football scholarship; his college years were spent working night jobs to send money home to support his parents and other 7 siblings; After Pearl Harbor, he enlisted in the navy, was made an officer, and spent 3 years hunting submarines in the Atlantic and Pacific and escorting Marines onto beaches in France and the South Pacific. He saw a lot of guys die. He spent a lot of time alone on the bridge of the ship crossing the great oceans, watching the stars all night. He was a boxer in the navy, was nicknamed 'Rocky' by his Sicilian brothers long before there was ever a movie about it, and he was all of that. At the end of the war, he was in the hospital for an operation, and my mom was a Navy nurse. The rest is easy to figure out; They married, and loved each other through good times and hard times for 50 years. The good times were very sweet between them. I would see them kiss almost every day of my childhood as the sun went down in the kitchen window and they would have their martini together. That was just about the only space they had together.

My mother was born on the opposite side of the USA, in a place called Worcester, a working-class industrial town not far from Boston. Her mother and father had newly arrived to America just before W.W. 1 from Lithuania, or Russia, we were never quite sure, as I only met my grandmother twice, and my grandfather, never, as he had died long before my birth. That side of the family, being thousands of miles away and relatively unknown, remained a mystery to me. My mother had been a nurse in the navy in the war, was very sharply intelligent, with a wry New England sarcastic wit, and a great deal of energy. I was the youngest of 4 children, and my memories of my mother are always of her being occupied with cooking, cleaning, washing, shopping for food, and caring for the illnesses and emotional upsets of all of us. She was always busy, emotionally distant at times, but very caring at others. As time went on, stress took its toll on her disposition, and her anger and frustration would become chronically present. I never understood why this was so, until much later in my life, at the end of hers...

As a child, my first 'meeting' with that mysterious event which we humans call 'death' was in 1960, at the passing of my Grandfather. He was the patriarch of a very large extended Italian family by that time, and I knew him as a stern and silent presence at the head of the table on Sunday afternoons, with all his children, grandchildren, great-grandchildren, and their respective spouses honoring him dutifully and respectfully, amidst the chaos of all those Italians talking all at the same time. He never spoke to me in English, but I spent much time playing with him as a young child, so we had our channels of communication. He died when I was 5. His death was accompanied by hysterical outbursts of wailing on the part of my grandmother and aunts during the funeral mass, and the beginning of them wearing only black for the next 7 years, the 'normal' way of grieving in a Sicilian family. I couldn't really understand why everyone was feeling so bad. Yes, it was a change, but it didn't register in me as sorrow, more like 'amazement' at the hysterical behavior of all the adults surrounding me.

In October of 1962 I was 7 years old. President Kennedy, a mythical and much-loved figure in the universe of my family, was on the TV, saying things about Cuba which I didn't really understand, but my parents were talking in soft fearful voices afterward. The house was suffused with a feeling of fear that just stayed in my guts, like a dull ache inside. We lived about 10 miles away from a huge Air-force base that was called March Field, a SAC headquarters tucked over the hills from the town in the desert, where, from the highway, you could always see out there on the runway a long line of B-52 bombers waiting, fully fueled, day and night. They had Hydrogen bombs in their bellies, very big H-bombs, measured in the Millions of Tons of TNT. Any one of those insanely perfected killing machines could wipe out several big cities and all the people in it and surrounding it. The generally agreed-upon rationale for having all those killing machines constantly ready and available to wipe out about half of the human race at a moment's notice, was that by having them waiting there on the runway, they are making it impossible for a real war to actually happen, and therefore, they are 'keeping us safe'. But now, they weren't waiting. They were all going in the air. The bombers and aerial tankers taking off from the base were in a scramble pattern flying low straight over our house, one every 15 seconds, for 20 long minutes, shaking the walls with the horrible roar of their 8 engines. That meant they were on 'alert', and they stayed in the air for days, loaded with Mega-death, refueling, circling, and waiting. Needless to say, that didn't make me feel very safe.

In school at that time we were handed little pamphlets that told us what to do if we saw a big white flash, and instructions about how to duck and hide in holes and ditches. The teacher trembled as she told us, "You p-p-probably w-w-won't n-need to use th-th-th-these!...". Her stuttering and wildly rolling eyes impressed me much more than the pamphlets. She was real shook up, and weighing about 200 pounds, it was a rather impressive picture embedded in my young mind. On Thursday mornings, at 10 a.m. there would be a drill, and the air-raid sirens would go off, a wailing sound so sad and fearful that it would make my bones shiver. That sound meant to me 'The End Of The World'. When we heard it, we would all jump under the desks and cover our heads. I asked someone, "Why do I have to tuck my head between my knees?" And one of the kids said: "To kiss your ass goodbye!"

I knew if I heard that wailing siren, and it wasn't Thursday morning 10 a.m., then I would be dead in 5 minutes. Not just dead, but probably evaporated, or melted, or just a faint darkness on the ground all that remains, like the photos of the sidewalks in Hiroshima, where little kids were reduced to shadows of neutrons. Those ghostly pictures haunted me. I knew there would be nowhere to hide when the flash came from the sky...

Those days, in October, the normally empty church which was next to the school was full of people praying at 7 in the morning, which was the most terrifying thing of all.

Then, on one of those October nights, I woke up at 2 in the morning, to the sound of those wailing sirens. I thought it was a nightmare. I pinched myself again and again to see if I was sleeping, but, no, I was awake, and they really were wailing. That meant it wasn't a drill: the Russian missiles were on their way, targeting the nearby base, and US! I laid there, with a knot in my belly, knowing I would be dead within a few minutes, and wondering why I had ever lived. These are unusual thoughts for a 7-year old boy I suppose, but on that night, I deeply felt that if I made it through the night, it would be a miracle, and certainly my life would not last beyond my 10th year, the world would be finished in a puff of nuclear smoke, and ash, and rubble.

From that day on, it became almost impossible for me to plan a future, the way that other children could. The hook inside my mind, that today leads to tomorrow and it goes on and on, and, "I'm going to be this when I grow up"... it just wasn't there. I could never really get my mind around the concept of a career, a family, having a long life and doing all the things that one does in 70 years or so. Instead, it became increasingly important for me to find out actually why I am here at all, before the time runs out.

A year later, on a sunny November morning, Sister Doretta came on the loudspeaker in the schoolroom to tell us to kneel down to pray; President Kennedy had been shot. We were Catholics, He was Catholic: in my mind it seemed like Jesus Christ getting killed all over again, the best and most loved one sacrificed for reasons I couldn't understand.

As we knelt there praying with all the fervor in our little hearts, Sister Doretta came on the loudspeaker again, to say that he was dead. School let out early, and my sister and I rode home on our bicycles, wondering what would happen. My father came home from work that day early, and he was sobbing. I never even imagined that he could cry. He was Rocky, in the flesh, a pillar of stone, and before that moment for me he was not subject to human vulnerability. But that day, he and everyone were shaken, and would never, ever again recover fully their faith in the structures that contained them. From that day on, the world that I knew, in the little house in Suburbia 20 miles from Disneyland with my siblings and parents, where everything was perfect and right and good and American and wholesome and pasteurized, homogenized grade-A like white milk, it all seemed to fall apart, more and more each day, like a gyroscope spinning more and more off-center. From that day on, the 'American Dream' that I had been born in started dying.

As I grew up, my fascination was with anything that flew, creating airplanes and kites and rockets and zeppelins all through my young days, wishing to be an astronaut, and travel far, far away. I dreamt of flying every night , flapping my arms and running in my dreams until I would clear the trees and lift off into the sky.

We lived on the San Andreas fault, and earthquakes were a common event. One summer evening I was watching the television set roll across the living room floor, and the lawn outside undulate in soft waves. Often I would wake up and watch the walls sway and shake, and hear the deep tremble in the earth, a sound which was more felt than heard. To feel the earth move was always as thrilling as it was frightening to me, that the very stability of the ground you take for granted at each moment suddenly is no more, and all is waving and wobbling...it is astounding, unsettling, and amazing all at the same time.

The constant backdrop in those years of the 1960's was the 'evening news', constantly worse, about Viet Nam. Neighbors would talk about this boy or that one getting drafted, getting sent 'over there'. The news came in every night. Walter Cronkheit, who was the most trusted and revered face on television at that time and practically had the status of a religious icon, the voice of Truth, would appear each night at 6 p.m. to sedately and logically explain the collective reality to the entire population at that hour, centered on what conflicts were happening and what our politicians were doing each day. Each day he would talk about the 'body count' in Viet Nam and the 'Search and destroy' missions, and 'pacification'. To my young mind, I thought those villages sure looked like they were getting napalmed, not pacified; and those children running naked, they didn't look so 'saved' from the Viet Cong. They looked more like they were screaming in terror at the American planes who just leveled their village. The body counts kept growing, as I did. Everyday, more bombs fell. Every night, the pictures told the horror story, my mind started to question, along with millions of others, "What's this all for? WHY??"

The 60's rocked on and gathered speed and momentum. The Beatles came to America. The Berkeley Free-speech movement erupted, a fist of dissent and the voice of youth saying 'NO' to the functioning of the grey war-and-money machine which had become 'the establishment'. Civil rights protesters were being fire-hosed and clubbed in Alabama and elsewhere, race riots exploding in LA, Detroit, Newark; all on the evening news. The 'Summer of Love' came and went, the antiwar movement gained momentum as each night the body counts rose and the bombers flew on the TV. From my 8th to my 18th birthday, my childhood passed with the backdrop of the terrible war each night as the soundtrack; Walter Cronkheit each day getting a little more sad, as the news got more and more unbelievable. 'Pacification' turned into devastation. Neighbor's sons were coming home in body bags. Agent Orange and the Ho Chi Minh trail, daisy cutters and Phantom jets: My brother was now just out of high school and coming up for the draft. Elsewhere in the world, in Peking, Prague, Paris, Rome, everywhere there was rebellion, turmoil; the youth of the world were in revolt. The drugs filtered back home with the amputees and Veterans, until my 13-year old friends were coming to school on LSD. Love was in the air, and in the music. The Beatles were singing ALL YOU NEED IS LOVE, the Doors, LIGHT MY FIRE, the Rolling Stones were Gettin' no Satisfaction...Jimi Hendrix was in a Purple Haze, the hair was getting longer day by day, and from every nook and corner, the rebellion of youth was exploding, like bright yellow flowers in the cracks in the grey asphalt.

Soon Soledad Brothers in prison and Black Panthers on the streets were raising their angry fists, and Jimi Hendrix, Jim Morrison and Janis Joplin were dead of drug overdoses, The Supremes were telling me you can't hurry love, Martin Luther King and Bobby Kennedy were dead on the floor in pools of blood, Chicago police were squirting pepper-spray in the faces of little old ladies on prime-time TV, while the crowd in the park chanted: "THE WHOLE WORLD IS WATCHING!" Then came Moonwalks and People's Park riots in Berkeley, and Ronald Reagan, the cowboy-actor now turned governor of our great and golden state, saying, "If it takes a bloodbath, let's get it over with!" The helicopters rolled out and the teargas sprayed, along with the buckshot, and the body count at home grew as well, in Berkeley, in Kent State, in Jackson State, in Attica. These were the daily visions of my childhood and adolescence. I could not dream of a future in this society. I could only wonder why I was here, in a world that killed its best ones, and seemed to delight in smashing the heads and dreams of those who long for peace and freedom.

The 60's rolled away and passed like a massive cultural tsunami. In their wake, you could try to pick up the pieces, but there was no way to fit the things back together. Many kids in my school got more and more into drugs and their eyes hollowed out and faces turned a 'much whiter shade of pale'. A few became Jesusfreaks and were 'born-again', waving Bibles, exactly at who I couldn't really figure out. And a lot of others, a whole lot of others, decided to fall asleep, and train for a job in one of those nameless, face-less office-buildings in one of those nameless, face-less endless suburban sprawls and shopping malls which by now had taken the place of all the orange groves of my childhood.

I played baseball or football everyday of my youth, depending on the season. But what was fun and thrilling in an open lot barefoot with 20 kids, became a very different story in high school under the organized direction of the coaches, who probably are a good bet to be the missing link between Australopithecus and homo-sapiens. American Football, a 'sport', as it is euphemistically called , is a right of passage, in a culture which sorely lacks those rituals. But this rite, rather than preparing adolescents for intelligent or responsible existence as adults, prepares them to dominate by force at the expense of others, nothing more or less. It is a violent and brutal game, breaking bones, destroying bodies, and minds, in a way which can be summed up as 'might makes right'; or in other words, training in how to be a psychopath. As I got more muscles and hormones, One day at age 15 I found myself on the practice field knocking people over rather easily, and looking down at the person on the ground with a feeling of disgust at myself. I felt revulsion at my act, and thought to myself: "This is incredibly stupid". It was a pivotal moment in my formation.

I was in the precarious position of coming home from football practice, picking up my flute, and reading Gandhi, Hesse, Dostoyevsky, Kerouac and Thoreau. "Simplify, simplify" said Thoreau, and I did it. I left the football team behind, telling the coach that I would rather spend my time playing my flute and doing yoga. I will never forget how his jaw dropped open! At that time, nearly 50 years ago, yoga was not the mainstream fad that it is today: It was 'weird'. Nobody had even heard of it there. I was a loner, mostly because there wasn't anyone else I could find interested in Walt Whitman, Lao-Tzu and Pranayama. One day, at age 16, out of the blue, I just decided that I didn't want to participate in killing anymore, and I stopped eating meat, forever. 'Cold Turkey': that is, from one day to the next, done deal. My mother was a bit taken aback, to say the least. This was akin to dietary sacrilege; after all, the Macdonald Brothers started their first hamburger joint about 10 miles from where I lived, and at that time not eating meat was equated with starvation in the 3rd world, in most people's minds. But for me, it was my statement of open rebellion, against the oncoming wave of mediocrity and business-as-usual that I saw closing in all around, along with the parking lots and shopping malls.

It was April, 1972. But my dear mother did her best to let me be who I was, and she slowly learned the wonders of tofu and vegetarian lasagna, long before it showed up on daytime TV.

As the years passed, and the cars and tract homes multiplied, the once deep-blue skies turned to deep brown. I was running four miles a day, coughing more and more as the 'smog alerts' came more and more often, when it was 'strongly advised' to stay indoors and avoid activity. In those days the gas was still leaded, and in Riverside, where all the air from LA backs up against the mountains every afternoon, you really couldn't breathe after the beginning of spring, or even see across the street, in the summer heat-waves. So, reading Thoreau and Gandhi, I set up my own unannounced civil disobedience campaign of one, and refused to participate in the car-culture that was creating all the smog. I rode my bicycle everywhere. At 17 I finished high school early and was already going to college, and the University where I took music classes was a ride of 25 kilometers. But I did it, everyday, and I got to love it, and my body got stronger, and my hair got longer.

I had taken up surfing the year before, and would often spend the days on the weekend at the beach, an hour from where I lived, with my wetsuit and surfboard. As time went by, I found myself sitting out just past the wave break-line, waiting, much more than catching waves. I became less and less interested in riding the waves, than in just sitting there, in absolute peace and silence, one with the vast and blue sea; Just digging it. I was the only person on the whole ocean, the whole enormous expanse of the huge and blue Pacific ocean; just feeling the rocking motion of the swells passing under me. Sometimes the sun would go down, the moon would come up, and I wouldn't come in until it was totally dark and shining with stars. It was mysterious, magical, silent. There was something that kept me there, just sitting alone on the water, all day. I did not know what the word meant at that time, but it had been my first experiences of something that I would later come to know as 'meditation'.

Music, particularly playing the flute, was my life-boat; it transported me to other worlds, beyond time and beyond the confining reality that I found myself in. In the rock band I had been in at age 15, my old friends were falling daily one-by-one to hard drugs and despair, and I took to my flute in earnest, as a doorway, as a hope, as a prayer. The sound was my sustenance. The dreamland of my childhood, Southern California, now with its multiplying tract homes and brown air, suffocating mentality, monotony, and heat, was a prison which I sought to leave forever and the sooner the better. I wanted OUT, and I wanted to go as far away as possible as quickly as possible, to San Francisco, that mythical city which seemed so different than anywhere else. I studied hard to be able to get into a good university, Berkeley, to become a composer, and make beautiful music, a kind that nobody had heard before.

With a friend who played the guitar and myself on the flute, we would spend long hours at night improvising together. One day in the torrid heat of summer, we decided to take off on our bicycles up the coast to get out of the smog, and miraculously, our parents let us go! We left one summer morning at 3 am, passing a long and smoggy day going all the way through greater LA on city streets, then made our way up the spectacular Big Sur coast to San Francisco. It was freedom. It was the wind in your hair on a long and empty highway. It was 'Easy-Rider' on bicycles. Nobody to tell us what to do or how to be. We would find a forest to camp in each night, and each day see new visions of blue sea, and the golden rolling hills of California.

We passed the Golden Gate, crossing the long red bridge of mystic foggy winds, and kept riding our bikes up the glorious coast of Northern California, on an adventure of discovery, a new world of redwood forests and mountains plunging to the sea. Then one afternoon, on a long downhill run, my wheels slipped in the gravel on the side of the road and I hit the pavement at high speed, losing most of the skin on the side of my left leg. I limped my way to a gas station, nearly fainting as I poured antiseptic all over the open wounds, and spent the next few days in shock in a sleeping bag on a hill outside of the town, waiting for my bike to get fixed and my leg to heal enough to walk.

I knew if I told my parents what had happened, the trip would be over, so I just stayed quiet, and shivered. When the scabs had formed, slowly, we made our way back south to San Francisco, and found a camping spot in the forest of the Presidio taking up residence there for some weeks. Each day my leg would get a little less stiff, and we would go downtown, and play music on the sidewalks, in Union Square, Chinatown, the Tenderloin, Golden Gate Park. People gave us money as we played, all day long, the lovely citizens of San Francisco. I will never forget one tall and beautiful woman, looking like a flower-adorned goddess with excess mascara and a long flowing skirt, slowly and silently placing a silver dollar in my flute case, with a big smile. Now, this was a nice way for a 17-year old boy to make a living. Just play my flute, and the world rewards me. "I can get into this!", I realized.

So suddenly, we two vagabonds pedaling our bikes between the foggy Presidio and the neon-lit Tenderloin found ourselves getting rich, relatively speaking. Each day we would meet the characters of this strange and delightful movie San Francisco, toothless Indian Chiefs with stories to tell , and kindly Russian grandmothers in the deli's, an old guy in a tweed suit playing Rachmaninoff concertos on the harmonica, friendly pickpockets on the cable cars, and burned-out trumpeters on Fisherman's wharf.

I went across the bay to see Berkeley, the famous hotbed of rebellion and my father's college. I was enchanted. Telegraph Avenue was full of milling crowds dressed like a militant carnival, street music of all kinds, people dancing, painting murals, blowing bubbles in the air: The exact antidote of pasteurized homogenized Southern Cal, with all the girls in Barbie-doll perfect makeup and all the guys stiffly acting like Ken dolls or Marine recruits. THIS was the place I wanted to be, and learn.

We stayed as long as we could in the city, until my father was boiling-over on the phone, yelling and threatening to come up there to bring me home. I decided to spare him the 1000 mile drive and me the whipping that would come, and we reluctantly got on our trusty bicycles and started pedaling south. I rode into the driveway of our house in smoggy Riverside one day in late August, and my father and mother looking at me like I wasn't a boy anymore, but a man.

That year I came up for the draft, as Nixon was in the full

spasms of his tyranny. Cambodia was getting invaded and Hanoi was being bombed into the stone age. My number in the draft-lottery was such that I was sure to be cannon-fodder wading through the jungle within a couple of months, I would be called up into the army when I turned 18, and I started preparing my case as a 'Conscientious Oobjector'. I knew I would choose to go to jail rather than be a robot with a rifle in my hands. One week before my 18th birthday, the draft was ended. I was spending my time in the election campaign for George McGovern, in the futile campaign to NOT re-elect Nixon. It was a bit like being a Greek in Thermopylae, with the millions of Persians and Xerxes coming on. The wave to re-elect the 'President', who to me was obviously a psychopath and criminal, was unstoppable. I would knock on doors, trying to talk to people about napalmed villages and Watergate, and more often than not, I was met by someone with a big beer belly and a six-pack in hand, telling me, "I don't give a fuck! Let's nuke' em!" The gap between my perceptions and those of my fellow human beings seemed to be growing wider by the minute.

Just as the social upheaval of the 60's was becoming a distant memory, and the Big Freeze was on, in September of 1973 I left for the University. My departure from Suburbia was a symbolic and real act of freedom. I left behind my parents, my childhood home, the town and all the friends I knew, television, surfing, shopping malls; everything. For the rest of my life I would never have a television in my home, or medical insurance, or a routine. The cultural hypnosis in which I grew up was odious to me, and I intentionally and fully left it behind, in whatever form I perceived it. I left on my bicycle again, and pedaled alone the 500 miles up the coast to Berkeley, feeling ecstatic. I pedaled 100 miles a day. When I got there, I jumped into my music classes with a fervor, plunging into a world of new sounds and experiences, drowned in Mozart, Wagner, Scriabin, Orlando di Lasso and Josquin de Prez.

But my other classes, in social sciences and 'general education', were disappointments to say the least, conducted in vast auditoriums with the professor on TV screens, exercises in squareness and a continuation of the same strange hypnosis I thought I had left behind. As the great cultural revolution of the 60s was fast fading beyond memory, it seemed like all the awakening which had held so many promises like flowers in the cracks in the pavement, was fast becoming deep sleep once again.

I tried to examine what I thought were relevant and real issues in my term papers, like the CIA backing of the coup in Chile, but my efforts were greeted by cold stares and ridicule by teachers and professors. American Government 1-A seemed to me to be American Hypnosis and Hegemony once again. I had the distinct nagging feeling, as I watched the white rats in the Psychology labs, that my mind was being channeled forcibly into a regimented and narrow way of thinking, that in the end would turn me into a robot, ready to take my place in the vast grey machinery of MONEY waiting like an abyss at the end of my primrose path in the university. Like a cow standing calmly in line at the slaughterhouse, or, as in the film METROPOLIS of Fritz Lang, I felt more and more like one of those zombies walking without resistance into the waiting mouth of MOLOCH, the ancient Sumerian god of money. In the guise of being prepared for 'life', these studies seemed to me to just be making me adjusted to a slow and boring death.

Before the blinders are put on the horse, does he not resist? That spark of life in all beings instinctively loves its freedom, and so it was with me. My resistance to the blinders methodically and systematically being imposed on me emerged yet more obstinately.

I drowned myself in music, studied Harmony, Counterpoint, Composition. I played Chopin, Stravinsky and Bartok on the

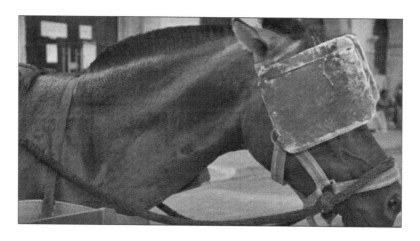

Piano and analyzed Bach fugues night and day, spending most of my time outside of classes in the basement practice rooms of the music department, hammering out Passacaglias and Sonatas with a pencil and a piano and was living on an occasional peanut butter sandwich. The coup became permanent in Chile, Nixon got caught lying and resigned, and was pardoned; A lot of ex-hippies-turned-yippies read the writing on the walls that made it clear the times were changing for the worse, and they started trading in their bell-bottoms for Brooks Brothers suits and a new career as yuppies. And I just kept wondering about it all. I pondered my history lessons as a child, spent a couple of terms observing behavior of white rats in the Psychology Lab, watched the profs in the enormous Sociology classes somewhere down there on the TV screen, as my music studies were channeled more and more away from the beauty and mystery that I loved and were forced into the mental abstraction of German modern composition a-la Shoenberg and Webern, which to me seemed nothing more than mind games expressed as ugly abstract sounds. My heart which longed for release through the magic of sound was drying up and becoming more distant day by day, and I realized this was not going to get me where I wanted to go. I didn't know where that was, but I could feel it when I was getting farther away. The beauty that I sought, that lift to another dimension, was disappearing into organized noise and mathematical mental cacaphony. I wanted life, not more hypnosis, not more brain-washing of which I had already had for 15 years since those nuns were whacking us in line.

In all my University Classes, my restlessness was growing, and my disillusionment was becoming total, as I looked at the world more each day in shades of darker and darker grey. My readings were no more of poetry and philosophy, but more of economic and social analyses, negation and revolution, Marx, Galbraith, Chomsky, Bertrand Russell, Bakunin, and Kropotkin; my mind searched for answers as to the 'why' of war and corruption and social injustice, and started to connect the dots between all the various manifestations of the MACHINE. And yet, the only 'answers' that social/economic revolution had produced, in our era, were Marxist disasters. The 'dictatorship of the proletariat', Marx's theoretical fantasy that 'the state will wither and die', turned out to be simply a blueprint for inhuman totalitarian structures to grow like parasites over the wishes of poor people trying for a better life, in Russia and in China. The antidote turns into the same poison as the original disease. There was no answer forthcoming in my music or psychology classes, and I decided it was time to try a different route.

There were demonstrations against the 'system', as whole departments were getting cut away if they had 'leftist' professors, and some of us, a very few, were enmeshed in a futile attempt at trying to revive the dying spirit of 'Free Speech'.

I protested, sat-in, got arrested, got pushed and shoved by the cops and the crowds and the clubs, and somehow got a strange feeling as the Alameda County Sheriffs Deputies, known locally as 'The Blue Meanies', rolled in on buses with clubs and shotguns. They were nicknamed 'The Blue Meanies' after the Beatles film Yellow Submarine. They were the sheriffs deputies of

Oakland, specially trained for anti-riot duty. They were generally big, mean, ugly and nasty tempered, dressed in baby-blue uniforms with full body armor and long clubs, and had lots of tear gas canisters, pepper spray, and shotguns. I started thinking this also wasn't my scene. The leaders of the demonstration seemed to be relishing their new-found authority and fame with a megaphone, and shouting slogans which seemed to echo Mao Tze-Tung rather than Lao Tzu, and upping the ante for a confrontation, to get them on the front pages of the San Francisco Chronicle.

It slowly occurred to me, that it was taking on the appearance of just another stupid movie, everybody playing their roll: The jock Police thugs dressed up as Nazis, with their helmets, flak-jackets, and tear-gas grenades, swinging their clubs; All of us shouting with fists raised, stupid slogans that nobody listens to, about a revolution that wasn't going to happen, the plainclothes FBI guys in grey suits taking pictures of everything, the University Chancellor peeking out of the window. It was just poor players with bit parts in a B-movie. I realized I had better things to do.

I left school, taking lessons from my piano prof in private, who was a marvelous classical pianist, and very expensive. Taking odd jobs digging ditches and running a jackhammer for 3 bucks an hour, and then paying 40 to him for a one-hour lesson, I was stretched, to say the least. I found an angel in the records of John Coltrane, and knew he had found something I was searching for. I studied Indian violin at the Berkeley Center for World Music. It was there that I first started to hear the sounds that would capture my soul, raga singing, Balinese Gamelan, Pentatonic scales on strange Chinese instruments, Shakuhachi, and Tibetan overtones. This was a new and enchanting world which opened before me. At the same time, I wished for more 'reality'. To me at that time, it meant participating somehow in the drama of 'human suffering'.

I worked as a volunteer in a special care home for severely disabled children, took jobs caring for quadraplegics, and trained and volunteered at the Berkeley Free Clinic as an assistant. The training and the actual work was a slice of 'real life'; The Dark Side of it. Mostly people on bad acid trips came in, attempted suicides, or guys on the edge of wanting to kill somebody, needing to talk. I just talked to people while notifying trained professionals to respond to the call. We were all volunteers, so there was not a whole lot of staff there. Sometimes it was just me at three in the morning. Sometimes just by listening to their story attentively, I helped the 'clients' to release, scream and yell. And sometimes, the depth of the depression and hopelessness that I would be facing in front of me would simply numb me, and I felt a total helplessness in the face of real human suffering.

The Berkeley Free Clinic; it's hard to say if we were the helpers or the 'crazies'. Truly, the borders got blurry at times. It was people trying to help other people, and sometimes the helpers became the ones who needed help. One weekend, all the staff went up to Tahoe to spend a couple of days in a cabin in the forest, getting to know each other. We all took 'acid': LSD. It was, after all, Berkeley, and psychedelics were the norm, not the exception. We did finger-paints, played in the mud, wandered in the woods, sang and banged on drums and pots and pans, made poetry, and had great fun. But the trouble was, one of the staff, a beautiful and extremely dynamic high-strung friend, on the way home went into a paranoic episode which became pretty serious, and she ended up in Highland hospital on the Psych ward for a couple of weeks. I visited her there, and was shocked to see a friend that I thought I knew, with a totally different personality, another 'persona' completely, occupying her body. Thorazine, shock treatment; I started to find out about how the society puts the lid back on the can when it starts opening, and it ain't too pretty.

At that time I was practicing my piano all day, studying Tai-Chi and Indian violin, growing vegetables and dabbling occasionally in psychedelics. I had a few good trips, and a couple of bad ones, in which I could clearly see from the forest at the crest of the Berkeley hills, the whole civilization covering the Bay Area as a growing cancer on the face of the earth. I knew that cancer was in me too, as a dark shadow living within me. It was shocking to me, and I cried and cried. I began to feel more and more distant from the scene of burned-out politicos I had known from school and people with axes to grind. Not that those axes weren't justified; but I didn't think it was doing anything to keep grinding them. Something else was calling out to me, something unknown to me yet, but beckoning from a place beyond.

The people whom I had respected, people whom I thought swere eeking a more just society now seem to be just playing new power games, changing hats and standing there with megaphones and 'Das Kapital', enjoying being in front of a crowd and being somebody important. It was just another game.

I sensed that there was an ocean of sorrow in me which I wasn't facing, that cancerous growth that was out there in the endless grey waves of concrete and steel encroaching on the green hills, it was in me too, and I didn't want to end up on the Highland Hospital Psych Ward. I decided it was time for me to start searching for real solutions, in earnest, not just on the piano. It was 1975.

The practice of Mantra and Perfections,
instructions in the Sutras and Precepts,
and teaching from the Schools and Scriptures
will not bring realization of the Innate Truth.
For if the mind when filled with some desire

should seek a goal, it only hides the Light.

Tilopa-Song of Mahamudra

I left the Bay Area, in search of a different kind of life, less of the mind, less of the negative, and more closer to the heart. I didn't know what that was, but I knew I had to find it. Hitch-hiking up the coast to Canada, by the autumn I settled in rural Oregon, outside of Eugene. There I found friends in artists, dancers, musicians like myself, looking for a way to express, in a simpler way, not so intellectual. There were music festivals, healing gatherings, new kinds of tribal rituals, really the beginning of 'New Age' before anybody called it that. People were trying to heal themselves with herbs, with natural food, to clean up their bodies, get the drugs out and get more real.

It was the time in the youth culture of 'going back to the Land'. I was living in a little cabin, with my piano, together with 5 other people nearby in a big old schoolhouse on some rural land. They were great characters. Ilana, Simon, Theresa, Curtis, Laura, I will never forget them. We were all looking for something; Nobody knew what, exactly. God? Our Souls? But we had all come out of the drug smoke and were experimenting with fasting, yoga, natural foods, raw foods, and NO foods. Ilana would invite all kinds of mini-gurus to come stay with us for a few days and do their thing, so we could find out what they were about. There were Rabbis, Raw-food faddists, Indian Chiefs, Evangelical-type prophets, Healers, Witches, Shamans, Astrologers, Kundalini Yogis... you name it, we invited them there. The Indian Chief was saying things like, "Earth Medicine changing, BIG purification coming...get ready, get Squaw, get Water!" This was almost 40 years before 2012. It sounded like everyone would die within a year or two. We would try their teachings for a week or so, and then somebody else would come, and we would try that. It was a real circus. I was fasting a lot, I didn't eat cooked food for about a year, and did yoga for

44

several hours everyday; Didn't have sex .... I think I was too weak from the fasting! We would go to different 'healing' festivals, the first Rainbow Festival, and things would happen. I would play my flute, babies would be born in tipis, Simon was making stained-glass windows and I was practicing my violin like crazy, sitting in trees.

I would visit different communities of people, like tribes, all experimenting, with trying to go 'back' to nature. Only, they were actually going 'back' to a nature that was just an absence of technology and culture, and intelligence. Everyone was looking for God, or the Revelation, but some of them seemed to be just devolving: As if losing vocabulary and syntax and just trying to keep warm was a step forward, as if WW3 had already happened and we were in the aftermath. There was a subtle guilt to the whole thing, new criteria for being judged; The more weird you were, the more feathers and colors you wore, the more 'in' you would be. Many were pretending to be shamans, claiming past lives as Native Americans; Dread-locks and lots of feathers, crummy clothes from Guatemala were the uniform, I realized somehow, that this wasn't 'it' either. This was also bullshit. The society, the anti-society, the non-society; it was all the same trap. Slowly I became disgusted and disenchanted with all the mini-gurus and self-styled shamans and their little followings of adoring groupies. It seemed so inane to me, the whole thing, somehow the REAL problem wasn't being addressed.

I was closing in on myself, becoming smaller and smaller, withdrawing more and more from life, becoming more and more lonely. I had been going through a deep emotional implosion, after the loss of a relationship, which I was trying to cover up with yoga, with fasting, with reading holy books. The real thing: I was a little kid hurting inside; Hurting from the loss of my dreams, the loss of the womb, physical, psychological, symbolic. The loss of the promises given to me in childhood, of happiness and comfort and safety, that God is up in heaven and America is good and just and doctors are there to help you and America is the land of the free and home of the brave…the whole deal. The whole collective dream had fallen down around my ears and left me bitter and lonely, hurting from the disillusionment with life, society, and the disillusionment with the antidotes to society, either political/social revolution or eclectic escapism. Joining it, changing it or running from it, it's still the same. Wherever you go, YOU are still there.

I heard from a friend about a new kind of therapy, and I wanted to give it a try. It was really simple: You just breathe, more and more, without gaps. After about 10 minutes of this, I just started crying, and crying and crying. That deep ocean of pain in me was starting to surface. At the end of the session, after 2 years in Oregon, I decided to go back to San Francisco,

One day, before I went back, my friend Simon invited me to experience something different. We hitchhiked up to Puget Sound in Canada, to a beautiful little island named Hornby. It was a summer day, on an empty beach on this little paradise of pine trees and bald eagles. It was unseasonably warm for that time and place, and there were long days of bright sunshine.

I was 22. We were there with our violins, and with a specific purpose, on that deserted, forested and wonderful beach. It was the full moon night, and we had chosen that night for him to initiate me into a ritual of passage, with a power plant, called peyote. I knew nothing about it, but I was curious about this magical plant, having heard of it for years through accounts from various people of their shamanic experiences, and I wanted to learn.

In a sacred and expectant way, we waited, for the setting sun. We slowly chewed on the dry and very bitter pieces of the cactus, ingesting it with a tiny bit of honey just to make it bearable. It was the most awful thing I had ever tasted, a bitterness which is impossible to describe. After eating it, after what may have been a half an hour, my body involuntarily started to vomit. I was told that it would be a natural cleansing process, so, I just let it happen, and in fact, there was no way to stop it. Vomiting, and laughing at the same time; it was the sign that the plant was starting to take effect.

I was not drunk in any way, I couldn't even call it intoxicated, as it had more the quality of crystal clarity. At first, it seemed that everything in my mind, including the fact that I was there on that beach, retching and waiting for 'something to happen', seemed utterly and absolutely comical...hilarious. Very quickly, the reaction of the body stopped, and everything changed. I was totally present, in that moment; but what a difference! I had always looked at Nature, like an outsider. I was looking at nature, thinking: "Isn't that beautiful!?" Or "How incredible!" I would have feelings of appreciation or awe, but I was outside of it. Now, Nature and I were not separated; there was no separation between 'me and it', not me looking at nature, just an inseparable oneness which I could only describe as 'Divine', or ALL THAT IS. I had the distinct sense, not a thought, but a deep feeling, that everything was 'sacred', everything suffused with a wonderful and tangible presence. I couldn't call it God, as I had left that idea behind 7 years before when I left Christianity. It was closer to 'Being', or Oneness, or LOVE, or IT, or whatever you want to call it, but it was beyond all those words, too, and unmistakably HERE and it was ENDLESS and TIMELESS and I was a part of it.

The full moon rose over the vast and empty beach, and I could not take my eyes off of it. A halo appeared in the sky, around the moon, one of those enormous hazy halos of light which happen when the air is moist, and the circle it described kept appearing to me as a large and radiant face, with the full moon as a brilliant point in the place where the two eyebrows meet. I had no conscious connection with Eastern mysticism, Buddhism, the idea of chakras or past lives or any of that, but as I looked, for hours, it appeared to me to be the face of the Buddha, although I did not know what that was, but yet there it was, clear and radiant, shining with love, in that marvelous sky.

We made a fire, and played our violins all through the night, and time disappeared, only music existed. Melodies grew and were born into the night sky, like birds flying into the infinite space. There again was that incredible warmth, rich in overtones, that sound that moved me as a small child listening to symphonies. As the eastern sky started to grow light, our music grew in intensity, delight, joy, and abandon. We weren't doing it, it was just 'happening'. The birds awakened with the dawn would fly down from the trees and land just in front of us, answering our melodies with their own! We communicated in this way, playing music to each other, Simon, me and the birds. In a certain moment, I had the distinct feeling, or knowing, that those birds, were not 'birds' as we think of them, as separate little creatures that eat worms and make nests, and live their lives. In fact, they were simply the sounding part of the whole universe right then and there, just like speakers of a huge sound system! They were that, little creatures whose task was to emit the sound of the universe at that location and moment...and we with them.

As the dawn came on, I went down to the beach, and found an enormous expanse covered with countless boulders. Barefoot, I leaped and ran on these boulders, my body pure energy, pure delight in motion, never losing balance, never hurting my feet, weightless, limitless, never tiring...simply flying, one with the flying...

As hours passed, slowly my body energy began to wane, and I lay under a pine tree to rest, and eventually sleep. The experience stayed in my memory, not as something that I wanted to repeat, but as a signpost, that something so very different than my ordinary consciousness really EXISTS, and is worth finding, and I resolved at that point, to find it, without the help of the plant medicine, but really find it, for REAL, in such a way that I would never have to lose it again. Thus began, my search, to find that divine reality.

I returned to the Bay Area, this time to Marin County, to study Indian music, in San Rafael, at the Ali Akbar College of Music. This was a different kind of music practice, not like reading Bach fugues or Beethoven Sonatas. It was starting again from the beginning, note for note, learning the pitches of the scales, the feeling of the raga in your heart. It was hard, it was devotional, you had to really practice and practice and practice to keep up with the pace. Ali Akbar Khan was certainly the greatest musician I had ever met. He was the son of Alauddhin Khan, the mythic great master of Indian music, and the founder of a 'school', or gharana, of a very star-studded line of great Indian musicians, including his daughter Srimad Annapurna Devi, her husband Ravi Shankar, Hariprasad Chaurasia, Nikhil Banerjee, Pannalal Gosh, and many others. Ali Akbar was a fountain of constant knowledge and inspiration, and he could hear which strings were out of tune in a roomful of 50 sarods and sitars, and each one of them has about 40 strings. I would practice, for hours, singing, and on the violin instead of the piano, and in the arduous boredom at which my mind rebels, I would wonder, "Why am I doing this?" I had no answer, but somehow deep inside I knew it was for my soul, for God. I didn't know how it would unfold, but I felt that it was for the universe, not just for me. That vague feeling inside me kept me going.

It's a different kind of practice, Indian music. The direction is IN, instead of out. We would start by singing one note: SA... for hours, and hours, and hours; Until you really got that note! Then slowly you learned the scale; not just Major and Minor, but dozens of variations on that; And then practice them, backwards, forwards, upside down, right-side up, broken into little patterns that repeat like sequences. It was maddening, and yet somehow nourishing at the same time.

As I was practicing hard once again for many hours each day, to learn now ragas instead of Chopin Nocturnes and Scriabin Preludes, my loneliness and sense of being a stranger was no less acute. In fact it was more. I was living in a house in Fairfax which oddly enough had once belonged to Janis Joplin, and I was working as a waiter in a restaurant to pay the bills. One night, there on the table as I brought the plates of food, was a open book that a customer was reading. I glanced at it, caught a few words, and instantly, in my heart, I knew the voice that was speaking. I read on, and on, and asked the customer what book it was.

"Tantra, Spirituality, and Sex" by Bhagwan Shree Rajneesh...

"Hmmmm. Funny name", thought I. But I had to find it and read it. I was spellbound. I knew that voice! It was speaking like it was my own heart.

A few days later, I was walking down the street in San Rafael, and there was a couple walking on the sidewalk, dressed in orange robes and wearing beads with a locket. I had to stop them to talk to them, I didn't know why. They had a strange and very light feeling to them, as if they weren't wearing the same masks that every one else seemed to have, and they seemed just 'here', in a simple sort of way. We got to talking, I found out they were disciples of this fellow Rajneesh, they had just been with him in India, and there was a meditation center of his teachings in San Francisco!

I was on the next bus to the City, to find that place. It was called Paras, up at the top of a hill on 24th street above the Mission District, and little did I know how much my life was about to change there.

The center leader was a crazy chinaman named Alok, also dressed in orange with that locket, and he was very friendly, and kind of dangerous at the same time. I couldn't put my finger on what it was, but there was something which was very disturbing in his demeanor: as if he could do anything at anytime. It was a weird feeling, yet his energy was somehow kind, inviting and soothing. That night, there was a 'dynamic meditation', and I decided to try it.

The big room filled up with all kinds of people, some of them businessmen in suits, joggers in sweats, some people wearing just underwear, and most of them had blindfolds. I put one on. It started with deep breathing, chaotic breathing, intense. The more you did it, the more it took you over. After ten minutes, a gong rang, and everybody started screaming, laughing, crying, beating pillows, pounding the floor, wailing: it was amazing! It was frightening, and wonderful at the same time: Total freedom to express WHATEVER was in you. And being in that room with all the rest of those mad people just made it come out more. There was 10 minutes of total insanity. Then, another gong, 10 minutes of jumping up and down and shouting. 'Hoo! Hoo!'. This did something even more strange: my mind was melting. The whole thing was so ridiculous, and intense, that it just pushed me over a cliff. Then there was another gong, and the most profound silence…peace…for 10 minutes; Then another bell, and some music, a soft dance, of gratitude for whatever had been 'found' inside.

It was astounding. It was profound. It was transforming. I no longer felt bottled up and confused. I could breathe, see, be.

I found another book there, that I started reading. It was called 'Only One Sky'. I opened the book, and the first thing I read was:

> *Mahamudra (enlightenment) rests on nothing.*
> *The Void needs no reliance....small teachings lead to acts...*
> *only follow teachings that are GREAT.*

Those words went off in me like a bomb. I had been following small teachings for 23 years, and millions of actions, all leading nowhere. And all the time, the real thing, which is the VOID, that thing which happened to me at age 6, needs no support, no action. How can Emptiness be supported?

There was a group that weekend, a 'Let-Go weekend', a residential intensive. I signed up for it. The things that happened in the group, the intense processes, encounters, provoking and releasing emotions, traumas, tensions, and the deep peace that I found in the silences after, melted everything in me. All the doubts, all the years of hopeless searching just evaporated. I knew this was what I had been looking for. This was addressing the 'real situation'. And the real situation was ME. That package that I called 'myself', all those emotions, projections, judgements, attractions, rejections, yes-and-no's, likes and dislikes, based on my past experiences, forming my experiences of the world. Now, for the first time, this was facing the real situation inside me, the garbage and the flowers too, and transforming them both, through experience, and understanding. This was not spiritualizing escape. This was grabbing the tiger by the tail, and riding it; Not avoiding emotions, Not putting the attention on false problems, like diet or lifestyle or learning physical contortions or social change. This was accepting what you are, NOW; accepting all the contradictions, honestly, and living it, and riding it into silence and a place deeper than the mind.

Within two weeks I had dyed my clothes orange and I was on the plane for India to meet and be with 'Bhagwan'.

It was June 7, 1978. I was 23.

CHAPTER 3

Meeting the Master

At that time long ago, 1978, it was a 24-hour flight to India, in two parts. As the plane door opened in Bombay, I was greeted by a fetid, smelly rush of warm air that strangely felt very familiar and 'homey', as much as it seemed disgusting. It was a paradox that I was to experience again and again in India, on many levels.

In the airport I found some other people going to Poona, which was easy enough to do as we were all dressed in bright orange, and we shared the long taxi ride up into the hills, past monkeys and beggars and funny-looking diesel trucks all painted with bright colors and strange signs, like, 'Horn please ok!' And, 'Don't say goodbye, say TA TA!' After the 24-hour plane ride and endless taxi passage, arriving in Poona seemed surrealistic; all the rickshaws, scooters, donkeys, buses and cows all mingling into a strange blurring vision, rather chaotic and somewhat soothing at the same time. I found a hotel near the train station, left my luggage and immediately went to the ashram, the place where Bhagwan was.

I can never forget the first time I saw the main gate of the ashram, and the street in front with dozens of orange-clad people, somehow moving differently, not so fast, not so driven, like other people are in America. There was a different vibe in the air. It wasn't just that people were wearing robes and many had long hair; there was something empty, and yet very alive in the people, that I couldn't quite figure out. They were running on something different.

I got to the office, and asked to take 'Sannyas Initiation', to become a disciple, that very day. I was given an appointment to meet Bhagwan in a day or so, but I would be sick on that day, and had to wait a week.

It was a magic feeling to be in the ashram at that time, I felt as if I was floating, on an unknown and yet tangible energy in the air; everything seemed more intense, more vibrant, more alive.

During that week, I was going to the discourse of Bhagwan in the morning, and meditating all day. I wrote my first letter to Bhagwan, like a nice American boy telling him something about me. I mentioned something about birth trauma, having always thought that my basic problems in life were caused by the fact that I was born a couple of months prematurely, thinking it would be helpful to him to know that about me. I was in for a surprise when I went to lecture the next day.

Bhagwan came in, and he seemed to shine; I couldn't say what it was, but I couldn't keep my eyes off of him. He was silently magnetic; he walked in perfect silence, slowly, with his hands in a gesture of greeting, called 'Namaste' in India, and sat down, smiling gently.

The series of discourses was called 'The Perfect Master'. That day the sutras had to do with a disciple who was searching the perfect master. Bhagwan started to speak so softly, and before long he was talking about how a disciple who searches a perfect Master is absolutely in the wrong search. The real search is to seek how to be a perfect disciple, and then the Master is there before you. At one point in the lecture, Bhagwan said, "And these days, you can't believe the kinds of people who come to me, the kinds of letters they write. I get letters, telling me about birth traumas, and all kinds of garbage and nonsense; the quality of seekers is simply not there...."

At that point, I wanted to crawl out of the Buddha Hall and disappear into the bamboos, as he was clearly describing my letter as a shining example of the low-level of intelligence and commitment of the modern seeker. Needless to say, it would be a while before I would be writing again, and I decided to keep quiet and see what's going on a bit more here before sticking my big foot into my bigger mouth!

A week later; it is now June 15th, 1978. The warm and wet air of evening signals the arrival of the monsoon, a rainy season of 3 months, hot and torrid rains drenching the thirsty earth after the long months of dry baking under the merciless sun of India. The monsoon comes in huge billowing stacks of clouds, purple and pink and orange in the sunset. Birds scream and the wind picks up, the air is thick and full, with the heat, the pressure of the dampness, the massive clouds that fill the sky with their immense and colossal forms. As the sun goes down in a blaze of orange and pink glory, the cries of the birds fill the air as they return to their roosts in the orange-flowered gulmohar trees. I am sitting in a small open-air auditorium surrounded by a lush garden, filled with the fresh scent of the newly wet earth, after the long summer's wait for the rain. I am waiting to meet Him personally for the first time, with my heart pounding in anticipation.

When Bhagwan walks in, silently smiling, his hands raised in the gesture of 'namaste', I am struck with how physically small he is. And yet, He seems so big, so enthralling with His presence. I wait, for what seems like a very long time, until my name is called, and I make my way to the front and sit just in front of him. He is sitting on a chair, with me on the floor at his feet. As I sit there, and look up at him, I notice that it seems like the whole universe is moving around him, there is this flow of energy, seen or unseen I cannot say, but it just seems like everything is moving around him, so alive. His each movement, of hands, or eyebrows, strikes me as remarkable. And his eyes are fathomless pools, in which I am taken in, deeper and deeper. There is a feeling of joy which surrounds him, and engulfs me, and makes me feel wonderfully at home, like I am wrapped in a HUGE LOVE.

He says to me, "Close your eyes, and listen to the sounds". I listen to the cries of the birds, which seem to me to be the most beautiful things I have ever heard. After some time, which seems very timeless, he says, "Come close", and as I lean forward, he puts a necklace of wooden beads around my neck, and touches my forehead between my eyes with his finger. I stay there for a timeless eternity, and what moves inside me I cannot describe, but it is the first taste of bliss that I have ever had in this life. I am gone for a little while. After some time, he says, "Come back... This will be your new name...Swami Deva Kant.....Deva means Divine, Kant means beloved. And from this time, feel that way, that you are beloved, the universe loves you, it takes care, it mothers you....". He continues for some time, telling me about the miracle of trust, and how once it takes root in the heart, everything changes. His words are like music, so soft, so full of something that I cannot name, but so real and deeply fulfilling.

For the next 3 months, I would spend all my time in the ashram all day, from 6 in the morning until 11 at night. Meditating every day, all day long, getting up at 5 in the morning to ride my rented bicycle through the monsoon downpours to get to dynamic meditation. 'Dynamic'....if I hear the word, I can never forget the sounds of those birds in the reddish-orange sunrise of India, surrounding the Buddha Hall, as several hundred people would spend an hour breathing-screaming-crying-laughing-jumping up and down shouting "Hoo! Hoo! Hoo!"...and then...silence. It was a silence so deep and tangible, only made more deep by the sounds of tropical nature exploding forth with the new day.

At that time, the first week of each month was spent in an intensive meditation camp, which means doing these meditations one after another all day long. The day would always start with 'Dynamic'. This technique, more than any other, simply melts the mind, and opens up a remarkable absence of thoughts. My first experiences of it were filled with fear, as the body is just not used to having that much oxygen in it. My mind would fight, complain of exhaustion, and muscle cramps. But after awhile, that all passed, and a tremendous and seemingly endless new energy seemed to take me over.

Throughout the day and week there were many other meditation techniques as well: dancing, laughing, singing, chanting, humming, shaking, running, retaining the breath while staring at blue flickering lights; all very powerful and strange methods to bypass, and detour beyond the defenses of my chattering mind, and reach to an inner silence. Sometimes in the pauses between these meditations, I would simply lie on the grass, face down in the ashram garden, my tears flowing into the earth, of sorrow, of loss, of anguish, of joy, of nothing in particular that I could put in words; of just being overwhelmed by all that was happening in me.

Much would happen inside me in the meditation camps. There wasn't much chance for the mind to control anything, just one meditation would finish, and within a few minutes, the next one would begin. It was overwhelming what was occurring within me: all the mental-emotional structures I had were melting all at once. I was usually in silence, not speaking for the whole of the camp.

The other 3 weeks of the month were spent participating in the therapy groups which Bhagwan had specifically written that I should do that night when I first went to see him. These were intense and vivid experiences, of encounter and confrontation, exposure, opening to the negative feelings and moods locked up inside, peeling off the superficial masks which I had learned to take as my real face, but which were simply a patterned and weak substitute for real feelings.

One of the first groups he gave me to do was called Enlighten-ment Intensive. We were about 60 people, sitting in rows facing one another, for 18 hours a day, for a week. The technique consisted of one person asking, "Tell me, who you are", and the other person, sitting just in front and facing the first, would sim-ply begin to talk, whatever he considered to be his 'identity'. In the beginning, you would say maybe your name, where you come from, what you do, your education, and on and on, dig-ging and digging into whatever files were there in the mind, in the past, with which one creates the package of personal identity that we use to make our world and our perceptions. Hours, endless hours would pass, entire days, repeating the same stupid ideas, until there would be absolute frustration at the absurd nar-rowness of this box that we live in, this mind.

The group was happening on the open roof of Krishna house, the main building in the ashram, under a canvas cover, and the storms of the monsoon would arrive, howling hurri-canes, thunder and lightning and wind and rain, and, "Tell me who you are!!!" on and on. Amida, the group leader would be there jumping and shouting out like a madwoman, "Use the en-ergy of the storm! Use it for your search!!" Really sometimes I didn't know whether I was going mad or everyone else was, but there was no turning back now. On and on it went, emp-tying the whole baggage of the mind, ...until beyond, something would happen, a silence, an emptiness, a profound and absolute sense of being without words.

Another group consisted of different kinds of confrontational games; walking with a partner, in the rain, on the streets, simply recounting honestly the flow of awareness. "Now I am aware of..." enumerating all the objects on which the attention would rest for a moment, being absolutely and mercilessly honest about it in that moment. "Now I am aware of... the diesel smoke from the truck passing... Now I am aware of... the feeling of the road under my shoes... Now I am aware of... the smell of shit and smoke... Now I am aware of... the tits of the woman walking by... Now I am aware of.... my stomach cramps... etc. etc. etc."

One night, we were sent into the middle of the town, (which was a busy city of 5 million at the time), with a mission, to walk on the busiest street of the marketplace, with a kind of jingle passing between myself and a partner. It had a non-sensical sequence, that had to be remembered exactly and followed at all times while walking. One partner would begin saying, "Chamawy". The other would say, "Chattatty"...the first would say, "Chattatty", and the second would say, "Chamawy"...The first would say, "Chattatty, Chamawy"..the second would say, "Chamawy Chattatty"...Etc. The sequence was a certain combination that really had no intrinsic logic, and no meaning, but needed to be remembered and repeated exactly as it was. Remembering and repeating this, between two people, had the strange effect of shutting off a certain part of the mind, which needed to stay with the sequence, and could not continue its usual discursive pattern of thought. So, it left one with the curious experience of presence, of being there, in action and movement, without thought, because the thought mechanism was being used to keep the sequence going. We started walking, and before very long, we found ourselves in the middle of a religious festival, there were perhaps 100,000 people packed into the narrow streets, walking, beating drums, cymbals, shouting, pushing, jostling. In my normal state of American control-freak-fear-of-anything-vaguely-alive, I would have panicked. But mysteriously, we just passed through that ocean of humanity, as if it wasn't there at all.

Other groups were given to me by the Master: 'Tantra'. The name conjures up visions of sexual orgies and unusual acrobatic positions in the love act, described in archaic manuscripts. 2000 years of Christianity has served very well to make sex a glamorous forbidden fruit in the mind. It's a good mutual business, between the priests and the porno-venders. But, dear friend, I must tell you, this group wasn't like that at all.

I was 23 years old, quite shy and self-conscious, and I hadn't a clue as to how to approach women. Suddenly I found myself with 30 men and women of all different nationalities, all naked, in a windowless padded room underground for 6 days, 24 hours a day. What I recall is that on the contrary, no-one made love during that entire group.

A few tried, but it would quickly lead to something else, acting more as a provocation, a trigger for the enormously charged emotions behind the sex act. An Italian man, smiling lasciviously, would flirtatiously approach a pretty blonde woman. Now, flirting like that perhaps looks cool when you are wearing an Armani suit and you are in a plush hotel bar in Milano, but it looks completely ridiculous when you and her are both stark naked and there are 30 irritated bored people watching. The animal reality, and the contradiction of the mind-game on top of it; the woman would snarl, "Was ist disse SHEISSE!?" and the fight would begin. What happened for the most part was struggle, verbal and physical, confrontation, encounter, catharsis; all the bitterness, frustration, rage, fear, lust, anger, resentment between men and women, hatred between different classes, nationalities, races, fear of rejection, fear of rape, hatred of the father or mother, painful memories of abuse, rage at being denied physical nourishment as a baby; you name it, it all came out, all the garbage of the mind involving bodies of others, physical territory and contact and need, it was expressed and lived and observed. It was a tremendously cleansing experience.

There was one woman I liked very much and felt very attracted to, she was German, and beautiful in a natural way, and seemed very honest, simple and real to me. At one point an enormous giant of a man, also German, started groping her. He was about 7 feet tall, must have weighed 300 pounds and had lots of muscles. She got very scared, and the more scared she got, the more aggressive he got. I watched this scene unfolding, and my American cowboy sense of protection, kicked in, full gear, like the 'Lone Ranger' saying, "I'll save you, Ma'am!" I grabbed him by the leg and started pulling him off of her, and we got into a fight: I was a pygmy next to him, like a mosquito picking a fight with an elephant, and at one point I just freaked out and screamed in the most blood-curdling, high-volume and desperate primal explosion straight from my guts, and I curled up in a ball on the floor, my 'crust' had shattered and I was sobbing.

Meanwhile, through the air conditioning vents, from all the other therapy rooms, came the sounds of cheering and sustained applause after my scream, and everybody in the room including me started laughing. It went like that, for 6 days.

By the end of it, I had the distinct feeling and sense of living as a natural being, with a body, amongst other beings with bodies. If you FEEL 'yes' you just move with it, without thought, and you see what happens, what response comes. If you feel 'no', you remain true to that, with no mind in between. No games of how to manipulate or charm or capture, or dominate, or be liked. Just...feeling, sensing, acting, responding...being, in the moment, no thought of past or future outcome. It was, after the deep catharsis and purification, an incredible relaxation.

Sudha, a lovely Cuban woman and extremely sharp therapist, was the group leader. She never interfered in processes, but somehow let things take their course and come to their natural climax. Ironically, 30 years later I would make a statue that would stand as the funerary marker over her ashes, in a forest in Tuscany. It was a way of saying, 'Thanks' for a life-changing experience. The statue is in the form of a sensuous and elegant South American woman, offering a symbol of infinite wisdom in her hands, the wisdom of the female, the Shakti energy which is the source of all creative power in the universe.

In between groups, there was often an evening meeting with Bhagwan, once every ten days or so. These meetings were small and intimate. He would call me in front of him, and ask me what I had been doing. Sometimes he would say, "Anything you want to say to me?", with his very sweet smile and incred-

Monument to Sudha:WISDOM

ible love. I usually couldn't say anything to him, finding it actually difficult to speak while I was in front of him. His energy had an enormous impact on me, and my mind simply had so much space in it when I was near him, I had difficulty actually putting together the words, for the first three months that I would see him. He seemed to understand that, and then he would smile, and say, "Come close..."and he arranged a few women, in a kind of geometrical spacial arrangement around me and Him; a woman sitting behind me, another by her side, and he touched my forehead for a timeless eternity, and energy changes would just happen. Once I was so full of energy, that we all started yelling, and I just fell to the floor, stunned. One woman was half under me, two or three other people fell over me too. Everybody laughed, and Bhagwan was shaking his head and laughing, and said:"Crazy!"

Eventually, I became more accustomed to the energy of being around him, and was able to actually talk to him. At another 'darshan', one of these meetings with the Master, He asked me again if I had something to say, and I said, "Yes I do, Bhagwan. I love to play music. I love it more than anything in the whole world. And sometimes, when I am playing and the music is starting to really happen, my ego comes in, and it kills the music. Can you tell me something about this?"

He answered: "Music is so real, and the ego is so unreal, there is no way the ego can stop the music. It's the THOUGHT, that, "If the ego comes in, it will stop the music.".. THAT is the problem. Don't take the ego so seriously. Your ego is there, other egos are there, what is the problem...what your poor ego can do? (laughing). Just say, "Hello!", and GO ON PLAYING YOUR MUSIC".

CHAPTER 4

Rivers of Light

The darkness of ages cannot shroud the glowing sun;
The long eons of Samsara
ne'er can hide the Mind's brilliant light.
Though words are spoken to explain the Void,
the Void as such can never be expressed.
Though we say, "the Mind is a bright light",
it is beyond all words and symbols.
Although the Mind is void
in essence, all things it embraces and contains.

Tilopa, Song of Mahamudra

I had been living in Poona for a few months by this time. My life consisted of getting up at 5 am, riding on my rented bicycle, usually in the rain, to the ashram before dawn, to do dynamic, and then continue meditating all day. All the day I would pass in the ashram, listening to Bhagwan speak in the morning, doing the various meditations that happened throughout the day in the Buddha-hall, or else participating in the therapy groups that he had given me to do on that first night when I became a sannyasin. At that time, Bhagwan was speaking on an cryptic esoteric text from ancient China, called 'The Secret of the Golden Flower'. It was a mysterious yet very pragmatic text about a technique of meditation from an ancient mystery school in China, consisting of focusing one's energy in meditation on

'The Circulation of the Light', a process of balancing the inner energy, male/female, yin/yang, or in the terminology of Carl Jung, Animus-Anima. Once the energy would begin to flow, then effort would be made in increasing the circulation of this energy, perceived as a mysterious inner light within. The backdrop of these discourses mysteriously fit perfectly with the process I was living at the time; intensive group processes, cathartic meditations, that were serving to awaken the Anima in me and increase dramatically the flow of energy within my body, especially male. This process was greatly amplified by Bhagwan's physical presence, both in the morning lectures, and in the darshans which were happening at night, at which time I would often be called up to sit in front of him face-to-face.

Many times, usually in fact, this would end with him directly transmitting energy into my body with his finger on my third eye. This was a kind of blissful electrocution. It moved energy inside me in such a way that I was starting to feel like a 100-watt lightbulb plugged into a 220-volt socket. LOTS of things were moving inside me, LOTS of emotions, LOTS of mood swings. I could not maintain anymore the small limits and borders which I was used to in my personality comfort zone. My control mechanisms were melting away, and I could not hide or repress anything that was surfacing in my psyche, being stirred up and released by the processes I was in, the powerful energy field which was the Poona Ashram at that time, and of course, the direct energetic interventions of Bhagwan, through these individual darshans, sitting in his lectures everyday, and meditating all day within a short distance of his physical presence. The whole milieu created a situation in me of 'immanent explosion'.

In these days during the monsoon months of 1978, I was living in a one-room building by the railroad tracks, a low-end housing of a few bungalows which probably had been servants quarters in the back of a large villa during the British Raj. Now it had been turned into inexpensive housing for the overflow of western disciples surrounding Koregaon Park, the wooded area where the ashram was located on the outskirts of Poona City.

My room was whitewashed and clean inside, but if you touched the walls, your hands or clothes were also white. Outside just a few yards away were the railroad tracks, and the passing steam trains were depositing loads of coal dust on everything all day long.

On that particular morning, I was in my room, that little building of mud bricks and whitewash, with the occasional visit of rats so big they would have passed for dogs, who would simply push the door open and stand there like football linebackers, looking for a quarterback to tackle. There was many a time passed chasing those vile and aggressive creatures around the room to get them out. They had the nasty habits of eating holes in my orange robes, of which I couldn't afford to buy new ones, so it was me or them who had to go, and I was going to make sure it would be them.

During those first months there in Bhagwan's energy field, I was continuing with Rebirthings, both in a group and individual sessions, and each was a unique, often very painful experience. This had been specifically given to me to do personally by Bhagwan, who that first night in darshan, had written down, amongst other groups, Rebirthing when he had made out the list of groups I would do, as he usually did with newcomers.

During these experiences, much emotional material was released in me, with accompanying 'memories' and visions:
I experienced the agony and extreme compression and discomfort of the birth process, even to the point of strongly smelling the vaginal fluids and anesthetic which must have been given to my mother during my birth, a smell resembling ether-alco-

hol. There was, at another time an explosive breath-release, and a memory of extreme pain, as I kept hearing my voice saying , "They've killed me, they've killed me!" I saw my body (actually it was not my body in this lifetime, it was the body I occupied in another life, as I apparently was experiencing a death-experience 'before' my birth in this lifetime). I was laying as a now-dead body on a large oak table, there was a Nazi flag on the wall facing me in the room I was in, and I felt that I had been tortured and killed in this place, as my consciousness was leaving this body. I cannot say actually that this was 'past-life', as the idea of time sequence flowing from past to present to future is actually just an idea. When I experienced it, it seemed as 'present' as any other experiential moment of my life.

Now on this rainy morning, I had woken up feeling peculiarly frustrated, as if everything was just bugging the shit out of me, and it seemed that the universe was intentionally designed to inflict mal-intent on me personally. The rain, the mud, the rats, the smell of excrement everywhere and always, (a constant in India), the steam trains passing by which would leave a film of soot on the white walls and my orange clothes; EVERY-THING was on my NERVES! In that state, I mounted my rickety rented bicycle, and pedaled off to Koregaon park, for another session of rebirthing.

So, dutifully, yet resentfully, in fact, completely and utterly pissed off, I went there that morning. The therapist was a little French man, very quiet, who started me breathing; long breathing, in and out connected, with no pause in-between the inhalation and exhalation. I slowly filled with energy, and my body took over the breathing automatically. I was laying down, and can remember the sensation of my body tensing up in the arms and hands, a kind of lock-up that happens to babies when they take too much air. It was excruciatingly painful. The breathing went on, faster and faster, I became hotter, and hotter, and my arms in more and more pain, until it was unbearable, or actually beyond unbearable: faster and faster...then...an Explosion!....just silence...and RIVERS OF LIGHT! Endless streams of energy crisscrossing in space...a wordless, timeless space: I had no thoughts, no body sensations, no body whatsoever, but I was seeing the universe all around me and me included as rivers of light...vibrations all crisscrossing and flowing in many colors...it was ecstasy...it was utterly beautiful, marvelous. It was sheer bliss. I didn't have any sense of time, or body, or space, nor pain nor pleasure, but when I 'came back', the quiet frenchman said that it had been about 3 hours that I was in that state, and it had taken over many other people who were having sessions in the room at the same time, like a great wave that engulfed us all. Gone was all that frustration of the morning; just I was left with a vast sense of wonder, oneness, awe, and gratitude...

One night outside of the ashram, walking on the back road, I heard a very magical music, a strange sound that was like the human soul crying out for union with God, and I followed the sound. In the garden of a big house, under a palm tree there was a man, dressed something like a Sadhu, an Indian monk, with his hair in a top knot, like Hindu monks wear. He was playing something, resembling a small odd-looking cello, with many strings. Its sound went straight to my soul. I sat for a long time listening, and then spoke to him. His name was Jitendra. He was British, spoke a bit like a gentleman with his little round glasses and steely blue eyes, and we became friends. He told me that the name of his little instrument was 'Sarangi', which means, 'the dancing voice of a thousand colors'. He lived there, in a hut in back of that garden, and said I could come to visit sometime.

He was a wonderful musician. He was English, with long white hair, long ago having chucked his passport away, and he had simply stayed in India, 15 years by then, playing music, and making wonderful music instruments and selling them to make a living. He had a very lovely and fairly well pregnant Scottish girlfriend named Yashodhara, and I spent many afternoons and evenings with them, playing music together, and hearing stories of their years in India. We would play often until 3 or 4 in the morning, late-night ragas, and Yashodhara would whip up some great tapioca pudding around that time, which would make the evenings pass very well indeed. I was looking for a teacher of classical Indian vocal music, and he knew someone in downtown Poona, and offered to bring me to him. So we went on our beat-up bicycles, long miles into the city, past the Red Fort, the Sari market by the river, into the swarming and crowded old center of Poona, named Laxmi road. Poona was not a large Indian city, but in actuality its population was more than 5 million then. It had vast stretches of slums, the houses being made of discarded metal and cardboard with open sewers in the streets, and we passed much of it on the way to the old center of town where lived the voice master. There in a back alley, up an old and broken stairway, we came into a little 'apartment', with two rooms and mud floors, very, very old and ramshackle. Outside the window was the crowd passing like a river below, with a massive Shiva temple visible in the window a few blocks away. There I met a smiling little old man with shining eyes, named Hindegandharva Divekar. We talked a little bit, drank some tea, and I asked if he would teach me how to sing. With a delighted and toothless smile, he said, "Yes!"

When Divekar used to sing, it was pure delight. He sang from a place of joy, and he was in bliss when he was making music. He came from a Gharana (a traditional school of Indian Classical music) that were Veena players, and his Rudra Veena was there in the room, along with a few ancient looking tambouras. 'Rudra' is another name of Shiva, and it is legend that this Divine Being actually created the instrument Veena thousands of years ago, wishing to find a way to give meditation to humanity. Shiva made the instrument from two pumpkins and a bamboo stick, and practiced in the forest until the deers themselves would cry from the beautiful sounds he was making.

Divekar played so marvelously in tune, and sang in the same way, it was a joy to hear, and it made you feel like everything was vibrating in harmony inside you. It was such soft music, so real, with such a pure vibration. I would go to see him every week for the next few months, with my violin.

I could never forget the sound of that sarangi, though. It haunted me, and called out to me. I asked around if anyone knew where to find one, as they have become rare and hard to find in India. I went to all the music shops, and instrument makers on Laxmi road, the chaotic and crowded center of the old town. One shopkeeper would send me here, another would send me there, into little alleyways and up and down stairs leading to little holes in the wall which on second inspection were shops crammed with all kinds of weird odds and ends. Nobody knew exactly where to find a Sarangi, and finally, the opinion of everyone was that, "You simply must go to Bombay!"

So I found out where the music shops with sarangis might be in Bombay. I would have to go to BINDI BAZAAR, a market section of Bombay where there were many instrument shops at that time. I guess in my mind it seemed like I was going to a mall in Southern California to buy something at Macy's; I had no idea what was about to happen, and it was good that it was that way.

I took the train at 6 a.m., a 3-hour journey through cool dripping forests with monkeys, down into the sweaty and steamy plains of Bombay. I was dressed in orange robes, with my hair tied up on my head, and my wooden mala on my neck, a string of beads with a locket and the picture of Bhagwan. To the other people on the train, they assumed I was a Hindu monk and gave me their seats, or offered me some of their breakfast. I was silent, and politely refused. When I got to Bombay, which at that time was a city of more than 15 million people, I had really no way to be prepared for the shock to my senses, all of them, which was Dadar station. A flood of sights, colors, smells, sounds, ranging from beautiful to utterly disgusting, all presented themselves to me at once. I felt like I had landed in a bad acid trip. I took a bus from Dadar station..and got off at Bindi Bazaar. It was more like 'Bindi BIZARRE'.

I found myself walking down a street that was... potatoes; Only potatoes... Mountains of them, on both sides of the street, as far and as high as the eye could see. And here and there were people, children, barefoot wearing rags, coming out from the piles of potatoes, living in them, under them; I walked and walked, and turned another street, and it was... Used car parts; Mountains of them! Bumpers and motors and wheels and headlights and doors, all piled up in surrealistic patterns, on both sides of the street as far as the eye can see, with people living in them, cooking in them, babies crying in them. There were no buildings, just piles and piles of every possible combination of ancient car parts that could ever be imagined... Dali would have loved it. The grey, steaming and dripping sky gave no sense of depth, or space, it only heightened the sense of desperation. A sense of panic overtook me, and I had to get out of the sea of car parts! I walked and walked, and came to a kind of 'park', but it was more like a disaster area, garbage and papers every-where, no trees, no grass; just a desolate emptiness surrounded by buildings that looked like they were all about to fall down, or already had. Hundreds of people milling here and there, all dressed in dirty rags; A little girl walked alongside me, taunting me, I don't know what she was saying, but it didn't feel good... someone passed by and slapped me... and I realized I look like a Hindu monk, and this must be a poor muslim section of town. I think to myself: "Oof, not good, I've heard stories of commu-nal violence in the slums in Bombay between Hindus and Mus-lims; this is definitely a slum, and I look like a Hindu...walk on, my friend and take no notice, take no notice." There must have been at least 400 people looking at me while the little girl went on taunting... I walked and walked....

I turned a corner, onto a dirt road with green slime in the gutters, and both sides of the street as far as I can see disappearing into the distance are lined with dirty cages with iron bars, and in them, thousands upon thousands of young women in saris, with intense makeup, reaching out their hands, making movements of eyes and hips and lips to me that make me feel like I am standing there completely naked. The gestures they are making are striking me in my sex chakra, in a way that is much deeper than my conscious mind. The putrid stench in the street, the vision of all the women behind bars as far as the eye can see, and the strange effect of their lips and eye movements, I don't know whether to vomit or run, so I stand and stare. I can't believe this is happening, in 1978, human sexual slaves, by the thousands. I had not the faintest idea that this existed on planet earth, now. "This sure doesn't look like Kansas, Toto..", to quote a popular movie of my childhood. I was shocked and disarmed too much to sit in judgement. Those women had an animal power which I did not have, I was swimming in the dark waters of which I knew nothing. It was a bottomless abyss, this dark side of human sexuality, and I was neither above it nor outside of it. It was part of me, I could feel it in the way my body reacted to their lewd and explicit gestures. Disgust, attraction, repulsion and fascination all were in me. The air reeked of decay, dissolution, putrefaction, a Dante-esque vision of the hell and slavery of lust, in 3d and technicolor. I walked on and on. I turn another corner, and there standing in front of me, is a beggar, wrapped in a white shroud. I cannot tell where or what is her face, there is only an open wound on most of her exposed flesh, featureless. She mutely reaches out her fingerless hand in my direction. I realize she is a leper. I only heard about this in stories as a kid, in movies like 'Ben

Hur'... But facing the reality is like facing a living corpse, all the pain and sorrow and horror of humanity standing there in a speechless plea before me.

I walk on, and on, and turn another corner, and finally there is a street of music shops! I go in the first one. They have no sarangis. They don't know where to find one. The second shop is the same. The third , the same answer. One by one I check all the 15 or so shops on the street. No sarangi. They say that everyone now wants to play electric guitar. By the evening, I am back on the train to Poona, speechless, with very empty hands and a head full of things that I still can't believe I saw. When I get to Poona late in the night, I decide to visit the music shop on Laxmi road before going home. There in the shop, on the table, waiting for me, was a beautiful old sarangi, so lovingly made, and the shopkeeper had a big smile as he says, "I was waiting for you."

I practiced that sarangi night and day. My fingers would bleed sometimes, from playing it too much. It was the most difficult instrument I had ever touched. There are 40 strings, most of them simply for resonance. It has 3 very thick and rough gut strings, that you played on the side with the cuticle of the fingers, which was very painful at first. It took awhile to build up callouses, and not cut or burn the delicate skin of the cuticles while playing. Jitendra helped me learn it, and I started to accompany my vocal lessons with Sarangi. It has an uncanny way of sounding just like a human voice, only more plaintive.

Sitting in Divekar's little room with him, the windows open to the endless flood of human life passing on the street below, the Shiva temple always present there in the window; this was the right doorway for me to learn Indian music. It was 'right'. It could not have been otherwise. The river of humanity passing below, the sounds and smells and impressions of the ancient life of India still present all around, in this atmosphere I drank in the ragas and joy of Divekar's sweet voice, his ancient Veena, like

74

the sweet chai made by his wife as the long afternoons would pass.

One of those days, coming home from my voice lessons in the center of Poona, I was sitting at a chai shop, facing a long highway, a dirt road, at 7 o'clock in the evening, outside the Red Fort, at the gates to the old city. Thousands upon thousands of people passed as I sat there, an endless sea of nameless faces, walking in the dust, wearing dusty clothes, some in rags, the queue endlessly walking and walking, disappearing in both directions into the fading grey sky. I then realized, deep in my heart, that all my adolescent dreams of worldwide social change were just idiotic. The problems of the world are so vast, and my mind so small to comprehend them; humans are a numberless sea, and each one a world in themselves, each one believing themselves to be the center of the known universe, and each of those universes is as numberless as grains of sand on an endless beach. Something just fell away from my mind, and I stopped to think of changing the world outside anymore.

Twelve years later, I would sit one night on that same Laxmi road, in a free public concert by Bhimsen Joshi, the master vocalist of India. The streets were packed, there were at least 100,000 people there that night, on every roof, balcony, window, sidewalk, and shop window filled with attentive and utterly silent, devoted listeners. There was only the sound of his voice, and one silent, ecstatic oceanic heart. Only through music can that happen, and then, only in India.

The daily rhythm of the ashram was centered around Bhagwan's morning discourses, which one month would be in English, and the next month in Hindi. I loved particularly when he was speaking in Hindi, because at that time his voice would enter into me like a musical soft rain, with no logical meaning to engage my mind. He spoke Hindi in a particularly beautiful way, with a poetic rhythm, and it would invariably put me into a kind of trance, a deep meditative space, where something mysterious would happen inside, movements of energy as such. I also loved hearing him in English, where I could actually understand what he was talking about, but that was a different experience that also engaged my mind, and I was naturally drawn to falling into him like an ocean without using the mind at all.

He would usually talk about a different master every month...Sufi, Zen, Christian, Buddhist, Hassidic, Bauls: it was amazing how he could weave a canvas with each of these different threads, and each time, you were left with the feeling that THIS is the really true path! And then next month, you felt that way about a completely different one. In short, there was no way to form a dogma or system inside your mind about his teaching. Everything he would say, he could say the paradoxical opposite of it, IN THE SAME LECTURE, and it would all make sense. It was not logical, it was not illogical: It was supralogical, beyond logic, and it worked in such a way to first fulfill and then break down all the boxes you were trying to form in your mind. There was no way to hang onto anything, you were left with the negation of the negation of the negation; just the emptiness, between his words, was filled with something so unexplainable and yet so tangibly real, that was a deep nourishment to the heart and soul.

Life in India at that time was different than it is now; there weren't clean Western-style cafes and bakeries and shops like there are now, there wasn't even toilet paper. The great mass of men on the streets were wearing white kurtas, a long simple shirt, and dhotis, a kind of loin cloth wrapped around the pelvis, and white gandhi caps. The women all wore saris. The only cars on the roads were Ambassadors, a kind of turtle-like car resembling a 1949 Oldsmobile. There were millions of bicycles, scooters, goats, an occasional elephant, and cows, cows, cows.

The cows would walk around freely, sometimes just sitting down in the middle of a busy road, and everybody would have to go around them. If you ate any food that wasn't cooked, even a little parsley on the top of the soup, you were taking your life in your hands, literally. Showering had to be done with a tightly closed mouth, and brushing the teeth with only bottled water. If you forgot this, just once, the consequences were disastrous. Typhoid, hepatitis, cholera, amoebic dysentery, all were endemic and water-borne. It was the last days of the monsoon, the cultural habit of the 800 million Hindus living there at that time was to defecate on the shores of all the rivers and streams. And in the monsoon rains, the rivers swelled, overflowed the banks, and obviously, every drop of water in the whole country was full of shit, literally. You got used to that, but you had to never forget it.

As for my social life, other than the music sessions at night, I actually had none at the time. I would participate fully in the ashram meditations, from 6 am until 11 pm, and what was happening inside me was really so much and so fulfilling that I was overfull. It was not my time to get involved romantically with someone. The ashram was full of lovely young people, in fact I had never seen such beautiful women in my whole life, but I was in such a process of uncovering parts of my psyche that I had no idea existed, it was not the time for me to be reaching out for 'outer' kinds of fulfillment or sharing. It just didn't happen. I was in a kind of energy-cocoon with myself, and that was fine. In a place that was world-renowned for being a center of free sex, I was a defacto monk, without even trying to be one. The close friends I had were Jitendra and Yashodhara, and our music that we played late into the nights, in the garden behind Bhagwan's residence.

I had done the many groups that Bhagwan had given me over 3 months time; Tantra, Rebirthing, Bio-energetics, Centering, Enlightenment Intensive, Tai-Chi, and others...the last on the list was Vipassana. This was a 10 day residential group in a long bungalow on the river, about a 20-minute walk from the ashram. It was to be a retreat of silent meditation. 'Vipassana' is a Pali word, and it was the main technique of Gautama the Buddha to attain enlightenment. It means to be watching the breath, from 6 in the morning until midnight, for 10 days. It was 3 months to the day that I had arrived in India. The monsoon was in its last days, the river was a brown and muddy torrent passing by the front of the long bungalow that was to be our place of retreat. I had given up my sooty hut by the railroad tracks, and my visa was about to expire. I went to the group with my backpack ready to return to the States, as I would leave for Bombay straight after the group...or so I thought!

As the group started, the long days of silent sitting seemed uncomfortable to me, I wasn't finding it easy to settle into myself. My body was getting more and more uncomfortable, painful in fact. I couldn't figure out what was happening. Meditation which had become a daily joy to me was more and more difficult to settle into. By the 5th day I was very weak, and low energy, and it was painful to sit. I didn't feel to eat anything, and I was feverish. I had to leave the group, and walked the few hundred yards to the medical center, with great difficulty. I was nearly fainting. When I arrived to the ashram medical center, Dr. DevaRaj was the one who saw me, and he looked in my eyes, and had me do a urine test. When I gave him the bottle back, my piss was as brown as coca-cola. He held it up, and without any further ado, said, "Ah, pepsi, is it? You've got hepatitis. Go to bed."

I had nowhere to go, very little money left, and an expiring visa, and a backpack. I somehow got into a rickshaw, and went to a big old Indian palace where was living a friend of mine named Neejara, a wonderfully crazy Danish lady who liked my music very much. She had hepatitis a couple of months before, and I thought she might know what to do. With my last strength, I knocked on her door. She opened the door, took one look and me, and said, "Oh my god...Come in!"

For the next 3 weeks I was pretty much in a delirious fever, I cannot actually remember any passage of time or events. I know that I must have eaten sometimes, but it all passed like a foggy nightmare. In my mind were angry visions, terrible dreams, it was a painful purification of all the repressed anger of my childhood. Neejara had her servant-lady take care of me, give me good simple food with no oil when I could eat, and slowly the fever passed. I would be weak for many more weeks, a strange and mystical time in which I had no physical strength, but a kind of high-frequency energy in my body which was not of my body. My body could do practically nothing, I could walk for short periods, and that's about all. But I felt very high and light inside. I couldn't sleep, and would walk in the night in Koregaon park playing my little sitar, and melodies would flow through my fingers all night. It was magical, and mysterious. The soul of Indian music was starting to penetrate into me, and it was a strangely blissful time.

As I recovered strength, and was no longer so yellow, and was well, I could start to see people again. I went to the ashram now for discourses , and I wrote to Bhagwan, saying that I came from a place called Oregon, and I thought that there were "many people there who could appreciate his presence". I was referring to his spiritual presence, but little did I know at that time how fateful those words were to be. He did not answer me in a discourse, but I was called into the office, and the message was given to me from him that I should start a center in Oregon. It would be called:'Anando'.

I used the last money I had to buy books, pictures, and things that I thought would help start the center, and packed my things once again.

As I boarded the plane for America, all my possessions including the sarangi, the books, other music instruments and all the materials for starting the center were in a big box on the plane, and my arm was in a sling from a hand operation I had just days before leaving. I landed in London, and I had a half a day before the flight back to the States, so I decided to have a look at the city. The quarantine officer was a little leery about letting me through immigration, as I was looking pretty bleak and thin and that arm in a sling seemed very dubious to him, but he eventually did let me in. I got off the 'Tube' (as they call the subway in London) in Piccadilly and wandered around the town, in early November in my thin cotton Indian kurta and pijamas, bright orange. I stopped, transfixed, in front of a huge bronze statue, Rodin's 'Burgers of Calais', and stayed there a long time, deeply moved by this masterpiece of shadow and light, emotion and silent testimony to human drama and courage in the face of death. In front of Buckingham Palace, a burly motorcycle cop stopped me, and asked me what was that on my back. I said, "It's a miniature sitar". He asked me if I could play it. I played a few minutes for him then he asked me if I played something other than miniature sitar. I said I played the violin. He said he was in a bluegrass band and they needed a second fiddle, and asked if I wanted to join the band, on Thursday nights. I said thanks, but I wouldn't be able to make it for Thursday.

The next day, when I arrived to San Francisco, all my luggage, including sarangi, books, and all my clothes and instruments, never showed up. It was lost by dear British Airways in an ironic parting gesture from India. I stepped off the plane in America with 5 dollars in my pocket and my arm in a sling, wearing orange robes, skinny as a rail, and no other possessions but my memories of those 6 months with me.

CHAPTER 5

A Passage In San Francisco

Woman:	Let me through, Let me through!!
	Where does this narrow road lead?
Gatekeeper:	It leads to the Shrine of Heaven.
Woman:	Let me through!!
Gatekeeper:	It's fine to go, but it's frightening to come back.
Woman:	Even if it's scary...Let me through!

('Toryanse': children's song from ancient Japan)

When I arrived back in the USA, the real work began, in the sense that it had been an idyllic atmosphere for entering the 'inner world' of meditation in Poona. There, deep psychic experiences were frequent, and easy; just you had to tune inwards a little bit, and persons you had known in past lives almost would bump into you on the street. There is a deep undercurrent in India, nourished by 20,000 years of yoga and meditation; it EXISTS there hidden under the surface of the collective, and it's available still, to tap into, like a river. But in materialistic America? That's a different story...

Back in the USA, I found that I had changed more than I had realized. The City of San Francisco, once interesting to me, now seemed hard, cold, lonely, and sterile after the intense colors, sights , sounds and smells of India. I went up to Oregon, to start the center as I had been advised by Bhagwan, and that was a good project for awhile, for me to recuperate my physical energy and come 'back to earth'. I found an old house in Eugene, the rent was $50 a month which I paid for with gardening jobs, and the landlord had no objections that I take out the inner walls and turn it into a big meditation room.

Doing the carpentry to fix the house up made my body slowly get stronger after the illnesses in India, and soon I opened the meditation center in Eugene, Oregon. People would stop by in that little center, come for Kundalini meditation, a cup of tea, a rebirthing session; it was simple and heartful. Travelers would come and stay for a day, and tell their stories, and move on. I reconnected with old friends I had known in Eugene before I went to India, but there was a widening gap between us. I was crazy in love with Bhagwan, and there were many pictures of him in the house, and that didn't go over too well with my Oregonian friends. No matter how 'alternative' they might have been, they felt offended by pictures of my guru and my new name. So, we drifted apart, and I settled more into my new path, and accepted the change.

After many months, I longed to reconnect with other sannyasins, (the name Bhagwan would usually use for his disciples, as a group), and eventually somehow get back to India. I was going through much 'purification' after the intense experiences of India. Sometimes I would cry for days nonstop, without really a reason, just a letting-go. People there in Eugene couldn't really understand it. Old friends thought I was losing my marbles, but I felt I was finding them. I longed to get back to the ashram, to drink in Bhagwan's presence like a healing ocean. India was far from San Francisco, but it was light-years away from Oregon, in those days. In Eugene, running a meditation center, if you even could survive it was a miracle, but to save money to travel was impossible. After a year's seasonal changes, from the roses of spring to the brilliant colors of autumn and frosts of winter, I decided to pack it in and go back to the Bay Area, and see what happens.

I returned to Marin County, and was living for a time in a small cabin on the top of Mt. Tamalpais. I was re-birthing almost daily, training with people from the Rebirthing Center in San Francisco, students of Leonard Orr. The re-birthing process opens and releases much 'shadow material', emotional memories in the psyche. Many times I would feel the same sense of frustration and helplessness as a newborn baby, inability to deal with the 3d aspects of my life as such. This was the real work, digging into the unconscious while integrating into the reality of here-now in THIS world. This was a huge challenge to me, and it was very necessary the support system of rebirthers and other sannyasins in the Bay Area, who were in the same boat so to speak, of unearthing their shadow material inside and releasing past internal wounds and programs.

In my inner search, and confusion about what was actually happening to me in this process of emotional-and-psychic-purification that I was in the middle of, I felt I needed the closer support of the sannyasin community in San Francisco. So I went to live at the Paras Center. It was a big old house on 24th street, with 3 floors, a big meditation room, a hot tub in the basement, and about 20 people living there at a time. It was a totally new experience for me, having lived always a kind of monastic life. The style of communal sannyas life was very confrontative at that time; you didn't hold anything back in words, either positive nor negative. What you felt about somebody, you said with all the emotions behind it, or screamed it, and then lived with the aftermath. Sometimes it was really a mess.

The emphasis in Bhagwan's work at that time was going beyond fear and being 'real', peeling off the masks of hypocrisy and expressing what you truly felt, come what may, regardless of the consequences. It was a lot of egos colliding, like a hall of mirrors, with every one of them pushing all the buttons you had. We had weekly encounter groups, and sannyasins from the outside community would come too. Sometimes those groups were 50 people on an evening, and they got pretty wild. Amitabh was the facilitator; he was the 'papa of the tribe' in the Bay Area, having been with Bhagwan a long time and in fact he was a very gifted and insightful therapist and great human being. We moved through much emotional baggage in those days. It was a time of peeling layers off the personality, dramatically, and I learned a great deal.

At the same time, with a few of the musicians I was getting to know in town, we started up a rock band, and played gigs here and there in the City, usually parties, sometimes meditation weekends. That was great fun. I was playing my flute, and fiddle, and singing, and I enjoyed it when the music wasn't too grungy. Those were the days of the start of Punk, and sometimes the band got pretty raunchy and I would step out until things got a little more harmonic. I grew up on rock and roll, and I love it, but I don't love noise, so…when things get too loud and disharmonic, I just don't hear music in it. That was a dilemma in that band. Sometimes it worked, sometimes it didn't. We served as a focal point of energy for the hundreds of sannyasins in the city at that time, and sometimes it was really a blast.

At that time I was in what I could only call 'a difficult relationship'. Looking back at it with the understanding I have now, I certainly can't call it 'love'. It was more like hormonal inundation-drama-conflict-sex-and self abuse. Her name was 'Triste'. She was a very tough and sexy lady (I use this term euphemistically…she was no lady!) from Queens, the 'Queen of Queens' I would call her, In my childhood this was a title given to the Virgin Mary, and ironically, this woman now came into my life as a total anti-archetype to that Virgin Mother image I grew up with. She was more like Durga the Destroyer, changing all the ideas I had about who I was and why I was living. She was a few years older than me, from New York, and me a too-nice-guy from the suburbs of LA. She was a Scorpio and I an Aquarian. She was a part-time stripper and film actress, and me a budding new-age musician and poet. We didn't fit together, but she definitely pushed every button I had in me, including the ones that blinded me with hormones, and I got to see a lot of the darker sides of myself which I never knew existed before that time.

For that I can be ironically grateful. That she nearly destroyed my life and made me realize that I was in a life-and-death struggle for my psychic survival, I can't say that I feel grateful, but it had to happen. I learned much through it, namely that I would never wish to relate or live in that manner again, from the dark side. It was a perfect reflection of what I was going through in my therapy processes, opening up and cleaning many wounds hidden inside me, and it was a mirror of all the emotional garbage that had been repressed in me, all the anger and inhibitions and rage that I had never acknowledged from 24 years of denying my real feelings. I was living the dark movie of my inner shadow, projected out on the screen of my outer life including my girl friend. It was a tough way to go through it, but it worked, Fastrack...it's like an old Italian saying :

"If it doesn't kill you, it makes you more strong".

This was the process we were going through; whatever was happening to us, we expressed: with very little consideration for the consequences. Anger, jealousy, possessiveness, rage, frustration, every reaction, every emotion, it all got projected outwards, day by day. We were groping in the dark, for a light, and the dark seemed bottomless, but in the midst of the worst moments of that unhappy and hellish time, I found a base inside myself, in the silence after the storms; a kind of bedrock, which would not be lost. I was not reaching for some spirituality in the sky, but standing on the solid ground, accepting the mud in me for the first time and starting to live from there. I knew I was not where I 'wanted to be', I had no way yet to absorb and transform these negative emotions I was experiencing. I was drowning in them, but every day doing Bhagwans meditations and going through therapy processes in the center were helping, as well as provoking and intensifying the process. Where was I going in this? Where was leading this road? I could only dimly sense a light somewhere at the end of the tunnel of this process, yet I didn't have enough understanding to get there on my own. I did feel I was unburdening my consciousness of much heavy baggage. The processes I was in were exposing gaping holes in me, worthlessness, shame, resentment at everything, especially the 'system'. At the same time, Bhagwan's constant message was to not take oneself seriously, to celebrate, to rejoice in life. Yet I couldn't get it. I was wearing orange and red clothes, with a mala around my neck: trying to get carpentry jobs looking like that, I would more often get laughed at than hired. I had no interest in fitting into life in America, my heart and soul were deeply involved in something totally different, a process of trans-formation which at times was fascinating and joyful, and at times extremely painful and confusing with what was being uncov-ered in me. And to live there, in between those two worlds, but being really in neither, was an impossible position. I had no in-terest to re-enter life in America and get into making money-money-money, and yet to get back to India and Bhagwan meant crossing that river somehow. My past reference points were dis-appearing, I couldn't see who I used to be. And who I was com-ing to be was not at all clear to me yet. It was a strange time.

"When a man begins the path of a warrior,
he becomes gradually aware to have turned his back forever
on normal life.
That means that the ordinary reality can no longer protect him,

and to survive he must adopt a new way of life.. ".

Don Juan as told to Carlos Castaneda

In what were those strange days of transition in San Francisco, rumors were coming from India that Bhagwan was ill, that he would soon stop working with people, that the commune would close down and he would disappear with a few chosen disciples in the Himalayas, all kinds of things were being said, and nobody knew what was the truth. I was becoming desperate to get back to India, I was still half-cooked on this path, and needed to be near him.

At that time my girlfriend left for Korea, on her way to India. She had no qualms about leaving me behind, and I should have taken that as a blessing. But within a few days I started getting calls from her, urging me to come there, there was a business deal that I could be in that would give me the money to go to India. She sent me a ticket to Korea. Like a fool, I accepted, and got on a flight for Seoul. Within 5 days that I was there, my part in it evaporated, and she left again, this time for India, leaving me alone and just about penniless in the YMCA hotel in Seoul, waiting for a connection which would never come. The ridiculousness and absolute stupidity of my situation started to dawn on me, that I was depending on and basing my life around someone who actually cared nothing for whether I lived or died, and in the end, leaving me for her own impatient and selfish motives. Sometimes, lessons come the hard way. This was my time for that.

CHAPTER 6

The Eel and the Lid

Seoul, South Korea, in 1980: at that time it was a city of more than 10 million, still recovering from the terrible war which devastated the country 30 years before, the city having changed hands a few times between the South and the North during the horrible years of battle. After the vacuum left in the wake of the Japanese occupation of WWII, the country was divided into factions of communists in the North and capitalists in the South. The South was backed by the USA, and the North by the Soviet Union and then the new China of Mao-tse Tung, and a local conflict became a standoff between nuclear powers in the Cold War now-turned-hot. The Americans under MacArthur nearly won, having pushed the Northern forces back to the Chinese border. Then came the army of Mao's People's Republic of China, flooding in human waves, basically throwing more men at the American machine guns than there were bullets to kill them. MacArthur got fired for wanting to 'nuke' them, and the Americans were pushed back and back, the population being massacred by both armies using every terrible means at their disposal, including biological weapons. The war ground on in a kind of hellish see-saw for 3 years, until an uneasy ceasefire fixed the border just 25 miles from Seoul. When I got to Seoul, even after so many years, I felt the uneasy tension, the barbed-wire and guard-posts, the soldiers everywhere, the curfews at night, the people living still with very little in the sense of needs and nothing in the sense of abundance. But never had I seen such simple and generous people, willing to share what little they had with a total stranger. And yet, there was the uncanny feeling, this my first time in Eastern Asia, that I never really knew what anyone was feeling when they were speaking to me, at any time. What they were saying, and what was actually going on, I uncomfortably sensed was never really the same.

In my hotel room in Seoul, the rats would shinny down the heating vent at night, and nose around the room, seeing if anything was worthwhile there. It was a dark and small room, to which I would be confined each night after 9 pm, as the military trucks moved through the streets announcing the curfew time, and everyone disappears inside. It is a room for which I could no longer pay, as each day I would sink more into debt, as the business connection who arranged the room had suddenly disappeared, with no explanation or contact number. Each day I wait hopefully and expectantly for a call that would signal my release from this jail, each day the call comes at 5 pm, each day a voice with a thick oriental accent says, 'NO TODAY!' and hangs up.

The Kafka-esque quality of my situation became more surreal with each passing moment. The city is a mass of millions of faces without names to me, moving in the streets, in polyester business suits, the air reeking of fish, kim chee, charcoal smoke, and diesel. In the day I am alone in the endless sea of black heads moving like fish on the crowded streets. I haven't spoken to another human being in days. In a park a man walks up to me to shake my hand and says: "I Rike basuboru belly much... do you Rike basuboru?" and walks away. I realize after a minute or two he must have been talking about baseball. Two women looking like China dolls approach me: they are wearing so much makeup that I cannot tell where are their real eyebrows or lips. They hand me a small camera, and indicate for me to take their picture. I do so, and they leave. These kinds of interactions, which were quite sincere on the part of the others in their world and habits, were interpreted by me as 'vacuous', simply making me more acutely aware of my loneliness and depression. Wanting air, and space, I walk uphill, to the ring of forested hills on the edge of the city. From a hole in the ground, a voice shouts to me, "HALT, DON'T MOVE!"...and the helmeted man in green fatigues who owns this voice is pointing a loaded rifle at my head. I say, "I am just going for a walk". He replies, "NO CAN GO!!" So I return down to the city, sinking even deeper into the morass of hopelessness that is this depressing fascist hell I find myself in.

In an alley a drunk is being carried away by his two friends, cursing and vomiting as he goes. I am passing the large market, the now familiar Asian market smell of dying fish and spices and soot lingers in my nose and brain. On a long street beside a river, I pass a fish-sellers shop. In the window is a large tank, with some eels boringly and hopelessly waiting their demise, being visible and available to the choice of prospective buyers.

I drift a bit closer, as I am drawn by the face of one particular eel behind the glass just in front of me. Such a depressed and despondent look is there in his eyes, as he stares vacantly into the distance, awaiting his death. I immediately identify with this character, feeling that same despondent and hopeless look in my own heart, and on my own face. I too stare vacuously into the distance, a distance of time which seems to have no signposts or milestones in the endless expanse of loneliness and closed doors which spreads out before me in all directions like the sea of black heads on the sidewalks.

As I look into his eyes, the eel slowly begins to nose into the corners of the tank, searching here, searching there, searching for something which I cannot even imagine. He stretches upward, and gets his nose into the top corner of the tank, where he manages to edge the lid off just enough to get his snout in between the lid and the edge of the tank. He wriggles, and struggles, and widens the gap, moving ever so slightly the lid, until his head and body begin to push through the opening; his body electrifies into motion as the lid slips off the tank and crashes to the floor, and he stretches over the edge of the tank, across three feet of air to the top of the transom, which is open. He shoots his whole length like a lightening bolt through that transom window and finds himself on the sidewalk, in front of my astonished eyes! He wriggles in every direction, gets to the gutter, slips down a covered grate into a storm drain to the river, and is gone!

I stand transfixed, knowing that this is a direct message to me, from the Source, telling me, "Wake up! Move! Just get going and stop depressing, move in any direction until you get the lid to budge!"

Walking back to my hotel room, I find a piece of wood on the sidewalk, and with my pocketknife in my room, I begin carving a man, and a woman. The man is robust, a stocky powerful body with a healthy erection, and the woman, a kind of Venus with maternal breasts and a pregnant belly. Each day they come more into life, and the simple joy of doing it changes my world, I begin to notice the coming of the spring in Seoul, the smell of blossoms in the fresh wind. The maids come in to sweep up the shavings I am making on the carpet, and they point to the erection of the wooden man and laugh very sweetly.

Down on the street, in a busy intersection, a man approaches me and asks, "YOU SPEAK ENGRISH?" I say yes, and he asks me in broken English if I would like to teach conversational English, as one of the teachers in his school has just quit. I say, "Sure!" and that very day I hold my first class of about 60 people, mixed with housewives, soldiers, businessmen, secretaries, all people hopeful of starting a new life somewhere else. The classes are fun, I read to them anything I like, and we talk about it, they doing their best to use what little English they know, and me correcting them and suggesting new ways of saying the same ideas. I read to them from Bhagwan, and they sit dazed, amazed, asking who is this man, and where is he. I tell them about Him, show them his pictures, and tell them that I am on my way to India to see him. They all ask me to dinner, all 60 of them, and we sit for hours drinking soju, the local rice liquor, and talking about this man who they say is a living Buddha, by the pictures they see and the words they hear....

My classes went on for a few weeks. In the meanwhile, I became friends with the man who botched up the business connection when I arrived in Seoul, and he invited me to come stay with him in the country. He lived in a little house far from the city, outside of Seoul, near a big US airbase. I lived with his family for some days, eating their food and living their life. It is only white rice 3 times a day, with Kim Chee, a spicy fermented cabbage mixture. On Sunday: rice with butter; that's the big feast. The grandmother had an old non-electric pedal-type sewing machine, and I asked her through sign language to teach me how to use it. I carved a few things for the house, little sculpture things, and went for walks in the countryside, as the U2s passed overhead, coming in at treetop level from spying on China and Russia for landings at the nearby base. I began playing my fiddle and singing in the coffeeshops, chitchatting with the waitresses, and realized with each passing day the warmth and simplicity of these country people. I returned to Seoul, and my English classes, and soon I made enough money to go on to India. As spring came to Seoul with the blossoms, by late May I was elated and happy to be on the plane to Hong Kong, Bangkok, and then Bombay.

CHAPTER 7

The Last Mango in Poona

If one looks for naught when staring into space;
If with the mind one then observes the mind;
One destroys distinctions and reaches Buddhahood.
The clouds that wander through the sky
have no roots, no home,
Nor do the distinctive thoughts floating through the mind.
Once the Self-mind is seen, Discrimination stops.

Tilopa, Song of Mahamudra

When I arrived in Poona, much had changed in the time since I had left. There were many, many more people, everything was more organized, and it was no more possible to have the intimate meetings with Bhagwan that happened in the first time I was there. Instead, there was something called 'Energy Darshan'. For the people who had just come back from the West, this was a very brief meeting, called 'CHARAN SPARSH'; consisting of being called up to sit in front of Bhagwan in the evening darshan, two at a time. He would put his finger on your forehead while the music played for a little while. As 'luck' would have it, (and there is no such thing as luck in this synchronistic universe, I am sure), I was called up with the very guy with whom my wonderful girlfriend had an affair while I was chewing my lonely heart out in Seoul. So there we were, the two of us sitting in front of Bhagwan side by side, my imagined 'rival' seemed flowing and open with the situation, and myself I was stewing in my jealousy and irritation that of all the thousands of people in the ashram, it had to be with him at that moment. Needless to say, that attitude made me about as open as the Berlin Wall before perestroika…like, zilch. Not only did I not feel blissful, but I felt a kind of amplification of my bad mood, as if it was being broadcast over loudspeakers straight to Bhagwan. I realized this time in Poona was going to be different for me.

My first wish in being there was to finish the group that Bhagwan had given me two years before that I had left in illness during my first visit. I did the Vipassana group, and when I wasn't obsessing about who might be enjoying my everyday-more-distant girlfriend that night, I was falling into a peace inside, the long days of silent sitting slowly settled into me and by the end of the 10-day group, I was ready to be there again, in that storm of energy and silence which was the ashram in 1980. It was the wildest time, energy darshans were powerful events in the night with wild music and hundreds of people. Bhagwan had 'mediums' surrounding him, beautiful women who would dance and act as transmitters of his energy. The whole scene was very impressive, shocking in fact. I was sitting outside Lao Tzu gate one evening, the gate to Bhagwan's house and the small auditorium where the evening meetings with him would happen. When the first energy darshan happened, the lights all over the ashram were turned off. The energy was almost visible, as it rolled out of Lao Tzu gate in waves with the music, and people were visibly affected by it. It was beautiful, mysterious, and weird at one and the same time to me.

I had finished my groups now, and the natural avenue to be more involved with Bhagwan would be to start working in the ashram. At that time there was a music department, with an orchestra, and they needed a viola player, so that became my 'work'. It consisted mostly of practicing alone, in a hut behind Bhagwan's garden, ironically enough where had been Jitendra and Yashodhara's hut 2 years before. Nobody knew where they had gone, and the garden had been purchased by the ashram and turned into living spaces, in the form of bamboo-hut residences, one of which I was given the use of during the day to practice my viola. So there I was, practicing Bach Sonatas in the garden behind Bhagwan's house 6 hours a day, alone. We had a big performance of the Bach B-minor mass in Buddha Hall coming up, and I had to get ready for it, playing all day those wonderful and deeply transcendental melodies from that unearthly and deeply spiritual masterpiece. I loved the performance, there were thousands of people there, the Buddha Hall was full, and that glorious music with all those crazy red-clad sannyasins there and the little kids of the ashram all dancing in front was an amazing and memorable scene.

At times we in the music department would gather together, about 10 at a time, and sing; spontaneous, wordless voices together, harmonizing and listening to the silence. It was led by Anuprada, a wonderful pianist who had studied with Nadia Boulanger in Paris. This was magic, mysterious and wonderful, and the power of harmony stirred my soul in those days. But our 'work' as a music department was always unsure and nebulous, nobody seemed to know what we were supposed to do and there was the feeling in the air that all would soon change and any day we might be carrying rocks in Gujarat. I enjoyed very much that music time, we often played string quartets through the afternoon, joined by very high-level players who would come to visit the ashram; a violinist from the Berlin Philharmonic or cellist from Radio Netherlands. It was a fun and rich atmosphere for me. As a violist, I was nowhere on a level with them, but it's a bit like playing ping-pong: even if you are a lousy player, when you play with a great ping-pong player, suddenly you play MUCH better than usual.

I had very little money, and was a wanderer at that time, in the sense that I lived wherever I could, accepting what came my way from friends who were going away for a couple of weeks or a month. For a time I was given a huge room with a grand piano in the 'Dutch Palace', for a time, a balcony on the side of the pottery shop, for a time a very rainy hut with a leaking roof in the monsoon. I accepted what came my way, as I wanted to be there in any possible way, and absorb what I could from that energy field at the peak of its intensity and the edge of dissolution, which I felt was reaching its climax and would not be repeated.

Sure enough, the end of our music department came soon. One day, we were suddenly absorbed into the Groups department, under the management of a woman named Susheela, and I was given a job as a carpenter. From one day to the next my viola bow was replaced with a hammer. Susheela was already notorious by that time, and my introduction to her methods of management was abrupt. Everything had a sense of urgency, intensity, and 'DO IT NOW'! She had an uncanny ability to talk like a very sweet Jewish mother while pushing every button in your psyche, managing to make you feel totally uncomfortable and irritated without really knowing exactly what it was that had done it.

One afternoon at the end of a long day's work, we got urgent instructions to tear down a brick wall separating two group rooms, and make them beautiful and useable for the next day. Just as we finished at about one o'clock in the morning, we got an urgent message, that it had all been a misunderstanding. In fact, we had to rebuild the wall and paint it and have it ready by 8 the next morning. So we worked like maniacs all day and night around the clock, just to get back to the zero point where we had been the day before. It was often like that: digging holes, and filling them in, and learning not to take it too seriously. That was the training. And meanwhile, you watch your mind's reactions, and your emotions, and your belly getting bloated with gas from the amoebas, and strange energy experiences resulting from being in that very intense field of transformation.

At that point I withdrew from work, having reached a point of obstruction inside me with ashram life for the time being. I didn't want to be involved with the hierarchy of work and all that it entailed, getting embroiled in the expanding hierarchical power-structure of the ashram management. I had a few interactions with the ashram 'Brass' at that time, and my rebellious nature intuitively reared away like an alarmed horse from the interactions.

Susheela…Deeksha…Lakshmi…..Sheela…Aruno…Vidya… Who were these people in the positions of power in the ashram at that time, characters in the large drama which was unfolding out of sight from my small personal world where I lived? About Aruno I will speak later. I experienced Vidya as someone who provoked my feeling of fear. It's not that she was terrible or evil in any way, she was not that. But on a subtle level of 'the emotional body', her presence would mirror and vibrate this in me; ferret it out, bring it to the surface, play upon it, use it. She was South African. Being around her made me nervous, as it seemed to me like she was on the edge of some kind of hysteria always. It triggered in me the memory of the nuns in my grade school, Sister Doretta in fact, someone capable of very nasty action if provoked, a latent explosive potential that remains there just under the surface as a hidden threat. And yet, she was often very friendly, charming, jovial. I went to her office one day, not knowing who she was at all, but I had heard it through the grapevine that she could arrange for visa extensions. She was furious that I had come to her, and flat-out denied vehemently that she ever did anything like that: not only denied it, but was extremely pissed off at me for inquiring to her. I felt like I was unwittingly sticking my hand into the nest of a viper, I just wanted to get out of that office as quick as possible, and I did.

Deeksha was a person I didn't know directly. Second-hand,

I had a friend, a very talented professional violinist, that had been sent to Deeksha's kitchen at the demise of the music department. She had refused to do something that she had been told to do, as she felt it was harmful to her hands; at which point Deeksha slapped her. My friend slapped her back, and was immediately kicked out of the ashram. Deeksha was notorious for her hard-style methods of neo-Zen: hitting disciples, insulting them, over-working them as punishment. In the discourses Bhagwan would often give her his full support, saying that the only thing to do is to surrender to her, he is working through her.

As for Sheela, I never met her face to face in Poona 1, al-though I was aware as well as everyone else of her presence. It was her decree that ended the music department, it was her de-cree that ended music at the 'Music House', a popular place where musicians would gather near the ashram to play together, until one night she stormed in and said: "No more music at the music house!" And it became an overflow residence for ashramites. So, my impressions of her were not so positive from the start, it was more trepidation than curiosity.

There was a definite message being given at various times in discourse by Bhagwan at that time, that these people were 'de-vices' set up by him in order to provoke the abandonment of the ego, a situation to surrender one's defenses, and that was his way of working. That was a hard pill to swallow, given my youthful years as a taciturn rebellious hippy with anarchistic tendencies. It's relatively easy to surrender at least in theory to someone as charismatic and beautiful as Bhagwan; but to surrender to Aruno, Susheela, Deeksha, Sheela? That is another story entirely. My natural disinclination and rebellion towards authority definitely didn't like the feeling of absolute power which they wielded in the world of the ashram. They were petty tyrants fighting for turf in a small domain, it seemed to me, and I wanted no part in it.

At this time Bhagwan had been speaking in discourse of the seven valleys in the life of a seeker: that is, how a disciple has to pass many peaks and valleys, the peaks being love and consciousness, and the valleys being a 'dark night of the soul', when the disciple loses trust, and distances himself from the Master's energy and presence. I was in the midst of the valleys, and my rebellious nature and non-acceptance of authority were in direct conflict with my deeper need to be near Him and involved in his energy.

My money was just about finished, and I found a very cheap hut to live in, made of bamboo with a dirt-floor in a sugar-cane field. Every day in discourse, listening to Bhagwan's voice, I would fall into a deep trancelike state, in which I constantly heard harp-music. It was bewitching, mesmerizing. One of those mornings in Buddha hall I was jolted from my 'reverie' when an Indian man suddenly stood up in the middle of the discourse a few feet away from me, shouted at Bhagwan in Hindi, and hurled a knife at him. As Bhagwan's bodyguards stood up around him to block the knife, I heard it strike the roof of the podium above his head, and fall to the floor. But the shock of the incident reverberated inside me for a much longer time, and would be echoed again and again in scenes that would unfold in the near future.

It was a strange time for me, I had fallen into a kind of Indian sadhu-limbo of non-materiality. I had lost a large part of my conditioning, my Western mind and its drive and ambition to 'get-it-together'. But a new personal reality hadn't yet formed in me, a new vision, and instead I was lost in Indian collective thought-forms, a social conditioning of renunciation or helplessness in the face of the ocean of poverty surrounding and pervading everything in India. It was familiar to me, perhaps from another lifetime, and I was drowning in it. But I was not unhappy. It was so well-known to me, an inner emptiness and will-lessness which was neither good nor bad. I had little to eat, but it didn't matter much to me then.

I know now in retrospect that it was a very dangerous state I was in. I was like a loaf of half-baked bread. It can't become flour again, it's gone too far, but it's not yet bread. If it doesn't keep in the fire, it will spoil. And that was happening to me. The human dream—the collective mind that one is conditioned into—is a delicate and sophisticated construct. Through all the meditations and groups, I had lost some parts of that burdensome mind. But as yet my consciousness was not my guide: I was not at all the master of my life from my inner being, and was subject to waves and tides from the subconscious and unconscious mind of which I had no awareness at all. I was like a bush being blown in the wind. I had no more roots in my past, and I was not yet rooted in the present either. That is a very dangerous moment for the seeker. Bhagwan, as my Master and the guide through this difficult sea, was available, but that availability to his energy and guidance was through work in the commune, and my resistance to authority was like a rock standing in the way of me totally allowing myself to flow into the Master, and him to flow in me.

There is a Sufi story, about a stream that came to the desert, and could not cross it. It's only possibility was to become a quagmire, stagnant and static. But a swamp is not a stream at all. The stream had to stop and listen to the wind, which was saying to surrender to the arms of the wind and let itself be carried as vapor across the desert, and re-form as rain on the distant mountains. It was exactly the situation I was in: following my mind, my personality, I was in the state of a quagmire, a swamp, and in my heart was whispering the wind, to surrender into its arms, and be re-formed across the desert as rain...

As the days moved into December, change was in the wind in the ashram, underground: rumors of change, rumors of Bhagwan being ill, rumors of land being purchased elsewhere. Bhag-wan was often talking about what would be "In the new com-mune...". The commune which for seven years in Poona had been growing in intensity and numbers suddenly started to wobble, become insecure. I left Poona very shortly after, bound for California, a bit confused, not knowing what would happen with myself, the ashram, or Bhagwan.

CHAPTER 8

In the Arms of the Desert Winds

After this, my second passage to India, I arrived back to San Francisco at the start of 1981. Back in the City, as we started up the band again, there were more and more sannyasins flowing in from India. With the situation in the ashram in Poona changing, many people were being sent away 'To the West', and the gatherings which we were playing for suddenly grew bigger and bigger. Famous therapists from the ashram started showing up, and there were fundraisers happening for the 'New Commune'. Our audiences went from the dozens to the hundreds, then to the thousands, very quickly.

It was early spring. I was playing flute, and violin, and singing in the band at night, while in the days I was working in the shop of a sannyasin friend who had a business making little lamps with buddha and tara figures on them.

I was the carpenter, and as I ran a table saw, I listened to Bhagwan's discourses under my earmuffs. It was a strange kind of meditation; repetitive, monotonous actions with my hands and body, which occupied that part of my mind that would normally be talking, and 'I' was left free, to observe my breathing, observe my thoughts, and often listen to Bhagwan. Doing this work, something in me was settling deeper in myself, with this very simple and apparently boring labor, in which I could 'turn off' my mind and simply watch my body and feelings, and hear Bhagwan's voice from time to time.

There was a change in the wind. Rumors abounded again,

about Bhagwan stopping his work and leaving for the Himalayas with a few disciples. Other rumors came, of something being prepared in the West. Other news came, of the Poona ashram relocating to the north. No-one knew what was happening, but the commune in Poona was definitely disbanding and being dismantled. All was unstable, unknown, as such an important part of our lives was no longer there as a center-point to revolve around. Suddenly, one day, we who were living in a big communal sannyasin house in Oakland, started to feel incredibly and uncannily happy, to the point of being ecstatically 'blissed-out'. I knew in my heart, and we all knew, silently inside us, without talking about it, that Bhagwan was in the USA. A few days later, came the word, that he had landed in New York and was staying in a big estate in New Jersey with a number of disciples, which had been arranged by Deeksha. Few details were known, but that it was a temporary situation, and something much bigger was in the works.

A big event was being prepared on the West Coast, in Berkeley at the University, and I was to be one of the musicians playing in it. Lots of 'important' therapists would be there, Teertha, Rajen, and others. It was a rally and fund-raiser, for the New Commune, gathering energy, money, volunteers. Laxmi, Bhagwan's long-time secretary and head of the now disbanding Poona commune, was in the event, on telephone, giving a kind of pep talk, that this new step wasn't just for us, this was "For the Universe!" Rumors were that there was a new Land, with ten miles of riverfront, and a thousand streams, 100 square miles, and this would be the new commune, in the Pacific Northwest. It was ironic and strange for me that this event was taking place in Sproul Auditorium, at U.C.Berkeley, my own university, and to see all these sannyasins dressed in orange, and Teertha, the most prestigious therapist and other landmark personalities of Poona there, was an odd and unexpected turn of events, my 'new life' entering into and merging with my old life.

At that time, I had a strange feeling that my life would change drastically, and I didn't know how. One day, without knowing why, I just packed my backpack at home, sat, and waited. That very day, a call came for me, from Amitabh and Susheela, inviting me to join the commune in Geetam, in the Mojave desert of Southern California. I left that same night.

The first stop was Utsavo, a church in Laguna Beach that had been in a hotly disputed hand-over to the sannyasin movement by the pastor of the flock, when he had become a sannyasin a few months earlier. He had whole-heartedly thrown himself into his new life and spiritual path, donning orange robes and a mala and inviting the commune to use the premises for therapy groups. His very conservative flock in Laguna Beach however didn't really take to this idea very well, shall we say, and the whole place was vehemently polarized about 50-50: rabidly so. I was there for 4 weeks, playing music and building bathrooms for the groups which were being planned, while meanwhile there were volatile shouting matches in the church between dissident members, among whom some were sannyasins, usually not shouting but being loudly shouted at, and other older church members who would scream things like, "You are a bunch of dirty red commies!" and similar sentiments. After about a month of this, I was called to go to Geetam, a commune which had already been flourishing in the Mojave Desert for a few years, and now was rapidly filling up with the groups department which was translocating from Poona. And with the group department, came all the major therapists, Teertha, Rajen, Turiya, Mallika, and many, many others. We were about 120 in all. I was a carpenter and musician there. I had a tough time at first, adjusting to the seemingly endless hours of work, twelve hour days, and sometimes more, and the difficult living conditions. We lived in tents, and the desert nights got cold. I was used to being a musician, and the only music I would play now would be my flute or violin for a few minutes, sitting on

Fiddler on the roof, age 24, at Geetam

the roof of a building I was making, during the tea-break.

At Geetam, for the staff, the workers, and the therapists it was 'head-hunting' time; death-to-the-ego, surgery without anesthesia. Priveleges for those that had risen in the ranks of fame at the ashram, that had grown to be assumptions in Poona, suddenly didn't exist anymore: no front seats at discourse, no discourses either. Nobody was special now. Couples were separated and were sent apart, including the one I had been in. Personal possessions and attachments were dumped in the garbage, literally, as I watched the clothes and gifts to which I had sentimental ties, which friends had given me over the years, being carted away in a dumpster. The cozy and privileged life of those who were once 'Ashram-ites' in Poona, especially the therapists who were used to living in the ashram with the fame of rock-stars, was now over, and they were suddenly having to sand and paint bathroom cabinets in the carpentry shop or stir big pots of soup in the kitchen, twelve hours a day. The long looks and miserable expressions on the faces of some of these people whom I had seen as demi-gods in Poona told the tale. It was a gift for me in fact to see this, because it ended all my projections on them, then and there. I had believed some of the ashram therapists to be nearly enlightened, certainly very wise and knowledgeable, and this was a remarkable opportunity to see that they were just like anybody else, the same jealousies, attachments, possessiveness, limitations, like anybody else. I started to see them as people. I realized that 'therapy' as a profession, is not particularly more self-revealing than say, being a car mechanic. In fact, in the intervening years, I have found a few car mechanics I have met to be quite nearly enlightened, certainly bodhisattvas, full of compassion and true ego-less service to humanity with little recompense, and a few therapists to be regularly dwelling somewhere near the 'doors of hell and the river of death', to put it poetically. Needless to say, it's possible for a great car mechanic to have a personal car that doesn't work well even though his work is impeccable on other people's cars; and it's also possible to have a therapist who prefers to work on others psyche instead of him or herself. Things are not always what they seem.

One very good therapist who became a very dear friend to me in those Geetam days was Vasumati. She is a South-African lady with a beautiful smile, has a deep wisdom, a great sense of humor, the sweet love of a caring mother and a wonderful sarcastic wit as sharp as the teeth of a lion on the Serengeti Plain. In short, she is a delightful being, who remained a friend, counselor and mirror for many years, both at Geetam and in the years to come. Often in the midst of my most confusing and dark moments living in the commune, we would run into each other, and over a cup of tea she would make me easily see a path through the tangled underbrush, in my journey through the labyrinths of personal relationships and struggles of political power, in which I would often unwittingly step like a clown in a minefield. Her caring friendship would give me a very welcome sense of home and peace, for a little while. She was one of many such beautiful souls in the commune, it was by and large a gathering of loving friends on the path, willing to help each other when the occasion arose, willing to laugh and love together even in the midst of unimaginable outer storms and internal upheavals.

In the adjustment to commune life in that desert and extreme work conditions, seven days a week twelve hours a day, the hardship that I felt was in part physical, but more than that was the misery generated in my own mind by the friction of the external situation with my mental habits, my ideas about who I was. Working all day every day is not in and of itself a terrible thing, one is always working anyway, at something or another. But RESENTING the work: THAT is a great drain of energy, that makes one very unhappy.

Geetam was a training-ground, in dropping the personality, even a little bit, in the guise of an external task that had to be done. We were all pulling together so to speak, to make this thing work. The more I flowed with it, the easier it was. The more I resisted, and resented, the difficulties would multiply within me.

Along with the friction I was encountering with myself, at having to follow orders all day long and live in an extremely disciplined way in the sense of not having the 'freedom' to do what I would like all the time, the up-side of this balance was the many lovers and friendships which formed for me there in that empty desert. There were so many beautiful people, some of whom became friends for life, and many of whom I never saw again. It was a great learning in how to share and love and relate without attachment or bondage or drama, for the first time in my life. It began to give me a sense of the fellow-travellers on the path, the 'sangha', the community of seekers, this group of souls that were not just there by chance or random events. We have been together before, it is a re-gathering, a re-membering and pooling of energies around the Master that was happening.

Every evening, after the long day of work, everybody would gather in the main building, which served as a kind of bar, and I would play the flute, my friend Doug would play guitar, and it was a much-needed respite from the sawdust and the sand and the blazing sun.

Susheela was my boss again. Ah, Susheela; How she had endeared herself to me now even more than ever! She wasn't there at Geetam usually, preferring to rule by fiat and spend her time elsewhere, usually psychologically holding potential donors up by the ankles and shaking them to see what would fall out of their pockets, but once in awhile she would show up at Geetam, and do her 'tricks'. These were glorious days indeed. Her tricks would consist of her fore-mentioned uncanny knack to irritate, manipulate, and push every button you might have inside you, all with a smile like a sweet Jewish mother, while you never really sensed what was actually going on, until it was much too late to shield yourself.

One time, when we were in the midst of a particularly heavy and difficult time of work, with long extended hours of construction late into the nights, the commune was particularly full of grumblings and frustrations and on the verge of revolution. There was a general irritation among the population at the state of affairs, particularly the cutting off of the usual ration of one glass of wine per person per day. At that point, Susheela suddenly showed up, and gleefully announced: "Party tonight! Free drinks! All you want!" And the bottles of Champagne and hard liquor from the 'hill-house' where the rulers and managers of Geetam were living were duly brought out and opened up for all to partake of liberally and without restraint.

Well, it's easy to picture what happened: after prohibition, suddenly all is available in abundance, and it's the first night of no-work in months. By midnight everybody was completely smashed. Suddenly, at half past midnight, the announcement was made. "General Meeting! General Meeting! Everybody has to come to the main tent!" So we did, and there we were, at 1 o'clock in the morning, all 120 of us, bleary-eyed and stupefied, laying on the floor, and completely drunk. And dear Susheela came to the podium and said into the microphone in her unforgettable Jewish-mother voice: "Well, I've heard that there's been some negativity and grumbling. Let's talk about it! What's the problem? Now's your chance to speak your mind! Go ahead! Who's first?" Nobody could move or speak, and in the dim fog of alcohol-pickled brains, we all realized she had got our goat, and resistance was crushed without firing a shot, by our own stupidity. It was a masterstroke in the style of Gurdjieff.

Geetam was a mixed experience always; beautiful friendships, many lovers, the simplicity and beauty of the desert sky, and the long and deadening hours of endless work and endless psychological games played by the budding therapists vying for recognition as capable power-wielders in the ashram hierarchy. Many, many times I was ready to leave. But something was happening within me that kept me, in a constant struggle between my desire for relative (immediate) freedom, and ultimate freedom—freedom from the mind itself, which I knew was still very far from my reach. I had the clear and urgent feeling that I needed to be with Bhagwan, and could put up with much in order to get there.

I did put up with this, for about 6 months, hearing tales about how already people were going to the Ranch in Oregon, and I seemed to be 'stuck' in this cul-de-sac in the Mojave Desert, a side-stream not in the main river. And we would hear other stories, that the first winter up there in Oregon was grueling, people were also living in tents and it was 20 degrees below zero. It was pretty bloody cold at Geetam, I would wake up with ice in my hair, and colder than that I didn't really fancy to be in. At the same time, I was seriously getting psychologically and verbally worked-over by the behavior-modification squad, which consisted of the female boss of the carpentry shop. Let's call her for convenience sake, 'The Shrew', and her helper, a mousy fellow who would finger the notebook with all the information about us, while on the rounds with the Shrew, his boss.

Her actual name which means 'poetry', was about as far from her personality as a name can get. She was a budding therapist who was not particularly successful, nor well liked, and either because of that, or adding to that, she had a particularly nasty disposition. She would usually speak in a kind of screech, basically lived in her emotional body and constantly used it to manipulate everyone and everything around her. Those kinds of females often rose easily to positions of power in the commune. In the terms of the Toltecs, seers and mystics of ancient Mexico, these kinds of people who appear along one's spiritual journey, would be called 'petty tyrants'. They are persons who, through their inherent unpredictability and tendencies to enjoy creating problems in the lives of people over whom they exercise nearly absolute power, can make one's life either a veritable hell, or a crucible of transformation, depending on how you take it. I wasn't yet there, as far as the transformation part goes, and the hell part of it was sitting pretty heavy on my head and really did

110

not go over too well with me during my time at Geetam.

This person of the screeching voice, basically sensing my inner resistance to everything she would say or stood for, would relegate to me the most menial tasks and remove me from any activity which might have a semblance of personal satisfaction throughout the 12-to-14 hour workday.

One case in point: there was a big log cabin being built as a group room, and I was the one who would carry the logs, and carry the logs, and carry the logs…it went on for months, with constant harassment about my 'quality of work'. I looked, with my thick beard at that time, a bit Biblical and with those logs on my back it could have been a scene from the 'Stations of the Cross', at least in my very tired and irritated mind. It was my 'crucifixion', in my own inner-movie. These logs were 8-10 feet long and as big as tree-trunks, and were not light as a feather to say the least. After building them up for weeks and nailing them in with railroad spikes to the height of 9 feet, the building was framed, fitted, roofed, and about to receive the finishing touches and last touches of sandpaper on the final night. Just as the building was about to be finished, as a final touch to her petty-tyranny after I had been sweating under these logs for the better part of an autumn and winter under the desert sun and moon, on the night of completion I was forbidden to be there, in the all-too-obvious manner of being relegated to sweep the carpentry shop at midnight, of course an 'urgent' task, instead of gaining even a minimum crumb of psychological satisfaction over seeing the completion of the job. The message was clear: "You are nothing and nobody. And don't forget it."

The point was made, my tipping point had come and passed; that is to say, I was fed up, the camel's back had been broken by quite a lot of straws. I remembered Bhagwan's words, "Why wait for boats which may not come, when with your own efforts you can start swimming?" The next day, without telling anyone, I packed up my personal belongings, emptied my tent, and went in the evening to play, for what I knew would be the last time, to all the dear friends there. As I played the flute, nearly every person in Geetam came and passed wordlessly in front of me, and we connected hearts; I wanted to leave without goodbyes in part to not encounter obstacles for departure, and in part, just remembering everything as it exactly was, and this was the only way I could say goodbye to all those people with whom I had passed a difficult and beautiful time. The next morning, very early, I went and told Amitabh I was leaving, and said goodbye and thanks, and I headed out on the highway and abandoned that place of so many beautiful friends, lovers and enemies. I went up to my beloved Big Sur coast, to Northern California, starting up a band, playing string quartets on the street, and taking carpentry jobs in Santa Cruz while waiting a change of weather up at the Ranch in Oregon. It came, fairly soon.

I had left Geetam in late January, and word went out in early April that people were needed to come to work at the Ranch, preparing for the First Annual World Celebration, a summer festival of a week in which Bhagwan would come out for Satsang... a silent meditation of sitting with the Master. I bought a tent and a sleeping bag, and got a ride up to NorthEast Oregon, to a place on the John Day River called the Big Muddy Ranch, now renamed Rajneeshpuram.

CHAPTER 9

In the New Commune

The clouds that wander through the sky
Have no roots, no home, nor do the distinctive thoughts
Floating through the mind.
Once the Self-mind is seen,
Discrimination stops. ..

Tilopa-Song of Mahamudra

As I write this, I watch high wispy clouds passing in the desert winds of Andalucia, Spain. I am in an oasis in the desert of Tavernas, in a place called Cortijos Los Banos, a green valley of palm and olive trees, and, a Juniper tree, just off the balcony outside which opens out from this little room in the white stone building in which I am staying. The winds of the desert, the rocky hills all around, and the Juniper, brings me to a time and place which I shall never forget, in another desert, of North-Eastern Oregon. Rajneeshpuram. 'The Ranch' as we would all come to call it. The time I shall talk of is May, 1982.

I arrived in the early afternoon on a beautiful day in mid-May to the top of the Ranch, and looked down on 100,000 acres of dry hills, rocky buttes and Juniper trees, disappearing into infinity. It was beautiful, stunning in fact. It was dusty, it was wild, it was wide open. You could almost hear the theme from 'The Good, the Bad, and the Ugly' as we drove the winding dirt road down into The Ranch. When we arrived, I got out of the car, and there, at the reception, was a big yellow bus that had just arrived with some of the people from Geetam. We all had an enormous hug right there in the middle of the dusty road, about 40 people in all, overjoyed to see me and me to see them. Someone ran out of the reception and said, "You can't do this sort of thing here! You can't!" And how little I could know at that moment how much that would symbolize my time at the ranch: an overflowing energy of love, and at the same time an intense effort to cap and squelch and channel it into something more 'useful', for lack of better terms.

As I registered at the reception desk, they learned from my registration form that I was a carpenter and a musician, and the next day I was back in the carpentry shop. The work was all day, every day, but it was different this time. There was as yet no misguided therapist trying to do psychological surgery on me during the hours of work. It was just things that needed to get done. No digging holes and filling them in: rather, it was making buildings, and more buildings... and more buildings. At that time it was very fun and creative, a wide-open situation, wild-west style. If you had to build something, you could just go toss the wood in a pickup truck and drive off and make it, surrounded by the magnificent rocky landscapes and big skies. I worked hard and well without the psychological pressure of the group department, and I was trusted more and more, and given more and more interesting jobs. And in the night, like in the old cowboy movies, I would play my fiddle under the starry skies. There was such a big burst of love and life happening in everyone involved, it was unforgettable. It seemed like the more you worked, the more energy you had, it was not tiring, it was thrilling.

Each day at 2 pm, we would line up in silence along the dusty roads of the Ranch, and wait for Bhagwan to pass on his daily drive. He was driving a Rolls Royce, and it was a special moment, as often when he would pass, our eyes would meet in a brief glimpse, a silent communion. There was much love in that time. He was not speaking, and the communion with him was extremely energetic, happening through the work, the sharing with many, many friends, and the silent and beautiful moments of his drive-by each day.

That burst of love would reach a crescendo in the First Annual World Celebration, a festival where Bhagwan would be coming out to sit in silence with everyone once a day. This would be the first time in almost two years that people could be with him again in meditation, and it was expected that many thousands would come. And they did come, in abundance.

I was busy pounding nails in preparation, making pumphouses and little buildings here and there to house supplies or electric transformers. About two weeks before the festival, I was relieved of my hammer and asked to be one of a crew of 7 musicians whose job it would be to play all the music for the happening, for the 6 days it would last. Suddenly, the 7 of us got two weeks to just play music, and start practicing night and day to put it all together.

The band was multinational; many of them were musicians who had been playing for Bhagwan in Poona, and it was a fun new experience for me to be with them, playing in all different styles of music, from New Age to Rock to Funk to Chinese Western. I was composing tunes, and playing flute, violin and keyboards. We worked all day, everyday and long into the nights. In the last few days, we didn't sleep at all, such was the fever to make the music really beautiful. And then, the people started coming, and coming and coming, about 14,000 in all. The new Buddha Hall, recently completed, was 2 acres of space, and it was full, with people sitting on the floor.

I will never forget that first morning, the first time I ever played for Bhagwan. I was playing the piano, in the beginning, a solo improvisation piece, a very quiet and simple tune that was very spacious. I began to play, and then I felt as if I was surrounded by such a light, inside me or outside me I cannot say, but it was as if an enormous light was turned on, that HUGE LOVE that I had felt that night 5 years before when he first gave me my name and mala. It was on me, flooding me and filling me up. And then I realized, it was His attention, listening. It was as if the whole universe was listening, and the notes I was playing became so wide apart, so much space and silence in-between them. It was a feeling of timelessness, vastness, acute presence, I would get to know this feeling many of the times I would play for Him. It was transporting, magical, and wonderful.

The 6 days of the festival passed like a beautiful dream, and we would play each morning for Him in a morning meditation of one hour, called 'Satsang', which means a heart-to-heart communion with the Master. We received specific directions from him via our 'co-ordinator' about the music, that it should be flowing and beautiful, and we did our best. After the Satsang, there would be a sannyas initiation ceremony with Teertha giving malas and new names, sometimes for 200 people a day. I would play for this, improvised solo piano, and often it lasted 2 hours. That was magical for me, there was so much energy present and so much love, and thousands of people, that the music just flowed, I didn't have to make it or think about it, it was more like jumping into a river and surfing it. Each night the band would play for the whole crowd in a celebration led by Anubhavo, a much-loved German singer who had done the same kind of music group every night for years in Poona.

The whole festival came to a climax on July 6, called 'Master's Day', a reflection of 'Guru Poornima' festival in India, which is the full moon celebration in July. It is a day which is traditionally dedicated to devotion for the spiritual guru, or master. That day was literally 'out of this world'. As Bhagwan was arriving in his Rolls Royce, 15,000 people were dancing ecstatically and singing in Buddha Hall. It was sunset, the colors all around in the sky were dramatically red and orange, there was a sudden storm with lightning and thunder and wind just as Bhagwan stepped out of his car. It couldn't have been more dramatically timed by Cecil B. Demille for the arrival of Jehovah to meet Moses on the mountain. It was, literally, awesome, and a gas, and so fun, as if the whole universe was celebrating with us.

The festival came to its end, the crowds thinned and left. We who stayed were working to clean it up for a week or so, living on thousands of cheese sandwiches which had been prepared for the multitudes and not used up. Cheese sandwiches, sometimes 3 times a day, every day. It was a comic post-script to a beautiful high that had passed its peak, and we were living in its wake. We were so very tired, but happy, the time passed in the afterglow of the joy that had been to see Bhagwan again and be with Him. But, thankfully, the cheese sandwiches passed too, and we were eventually given 3 days off of work to recover. I did not know it then, but that would be the last time off I would have for the next 4 years.

From May until late September, I had been living in a tent near the top of a hill above the main valley of the Ranch. When the autumn came, the weather rapidly turned colder and colder, and again I would wake up with ice in my hair. It was 'decided' by the higher-ups who decided such things that I could stay permanently, and become a resident of the Commune, and I was moved into a trailer, in a part of the ranch called Subhuti grove. At the same time, my jobs began revolving more and more around Bhagwan's house: fixing his roof, adding a porch, building a clothesline or a deck, doing things that were too small for the construction crews but too big for someone who was just a cabinet-maker. I was kind of in the middle, and I could take off with a pickup truck and find what I needed myself and do it pretty quickly, without much fuss, budget, blueprints, or problems. Sometimes when Bhagwan would come out of the house to go for his drive, those of us who were working up at his house would play music on the lawn for him, with the peacocks dancing around him. I was playing violin. I loved to play for him, but in that love was mixed up a big dose of 'the wish for recognition'. I wanted him to know who I was. I was soon to get it, in an unexpected way.

At that time, we started preparing music for the coming celebration for Bhagwan's birthday in December, and we received a message from him about some directions for the music. There was some very particular comments about not playing in a rough and rowdy way, and not playing violin solos that are scratchy and not beautiful! Of course, it was me who he was talking about, because I had been the violin player in the recent Satsangs with him in the Summer Festival, and the one he had seen on the lawn the week before as he came out for his daily drive. I felt terribly guilty; I would have liked to disappear from existence, if such a thing was possible, as the last thing I ever wished was to displease Him. So I wrote an apology to him, and basically felt wretched for some time, wishing I could just vanish as quickly as possible from the face of the planet, and melt away into the sagebrush and sand. But, instead, I got a message back from him, saying not to worry about it, and to put my energy into playing music that is more meditative and helps people to go 'inside'. So, what started as an extremely painful exchange for me, became a life-direction in fact, as all the music I have made since that time has been with that message in mind and heart.

The following Darshan, or meeting-with-the-Master, was on Bhagwan's birthday on the 11th of December. As Buddha Hall was still an unfinished open-roofed area not prepared for the harsh winters of Northern Oregon, and far too cold at this time of year, the Darshan would be in the nearly finished airplane hangar at the airstrip of the Ranch. As the hangar filled and filled with people, we were playing very sweet music for him; a birthday song, the words being: 'Sweet Sweet Bhagwan, we love your love, we love your song...happy birthday to you'. And as he came in, in black robes, the whole place was simply a melting overflow of love. It was so tangible and full, the wonderful feeling of love in the air. Playing music on that night was to be flying into the sky on those wings of love. But, this time, maybe for the first time, I really didn't WANT him to know who I was. No recognition! Better to be nobody, or nothing, but just PLAY!

I had fallen in love with a very beautiful woman named Kasi. In her daily work, she was Sheela's laundry lady. Sheela was now the absolute ruler of the Ranch, being now Bhagwan's personal secretary. Bhagwan had gone into public silence around the time that he left India, and since then, was not speaking to disciples other than his personal caretaker Vivek, his doctor DevaRaj, and his secretary, Sheela. So, she was now the only person who would be speaking to Bhagwan everyday about the direction of the Ranch, and relaying his messages to all the rest of us, and the world. In the context of the commune which was now growing up in Oregon, at that time about 1500 people, this gave her a very special position. That is, Sheela was elevated to a special status as the spokesperson for Bhagwan. Hence, every communication to Him or from Him, personal or public, went through her.

Kasi's job was to do her laundry, but Kasi being a headstrong Taurus and very stubborn, Sheela would call Kasi 'Boss', the only person whom Sheela would address in that way. We delighted in each other. Being together, I often would go to meet Kasi after work at Jesus Grove, Sheela's residence, after Sheela had just come back from seeing Bhagwan, and she would be surrounded by her staff, which took on the aspect of a bunch of adoring groupies adulating her, and something in me felt uncomfortable there and didn't want to be around that. I had a funny feeling that somehow the real direction of adulation was getting distorted, the disciple/secretary was being treated like she was the source of the happening. She wasn't, never was, and never could be. And yet, she was, at that time, the only doorway to Bhagwan's messages. Hence, being at the pivotal point of contact between the great mass of followers and the Master, she was in a position of tremendous 'power', albeit borrowed. And those around her would start adulating, almost adoring her. I started spending less and less time around Jesus Grove, feeling a strange sense of caution about the way things were unfolding there. Although those people were not unkind to me and were very friendly at that time, something about the way everyone was figuratively kissing Sheela's butt so obsequiously, while the rest of us on the Ranch were there because that mysterious man was silently there, driving by in his Rolls Royce once a day. A caution bell was starting to make little sounds inside me.

Kasi loved my music, and was an extremely caring and wonderful person. A friend of hers, an older Indian sannyasin of Bhagwan named Jyanti-Bhai, was coming from India and asked her if she wanted something, to which she gave me the opportunity to get a sarangi. I borrowed from my musician friend Doug the 70 bucks that it would cost, and some weeks later Jyanti Bhai showed up from India with a beautiful old Sarangi. I was enchanted with it, as I hadn't been able to play that instrument since British Airways had lost all my luggage 4 years before. I would get up an hour earlier now, and in the pre-dawn light go out under some juniper trees on the hills near where I lived, and practice the Sarangi once again, as the dawn would arrive over the Ranch, and the buses would start to roll to work.

Shortly afterward, Bhagwan changed the name of our music-department to 'Baiju Bawara'. This was the name of an Indian beggar-musician from ancient times, who apparently could play so beautifully, he would not only bring tears to the audience, but the nearby marble statues would melt. The significance of this was not known to me at that time, shrouded in the foggy mists of the future, but it would be driven deeply into my heart after a few years.

At that time, as autumn unfolded in the softening of the desert sun and rains would come on occasion, I began working not just on the roof or grounds of Bhagwan's house, but IN the house. And at the same time, the work went deeper in me. I was often building or modifying things in his living space, and always it was part of my job to not be intrusive on that space, to not disturb his privacy. So I would be a kind of non-entity, like a mouse disappearing when He would be there. Sometimes I would be fixing the floor, and would have to duck into another room when He would walk by. Or I would be sanding some wood in a cabinet, and would duck into the clothes closet as he would be passing by in the hallway. Again and again, I would have this experience of the nearby presence of Him, but not actually seeing Him. It was a very familiar feeling in my heart, of light and warmth, almost a physical glow. I could sense where he was, by this feeling in my heart.

In the 3 months between the festivals, once a week we musicians from the Satsang band would play Kirtan in the Buddha Hall. This is a form of devotional singing, in which the lead singer sings a phrase, usually names of the Divine or truth, Shiva, Krishna, Narayana, Om, and the audience repeats the phrases. It goes faster and faster, with instrumental interludes in between the verses. It gets very intense, and builds to a climax, with everyone dancing like crazy and losing themselves in an ecstatic frenzy of devotion to the Divine. The leader of the Kirtan was a very 'BIG' Indian woman named Taru, who was really an incredible performer. She was simply unique. She would sing a phrase in the sweetest of voices and a heavenly expression on her face, and turn to us, the band, with a look like Kali or Durga, and scream at us, "Come On, COME ON!!!!" to play faster. Really, her facial expressions could have made a lion piss in his proverbial pants, she could really be intense. And she was so solid in her voice, that if her keynote was a little lower than the band, we would have to tune every instrument, including the piano, down to her note, she wouldn't budge for the Queen of England. But when she got going, the whole house would fly with her, she had an internal power of Shakti, the primordial power of the feminine, that was simply phenomenal.

Playing in the Kirtans, I met a little Indian woman named Priya, who was the wife of Bhagwan's brother. She was a clas-

The Band, first Festival at the Ranch. That's me, at the piano…

sical raga singer, and we got to practicing together, her singing and me playing sarangi. I would go to her house, she lived with her husband Shailendra and Bhagwan's mother, and we would play together on winter nights. Sometimes we would be playing night-ragas, mysterious melodies especially apt for the hours of darkness, and Bhagwan's mother would come in the room to listen, for hours. It was as if no-one was sitting there, she was such a silent and ego-less presence. When she would leave, it was just as if a silence and an emptiness had left the room, the room was more crowded when she wasn't there. It was very sweet and fulfilling to be there and involved with this very special family, and a great gift.

CHAPTER 10

Visitors

It was now April of 1983. I had been living in Rajneeshpuram for almost a year. I was a carpenter during the months between festivals when I would be playing the music, and by that time our carpentry shop had moved to a new industrial area at the end of a large valley which also contained the airport.

Although we saw ourselves as an 'alternative community', as we certainly were outside of the mainstream American culture, we were as well outside of, and even farther from the New-Age culture. UFOs and other 'esoteric' phenomena were definitely not a part of our social context, and in our particular subculture it was definitely 'not cool' to talk about such things. It was a time of hard physical work, being very down-to-earth and giving very little energy, time or thought to philosophical or metaphysical speculation, to put it mildly. Oddly enough, although we were all there fundamentally for the experience of meditation, even to talk about meditation was 'out'. In great part due to the personality of Sheela who vehemently disdained anything esoteric, those things were taboo at the Ranch, at least in public.

I personally at that time had never believed in UFO experiences and was on the contrary very skeptical of anybody who talked about such things. I basically consigned them in my mind to the category of 'wackos' and 'needy people hungry for attention', or something like that.

One evening around 11 pm, I was outside the carpentry shop where I worked, waiting for a taxi home with my beloved Kasi. I had been working late at night on a musical instrument, a sarod I had begun at Geetam some years before, which was now nearing completion, and I was working on it in my 'spare time' which was after 10 pm at night. Kasi had stopped by to help me in the night. She liked to do the little jobs of finely polishing tuning pegs and things like that, which were repetitive jobs which I found tedious, but for her it was a welcome creative change from her long days doing Sheela's laundry. We were the only ones there in the building at the time. The carpentry shop was down at the end of a long deep valley in the desert hills, which was also occupied by a small airstrip, in the direction of the town from where we stood.

The commune had recently bought a new airplane. While it was 'new' for us, it actually was a 50-year-old DC3 built before WWII. We were looking down the runway towards town, and the headlights of what seemed to be this airplane were slowly coming down the runway towards us. I thought to myself, "it must be the DC3 coming in for a landing". It was about a mile away. Slowly the lights of the aircraft started sliding sideways perpendicular to the runway, and both of us started staring at it. The lights kept coming our way, as the 'aircraft' started rising higher in the air and approaching closer to where we were. It very slowly passed over a building about half way in-between the runway, and us. This was a large office building called 'Socrates', and by the juxtaposition of the craft above that, I could get a general idea about how big it was. It was at least 300 feet long, and by that time was about 200 feet up in the air. It had a pattern of lights all over it, something like triangles marked with points of light. It was not circular, but rather oval, longer from back-to-front than it was in width. There was some kind of energy-phenomenon happening in the 'back' end of it, of which actually my eyes and brain could not give any description of; it was not flames, it was not exhaust, but it registered to my brain as some kind of 'energy happening'.

I was awestruck as it silently rose higher and nearer to us, and its colossal dimensions became more clear to me. Kasi started to panic, and I definitely felt that was not a good idea to do at that moment, as we were the only people in front of this thing, and I instinctively felt that fear was not the best way to meet it. So I told her something like, "Stop it! Just watch the thing!" She got the point, and just stood there like me.

It's not that I wasn't scared, but I felt something like, "What the hell? This thing is obviously way beyond any thing we could possibly do to protect ourselves from it, we may as well just watch the show".

And that's just what we did. It was a Spielberg movie, in real life, right before our eyes. Before that happens, you never can really believe it will happen, it's just too 'unreal'. But here it was, bigger than life, and very much HAPPENING! It slowly came closer and closer, passing almost straight overhead from us, about 300 feet up, as it moved very slowly and silently off over the low hills to the right of us. It was absolutely silent, it moved effortlessly, although it was probably as big as an oil tanker up there in the sky. To my feelings, it radiated what I would call 'HIGHER INTELLIGENCE'. It had absolutely no vibe of military, spy, stealth, or human flight machine. Nothing sinister, or helicopter-ish, it moved freely, silently, and without any show of resistance to gravity.

I had grown up near a huge Air Force base, and was very well acquainted with any kind of military flight or spacecraft as a boy, as it was my fascination to watch rockets and jets in flight and study any kind of flight machine known to man. This was nothing like that. This thing moved effortlessly, it was not struggling to overcome gravity like human machines, but it was simply moving silently by some unknown higher force. It just CRUISED.

It passed over us and slowly disappeared over the hills to the right. We looked at each other, and both of us promised to not talk about it to anybody, as we would certainly be labelled as 'crazies' by the ranch Brass. A couple of minutes later, the taxi we had been waiting for pulled up, and as the driver opened the door, she slumped over in the seat with very shocked wide-open eyes, and said, "Did you SEE that thing in the sky!?!?" We said we did, and the three of us silently drove into town. As we entered the village, there was a guard-post with a young policeman standing outside of it, and he was obviously in a state of great distress. He asked us, "Did you SEE that thing in the sky??!!!". We said we did, and we went on home.

The next day I talked to at least two other people that saw it, and there was also printed in the Portland newspaper a disclaimer by an Air Force spokesperson, saying that there had been thousands of calls in the night before about a UFO in the skies of the Pacific Northwest, and it had been a vehicle from a Russian spaceflight burning up on re-entry.

I witnessed as a boy many re-entry vehicles re-entering the atmosphere, I grew up downrange from Vandenburg AFB where rockets were constantly being tested. I could see their contrails at sunset. This had as much to do with a rocket-test, as blue cheese has to do with the moon: namely, nothing. Rockets on the way up leave contrails with a zigzag pattern high in the upper atmosphere from the intense winds up there, or they burn up like a meteor on the way down. This thing slowly cruised within 300 feet of me, rising upward and turning. I had a clear view of it, with triangulation of the hills on the side and the building between me and it, so there was no question for me about a visual distortion from something high in space. It started out at almost ground level, blocking my view of the things behind it, and rose to pass over me and the nearby hills. I felt elated watching it, I waited many sleepless nights after that hoping to see its return, but it never came back.

After some years, talking with other friends at the Ranch I came to know that sightings of UFOs were common there. One close friend had been walking past Buddha Hall one night, and saw a craft parked there. She hurriedly walked past it, not wanting to see it. Another was in a car that was coming from Antelope down into the Ranch, and they had been followed the whole 20-minute ride down into the Ranch by a very obvious and nearby Extraterrestrial vehicle; that is, it was not anything that was known at the time to be flown by humans from planet earth. None of these things were ever talked about publicly, but word was out through the grapevine that we were not to talk about it, as it would only make our position there in Eastern Oregon more tenuous and delicate if the locals came to know that we were attracting these things to us.

CHAPTER 11

Church and State

As I write this I sit in a small cafe on the only street in a tiny town in the middle of Spain. I am traveling in-between concerts, in the mid-summer heat. Somewhere between Barcelona and Valencia, the fan belt of my aging but trustworthy auto has dissolved into shreds. I somehow got to this little town and found the only mechanic with a shop open, a very honest and sincere person, available to fix my trusty steed. It's about 45 degrees Celsius outside, and the stone streets are nearly deserted. There's just me in this little shady cafe, and the somber and very big Moroccan owner who looks at me now and again suspiciously to see if I am going to pay. Eventually I do, and when I buy 3 or 4 more cups of tea, as the stultifying hot afternoon wears on, he relaxes and even begins to smile a little. As the evening approaches, my car is repaired and ready to go, and I drive on in the now waning heat of twilight, to the far south of Spain, following the coast. I have a concert arranged in a very special place, in Malaga. It will be about 50 feet underground in an ancient cave complex, called Cuevas del Tesoro (Caves of the Treasure). As the story goes, it was used 30,000 years ago for ritual practices, particularly by female shamans, who left their cave paintings and ritual implements there, as well as their mysterious energy. Now the caves are a tourist attraction, albeit a very quiet one. You go down an elevator several floors to the cool depths of the caves, which are fantastic grottos of large and small chambers, with a small stream connecting them. My concert is in an especially large cavern, bathed in a reddish glow from the color of the stone cavern walls. As I begin to play for the small public which has gathered in this unique place, I am struck by the quality of the sound. It is pure, penetrating, pristine and wonderful. It is the most perfect and beautiful sound I have ever had in a concert place, more beautiful, resonant and clear than any cathedral, and I have played in many. At a certain point in the concert, as I play with eyes closed, I have the distinct and startling sensation that a spirit or entity has come forth right in front of me and is listening attentively. It is such a clear and uncanny feeling, as if someone

Malaga cave concert

abruptly appeared and put their face right in front of me as I played with my eyes closed. The feeling was so startling that, in fact, 3 or 4 people in the audience got up and left abruptly at that moment, as for them it was a 'weird' presence. I was not the only one who felt this, as many people in the audience told me afterwards they had a similar impression. Although it shocked me, I relaxed into it, and realized that it was the spirits

130

or entities who dwell in the cave who were there to check out was happening in their space, and they in fact were enjoying the music. It was not a negative entity, but a curious one. I have often felt in my concerts that the public presence there are not only human beings, but also spirits and entities who are residing in those places, and the music is a healing force on many dimensions. I have played in Hiroshima, Nagasaki, Dresden and Berlin, sites of great suffering and traumatic loss of human life in the recent past, and felt that the music was somehow healing the astral space, on a dimension which I do not fully understand but accept, as I seem to be destined to be a player in a greater orchestra whose designs I do not fully grasp.

And now, back to my tale, at the Ranch: while I was working in Bhagwan's house each day, I became slowly aware of a first hidden, then rapidly widening schism happening in the commune. Until that time, I had been fairly oblivious to the internal political situation in the commune itself. I had basically, albeit reluctantly, accepted the fact that there were people in positions of power, even absolute power, in the sense of having total control over where I lived, what room I slept in, what color of clothes I wore, when and where and what I would eat; all the physical manifestations of daily life were controlled and organized as part of this hierarchy in the commune, which I 'accepted' as a part of the rules of the game. That was, in fact, 'no big deal'. The game was 'surrender': giving up the small ego, as a gesture of allowing 'The Bigger Thing' to happen, and that being a real energetic meeting with the Master, and hence, the existence—the universal energy behind everything. It all sounds logical, but in the day to day living of it, you forget what's beneath it all. It becomes your mundane reality. Slowly, the little manifestations of individual life got washed away in the flood of experiences. Although I never sought to be close to the people in power at the Ranch, I also did not hate them, but rather did my best to avoid involvement with them, instinctively. It was my nature to not gravitate towards power, and in fact to gravitate away from those who hunger for it. I just don't vibe with them, and feel instinctively that it's a bad idea to suck up to them, or fight them. It seems to me, either you are into meditation, or power. It can't be both. One precludes the other. If you are seeking power on the outside, it means you haven't found the real thing inside, the real contact with your source of energy. And if you haven't found the real thing inside, you probably are still seeking power or symbols of it outside. I was interested in meditation, not being part of any hierarchy or being in any position of power over anybody else. But I accepted the hierarchical situation of the ranch, though I did not love it. It was simply a part of the game I had to play to be there. I wanted to be there, physically close to the Master, and if that was the price I had to pay, to give my time and energy to the happening 100 % without holding back, yes, I accepted that, I was willing to pay that price.

Those people in positions of 'power' as it were, were not perceived by me to be evil as such. At least at the beginning of the Ranch, they seemed to be very sincere, and working diligently and thoroughly to fulfill THEIR inner programs, of manifesting this City in the Desert for the 'Buddhafield' of an enlightened master. They as well as I were simply living out in the best manner they could the results of their conditionings and propensities, which put them into the roles they were in, as well as I in mine. Tyrant, victim, manager, worker... these were roles we were playing, although the dimly perceived knowledge of that somewhere in my deepest silence within me, in no way dulled my emotional reactions to daily events, at that time.

And yet, my daily reality although it was of long hours of physical labor was not one of oppression. It was primarily joy. If I would discount the fact that I was getting physically tired, my life was very enjoyable. Working, living, eating, was mostly fun, full of jokes, interesting people from all over the world, laughter, and many hugs and kisses. Even in the hardest of times, while we would be pouring concrete 16 hours a day or more, we would be laughing all day, even about Sheela and her stupid gang of followers. There was a love between most of us who worked side by side, day-in-day-out, and a hilarity in the face of the ironic and harder aspects of the life we were living, that was infinitely preferable to the life I had known up to then, isolated and with not much luck in the heartless and hard struggle for survival as a musician in America of the 1980s.

Living a 'normal' life out in the world, one is actually working most of the time also. You do a million things, you make your living, you shop for food, you drive your car or in my case, your motorbike, you keep your vehicle repaired and running, you pay the bills, and the parking tickets, you go to the bank, you cook the food, wash your clothes, clean the house, etc. The only difference was that in the commune, you just do ONE thing: your job. And everything else is somebody else's job. So, in a way, life was much simpler, you focused on what you needed to do, and the rest was taken care of. Survival was guaranteed, your room was clean, the food was ready, and your washed clothes were waiting for you at night, friendships and love were plentiful and abundant, and actually life was fairly delightful. Relationships took on a different format, you weren't 'stuck' together living in a house or apartment with your partner-of-intimacy, if you didn't feel like seeing each other HERE AND NOW, there was absolutely no reason to do so. So there was a flow to social interactions which made them easier, lighter, you didn't glue yourself to somebody in order to not be lonely, there was no need of that. It made the energetic of the relationship more honest. The other side of it was, there just wasn't much time for intimate relations or dramas, you couldn't spend more than a few hours together at a time with your 'partner', if you chose to have one, just because the hours of work were so very long, and there wasn't much energy or time available for personal conflicts. The emotional indulgence that was common in the days of the Poona Ashram was less and less possible, you simply could not spend much time or energy feeling sorry for yourself or discharging emotions. There was always too much more to be done, objectively, outside of you. This was a kind of 'Paramita' as they call it in Buddhism, a bridge that carried one over to another place, figuratively speaking; an objective physical activity that gave a focus for one's energy and creativity, the actual 'Work' to be done, of building this city, this energy-field, and all the millions of actions that it would entail. It served as a bridge, to take us out of the 'personal wallowing in our small selves,' and into a field of intense, impersonal energy and action.

As for the politics of the commune at that time, my own reservations were kept inside me. I did not believe in the rap that was going down from the ashram Brass, the creation of the new religion called 'Rajneeshism'. I thought that was all PR, legal games they had to play to qualify as a church or some sort of religious institution according to US law. There were frequent meetings in every workplace where information and direction was disseminated, a kind of pep-talk and propaganda format, albeit very gentle in the beginning years, more like a 'sharing'. The crew leaders, those who managed people on the immediate and practical day-to-day level in the workplace, were of both sexes, but the coordinators above them were mostly women, and they had overseers higher up, ONLY women, higher up in the pyramid of power, and closer to Sheela. These people would come to be known as her 'gang' over the months and years. This predominant attitude being promoted by this gang was to place more and more initiative in the structure rather than in the individual. As the months became years, it became a kind of 'party line' that was against my basic nature. I'm not a communist, nor a soldier, nor a true believer. If I had to state my political affiliation, it would be natural anarchism, but even that, I'm not waving a flag about it or printing it on my t-shirt. I think hierarchies work very well for brainless creatures with no individuality, like bees or ants or sheep, but for the rest of us born with all that it entails in being a homo-sapiens, it's better to use your own thinking mechanism.

Human beings are born with a capacity for their own unique and independent perceptions and decisions, and that's a big part of the reason why we come into these bodies, to USE them and learn from them. Through this long chain of mistakes and 'learning experiences' which unfold through all the days of one's life, we learn. That IS the life process. To make our own mistakes, and learn by them, and grow up our consciousness, in so doing: this is a big part of the reason for being in this spacesuit we call 'A Human Body'. Throughout history, all the attempts to make humans into something like sheep or ants mindlessly following a leader, have only served to increase the great quantity of human misery on planet Earth by leaps and bounds. Great collections of human energy and numbers have led to great quantities of responsibility being abdicated to religions, legal systems, kings, presidents, commissars, bureaucrats, and bankers. Whatever name was fashionable with the passage of time, the simple power of making real decisions about how you live has been generally shunted into the hands of a few, and that power has always and always and always led to absolute corruption and destruction by those hands. If there is or ever was a devil who delights in making humans suffer, then certainly that entity has taken much delight in governments, and their business of managing people. I take what is happening and the way it is being presented with a good grain of salt always. I was there at the Ranch, by my choice, and many, many, many times it rubbed me the wrong way. But my YES in trust towards the absolutely real energy experience which I have with Bhagwan was always there, without any question from me. To all the happenings around that, I had my 'yes' and I had my 'no', and never relinquished or denied my personal feelings about it. If I felt like hell, I didn't rationalize it away, I felt it, intensely, and often would wander out into the sagebrush under the stars at night to let things settle inside me.

I slowly became aware of a cold-war which was hidden under the blankets, there in North-Eastern Oregon, and this one was in the family. There was this 'Rah-rah' spiel about building the commune and Rashneeshism and Us-against-them, (the people in the world outside), and 'not being negative'. This was slowly spun by the people who actually managed the commune. These people, although I had many opportunities to know and become friends with, I never felt to be close to them. And there was another distinct group, of around 10 people who actually physically served Bhagwan, personally in his house, who worked with extreme care and love, and these people I felt an instinctive kinship with. I didn't know why, but in a certain moment, I realized that if I had to choose between these people, who lived in His house, Lao-Tzu grove, and the organizers of the commune, the people who lived in Jesus Grove, of course I would choose the people of Bhagwan's house, the Lao Tzu house people. It was a clear moment in my mind, because after that, it slowly became evident to me that I WOULD have to choose where to put my allegiance and friendship.

In little ways, little things being said, little slips during meetings, furtive glances full of tension, pregnant silences, all these clues started to point out to me that in fact there was a tangible and ugly pressure being put on the servants of Bhagwan, by the rulers of the commune. These rulers, lets call them, Sheela's Gang, were a group of about 20 people who had clustered around her from years before in Poona, and had become her trustees of sorts. Her power grew as she rose in the ranks of the organization, and those whom she trusted rose with her. As Sheela's power became absolute at the Ranch, commanding the economic control of Bhagwan's worldwide movement of hundreds of thousands of sannyasins at that time, so too did the relative power of those acting as middle-men (This is euphemistic, at the ranch they were all women). At the ranch, this hierarchy was clearly evident, as much as it would be in Stalinist Russia of the 1930s. Just you had to see who was driving their own car at the ranch. If you were driving a new Jimmy or Bronco, you were one of them. If you were riding a public schoolbus, you weren't one of them: clear division. The only other person I can think of with her own car, was Vivek, the personal companion of Bhagwan, who was driving a Rolls which Bhagwan gave her. Needless to say, this certainly did not help the situation of the mounting green wave of jealousy floating from Jesus Grove, the center of political power, to Lao Tzu grove, the place where Bhagwan lived with Vivek and the rest of his caretakers, the women and men who cleaned his room, washed his clothes, made his robes and shoes, made his chairs and tables, his doctor and nurse, etc.

As time went on, the divisions got clearer. The gang members had silk scarves, nice clothes, were mostly fat, and sooner or later, had pistols on their belts. It was reminiscent of the pigs in George Orwell's 'Animal Farm'. We had grubby clothes, sometimes ate well and sometimes ate very thin cheese sandwiches 3 times a day while working 18 hours during the festival crunches, and we waited 6 months or so for a pair of tennis shoes or plastic sunglasses: no exaggeration there, I can testify to it. Sounds like a scenario Orwell could have enjoyed as a model to write about.

I often thought, "Why am I doing this? I HATE communes!" I hated living in a room which some bureaucrat in an office decided I have to share with somebody I would rather remain strangers with. I hated eating at fixed mealtimes, always in the same place, getting on the same bus, to go to the same work, day after day. I hated being told when and how long to work, even if I was so exhausted I couldn't see straight. I hated playing music I was told to play and wearing clothes I was told to wear. But the answer that I came up with, from inside me, was simply, that this is the price I have to pay. I want to be near Him. I felt instinctively that this man holds a key to my gaining freedom from the miserable bondage of my mind. And all these hatreds and dislikes in me are exactly the clothes that my mind wears, its operating system, its 'OSX', so to speak. No matter what is happening outside me, with his presence, with his words, with his energy, and with all these irritating aspects of the commune I was living in, he was provoking me to get out of the prison of the mind, into an inner freedom which I could not yet understand or explain or deny. Knowing that He wouldn't be here forever, I realized the time is precious and decided that I will stick it out and see what happens. I will accept a temporary physical bondage, on the gamble of seeking ultimate liberation.

The interesting thing for me, as I slowly realized that I was living in a mild form of concentration camp, was that I could actually face my oppressors. They were not nameless faceless distant bureaucrats in Washington or Moscow, but they were people that I would meet on the street downtown at the Mall, or would talk to in meetings during work. I could see them, see their weakness, see their inner emptiness and insecurity, and it made me see the futility of hating them. It was a drama being played out, and I knew I would outlast them. I knew they would be gone one day, and I still would be there.

I was living in a place called Subhuti grove at that time, and it was a group of trailers situated in a high mountain valley. At night, except for the trailers, it was an endless expanse of black under the intensely starry skies. One night, there was a flickering in the sky, and huge vast columns of green light shot out from the Northern horizon, waving and undulating, changing into dancing waves of greenish ghostly glow. It was unearthly, spellbinding. They were so alive, so vast and mysterious. I realized it was the Northern Lights. I watched for a long, long time, spellbound in the silence of those hills...

My days were spent working on carpentry projects, usually alone, here and there in that great expanse of Juniper covered hills, with more and more frequency being at Bhagwan's house or garden. For several months I was helping to build the garages for the ever-more numerous Rolls Royces. They were arriving so quickly that we didn't have time to make real buildings, they were more like framed warehouses covered with tent-like material. As soon as we had finished one, it was necessary to make more, to accommodate the growing number of cars.

As time went by, many of the projects I was involved in were set up in such a way as to be a part of this mounting pressure from Sheela against the housekeepers. I was in a crew of 3, whose job it was to build a guard tower on the roof of Bhagwan's house. It was told to us that it was to protect Bhagwan. But after the building of it, it became clear that the main purpose was not to protect Bhagwan, but for someone in Sheela's gang to watch and monitor the movements of each and every person who lived with him, as if they were going to be the 'betrayers'. So, I was being used by the managers, but my work every day in the house made me more and more friends with the people who lived there, with them I chit-chatted during the day, with them I shared a cup of tea, with them I became close friends and beloveds, with them I felt solidarity, and the feeling that if push came to shove, I would be pushing with them.

CHAPTER 12

Vivek

I take a break from my writing, and I climb the hill slowly, in the fading sun of late afternoon, above the wooded river gorge, as the road, this endless brocade of little river stones set in patterns and arabesques of grey and black and white, winds upward into the hills. Passing white stone facades and balconies clinging to the hillside I begin to see openings to caves dug into the mountain centuries ago. Each pass of the road reveals more views of the high red stone walls on the hillside across the gorge. Those walls, tapering ever so slightly as they rise upward in symmetrical perfection, are the impeccable mathematical geometry and poetry of the building that graces the top of the next hill, the Alhambra. Here, on this side, from small windows in the white stone walls covered with iron gratings amid the bouganvileas, the magnetic and irresistible sounds of flamenco music drifts out into the hillsides covered with cactus and pepper trees, the penetrating rhythms of many clapping hands and drumming feet in overlapping patterns of twos and threes which I cannot follow with my mind, but can only delight in from some place deep in my soul. It is an incessant wind here in Granada, which blows upon the coals of passion inside the heart, kindling them into a living flame.

The canyon echoes in the distance with the encroaching night, muffled handclaps and guitars, and the wailing voices of men crying out to the stars in elaborate mesmerizing melodies about the women they have loved and to whom they have lost their souls. The voices are a deep cry straight from the guts, which grabs me in the same place.

The music that fills the air with passion and mystery is an outpouring of a people who wandered for centuries, from the deserts of Rajasthan, across the middle East, to Egypt, North Africa, and then into Spain. Their rhythms speak of India, Arabia, thousands of years of songs and deserts and gatherings in the night under the great mystery of the millions of stars reaching from horizon to horizon. These people of the hills and caves, although their bodies were enslaved by kings and conquerors and oppressors, in their souls they remained free, and proud, and strong, unconquered in their music, and their passion, and their love.

The soft winds of evening move over the olive groves and palm trees disappearing into the distance. The red rocky cliffs all around seem to soften with the heat of day now fading. The moon rises, a crystal clear half-circle in the empty sky, slowly filling with stars in this Andalusian night. I gaze out from under this elm tree which serves as my friend, protector and harbor in the summer's heat, as I write these words.

My dear reader, from these musings amidst the cactuses and stones, I return to my tale, and here in so doing my thoughts regress to a day in 1982.

That was the first day I ever saw her: it was in the autumn, an autumn which comes in that Northern high desert place as a sweet dying feeling in the afternoon golden glow of the sun. All power and force in the heat is gone, and only the light remains, the wind growing cold around sunset, and the days marvelously soft with the approaching winter. I was building a little roof over the back porch at Bhagwan's house, so the ladies who worked inside taking care of him could smoke outdoors without sitting exposed in the rain and snow in the cold winter. At the Ranch, no-one could smoke indoors, one would have to go outside to a designated 'smoking temple', and there it was the back porch of the house, so the women who were his robe-makers and shoe-makers and cooks and cleaners up to that time had been smoking on their brief work-breaks out in the rain and snow.

It was a good job I had. I was free to figure it out as I went along, improvising along the way, and enjoying the wonderful atmosphere of being nearby to Him, as the room where He spent nearly all his time was about 10 meters away, which was a kind of silent joy inside me, as if all was at peace with the world.

She was already a legend by that time: 'Bhagwan's companion'; Mysterious, British, beautiful, distant; you name it, all the things that could make me nervous, I already thought about her, just on hearsay alone. I was nailing a board to the floor of the porch, I turned around to get my hammer, and suddenly there she stood, about 6 feet away from me: beautiful, dressed in purple, very pale, solemn, imperial, not exactly friendly, silently looking at me reproachfully, as if to say, "And WHO is this lump of crud on the porch where I want to be alone?" Not wanting to be mistaken for a lump of crud, I said, "Hi!", to which she replied in marvelously perfect British fashion... absolutely nothing! All she gave me was an icy look that would wither the balls off a brass monkey, to quote an old and very useful saying. But if I could hear that look in words, it would say: "How DARE you speak to me, you impudent, worthless and crummy barbarian!?"

Well, that pretty much finished the silent conversation right there and then, and I gave up any ideas about not being a lump of crud, as that is exactly what I felt like, and I skulked off to find something else to do, pretty quick.

As it was, I would still be around, day after day, and I took great pains to not bump into her, or even pass by, if it was at all in my power to avoid. I kept my eyes to myself, and spent most of the days up on the roof, fixing the leaks between trailers so the rain would not dribble into my Master's room. I took care to walk softly on that roof, not dropping anything, basically taking the attitude of a mouse as best I could. The view was very beautiful from my mouse-perch, the red and purple rocks of the hills all around dramatically set against masses of purple and black clouds. I could breathe up there... Sitting on the roof, Bhagwan in his room underneath me, the vast desert and purple mountains all around me; it was a wonderful scene, I must say, and I forgot all about commune Politics for the time being. Sometimes at the end of work, instead of walking down the path from Bhagwan's house to the valley of the Ranch, I would take the opposite path, and head up unseen into the beautiful rocky cliffs above his house, and sit up there for awhile in the twilight afterglow, feeling like an eagle on its rocky perch, surveying the magnificent valleys and peaks all around, and His house nestled in the trees in its beautiful little valley below.

One afternoon, about a year later, I was passing down the long and silent corridor in the house on the way to the balcony where I was working on another job, and she was passing down the same corridor, going the opposite way. My eyes were to myself, and I was going my own way. As we passed, suddenly, she stopped in her tracks and declared in a loud voice which actually raised the hairs on the back of my neck:

"I had a DREAM about you!"

I said quietly, "What did you dream?"

She paused, and said, in an even louder voice and an embarrassed smile:

"I'M NOT TELLING!"

Well, I suppose one could be happy about such things, and in truth it was not unhappiness that I felt, but as these words echoed down the long corridor, the fact that this was happening in Bhagwan's house just outside his room made me incredibly shocked, shy and nervous. I didn't say anything, and it was a few days before I saw her again.

At this time, I was working just next to Bhagwan's room everyday, in a balcony which was being turned into a bathroom, and was nicknamed by us 'The Cave', as it resembled that, in the dark, silent and intensive way that we would be working there all day long, each day.

A few days after the passing in the corridor, we ran into each other again. This time it was outside, in the afternoon, around 2 o'clock. It was when He would leave on His daily drive, and we, (Vidhan and myself), would use that time to do whatever we needed to do in His house that required making noise, like drilling holes or pounding on things. So I was walking hurriedly up the driveway on my way to the Cave. In the young poplar trees, she was suddenly standing there in front of me, wearing a long dress which made her movements incredibly feminine, as it blew softly in the warm afternoon breeze.

I was surprised to see her, as usually it was she who went on the drive in the car with Him, but this day, obviously, she had not. She stopped in front of me, not saying a word, and smiled with the biggest and most beautiful smile I had ever seen in my whole life. I felt as if the whole universe was smiling at me. I stopped in my tracks, and my whole body involuntarily shivered, just like the poplars in the wind all around me.

I remember now those words of Shiva from the ancient Tantra sutras, "When senses are shaken as leaves, ENTER this shaking". And I knew now what it meant, to be moved by a force greater than my mind could grasp.

In truth, I didn't want this to be happening. And I wanted it with all my heart. I felt I would DIE in this door opening between us, like paddling a little canoe into the middle of the Pacific ocean: no escape. Nowhere to run, nowhere to hide. I felt completely exposed in front of that smile, which was actually so honest, so huge and real, that I knew it demanded just as

144

much realness from me. It completely freaked me out. (For those of you who are not familiar with 'California dialect', this means, "It scared the hell out of me".)

A few days later, at sunset I was walking out the gate of Lao-Tzu grove after work, and quietly behind me there pulled up a black Rolls Royce; her Rolls. Silently the window rolled down, she looked out at me and said, "You want a ride?" and pointed towards the Ranch. I said, like an absolute idiot, "I'm going the other way", which was a fact, but really not the absolute truth. The truth was, whichever way she was going would have been the right way, if I had the guts at the moment. There was a million reasons to say no, and only one to say yes, but that yes would have to wait three years and a huge amount of suffering and 'water down the river' before I could say it. So, she drove on, and I was left to ponder my stupidity for a very, very long time.

CHAPTER 13

Distant Thunder

As I write this, I am in Sicily, traveling this beautiful island for the first time in my life, the land of my father and of my fathers' fathers. And it is true that everywhere I go in this marvelous island, my blood is stirred by the beauty of the land, the smells and sights and colors, and the faces and strength of the people. All the cells of my body feel at home here. The orange blossoms and the volcano and the rocky shores of the sea all speak directly to my heart. I am stirred to my roots, as I find myself in places which I dreamt of as a youth, reading Homer's Odyssey and wandering on the cliffs of Big Sur. Now I find myself in the very places where Odysseus' ship passed the island of Circe the sorceress, the cave of the Cyclops, and where he heard the wailing other-worldly songs of the Sirens.

I am playing a few concerts, one of which is on the side of the volcano Mt. Aetna, in a domed small meditation center. During the concert, I hear what seems to be thunder, and as I come out the door after the end of the show, I am greeted with the sight in the night sky of a Roman candle of lava pouring forth some distance away! The thunder I heard was the volcano on which we were, erupting during the concert.

In the morning I had been wandering in the ruins of ancient temples, in the south of the island. The signs written for the tourists by the 'experts' say they are 'Greek' temples from 600 BC, but it is difficult for me to believe that the Greeks as we know of them could have built these. The temples have fallen into ruins, either through earthquakes or some man-made disaster. Some of the columns remain intact and in place, but as I look at the ancient stones piled on top of one another, some things become clear. The columns, of which there were at least 60, were enormous. They are as big in circumference as a small room, each one perfectly flat on top and bottom and perfectly cylindrical. The stones sit one upon another, without even the possibility of a piece of paper fitting in between, and they were piled up 10 high. Each one is about 2 meters high and 3 meters in diameter, and weighs at least 10 tons, in my estimation of stone and volume. How did Greeks, 25 centuries ago, using ropes and oxen, raise a block of stone weighing 10 tons, 20 meters into the air and place it perfectly on top of a column of the same stones, 600 times? And then place huge lintel stones on top, connecting those columns, and more stone on top of that, beautifully carved, without any of it falling down? No, my dear archaeologists, your theories are nice in books, but if you have ever worked with stone, you would know what it takes to make a perfectly flat surface, perfectly perpendicular to a plumb, and on a perfectly round fluted surface. Without high-tech tools, higher than our present technology, it could not happen. Especially if you only have bronze chisels, ropes and muscle-power. Add to that, the fact that the stones were quarried from several kilometers away, and you have an engineering job which would have taken thousands of men many, many years. Look to another answer for the riddle of these stones. We are not alone in this universe, and someone with much greater knowledge and skill and strength than ourselves must have made this happen: Someone we have forgotten about, or purposely erased from our collective memories. Traces remain in tales of giants and gods in our ancient collective memory; do not overlook them when you gather all the clues to the mysteries which lie before our eyes, written in stone on the face of our planet. Stones do not lie. Just they wait to be deciphered.

Now, back to my story:

In the words of the Master:

"I am absolutely unreliable.
I have not given any excuse for my people to be around me.
In fact, I have given them every excuse
to escape from me, to avoid me.
Being with me does not bring you respectability.
That was well-considered by me from the very beginning,
that with me you should have to lose your respect,
your honor, your morality.
These will be the tests
whether you are going to risk anything to be with me.
And if thousands of people have decided
to be with me at any cost,
that is a determination, a commitment of tremendous import.
That means they have tasted something of my presence.
The people who are now around me
are not here just for my words.
By now they are perfectly aware,
that you can play with the words, there is nothing in it.
They are perfectly aware that they are not to cling to my words,
because tomorrow I am going to change.
Why cling unnecessarily?
I am absolutely unreliable.
And to trust in a man who is so unreliable is authentic trust.
It goes beyond thinking of consequences.
It goes beyond fear.
It goes beyond all words.
I may contradict,
I may say anything, it does not matter to my people.
What matters is my presence,
my love towards them, their love towards me.
And that is going to create a whirlwind of awakening around the
whole world. It is just the beginning."...

Osho

At this point in my narrative, I shall no longer use the name Bhagwan, but rather 'Osho', in reference to that mysterious entity which for a time the world called 'Bhagwan Shree Rajneesh'.

Throughout his lifetime, his name changed several times. The name he was given at birth was Rajneesh Chandra Mohan, which translates as 'The Lord of the Full Moon'. When he was teaching and traveling in India, he came to be known as 'Acharya Rajneesh', which means, 'Great Teacher'. As more and more disciples gathered around him in the Bombay years, they began to call him 'Bhagwan', a traditional name that is used in India for the Master. Later, the term 'Shree' was added, which is an additional term of respect in India. But at a certain point in time, in 1989, he began to change his name, saying that he had never liked the name 'Bhagwan', as its Sanskrit roots allude to the sexual imagery of the Shiva lingam and the yoni, the ancient symbols of transcendent experience in Hinduism. For a brief time, he was called simply, 'Beloved Master', but eventually settled on the simple name 'Osho', which is a term of respect used in Japan for every Buddhist teacher or Master. It is not a personal name, as such, but more a pre-nominative term of respect. 'Osho' is a title which means simply 'respected sir', in Japan. This was, a bit later in the timeframe of this story, His wish, to be called in the ultimate period of His life on this earth, by that simple name, 'Osho'. From this point on in respect to that wish, I will use that name in reference to my beloved Master who up to this point in the narrative for reasons of historical veracity, I have referred to as 'Bhagwan'.

Osho's effect on people was hypnotic. His energy was deeply affective to me, and anybody near him. But it was equally affective on other kinds of creatures around him, non-human. I was a witness to this many times working around Him, on and in and under and over his house, I came to see many things which could not be explained away by those who would claim hypnotism, or mere charisma.

There were peacocks all around his house. They wandered here and there, and as peacocks do, occasionally would get to screaming. There were many peacocks, but there stood out in particular a white male. Every day when Osho would come back from his drive, this peacock would make it a point to plant himself in the driveway behind the house, where Osho would drive in to park at the end of his daily drive. The peacock would literally block the road in front of Osho's car, and open his tail feathers, and dance around the car, until Vivek would have to get out of the car and shoo it away   And it just didn't want to go, it wanted to stay there in front of Osho, dancing in full display.

Each day, when Osho would be out on his drive and far, far away in the dusty Oregonian distance, sometime around 3:30, the 15 or 20 peacocks would all start screaming, and line up in front of his house. About 5 minutes later, his car would appear coming around the curve entering into the valley a mile away. The peacocks would all stand at attention, display their tails, and sometimes dance when he would drive into the compound of his house. How they would know that his car was coming, when he was still a couple of miles away and hidden behind several mountains, was really unfathomable to me, as it was not at the same time each day, it could vary quite a lot.

I was working at that time on adding an extension to his house to shelter all the robes which were being made for him, and because of that I was usually just outside the window where his sitting room was, for several months. In front of the window near to where he would sit most of the day, there was a little tree, not more than 6 feet tall. By this time the winter had come on, and there was snow covering everything, including the little tree. All the peacocks had their home, a well heated A-frame on the compound, and they would pass their wintry days and nights inside there. But that white peacock wouldn't hear of it: He passed his winter roosting in that little tree out in the open, 6 feet outside Osho's window, the closest point to Osho that was not on the frozen ground, his back and tail covered with snow, facing Osho's room. It's quite a choice to make, for a tropical bird!

Along with doing construction in his house and being a handyman, part of my job was to take care that the mice population would not take over. They were drawn to his house like a magnet. Dozens would appear every day. Each morning, we would have to crawl around under the house, setting and taking in the mousetraps. Every day, there would be a dozen mice, dead in the traps. Each one, in a different attitude of death, frozen in that moment when the trap would snap on them. Some, a face of total shock and disbelief. Some, deep surrender. Some, the clearcut horror of "Why ME??". Or "Oh NO!!". Or, "Im just a poor little mouse, trying to make a living…" It got to me, seeing this every day, how they die, just like people. They, just like us, never believing they will die until that moment arrives, and we all feel it is unjust, unfair, a personal insult. Sometimes it was too much, the expressions on the faces of the mice, so undeniably human, it would tear at the heart…

Self-importance is the worst enemy of a man. It weakens him by making him feel offended by the deeds and misdeeds of his peers. Self-importance requires that one spends a great part of one's life feeling offended by something or someone.

(Don Juan, as told to Carlos Castaneda)

"Nothing others do is because of you. What others say and do is a projection of their own reality, their own dream. When you are im-

mune to the opinions and actions of others, you won't be the victim of needless suffering."

Don Miguel Ruiz

In the first year that I was playing music at the Ranch, the 'co-ordinator' of the Music department, if it could be called such, was a guy named PremGeet, whom I had met 3 years before in some of the therapy groups at the Paras center in San Francisco. He was a bass player from New York, and a very conscientious and care-taking administrator of our tasks as a band. His job was to see to it that we fit together as a band, as a functioning unit, coming from all different musical and cultural backgrounds, to melt our sound and get used to each other and compose and play all the various pieces of music which were needed for the festivals when Osho would come out for Satsang. It was 5 or 6 pieces of music per day in the morning, and song-lists for each night of the music group. So that was about 30 composed instrumental pieces, rehearsed and performed live in front of the Master and at least 15,000 other listeners, and another 50 or so songs rehearsed and ready for the 4 or 5 nights of music group, also for a public of about 15,000. The music group could last 2 hours, so it was a big bulk of music to get ready in the 10 days or so that we would have. PremGeet kept a good eye on the larger picture, watching the clock tick down as the days of the festival approached, and he was careful to support the inspiration, and cut away the weeds, giving space to everybody when they would share their creativity. He had a healthy practical skepticism which kept the whole thing from flying away, but he was also appreciative of good playing and he had a very good ear. In my opinion, he was a great co-ordinator, helping the creative, keeping an eye on the bigger picture, with no real personal baggage that would cut anybody's wings, and he had no pretensions about playing therapy games with us.

'Above' him, was another shall we say 'archangel', without

wings, who was a part of the dominant power structure at the time, although she was a somewhat rival and dissonant note to it, never being quite 'in' with the inner circle of Sheela. Her name was Aruno. She had the curious ability to survive every regime change in the commune that I witnessed and suddenly appear as fresh as a daisy in the new power structure, always as number 2 or 3. During my 4 years at the Ranch, she was one of my principal petty tyrants. We never liked each other. It's not that I was against her from day one, but certain things she would do in our interactions didn't exactly endear her to me, nor me to her, I would guess. Whatever was its cause, it was a mutual discomfort between us, like two persons from different planets that could not understand the other's perspective, eyeing each other warily, but she from a position of relatively absolute power over the external aspects of my life at the time. That greatly contributed to my feeling of discomfort.

For example, after the first day of the first festival, which was extremely successful and joyful from a musical point of view, she came straightaway after the morning satsang with the Master down to our music trailer behind Buddha Hall, and started yelling at us at length about the wastebasket being full. We had just been in the most meaningful hour of our lives, the first time that Osho had come out to sit with his people in more than a year. It was the first time that I had ever played for Osho, and I was deeply moved by the whole experience, being in a kind of 'ecstatic afterglow' at that moment. The wastebasket being full, was such an obvious triviality, the misdemeanor for which we were being castigated by her at full volume, that it definitely seemed like she was scraping the bottom of the barrel in order to find something to complain about and make us feel deflated in that golden glow of a beautiful morning.

I can appreciate her efforts to trim the egos of musicians, as they do have a tendency to over-inflate rapidly, like helium balloons at a county fair, floating off into infinity when the string slips out of the hand. But her efforts seemed kind of heavy-handed and mental, bordering on the theatrical. There is an old Chinese saying, that says, "An apprentice woodcutter, when cutting with the Master's axe, often cuts off his own foot". It seemed appropriate to me at that moment. She would go out of her way to nag at us, at every possible opportunity, instead of actually talking to us in a human-to-human way. It got to be a running joke between us musicians, about getting 'hosed down', which was our euphemism for when she would work us over verbally. Sometimes when we would see her Jeep would be approaching the music trailer on the dusty road from the Ranch, we would put on raincoats and sit and wait, just to emphasize the point, that it was predictable, our getting 'hosed down'. I wonder if she even noticed the yellow raincoats we were wearing while she was throwing insults our way.

But, a far more memorable episode was when the Ranch was short of funds, in between the first festival and the second one. Aruno and one of her higher-up cohorts named Savita, who controlled the ashram finances, had the lovely idea to require us all to 'donate' all our music instruments. They were then promptly auctioned away, and I lost several rare flutes, which had been personal gifts to me, from people who liked my music, from Japan and Chile. They had been gifted to me lovingly, and had been with me for years, and off they went along with several other instruments which had taken me most of my short life-time to assemble together and learn to play. I didn't really get the point at that time.

Granted, I can understand the importance of 'non-attachment', and from a Buddhist standpoint she certainly was aiding me on the path to emptiness. Even further, it was a great incentive to see that the duality of owning or not owning was created from the emptiness of my own Buddha Nature, right..., I get it, sure...but, hey, I had spent the last 40 dollars I had to buy some mud-boots to work all day long outdoors in the Ranch winter.

154

The instruments, I was using to play for Osho and the commune. They had a value because of that, but the monetary value they fetched was not much compared to that, or so I reckoned…the price they sold them for. was about the same as two pairs of mud-boots. Now many of those instruments were off to Munich in the luggage of some enterprising new sannyasin tourist who saw a good deal when it came his way, and the 100 bucks or so that the commune got was about the cost of one of Sheela's silk scarves that Kasi would be ironing in the long afternoons. It was for me, the experience of emptiness, with a pie in your face. Two birds killed with one stone, both of them arising from the illusion of ego.

But, the 'cork-in-the-bottle' in my formation of a fixed attitude towards this delightful petty tyrant, was an episode in March, as the spring grasses announced the ending of the cold desert winter in that Northern country. I had been practicing my violin early morning and late night_outside the 12 hours of daily work to play sweetly and not scratchy this time for the Master, and just a week before the festival, my hand slipped for a split-second while using a table saw, and off came the ends of two fingers on my left hand. I looked in disbelief at my shattered fingers as the blood was starting to pour forth, and for a few moments, I felt nothing. Then, all of a sudden, the pain began to throb from my hand. It was excruciating, not to mention the mental pain that my 'career' on the violin was there and then halted forever, as the soft pads that create the sound on the strings would now be hard scar tissue, and I would never have a good sound again. I was rushed to the Ranch hospital, and that day, after having surgery, I was in the hospital room with my arm tied to the wall to immobilize it, and my mind a bit foggy as the anesthetic was wearing off. But I was clear enough to understand and remember everything. Sometimes pain does that, it is like a hot knife going through butter, you stop focusing on non-essential thoughts and you see things as they are. Aruno came into my hospital room, and gleefully said to me, "I have a great idea! We can take out an insurance policy on your hands and cut off the rest of the fingers, to make some money easily for the Ranch!".

I didn't say anything. I realized that her humor was poorly timed and not exactly humor, and was not even funny. Lying in a hospital bed with my arm throbbing and tied to the wall, her using this situation to psychologically kick me in my most vulnerable moment was not much appreciated by me. It did reinforce my feeling that these characters who seek power-positions have some kind of psychological problem, whether it is an inferiority complex, or frustrated creativity, or sadism, that is, taking pleasure in the pain of others, I don't know. But it seemed to me to be a kind of mental disease, and the feeling that it evoked in me was not one of compassion, but rather a sense of organic dislike originating deep in my belly. But this reaction I felt and noted within me, and did not express. With such people, as they had the means at hand to make my life even worse, one could only watch inside oneself the reactions they would provoke, and do the best you could to not participate in their games.

The second annual World Celebration, in July of 1983, was the peak of the joy I would experience as being a musician at the Ranch. The band consisted of Govindas, a German, on guitar, and he played very beautifully and heartfully, Nivedano, a Brazilian, on drums, and he was a great drummer. He had a truly great sense of rhythm, energy, skill and the ability to hold it all together. Shiven, an Afro-American, was on congas, and he was a real joy to work with, always positive, always with new ideas. Yashu, a wonderful little Spanish woman, on flute, and she was one of the most soulful and unique flute players I have ever had the good fortune to hear; Toby, an American, on sax and other wind instruments and composing often; Shabda Nur, an American on

156

trumpet, a wonderful guy who played so sweet and was so knowl-edgeable about music as well as having a very balanced character that kept the equilibrium in moments when it seemed that Spain and Germany and Brazil were about to flair up into open warfare; Premda, a beautiful ethereal American lady on Tamboura, and me, a Californian, on keyboards, viola, a bit of flute and composing quite a bit. By the time the festival came, we were all melted into one, often living, eating and working together 24 hours a day. The music was simply beautiful, heartful, and unique. We were all carried together on the wings of a Great Bird. And I value that time as a precious memory, a sunlit mountain peak that pref-aced the very deep valley that was to come after.

The beautiful part of playing music for Osho was also the greatest and most difficult of challenges. Playing music for him was, in a way, flying on his energy, and yet, if you got inundated, delighting and drowning in it and not keeping the mind functioning and well centered, you couldn't play. It was a razor's edge, and it was very easy to fall from that edge. It happened to me once, a day I will never forget, although I wish I could sometimes.

It was Master's Day Darshan at the peak of the 2nd Annual World Celebration. I was playing the piano. The band was fly-ing, 20,000 red-robed people in Buddha Hall were ecstatically singing their hearts and souls, and Osho was there, clapping his hands. At the end of one massive musical climax, a song that had practically gone orgasmic, there was a pregnant silence, and I was to play solo the first several bars of the introduction to the next song. But something had happened to me. The over-whelming energy of the moment had simply and suddenly erased my mind: It was a total blank!

In stunned perplexity, I looked at the keyboard, those white and black keys in patterns of 2's and 3's, and I had no idea what it was…20 years of musical training had simply evaporated into nothing in that instant. It was like a psychic EMP, an electromagnetic surge that fries the circuitry of anything near it; this had happened to my brain. My hands came down on the keyboard like a cat jumping on the piano. Osho and 20,000 people listened in stunned and awkward silence as the cat chaotically walked around for a little while on the keys, until after a few moments, my bio-computer rebooted and my hands found the chords again to the song I was supposed to play, and everything started up again. Now, if I could have died in that moment, it would have been a great relief. But instead, I had to be called to the office a few days later by Aruno to listen to the recording of what had happened. It was agony; and her gloating smile in rubbing salt into the wound did not escape me.

How to be open to that overwhelming energy that flowed from Osho, and flow with it, but not be lost in it? That was the paradox: how to be totally in your heart, dissolving into the ocean, while maintaining the functioning of the mind, in the dimension of time? This was a riddle, an existential Zen koan, one of those impossible-to-solve puzzles given to Zen students as a means of going beyond the reasoning mind, which I would face time and time again, whenever playing music for Him.

As the summer passed away, and the heat faded into the cool breezes of autumn, a change came over the commune. We were constantly in a legal fight to have the right to make our city, and its existence was never assured. One day it seems we had won some court battle, the next day it seemed another threat had come, and we were in yet another legal struggle. Due to losing or winning some land-use decisions in the politics of Oregon, I actually could never be sure, but the fact was that due to some loophole in the laws, if we could finish buildings that were already started, then those buildings could remain. But there would be a cut-off period for this, about two weeks as I recall.

Suddenly, within those two weeks, the foundations were hastily put in place for our planned residences, 120 in all, a big hotel, and numerous other things. Everyone who was available was drafted into construction crews, from cleaning, farming, cooking, offices, everybody who could be spared was now in construction, and we started working around the clock to erect those buildings before the deadline. Some new techniques were invented, buildings were planned that would use up the thousands of tent platforms left over from the festival as roofs; walls were made in modular fashion, everything became a production line round-the-clock to get those buildings up.

So the construction crews now were full of hundreds of people with absolutely no experience holding a hammer or nail, whom a few days before were cleaners or typists or cooks or veggie farmers. As I was an experienced carpenter, I was put in charge of a crew framing the walls of these 120 houses. So it was not just a crash-course in carpentry; it was an existential experiment in hundreds of men and women working together, in extreme conditions, under pressure, and oddly enough, extremely fun. I never worked so hard in my life, and never laughed so much. The catch was, that you couldn't just pound the nails and get on with it. A lot of those women and men had a lot of emotions flowing having to do with pounding nails, cutting sheetrock and slapping on plaster and paint 14 hours a day. There was a lot of tears, a lot of newly aching muscles, a lot of sweat, and a great, great deal of jokes that went into those townhouses. It was intense, it was not easy at all, and we were all literally stretched to the limit; physically, emotionally, and in our spirits.

The days of October rains moved into late November snows, At that time I was placed in charge of another crew of about 20 people, to complete the framing of some more townhouses, in a small canyon in the hills near the airport. It was to be a job of 3 or 4 days. As we began working there in that little wooded canyon, the temperature started dropping as a blizzard moved in. By the next day, it was 24 below zero F, with 3 feet of snow on the ground. We were working outdoors, there being no heat or windows in the newly framed buildings. I was not used to this super-cold weather, and I found that I had very few thoughts, coming verrrrry slowly, feeling much like a cow must feel. All my energy seemed to be going to my body to keep warm. We all found ourselves feeling more and more giddy, not much able to concentrate, and at a certain point we all just started wandering here and there, off into the woods. It was a kind of collective spontaneous time-out, there was just no way to keep it together anymore, mentally or physically. We wandered in the snow, marveling silently at the frozen waterfalls on the water-pumping station, the long icicles everywhere, the snow hanging in the air, too cold to fall. I started to feel warmer and warmer, with a great desire to just lay down in the snow... to be warm, and still, and quiet...just as I was laying down, a voice inside me said, "DON'T DO IT! GET UP! GO BACK!"... and I did that, finding the others as we all fought off the hypothermia and got ourselves back to the trucks, all of us feeling that the houses could wait while we found something else to do indoors until the weather changed.

As the residential houses neared completion, I was pulled off from the townhouses and started another crew at the hotel, a huge quadrangular complex down at the end of the valley. When I arrived, it resembled a scene from Bombay Central Station: a jumbled chaos of movement, confusion, colors, madness and noise, sheet rock, plywood, wires, nails and paint moving in every direction from people going up and down ladders and stairs in the frozen mud and chaos. In the weeks that followed, miraculously it somehow all slowly came together. I was relieved to be most of the days up on the roof, putting on a few miles of asphalt tiles and tarpaper, as February moved into March and the first signs of spring appeared.

On one of those days of late February, I was pulled off my job for a one-day stint on a special crew gathered to finish a new cafeteria building 'immediately'. When we arrived there,

there was only the concrete slab, and we started framing walls, roof, sides, doors, and all that goes into a building usually taking the better part of a month to do. We worked all through the night, and after 24 hours, as the sun came up, it was done. I went home exhausted in the morning to sleep a few hours, and realized that it was my birthday. I woke in the afternoon, and heard that there was to be a 'Celebration' in Buddha Hall, and there I went, still somewhat dazed from the previous day and night marathon of work.

As I arrived to the hall, it was full of thousands of people, all the residents of the ranch, the band was playing, balloons were in the air, and I was amazed at this strange coincidence, of there being an actual party on the day of my birthday. I wondered what the party was all about, and then came the announcement, that in India they had found the original Adoption Papers, which had given Osho in adoption at the age of seven to a man named Bapuji. This man, in actuality, was Sheela's Father! So Osho was in effect legally the elder brother of Sheela. What a strange turn of events! I recalled that the event was corroborated in Osho's autobiography, he had mentioned the adoption which had occurred at that early age, as it had been foretold in his Astrological Birth Chart, that either he would become a World Teacher, or die at age seven. The adoption was the only way to avoid the latter outcome. He mentioned that he had lived a couple of years with this family in Bombay. And now, being legally in Sheela's family, his chances of obtaining a permanent resident visa in the US were greatly enhanced.

This explained the great trust which Osho was putting in Sheela's hands, her being the only channel of information to and from Him, as family relations in India are extremely important. But as many things that happened under Sheela's dominion at the Ranch took the air of theatre, one never knew if it was true, exaggerated, or staged. Either way, the circus grew in intensity and mystery.

CHAPTER 14

Storm Clouds Gathering

Nothing has happened, and nothing ever happens.
What is…IS.

Chandidas Baul

After the Townhouse and hotel 'crunch', as the spring began I was back at Osho's house, again making garages for the ever-growing fleet of Rolls Royces. That was a good job, in the sense of working outdoors in the spring sunshine, in the relative peace and tranquility of Osho's compound. The rest of the Ranch was subject to territorial oversight by members of Sheela's gang, but here in Osho's compound, there was another atmosphere, much more expansive and vast and free. In the crew there were three of us usually; Kavi, Raghuvira, and myself. Kavi I had met in that first Let-go weekend, years ago. He had been a bartender in San Francisco, and on the Ranch he had become one of the best construction crew-leaders. His sense of mechanical space and how to figure out blueprints and make them work was really awesome to me.

We had been pouring foundations in the land below Osho's house, which was a lovely forest of poplars with a view of the hills all around. We would pour, and pour, and pour, sometimes 3 truckloads of cement a day, from 6 am until 11 pm often, and it couldn't be fast enough to keep up with the new cars rolling in.

At this time, Osho released a statement to the commune,

which landed like a bombshell in the midst of the long silence he had been in.

It was a sudden announcement about lists of 'Enlightened people' in the commune, Mahasattvas, Bodhisattvas, and more such Sanskrit titles of respect given to the wise or illuminated in India. There was about 21 names as I recall. Now, some of those people could very well have been enlightened, some of them were longtime and very respected Indian disciples which had been with Osho since the beginning of his teaching. Others, well, who knows? They were long-term disciples, beautiful people, some having done obviously a great deal of inner work…others, hmmm, it was dubious, they seemed to be just like any other one of us, prone to bad moods, not particularly luminous in any visible manner. And some others, forget about it, it was impossible! Enlightenment? They were people who I just avoided so as not to get in a conversation with them in the lunch line.

My inner dialogue suddenly went into overdrive: "Now, if Osho says they are all enlightened, and some of them obviously couldn't be according to my unenlightened mind, what's that mean about the rest of them? If that's enlightenment, do I really WANT it? And that's why I'm doing all this work every day, the surrender, the endless labor, the petty tyrants, the insults from the hierarchy? All was suddenly thrown into doubt. If the Master is publishing this list, what's he doing it for? To throw us a curveball? To give protection from the commune bureaucracy to some worthy souls? Maybe enlightenment is not what I think it is! It's not like, Wham! Suddenly you are in bliss, one-with-the-intelligent-source-of-the-universe, like Osho. On the contrary, you stay the same idiot you always were, just with no ego! Wo…I don't know if I want that! "

It was a stroke of lightning, to show us our own judgements, preconceptions, misinformed opinions about our fellow humans. It was all of that, and more. Who could know? An edict coming at that time from Osho landed like thunder in the midst of a long silent calm, and my mind was somersaulting with it for quite some days, through the long hours of pounding thousands of 16-penny nails and pouring yet another concrete stemwall.

Pounding those nails became my constant meditation. I came to slowly realize, that when a thought would enter my head, the nail would get bent. If I reacted emotionally to the first bend of the nail, with the next hit it would get hopelessly twisted, and I would have to pull it out and start again with a new one. If I could stay thoughtless, centered, empty and relaxed, the nail would go straight in, every time. It was a flawless bio-feedback device. Zen archery with a hammer, all day long, 7 days a week, and sometimes nights too.

As the weeks and months went by, the atmosphere on the Ranch was visibly changing, as we were receiving more and more external threats from various sources. Posters with a Rolls-Royce in the crosshairs of a gunsight were seen in Eastern Oregon. There were rumors of black-ops being planned against Osho, from right-wing organizations and possibly the CIA. At that time I was working for two weeks in Antelope, the nearest town 20 miles outside the Ranch. We were remodeling the school, and one day as I watched Osho drive through town, a US Postal Service truck parked in front of me gunned its motor and headed straight for his Rolls as he approached an intersection. A crash was narrowly averted by the lead car in Osho's entourage, acting as a blocker to deter the Postal Truck. I flashed back to the knife-thrower a couple of years back in Poona discourse...Now I had seen yet another attempt on his life.

At that time we had a hotel in the middle of Portland, and one night there was a firebomb set off in it. Back at the Ranch, hastily, guard-posts and watch schedules were organized all over our community. I was sometimes guarding on roads in the Ranch, a job which was a welcome break from the relentlessness of the carpentry work. Four hours in a guard-booth on a lonely road at night, and then you could sleep in the morning the next day. That was a luxury. I craved the chance to be doing 'nothing', even for a few hours, just to 'be', without action.

Along with the appearance of guards and checkpoints, came weapons more visible in the daily driveby; now, the car that was following Osho's Rolls had an M-16 visible in the window. The helicopter which would hover over Osho's car as he would make his way through the ranch would visibly have an armed sniper in it. The members of Sheela's gang now would appear with pistols on their belts. It all served to very slowly increase the level of tension, paranoia, and suspicion. It was something like the frog in the cooking pot, never feeling the water was getting hotter, because it happens so slowly. So it was with us.

My alarm about the guns and security measures was not going off, as I actually knew and saw there were real threats to Osho's life being made, in the news media, in the rednecks driving by with shotguns in their pickups, in the hysterical Christian preachers screaming and practically frothing at the mouth from road-stops in Redmond as Osho would drive by, and in the fly-overs of F-16s at treetop levels. Things were heating up seriously. But just as it would come to be used in the society-at-large after 9-11, measures that were supposedly brought in to make us more 'secure' from outside threats, came to be clearly a message against any potential internal rebellion as well.

"And why were things heating up?", you might ask. We were first of all, a thorn in the side of the ranchers and neighbors in Eastern Oregon. They had their way of life: mostly they were farmers and ranchers, very conservative, and Christian. Most of them are what might be called 'redneck'…which can be loosely translated as bigoted, fundamentalist Christian, xenophobic, and territorial. But, in all fairness, we weren't taking any pains to make friends with them. On the contrary, Sheela was berating them, insulting them, irritating them in any possible way, and Osho seemed to be backing her up on that, or at least not stopping her from doing it. Slowly the nearby town of Antelope was taken over politically, in the sense of our greater numbers gained political control over the municipality in the local elections. That was akin to throwing a burning match at a dry field of grass. I don't blame them for being wary of 'us', the tactics of Sheela and her gang were more and more belligerent and openly hostile. This backfired in that it triggered the locals to seek support from the Oregon Senator in Washington, Mark Hatfield, and draw the attention of the IRS, the FBI, and Ronald Reagan, now the President of the USA. He was the ex-governor of California of my adolescence, the notorious cowboy cold-warrior of 'If it takes a bloodbath, let's get it over with' fame. He was mid-term in his installation of the new conservatism and cuthroat-capitalism-unchained: flashback to Peoples Park, Berkeley, 1969, when Reagan was governor and let loose his buckshot and teargas tactics; only now, it's 1984 and it's us coming up in the gunsight, and we are all dressed in bright red, dancing ecstatically, living in relative joy and happiness in a commune without money, consumerism, or Christianity there in the Oregon Desert, right in the plain eye of NBC, ABC, and CBS. All the national networks and anybody else who turned on the TV any given evening anywhere across the country would see us. We lived well and abundantly and mostly happy without dollars, without paychecks or taxes; we enjoyed our love without preachers, certificates and justices-of-the-peace, and danced like crazy every afternoon as there passed by a brown-skinned foreign guru in one of his many Rolls Royces whose books mercilessly exposed the hypocrisy and ridiculousness of every organized religion and political system on the planet. It's not hard to see why we were high on the list of public enemies for the FBI, Justice Department, 1000 Friends of Oregon, and probably a lot of others.

Spring moved into summer, and the crew of 4 that I was part of, kept making garages, and garages, and garages for Osho's ever-increasing fleet of Rolls Royces. As the next big festival approached, the availability of food started shrinking. There was always a tightening of the economic belt before the festivals: as resources were pooled and concentrated to prepare for the big party and all the 20,000 or so guests, we as residents came up sometimes on the short end of the equation at the coffee breaks: smaller cups for the tea, no cakes, sometimes we had bread, and sometimes not. But this time was getting difficult. My crew was working about 16 hours a day, pouring concrete and framing buildings, and that means burning a lot of calories. I was in charge of the tea-shack, where we would have a coffee and a bite to eat in the 6 hours between meals. But there was nothing available. We could not get any more bread, snacks, or fruit for the coffee break in the long afternoon between lunch and dinner. Myself and my crew were getting really hungry, and skinny, and feeling the effects of not having enough gas in the tank to keep running at full speed. So, I decided to 'take things into my own hands', and make a raid on the kitchen.

The central kitchen was now in the main valley of the Ranch, and was a huge open-air complex that could seat several thousand people at any given meal time. At 11 in the morning, I entered like a ninja, straight for the storage bins without saying a word to anybody, and managed to fill a couple of bags with granola and slices of bread. As quickly as I came in, I crept out, heading straight for the pickup I had left running in the parking lot.

Just before I got to my truck, there came blasting over the loudspeakers of the whole complex at a volume sufficient to waken the guards at the top of the ranch 8 miles away: "DE-VAKANT!! RETURN AT ONCE TO THE OFFICE! RETURN AT ONCE TO THE OFFICE!"

I froze in my tracks: I knew if I 'resisted arrest', the thing would never stop and just keep sliding downhill. Once you were openly demonstrating rebellion, it gave the 'moms', as the authorities of Sheela's gang were sarcastically called, an opening to set up all kinds of psychological torture for you: job changes, longer hours, hose-downs, etc. So, I came back to the office of the kitchen, silently and resentfully surrendered my bag of granola and bread-scraps, feeling like a resident of the Warsaw Ghetto, and went back empty-handed to my crew. That the 'moms' were getting fatter and fatter on the ice cream in the fridge at Jesus Grove, did not make the incident go down easier with me. I definitely started to feel that all was not right in the paradise of love and celebration…

As the preparations for the 3rd Annual World Celebration continued, we started preparing the music too. As bad as Aruno had been, she was a 'piece of cake' compared to what was about to come. PASHUPATHA! The name resounds in me like thunder; it was the ultimate weapon of the war in the Mahabharata, the ancient tale of destruction and dharma from Indian history. In that epic poem, 'Pashupatha' was a weapon that could neither be recalled nor disarmed once put into use, and would destroy the user as well as the enemy. And she was that. She was one of the 'big moms'…the inner circle of Sheela, which coincidentally, were all pretty big in fact. She was no petite lady. She ran the kitchens. And suddenly, one day in May, she was running the music department. My life was never the same after that, it was the beginning of the end, the arrival of the Ranch Kali-Yuga: the age of Darkness and Destruction.

One never knew if Pashupatha's ideas were her own, or Sheela's. Not that it mattered: the end result was the same: abrasion, idiocy, and salt on open wounds. PP would sit in the rehearsals, or rather sit ON them, and say yes or no to every single note or phrase that anyone played; total control, micromanaging, down to the atomic level, without any musical sense or inspiration or beauty. "Do this! Do that! Don't play that! You, on that, try something else". It was stultifying, frustrating, absolutely non-creative. And it sounded really like hell. There was no forming of a band, but people were taken in, taken out, put together randomly like interchangeable pieces of machinery. She single-handedly destroyed every shred of inspiration and creativity that was there among us musicians, and replaced it with kitschy Russian folk music. There was a very good violin player who had arrived from Russia, named Bhavito, and his music was the fad in the Ranch restaurant that spring, which Sheela took a liking to and decided to make it the music of the festival. Now, I don't have any problem with Russian folkmusic. I even like it sometimes. But, every song?... To meditate with?

So, like it or not, that's what was going to be played, the whole time, every song. Along with that, she wanted a big-band sound, lots of brass, like a Duke Ellington band in a Mafia bar in New York of the 1930s, apparently fulfilling some gangster fantasy in her mind. So that was the blend. I was playing in it still, trying to fit into it, and there was a bad feeling in my stomach. The way it was happening was weird. In the rehearsals in our music trailer, if we musicians started to get in an argument, within 5 minutes, one of the Ranch Moms would show up to hose us down. It was so uncanny, too much to be coincidence. And slowly we realized that they must have a bug in the room, and they would come down to give us a hard time when they heard from Jesus Grove that we were arguing.

At the same time, the legal department of the commune was becoming more and more important as the Ranch was facing a lot of litigation against Osho's immigration and the existence of the city, and the music department started to be used as a candy bar to reward the lawyers, they getting a chance to sing in front of the mike in Darshan, along with some of the brass like Vidya and Aruno. They had not very musical and somewhat out-of-tune voices, and we still had to keep playing, and smile, brother, smile. The kitschy Russian tunes were the rage, so, I was not exactly one-with-the-happening. I took a side seat and I spent most of the festival playing piano in the restaurant along with a dutch Oboist, and 2 German violinists, where at least there I could be free to play melodious music, and we had some beautiful improvisations. But the music that was happening in Satsang and Darshan was just getting worse and worse. Sheela would be standing by the side of Osho in front of the multitudes seated there, 'interpreting' him to us, and making signs to us in the back to play faster and faster, when actually it didn't seem like that's what he was indicating at all. The overall effect was a kind of forced tension, which went nowhere, and left me feeling weirder and weirder, like a bad acid trip. To see this happen was a kind of ego-death to me, to watch music being killed in this way gave me great sorrow.

Howsoever, my perceptions seemed to be just my own. It seemed a lot of people really liked what was happening, and I was left to ponder the demise of my good times. I let it go, giving up any dream about being part of the festivals anymore as a musician. It just meant that the tremendous release and uplift I would get from playing music for Osho was not going to happen, and I poured myself into the work I was doing as a carpenter, and there began for me the last, and hardest, and most mysterious of my tasks in Oregon.

By that time, Osho's daily drive-by's had become an even more important ritual of the day, and with the swelling of the numbers of people at the Ranch to something around 20,000 at festival time, all the road was lined shoulder to shoulder for miles with adoring red-clad disciples, with Osho passing very slowly and lovingly the whole way. We would stand in the heat, which was remarkable in July, and wait for those few moments when He would come by. It was always a very special and silent moment in the day. But one day just before the last day of that festival, it changed character, and became a totally different experience.

It all started with two Italians, who had the idea to bring a guitar to the drive-by, and they started playing and singing when Osho came by. He stopped, and stayed with them for a good while, keeping time with his hands and smiling. The news spread quickly, and the next day, dozens of people were here and there with guitars, and tambourines. The next day it was hundreds, and the next, thousands, everybody started showing up with drums, flutes, trumpets, saxophones, bassoons, kazoos, tin cans full of rocks, ANYTHING that could carry a tune or rhythm, and the whole line was a massive celebration. It was wild. Osho apparently delighted in it, and it became a kind of energy Darshan. He would stop and do a kind of dance in the car with his hands, and smile and greet people he recognized, people would dance and jump and celebrate like crazy. The drive-by which used to last about 10 seconds was now lasting 2 hours. It was not a mental thing, of having him see you; It was a pure energy experience, a communion, a blast of energy that was more than physical, and very blissful.

CHAPTER 15

In the Eye of the Hurricane

As the festival wound down and we all went back to our normal jobs, I was working again up at Lao Tzu House, building more closet space for Osho's ever-increasing robes, hats and shoes. I was in His house all day long, everyday, working in those closets, or other small projects that were needed there. As all what I was doing at that time was visible to Him and part of his home, it began to lift up out of the world of carpentry which I had known, and became more and more like art. Everything was done as perfectly as possible, with every effort made towards beauty and no corners cut. I loved this way of working , the precision of it, the pouring of oneself totally into the task, and the drive for perfection.

Sometimes, especially on the day of full moons, Osho would become very unpredictable and start walking around the house. When that would happen, it was our 'practice' to duck into the closet behind the robes, or hide behind a door, so as not to disturb his 'space'. As I hid there in the dark, I could very clearly feel him passing by, like a wave of energy, a glow inside me that I could feel in my heart. I came to know frequently this feeling, and it became more clear to me with each passing day.

As the closets were completed, I was called in to the downtown offices of Chuang Tzu, the construction department of the Ranch, for a special meeting. I had been chosen to be part of a very small crew, two of us in fact, sometimes three, to do a special project in Osho's house again. It would mean working very close to Him physically; exactly two meters away, in fact, behind a curtained window. We would be turning a small balcony outside his sitting room into a bathroom, complete with armor plating. The armor was an incredibly dense fiberglass which would prevent bullets from passing through it, and each sheet literally weighed a ton. At that time I was 29, my body was very strong, and I was a fairly unsocial and independent character, in fact something of a grouchy bear. I was usually in a morose mood from physical exhaustion, which probably was ideal for that kind of job, as one of the requirements was that for the length of the project, perhaps 5 months, we were to talk to no-one about it, so as not to provide information for possible informants which could be dangerous for Osho's life. Since the hours of work were all the hours in the day, and we had no radio or television or books to read, and cell-phones didn't exist yet, hence our work was our whole life, there wasn't really anything else to talk about. So that meant that practically speaking I would be remaining in silence for 5 months.

The armor plating was to provide a safe room, in case that Osho was attacked. It was expected, now with the serious governmental threats and lawsuits that were coming each day more and more, that sooner or later law enforcement agencies could come in shooting, and this would provide a place for Osho to be and not get hit in the melee. The wall sections weighed probably 400 pounds each, were about 6 feet long by 7 feet high. The whole thing had been designed and planned and put together by the crew leader Vidhan, who was sometimes my friend, sometimes my very overbearing boss, and sometimes my dear brother. He was extremely intelligent with a mind better organized than the British Museum. His visual memory and ability to solve mechanical problems were extreme. He was a great singer-songwriter as well, and I had known him from the Darshan's in the first year of the ranch when he was sometimes the lead singer.

We would work together intensely for months on end in that

little balcony, he the leader and me the helper. The more I knew him, the more I liked him, even though he could be a real pain-in-the-neck as a boss. But the thing that endeared me to him was his rebellious attitude. He and Sheela were constantly fighting, but he was one of the few people at the Ranch that she couldn't afford to get rid of, as she had done to so many others. Those whom she didn't like, she would eliminate, either send them away, 'To help Osho's people in Dubrovnik' as we would jokingly say, or else lock them up in strange situations where they suddenly had inexplicable medical problems and needed constant care, or they were simply told, "This is not the place for you, swami." But she couldn't do that to Vidhan, as much as she hated him. He worked too closely for Osho, and was probably the only guy with the mental spatial capacity and physical dexterity to do those jobs on the whole Ranch. He was, in short a genius, and nobody else could fill his shoes, and that served to exasperate Sheela even more.

When I got on the project, it was nearly ready for its final stage. Vidhan had built it in a warehouse, and it was close to completion. Our task was to dismantle this armor-plated bathroom carefully, transport it piece by piece through Osho's house and carry it to the balcony, and reassemble it, solving all the spatial and mechanical problems that would arise when the gap between theory and reality would become evident. And then we would tile all the walls and make it into a real bathroom, beautiful and suitable for Osho. As any carpenter knows, flat planes in a building are flat on paper, but in 3-D are not wholly flat, right angles are not totally right, things that seem to fit by measure sometimes don't when they are put in place. And we had to work those things out, silently, carefully, under intense scrutiny, and all within 2 meters of Osho behind a window, all day long. Those days were of carrying enormously heavy wall sections silently through the house, and gingerly placing them in that balcony, slowing forming a new room; screwing them together and doing the plumbing in impossible positions and crawlspaces; working silently, putting a cloth between the nail and the hammer so as to muffle the sound, speaking in signs instead of words. I had heard of meditation retreats in mountain caves, Zen monks cleaning rice grains in the kitchen, but this was a different kind of cave, a totally silent retreat, a pressure cooker at times, and a blissful bath at others, every moment different...a constant and intense totality of attention and effort, within a few feet of the Master's constant and very tangible energetic presence.

His very close physical presence had a curious effect on me. It was a mirror and an amplifier to my mind, both thoughts and emotions. If I was in a good mood, the mood was elated, vast, wonderful; as if the whole universe was shining with joy and possibility. If I was in a negative mood, it was a gaping and vast black hole, with the thoughts howling like banshees inside my mind. In short, each day in that cave was to be in front of a huge mirror, showing me everything that was inside me.

One day was particularly filled with intensely self-negative thoughts, feelings of self-judgement, shame and unworthiness. The three of us were sitting having a coffee break, and someone just happened to mention that they were having a tough day, beating himself up mentally. The other two of us said, "Yeah, me too!" And we realized that these moods were coming like a wave, we would fall into them all together, like a contact high or low. I started to understand that thoughts are not really MY OWN, but more like a wave that passes through me, and that I believe in them and take them personally as my own.

We would always try to enter and exit when Osho would not be passing by, but sometimes it happened, the timings got a little skewed, or he would be leaving for the drive-by a few minutes late, and sometimes I would come strolling down the hallway and just about run into Him face to face. I would quickly change course and duck into a doorway, always trying to respect his privacy and not be an obvious nuisance. It was bad enough that we were there making muffled noises a few feet away from Him all the time. Other than that we tried to be as invisible as possible.

During the time of this very intense and long project just next to his room, I was more and more deeply affected by the presence of Vivek, Osho's companion and nurse, in the house. Many times we would pass in the house, in the corridor, or on the pathway, and always our meeting would leave me deeply moved, shaken in fact, in ways that I could not understand yet. My physical body, or several of 'my bodies', including emotional and 'etheric', would always receive a shock. Physically, emotionally, energetically… There was nothing I could do about it.

My relations with Kasi had become strained and distant over the last several months, as she was more and more deeply involved in projects for Sheela, now being a part of the self-defense force on the Ranch, including training in using firearms. My time was completely absorbed in my work up at Osho's house. We saw each other very infrequently, and were less and less able to enjoy each other's company. Our relating became less and less happy, and more and more difficult in the rare times that we would see each other. She was all day in Sheela's world, and I all day in the extremely different world of Osho's house, she couldn't talk to me about what was happening in her world, and I couldn't talk to her about what was happening in the one I was in, and the gap between us reflected that on every level. My heart was more up there at Osho's house, and less in the relationship.

In parallel to this silent mounting volcano in my heart, was a mounting pressure on my head, intentionally put there by the people at Jesus Grove, where Kasi worked. Each morning, at 7 a.m., before beginning our work, we three in the crew would have to go downtown to be grilled and drilled by the top bosses of the Ranch about what we were doing. Sheela, Vidya, Padma, they each took their turns. Our day, for the three of us, was planned down to the minute by these rather domineering and sometimes aggressive characters, our each action impaled on a skewer of questions and recriminations, why we did this, who we talked to in the house, where we went to get a cup of tea, etc. ad infinitum. It became clear to me that we were in the midst of the unspoken war, between the Organization and the Caretakers. The people who ran the commune were tightening the screws on the people around Osho, and we, being friendly to them, were the football caught in the middle. I can remember one of these grilling sessions, one of those 'poo-bahs' just digging left and right in me to find some thing that I could be accused of doing wrong, and I remember looking in her eyes, and seeing the fear there, this quite overblown and insecure person wearing a Gestapo suit of armor of false authority, authority which was not hers. It did not come from her being, but was just a social position, and I realized that there was a place inside me which she could not touch, which nobody could touch, nobody could mess with. That was the real place. And she saw it too in that moment, and became silent, and stopped the harassment.

The days were spent in the silent pressure cooker of the cave, together with one spy each day sent from the commune management, the 'dictatorship' as it now appeared to be, who would monitor our actions, watching our every move. The spy would be different each day, and seemed to be there on a rotational-basis. This person would be there in the cave with us, inactive, silent, simply staring at us all day long. The best way I found to relate to this, was to learn to simply ignore it. The fact that it was happening right next to Him was to be next to a huge amplifier all day long. Any negative space in my mind, any self-defeating or irritated or destructive thoughts were broadcast to me like a loudspeaker at 120db, with no escape, and I didn't want to give energy to any divergent stream, maintaining as best I could my awareness in the moment, and in my body.

And of course, there was the other side, days and weeks of remarkable peace and silence, even in the midst of the outward pressure, a deep peace that cannot be spoken of, in which time passed as if it was not passing at all, simply the day would be gone, without any recollection in me of having worked all the time.

I remember very clearly the feeling of being in his house, walking those hallways, always cool and with a silence that was not simply the absence of noise. I felt that I was walking in 'Halls of Eternity'. There was some tangible presence of the cool, vast silence of infinity, the emptiness, the absolute...the ineffable. I felt that Osho had faced infinity, and had absorbed it, and been absorbed by it, and WAS it.

I don't know how he had done it. I don't know if I wanted that to happen to me. But feeling that it existed, that it IS there, the really REAL, waiting as the inevitable, the unavoidable truth that is the real purpose, destiny, and origin of human life, made all other endeavors seem like playing with toys. One goes on doing it, but deep down, the days of toys are numbered...

One afternoon, I was holding one section of wall in place while it was being bolted in, and my face was up against the glass window, the curtained window which I knew was to His sitting room. But after months of being there every day, it had become a kind of automatic knowledge, with no more emotional impact on my mind. With my hands holding the wall, and my face against the glass, my eyes ambled upwards by chance, and fell upon a golden colored globular light fixture INSIDE the window on the other side, higher up on the wall. Without thinking, as my mind was occupied with the weight I was holding in place, my eyes starting puzzling over what they were seeing, an upside down image on the ball of the lamp. Suddenly, before I could think, my brain assembled the Gestalt of it and I realized what it was that I was seeing. There was Osho, who had just come in and was sitting in all His glorious splendor exactly as he did in Buddha Hall, just 6 feet in front and facing me. I was filled with a strange mixture of guilt, embarrassment, and exhilaration at one and the same moment, before I pulled my eyes away from that stolen glimpse, that violation of his privacy to which I was committed to protect. And the assumption that had become automatic in me, that HE was always physically right there in front of me all day long, became a very clear reality not only in my heart, but in my mind and body as well.

Soon afterward, came the day that changed my physical life forever. It was the last thing to be carried in, the sliding door of the bathroom. It weighed about 300 pounds, I would guess. It had to be brought in while Osho was sleeping in his bed, in the room we would cross in the early afternoon. I don't exactly know why, but that's the way the logic was worked out by the dictators, that would be the only possible time to do it. The three of us were carrying it, silently, slowly, heavily step by step, across Osho's room as He slept there in the bed. As often happens when 3 people carry something, suddenly a shift in weight, a misplaced step, and the weight is more in one person's hands. It happened to be mine.

If I had dropped it, it would have broken three pairs of feet, the floorboards, and would have been really embarrassing and hard to explain to Osho as He woke up from sleep and we groaned in bloodied agony on His floor. So, I held it as best I could for some moments, and we recovered balance and put it in place. As I straightened up, there was an audible click deep in my lower back. "Funny", I thought; "Never felt that before".

It was November 24th, 1984.

On the next day, the bathroom was complete, the set of keys was to go to Sheela, and instead of bringing them to her, I handed them with a smile and a bow to Vivek. After all, she was taking care of HIM, and she was the head of the household, so, in my mind, she was the one to get them. That squelched Sheela's hidden plan to have her own backdoor into Osho's bedroom. That was the last act I was to play in the house of the Master in Oregon.

I didn't know it then, as all I noticed was a grabbing pain in the back of my leg. I thought it was a cramp, ever-more-constant. But I had broken my back. Technically, it was a herniated hard disc, perhaps two of them. They simply and quietly broke, from the weight I was holding, like bamboo, with a deep clicking sound at the base of my spine, Not very dramatic. Just day by day, my legs started hurting, and slowly stopped functioning.

At that same time, there began in the commune a project called 'SHARE A HOME'. It might have been more aptly named 'LOSE A HOME', because that's what ultimately happened, from the imbalances that it provoked, reflected, and exaggerated.

One autumn day, we were called into the Buddha Hall, for a General Meeting. These were meetings of the whole community in which new rules or situations or regulations were laid out to everyone, a time at which The Party Line would be put forth by the Brass. It was a one-way communication which seemed to me to be strictly in favor of the Generals, and no kind of 'meeting' whatsoever. But it was there, in one of those General Meetings that we first heard about it. We were about 5000 residents then, the maximum population of what our city would reach. It had grown quickly, each year adding more and more residents, and all those who came were integrated and absorbed into the life of the commune. Now it was announced by Vidya that a new project was starting; that because the Oregonians had no interest in coming to the Ranch and experiencing the beautiful life that we had, the commune was going to reach out to street people all over America, the downtrodden and displaced and homeless, and invite them to come and share our life for a time.

"Hmmm…that's a strange idea". I wondered, "Who came up with that?" Sheela was away from the Ranch, in Germany at the time. She was by this time the General Manager of a worldwide movement of hundreds of thousands of people, amongst which the great majority were wishing and trying somehow to be there at the Ranch in Oregon. She would use that energy to build a worldwide labor movement, as disciples wishing to come to the Ranch were more and more 'directed' by her into large communes in Germany, Japan and elsewhere, with the purpose of concentrating capital and labor, and making them available in the end, to herself, as the CEO of the corporation. At this time she was on one of those journeys to Europe, closing, consolidating and drastically changing the communes of sannyasins which were already existing there.

Now at this time this Share-a-Home project was being announced in her absence: it wouldn't be announced while she was away if it was her idea, I thought, and I doubted that she could make such a huge change in the direction of the commune while she was not there. And Vidya, who made the announcement and was acting as the interim communicator with Osho, didn't have the power or vision to do anything drastic like that on her own. But I never heard Osho say anything like that, in the so far 7 years that I had been listening to him. He never said anything 'Ghandian' before, offering to do social service was not his strong point; he was often slamming with criticism those who do such things, that they use it as a hypocritical way of gaining political power, i.e. Mother Theresa, Ghandi, etc.

Osho was still in public silence, as he had been for 3 years, and there was no way to know what was really going on, and as always, there was no way to predict His actions or purposes.

But it happened, the 'ambassadors' were sent, to Chicago, New York, LA, Cleveland, and many, many other cities, and buses started rolling in with derelicts and street types suddenly walking around the Ranch. It was a big change, and not for the good. If you weren't working at the Ranch and were used to life in The Big Apple, our little utopian experiment in northeastern Oregon was a pretty boring place, after all. One club, one bar, one restaurant, one disco, one pizzeria, no prostitutes, banks, drugs, pharmacies, liquor stores, money or movie theaters. There was some adjustments implied, both for the new population, and for us. Segregation was the unspoken plan devised by the Brass. Most of us ate dinner at Magdalena cafeteria, down around the residential section of the Ranch. The new arrivals were housed at the other end, near the more industrial area, in the sense of that's where the motor-division, airport, carpentry shop and pipe crew were based. There was another cafeteria there, where the new arrivals could eat, and get their beer, and hangout together.

As usual, none of this happened with any input or discussion on 'our' part, the 5000 of us who built the city and were now living there. It was handed down from above, like everything else. Up to then, the things that happened, being told where to live and what to wear and having elections for mayor with only one candidate, it was all 'o.k.', I knew it was a game, a part of the 'spiritual discipline', like another kind of therapy group. It put my mind through a lot of changes. Some things, I enjoyed, some things I laughed at and some things I vehemently disliked, and I basically got more distant from the whole thing and stayed in my own 'center' energetically, as best I could. I would often use the General Meetings as a great chance to wander out into the silent nearby hills to meditate. I never felt involved in the whole myth of Rajneeshism, the religion-culture that Sheela was promoting and building around her idea of Osho's work. But this was different. This was playing with other people's lives. I thought it sounded weird from the start.

As time went by, it became apparent from the brief national news clips we would see from time to time that these 3000 or so people were being registered to vote, by way of an unusual state law in Oregon that allowed you to vote without any residence requirement. With county elections coming up and a couple of supervisors seats getting available, it looked like Sheela's gang was preparing to stack the deck at the polls and win a seat or two on the board of supervisors. By this time she was back at the ranch, and engineering the now often General Meetings, as well as making belligerent statements to the press about protecting 'our people', which now included the 3000 or so new arrivals from 'America's Outcasts'. It clearly appeared like the game of politics in Wasco county was going hardball, and many, many voices were raising in outcry from the local residents, and national news media.

I often thought, "What is Osho doing?" He seemed to be turning up the flame on the water in the pot, bringing this situation to a boiling point ever more rapidly. What was his intention? I could never know that, but creating controversy had always been his way of working. Never content to let things be as they are, like Krishna in the Mahabharata, Osho would push and provoke and expose constantly, acting in unreasonable and unpredictable ways, to force the facade off of situations, people, and beliefs. He was never simply good, or bad. He was both, and much of both, and beyond both. This was happening now in fast forward, the movie was getting surreal, and starting to involve the whole country. Where was this going? Did we work all these years, just to drive the car down a blind alley at full speed? My mind could not grasp the overview, but it was clear that this utopia was not meant as a permanent residence, that the bubble would soon burst. It's easy to 'surrender' and be devoted to a rational harmonious life of peace and love far away from 'the world', but to surrender and be devoted to an unpredictable 'crazy wisdom' master is another story. You cannot go on auto-pilot, the turbulences would arrive like hurricanes and the plane would start diving, and every moment one had to decide, "Am I in it, or not?"

I was distant from the life of the general population in the commune at that time, as I was all day up at Osho's house and not prone to gossiping or involving myself socially, as I had to keep my mouth shut about everything that happened at his house and everything that I did, all day long. 'Loose lips sink ships' was a saying from my parents wartime experience. Osho was under threat, from the FBI, the INS, from ultra-rightwing groups, and from Oregon rednecks, and it was clear that information about his personal routines was not to be spread around like small change on the bar-counter. So I became more and more isolated, by choice in a way, but also by circumstance of my position rather close to him physically all day long. The few scenarios that I would overhear regarding the Share-a-Home project really put me off. I heard about the beer in the cafeteria for the 'visitors' being laced with Haldol to keep things calm, about fights being put down by ashram police with difficulty and people getting quickly shipped off the ranch, and I could smell thousands of pairs of unwashed feet greeting me when I walked into Buddha Hall one day, a place which had always been impeccably clean and pristine and a temple of silence. The situation seemed to be spinning more and more out of control.

One day near the end of the bathroom project, a 'share-a-homer' had gotten through the security precautions around Osho's house and had been found standing on His front porch at night. Alarms went off in the commune management, and it was immediately decided to build a 12-foot high fence around Osho's compound, which was not small by any means, it was the size of a large municipal park in any big American city. The day after the bathroom was finished and I gave the keys to Vivek, I was given the job of making the fence, heading the crew along with two other people. We started immediately. Huge sections of chain link fence were brought in, surveyors plotted things out, poles trucked in, holes drilled through the solid rock we found in many places, and more and more people were brought into the project. Each day my legs were hurting more, and I couldn't figure out what was happening to me. The pain was becoming constant, and worse day by day. I continued moving heavy things, using a jackhammer to put poles in the rocks, positioning large rolls of fencing, all things which were aggravating my back condition without me knowing, because I thought I just had muscle cramps in my legs.

As the month went on, and the work on the fence was nearing completion, my steps became shorter, until by the end of a month I could not put one foot in front of the other. I was admitted into the Ranch hospital on Christmas Day 1984, and didn't come out until early February, 1985, spending nearly the entire time flat on my back in bed.

CHAPTER 16

Revelations and Mysteries

Sacsayhuaman

I am on a promontory overlooking the ruins of Sacsayhuaman, in Cuzco, Peru. I wander amid the zig-zagging enormous stone walls, made of huge irregular blocks of stone, some weighing tens of tons each. There are thousands of them, perfectly fitting together, multi-faceted and perfect stonework, into which one cannot insert even a knife-blade. Some of the stones are meeting and interlocking with 12 or more irregular angles, and no mortar used whatsoever. The stones have remained in position for at least 7 centuries, and perhaps many many more, in a land which is characteristic for its frequent and very large earthquakes. It is impossible to know how or why this stonework was done, with such precision and perfection, even by our modern technology. To lift those blocks, each weighing many tons, several meters in the air and set them in place, some of them with 12 interlocking angles, and no gaps in between, is an impossible feat of engineering for our present technology. The stones themselves show innumerable signs of high speed drilling and even melting of the rocks in many areas. Who could have done this magic work? Certainly it was not the Incas, in their brief reign over the empire which bears their name, just a few centuries ago. There were not enough people among them, to build these monuments, cultivate their lands, lay their stone roads all over their empire reaching from Chile to Ecuador, and maintain their political power. Even in their own sacred valley, between Cuzco and Ollantaytambo, and on the heights of Machu Picchu beyond, the number of stone ruins and terraces was far beyond what would have been possible or necessary for their entire population. The mysterious riddle of these stones, everywhere visible here, remains an unsolved puzzle constantly within me...

It becomes more clear to me, with each passing day and each silly theory I read at every archaeological site visited, written there as if it is the very 'word of god', that the huge elephant sitting in the living room all over our planet, is just these stone ruins existing in our midst. Impossible to explain, far beyond the capacity of our own technologies to construct, and pointing a very obvious finger to the gaps in our knowledge of our own origins. We do not know who we are, or where we have come from, and purposefully we have been kept in the dark about it.

Do naught with the body but relax;
Shut firm the mouth and silent remain;
Empty your mind and think of naught.
Like a hollow bamboo rest at ease your body.

Giving not nor taking, put your mind at rest.
Mahamudra is like a mind that clings to naught. .

Tilopa-Song of Mahamudra

Returning to my saga: entering the hospital on Christmas Day, 1984, It was going to be for me a very, very long 7 weeks, of sleep, traction, and epideral injections which it seemed to me would have made horses commit suicide. Traction was a medieval torture invented by the Inquisition I suppose. One is tied to a machine, strapped under the armpits, and another harness is strapped around the pelvis, and the machine slowly ratchets up with excruciating pressure as you are pulled in opposite directions stretching your spinal column. It's "Not Very Fun". Probably by chance it fixed somebody's back problem before he confessed to witchcraft or heresy, and another page was added to the annals of Western medical science. The epideral injections were with a needle so large it resembled those used to inflate basketballs; this was inserted into my pelvic bone, pushing salt water under pressure up my spine to force the wayward bits of soft disc off of my nerves. Needless to say, this didn't really go over too well with the nerves, and they definitely let me know that. In the shower I would see whole clumps of hair falling out from my head, and I was on the threshold of weeping with the pain nearly constantly, all day long. I didn't take most of the pain killers that the doctors would give me, as I very much dislike the feeling of being drugged and really didn't want to be doped all the way through this, but wanted to somehow see why it had happened, why I had called this to myself. The traction made me feel incredibly vulnerable and 'broken up', like I was literally being pulled apart and violated.

It was a kind of nightmare, and the atmosphere in the Ranch hospital was equally strange to me. I couldn't say what it was, but I instinctively felt not at ease being there, something weird was happening in that place. This feeling was slightly mitigated by the fact that after three or four weeks of badly needed sleep in the hospital, I could at least walk a little bit. So, as time went by and I was able to walk a little more, I was allowed to take short walks outside of the hospital for a few minutes, and I shuffled outside into the grey and frozen hills in January, briefly, catching moments of sanity from the welcome and much needed embrace of the natural world.

In the dry wintry landscape, I passed a juniper tree, with a strange shape, split in two and growing in two opposite directions. Looking closely, it appeared that it had burned at one time at the split, and I reasoned it must have been struck by lightning, and began growing again from that split. I realized that what had happened to me was a life-changing event, and I would have to be brave to face what was to come, the convalescence, the handicap, the pain. And I realized deep inside me, that I too had been struck by some kind of lightning, and I too could grow again, live again, and make the most of my new life.

I would be six months lying in bed, and a year-and-a-half of wearing a steel brace. I would have 14 years of intermittent pain. But I would recover, and walk, and even use my body, like a "normal" person again, although the pain would for a very long time not disappear completely, and would remain as a reminder, sometimes in the background and sometimes right in my face, of the fallibility and mortality of the body.

As I write this, it is more than 34 years later. I have known incredible moments of freedom and joy, ecstasy and fulfillment in those years, and the presence of the back pain has not been an impossible price to pay, for the life I have lived. It is a soft and windy June evening, as the desert winds blow against the side of the little house where I live. Outside the window, the palms and olive trees sway in the warm breezes.

'Sitting in the midst of bondage, I have set myself free.'...

Kabir, 12th century Indian Mystic poet

Months passed. Although it would never go away in those months, I would hold the pain at arms length by walking, and at lunch time I would lay down under a tree, and do the re-birthing breathing I had learned years before. The oxygen did something beneficial to my nervous system, it seemed to make space between me and the pain, and I could get through the day, and find a brief respite of peace inside me.

So from silently working just within arms reach of Osho every day, I was rather abruptly 'working' prone on my back, in a tiny stationery store in the basement of the Ranch office building, Socrates. This little shop was called 'Emerson'. It was about two meters by three meters, crammed with pencils, papers, eraser, staplers, file folders, myself, and my boss, a recent arrival at the Ranch, an ex-New York cop who now was managing the stationery store. He was kindly to me, sometimes a little too friendly for my comfort, and I was really not feeling very blessed by being there. Emerson was a kind of limbo for disabled workers, the dictators put you there when they didn't know what else to do with you, and being in the basement of the main office building, the Brass could come downstairs and keep an eye on you to see if you were going 'negative' or not. As I had been very close to Osho physically, and knew a lot about his life and routines, I was a potential danger if I had reacted to my injury by turning against the commune management. This was hinted at in a few comments which I picked up when various members of the ruling gang would stop in to get pencils or plastic file-folders. The juxtaposition of my life of two months ago, building and creating and working artistically and constantly in the very rarefied atmosphere of Osho's physical presence, was now contrasted by this new jail, lying on my back in a 6-square meter stationery store, selling pencils to the very people that I thoroughly disdained with every fiber of my being.

This new situation and its quality of total boredom, constant pain, and confinement in a world of triviality, forced me, in order to maintain my sanity, to get into dis-attachment and witnessing BIG TIME, right away. My back was killing me, my mind was bored to the extreme, and there was nothing I could do but lay there and sell pencils, all day long, wearing a steel brace on my back and occasionally having to take a fetal position when I would get spasms in my spinal column.

Luckily for me, there was another guy 'stationed' there in Emerson, recovering from a hernia operation. His name was Sargam, and he was hilarious; that is, when he wasn't giving monologues about nights on patrol as a gunner in Vietnam and the things they had to do. It was a little unnerving, how suddenly his face would change and he would go into one of those flashback monologues, describing how he had to wait in the jungle with his machine-gun all night long and blast away at anything that moved. It has a name now, 'Post-Trauma-Stress-Disorder', but then I had no idea about such things. In his lighter moments he was extremely entertaining. It was a welcome relief from the boredom of the pencil-shop, and his being there seemed to temper the situation greatly.

About that time it was 'discovered' that I did have typing skills, and wasn't just a Neanderthal injured carpenter and could actually put sentences together, so I was given small writing jobs for the magazine, music and book reviews, and follow-ups on tracking down videos of Osho that TV stations weren't returning, etc.

Suddenly, without warning, Osho began speaking again after 3 years of silence, in a room up at his house, for a select group of about 20 disciples each night! I was given the job to get the transcript of the raw unedited discourse the next morning and find out what He was actually talking about: the topic, that is. This is no small task. I had been acquainted with Osho's energy, that silent glow inside me that it provoked, and now I was to become acquainted with His mind, which was no less a marvel to me.

I would sort through all the words of a discourse lasting two hours, find the thread between the sentences that was the actual answer to the question, and would send that off to the Library of Congress to be copyrighted, each day.

His discourses would begin with a brief question, which Osho would begin to answer, and slowly He would weave circles and ever greater circles in an ever-widening spiral, circumambulating the point of the question like a vast mandala in the sky. He could begin talking about the most mundane and ordinary thing imaginable, and end up talking about cosmic forces wider than the known universe. He could leave a topic in mid-sentence, digress in greater and greater circles for an hour and a half, and return to pick up the topic IN MID-SENTENCE exactly where He had left it behind more than an hour before. Never would there be a non-sequitur, an "ummm" or a fumbling pause, never was there a single phrase or word out of place, not adding to the whole. It was only on paper that I could come to know this, as I had to actually follow the threads of the story in order to send it off to be copyrighted. In short, He blew my mind with the vastness of His mind.

One day, in the discourse I was editing, I came upon the fateful words: and I paraphrase here: "Before I go I am not going to leave you in the hands of a fascist gang. If anybody is doing anything against the spirit of rebellion in the commune it is not going against the commune to stand up and confront it. It is upholding the rebellious spirit of freedom that the commune is based on".

192

Reading those words, I felt as if a bomb had gone off inside me. That night, instead of showing that discourse to the commune in the Buddha hall like all the other nights, the message was given by Sheela that the master tape had been damaged in the recording. My 'shit-detector' was ringing loud and clear within my brain. The tape obviously hadn't been damaged, because here I had read the typed transcription of it that morning, done by somebody in Osho's house who obviously had listened to the tape. It was a bald-faced lie. Osho was telling us all to stand up to Sheela's fascism, and Sheela is claiming the tape did not get recorded. This is fascism, pure and simple. The commune leaders were murdering truth, they had claimed he master tape destroyed to keep us from hearing that message about THEM, and were covering their tracks in the process. A coup was happening, a silent strangling of the Voice of Truth. I secretly copied the words and stashed them out of sight of my boss, sharing them with closest friends, and watched the signs of the growing and fast-approaching calamity.

There had just arrived in the commune a very unique man named Dhiraj, who had developed or 'channeled' a new form of healing, which involved holding certain points in the body and feeling the pulse, for quite a long time. He was calling it 'Tibetan Pulsation', as it came to him in the form of a teaching delivered to him in dreams by a Tibetan Master. The Brass in charge of the ranch were skeptical of such things, but as he had a rather devoted following in LA, they wanted to see what he could do. As I was one of the cases whom the Ranch doctors could not help, and they wanted me to get back on my feet somehow, they agreed that Dhiraj could work on me for several sessions, as a kind of guinea pig. It was fine with me, I had nothing to lose and everything to gain, I was completely disgusted with the treatments that the doctors had been doing to me, and I only seemed to be in more pain because of it.

Dhiraj began working with his beautiful girlfriend and colleague Prabuddha, and we had a few sessions a week for some weeks. The sessions weren't painful, and almost immediately I began to feel a change in the energy in my body. Rather quickly, within 3 weeks all the pain that I was constantly feeling, had changed into sensations of a positive nature, vital energy, and I was even becoming interested in sex again, which was unthinkably far away in the midst of my agony of the months before. In short, my body quickly returned to the natural state of a 30-year old man, and all the pain which I had been in was moving in channels of pleasure, well-being, delight in being alive. I was thrilled. I started riding a bicycle, going for swims in the lake at lunch time, and walking whenever I could.

"The desire to rule over others, the will to power, is one of the greatest crimes that man has committed. My sannyasins have to be aware of it. Hence, my insistence for being just ordinary".

Osho

I had been living in a 'townhouse' called 'Townhouse 68'. There were others living there who also were close to Osho physically; DevaGeet his dentist and dental assistant Nityananda, Nandan who worked in his house, Sarita, Vani, and others, all people who had been with Osho for many years and worked in his gardens or house. Sometimes in the night we would meet casually, in passing in a hallway or the living room, and often talk about what was happening in the commune. I was pretty sure that the people in my house had the same 'view' of the commune management, and we would joke about it sometimes, thinking that we could safely, albeit quietly, talk about what we were seeing, amongst ourselves at home.

One day, we were suddenly all moved to another newer townhouse, in an adjacent valley just by the side of Osho's compound, much closer to his house. A week or so later, there was a General Meeting in Buddha Hall. By now I had come to hate General Meetings, as they were always more for the Generals than for the Meeting, occasions for some bullshit to come down from the management yet again, more rules, more directions.

This was no exception. In fact, it was a prime example. Sheela was giving the meeting, and she called off a list of 20 names. Those people had to come to the front of the meeting, in which there were probably 5000 people in attendance. The people who were called up were obviously newcomers. One of them I knew from the years before when I lived in Oakland in a big sannyasin house. His name was Visarjan, a very nice guy who worked as a breath therapist in the Bay Area, and had been a good friend to me in those transitions months of staying in that house. In front of everybody, these 20 people were told that Sheela had 'heard' they were being 'negative' and saying terrible things about the Ranch, and what did they have to say about it. It was an ugly moment of intense social pressure on these people, and we were all caught in it; it was the peak of Sheela's madness, the tension in the ranch was growing, as was the tiredness that we all felt with Sheela's ways and mentality, but nobody could venture forth and talk about it openly, or you would be immediately sent down the road. Or your life would be made into a living hell; the next day you would be working at the Rock Crusher or the garbage dump burning used toilet paper from the festival. It was the epitome of the totally Stalinist situation of the Ranch at that moment, everyone was fed-up with the dictatorship, but no-one was willing to be a martyr and sacrifice themselves by standing up alone against it. So there we were, watching this very stupid scene which would have fit more in the Politburo or the Inquisition than the commune of an enlightened Master, and those poor people had to stand up in front of everyone one-by-one and say something, like true confessions of having been a sinner in a Gospel revival meeting.

When Visarjan talked, it was obvious he didn't have a clue what was happening, he had just arrived a few days before and was working all day and late into the night, as a summer worker. What was going on? Who had squealed? Who had 'fingered' these innocent people to Sheela and her gang?

A couple of days later, as I walked by my old house and recognized someone now living there, I realized in a flash, that those people roasted in the meeting were now living in our old house, townhouse 68. We had been moved out 10 days before, and they had been moved in. Someone had been listening to our taped conversations, and that was meant to be US in front of that meeting! But the ineptitude of the bureaucracy had overlooked the fact that we had all been moved to another house by then, the list of names given to Sheela was the NEW people living in the house, a week later, and the people in that house were innocent newcomers. So, we were all being bugged. Now you couldn't even talk, the walls had ears. The puzzle started to fit together for me, the pattern of what was happening. But, we were being bugged by inept idiots, who couldn't keep the list straight about who they were listening too. This was classic for Sheela's gang, abuse of power and ineptitude based on emotionality.

Day by day, the pressure from the outside world increased on our little venture there in the hills. The situation had deteriorated between us and the residents of Antelope, and in fact the whole of eastern Oregon, on every front. I don't blame them. Not that I get along real well with Rednecks. But I prefer to leave them alone and do my thing, and let them do theirs if they aren't actually shooting at me. I've lived in Oregon long before the Ranch, I've been shot at by rednecks, but it was usually because I was unknowingly taking a walk across their farmland or forest. They are very territorial; stick your hand in a rattlesnake nest and you might get bitten, that's life in rural USA. But Sheela and her cohorts would take it to another extreme, they would go out of their way to provoke, harass, threaten, insult and irritate at any possible opportunity the people of the surrounding locality, 'them' as opposed to 'us'. I witnessed this first hand on several occasions.

On 'political' occasions, about 50 of us Ranch residents would be chosen at random, and granted a reprieve of sorts from work for the day, and taken in buses to be present at important events, courtroom things, public meetings: a kind of cannon-fodder event, more-of-us-in-the-courtroom-means-less-of-them. The two times that I was sent on one of these excursions was eye-opening to me, in that it definitely made an even greater distance between me and the commune management. My 'shit-detector' would be ringing very clearly. The first one I was in was a meeting to gain approval for building, fairly early on in my first few months at the ranch. Petitions for and against the city were presented, and the judge seemed to railroad our petition through, without giving any time or space to the dissensions. I thought that was odd, as I was more used to being on the underdog side of legal disputes, as the bitter fights at Utsavo in Laguna Beach had been. I later found out that the judge had gotten a very good deal on several dozen head of cattle from the Ranch. The second time was another petition a few years later, in the Dalles. In the middle of the courtroom, Shantibadra, one of Sheela's gang, started to speak, in a kind of weird way, very dramatically and slow and speaking rather over-pathetically about the recent death of a visitor to the commune. She got more and more full of herself and her words and spoke more fast and furiously, until by the end of her speech she was standing on top of the lawyer's desk in the courtroom, and ranting and raving hysterically. I was totally embarrassed to be associated with her side of the dispute, and I thought that she must appear to be some kind of evil witch to the Oregonians. She seemed to be that to me, and I'm not a Christian. She definitely acted like she had some form of spirit possession, some dark entity from the lower-astral realms having gotten into her. At that point I realized that the leaders of the commune were something to beware of, their fear-tactics, their pistols and secretive ways were definitely not a joke and not my idea of the representatives of my Master and his work. Something else was happening there in Jesus Grove, something at odds with Osho and His Vision, and I kept my distance from it and my guard up at all times. Never volunteer. Avoid them. Watch, and don't be observed. It was Lao Tzu who said that swords are best left in the scabbard: unseen, they survive, and I knew that to get through this, I would need to keep my wits and discrimination…the sword of my intelligence in the scabbard, but there: and take care to not get hit by the falling pieces of marble when the structure all around crumbles.

As Share-A-Home started to be more and more untenable, and there were more and more incidents, friction between the commune rulers and the newly ruled, more and more of these newcomers were being sent off the ranch, and dumped in the middle of the night at the bus station in Redmond, or Bend or elsewhere. One time I was ordered to be an escort for one of these events, with no explanation given. It's just that I was big.

I was in a car with 4 other male residents of the Ranch, and two Share-a-Homers, who apparently had been in a fistfight. They were being brought to the bus station in Redmond, and we left them there at midnight. To sum it up briefly, I thought this sucked. They took off in the night, I don't think they were getting on the next bus back to Chicago, and I pity the poor residents of Redmond who had to deal with this, as we deposited our refuse on their front porches. I realized the Ranch rulers were idiots for having created this, and my wholehearted participation in the direction of the Ranch was ended at that moment. I knew I was there to be alert, protect Osho from what was going to happen, and to see the end of the fascist regime, somehow, and hopefully soon.

Osho was speaking every night in the spring, at his house, usually with a select group of disciples, called The Chosen Few. The discourses continued to be videoed, and all the rest of us would see them the following night, in Buddha Hall. Everyone had been working 12-16 hours a day 7 days a week for years, so, it's easy to envision what was happening. As the video played, 5000 people were sleeping on the floor of Buddha Hall. But miraculously, whenever he would start talking about what was happening with us in the commune, all heads suddenly sat up, the snoring stopped, and attention was absolute. I had a hard time being there, as I could not sit on the floor comfortably with my steel brace on my back, and if I lay down, I could not stay awake. So I would walk outside, and cross the bridge to the other side of the creek, a place called 'Samadhi Grove', where there was the burial place of Osho's father's ashes, and the ashes of Vimalkirti, a disciple who had died enlightened in Poona in 1979.

There was a beautiful silent atmosphere in that place, unlike anywhere else on the Ranch, and I could still hear Osho speaking from the Buddha Hall about 50 yards away across the creek. I would prop myself up in the low branches of a Juniper tree, and with that support, I could stay sitting, using the tree branches to take the weight off my back, and I could meditate for the whole discourse. This, for me, was a gift from the gods; I found the peace and silence and the energetic connection with Osho that I had been missing throughout the nightmare of my body trauma.

With Osho speaking publicly now every day, Sheela was becoming more and more unimportant and impotent, and less the focus of attention. No more did Osho's words come to us through her and her filters, they came directly. Her unbalanced personality and hysteria was more and more evident, and nobody could 'believe' in her anymore. At the same time, nobody was openly rebelling, but riding it out, waiting, watching. Nobody could see the whole puzzle, just their little piece in it, and probably very few could realize the scope of what was happening, with Sheela, her gang, and the struggle between them, us, and the U.S. government. We heard rumors, about helicopters around the perimeter of the Ranch, infiltrators, bomb threats within the Ranch, but nobody could know for sure what was actually happening, who were not part of Sheela's inner circle. They had the information, and information is power.

One night I was among the 20 or so people in the audience at Osho's house, for his discourse. With some difficulty I could remain sitting, propping myself up against the wall. At one moment in the discourse, He was speaking about pleasure and pain, and how one looks at it from a different perspective just before dying, and He said, while looking straight into my eyes: "Your pleasures were as if written on water, and your pain, etched in granite. And you suffered all that pain for pleasures just written on water. You are going with empty hands." As he looked in my eyes and these words landed deep in my soul, I sensed that he was actually talking to me, but the entire picture was not revealed yet to my mind, as it existed in the fog of a future which had not yet come to pass.

As summer heated up, the preparations were made for the 4th Annual World Celebration. This was going to be bigger than ever. I was in a few of the rehearsals for the music, but it was horrible. Sheela was directing the rehearsal personally, and in it she was pushing the musicians, including me, to improvise without form or plan, playing more and more fast and intensely. It sounded like the worst form of avant-garde jazz, out of tune, non-harmonic, aggressive, ugly, and loud, like the sound track of a bad acid-trip. I withdrew from it, and spent the festival selling books and playing piano in the restaurant. The Darshans in Osho's presence were with that horrible music; Sheela was there in front of the whole crowd, spinning her hands and pushing the musicians to play faster and faster, and it seemed to me a clear reflection of what was happening energetically too, that things were spinning wildly out of control on all fronts, like the poem of 'The Second Coming' by W.B. Yeats:

> Turning and turning in the widening gyre
> The falcon cannot hear the falconer;
> Things fall apart; the centre cannot hold;
> Mere anarchy is loosed upon the world,
> The blood-dimmed tide is loosed, and everywhere
> The ceremony of innocence is drowned;
> The best lack all conviction, while the worst
> Are full of passionate intensity.

The second law of thermodynamics, as stated by dear old Isaac Newton, is that of 'entropy': the tendency in our universe for things to move from a state of order to one of chaos. This is experienced by all of us in daily life, perhaps expressed as Murphy's Law: that, 'Anything that Can Go Wrong, Will Eventually Go Wrong'. An easy example is when you have 5 new pairs of socks. You put them in the washing machine in a laundromat, and come home with 4 pairs of socks and two unmatched singles. Within a few weeks, you will find you have 10 unmatched socks. It's a mysterious force, unexplainable, but unavoidable. It's the same process that flings the myriad stars across the sky in an ever-expanding universe. Now, in our little venture in the desert, that state of entropy was in full play. The best of us lacked the conviction to take action against Sheela, while The Worst, Sheela's gang, were indeed full of passionate intensity, with plans to take over the county and more.

In the festival mornings, Osho would answer questions put to him by disciples, and one day there was a 'question' which was questionable in itself, submitted by Sheela. It consisted of a kind of tattle-tale attitude, "I have heard, that swami Anam was saying…etc." It was the same tone as the negativity General Meeting a month or so before. I was surprised at Osho's answer. I expected he would slam the questioner, throw it back upon itself and question why it was questioning. But instead, true to form, he unpredictably sided with the questioner: he went along with the direction of it and slammed Anam, against whom the gossip was directed. In that moment it appeared to me he was supporting Sheela and her attempts to stifle and control public opinion. So now here was another paradox. He has openly stated he opposes the fascist gang, implicitly, Sheela and her cohorts, and yet, in this discourse, he supports her methods, of public coercion and eavesdropping about the statements of others. Free speech? Not by a long shot. But that never was the rule; Who is on whose side? The only thing one could ever predict about Osho was that he was totally unpredictable. So his answer provoked more questions than it answered in me. If he is opposing her, why is he playing along with her hand this time? Is He buying time? Or maybe it is a flanking maneuver, to not directly attack her frontally, but appearing to be on her side until in a stronger position to dislodge her from her fortress? I had no idea anymore, but I knew things were reaching an impossible point of no return.

It was not predictable or fixed where was Osho's position in the game, at times it seemed opposing, at times it seemed supporting, at times both and neither. The only thing that was clear was that we were all living, under Sheela's government, in a system of government that could only be called a Pathocracy.

Definition: A system of government created by a small pathological minority that takes control over a society of normal people. A totalitarian form of government in which absolute political power is held by a psychopathic elite, and their effect on the people is such that the entire society is ruled and motivated by purely pathological values. A pathocracy can take many forms and can insinuate itself covertly into any seemingly just system or ideology. As such it can masquerade under the guise of a democracy or theocracy as well as more openly oppressive regimes.

(reprinted from www.veilofreality.com)

The final thrust of the forces of darkness within came at the darshan of September 8, 1985: the 'Poison Darshan' as it would come to be known. The music was under total control of Pashupatha and the lawyers, and was a cacaphonic mess.

There was always some idiot directing the music who had no idea about music, standing in front of the band and relaying the signals from Sheela up in front of the Buddha Hall, next to Osho. They even had microphones and started singing, Vidya, Padma, others. It was beyond horrible. The whole atmosphere was tinged with a color of weirdness.

Something had happened in the afternoon hours before the 'Celebration': the meal that was prepared for us to be taken home after the evening event, like a take-out dinner, had a fruit salad in it, in its own box. Just before the darshan, suddenly it was ordered that all the fruit salads had to be taken back to the cafeteria and gotten rid of, all 5000 of them. Rumors sprang up that the ones that were destined for Lao Tzu House had been poisoned, but the idiots of Sheela's gang who ran the kitchen got them mixed up with others, and now nobody knew what was what. That was typical; diabolical intentions and a lot of stupidity mixed together, that was a hallmark of the fascist gang. At the end of the darshan, something weird was happening up in the front, a crowd gathered; word came later that DevaRaj had a heart attack or something, nobody really knew what was going on in the ensuing chaos, but he was on the floor and a gathering of the 'gang' were around him, and energetically it was clear that a maximum low point had been reached in the life of the commune, that those precious moments when we could actually sit in the presence of Osho had been turned into a massive energetic disaster.

Three days later, on September 11 of 1985, to the great and righteous joy of the whole commune, Sheela and her entire fascist gang suddenly LEFT, and in leaving, left behind them a string of crimes longer than the road to Portland. I could physically feel that a dark umbrella of fear covering everyone had lifted off of the Ranch during the afternoon of their departure. After the last festival, Osho had been continually talking each morning to all 5000 of us in Buddha Hall, which definitely was a part of the reason Sheela left, because now questions could be submitted to Him directly. Two days after her and her gang's hasty and unannounced departure, in the morning discourse in front of the whole population of the Ranch, Osho unveiled a list of crimes that Sheela and her people had committed, including wiretapping and attempted murder, that now people were free to reveal their parts of the puzzle that they knew about, not in fear, but openness. Many people came forward at that time to tell their small part of the puzzle of the fascist shadow which had now past, and many, many shocking stories were revealed about Sheela's extremes, hidden bunkers, attempts to kill both members of the commune and U.S. government officials, and even secret meetings her gang were having with government agents. At the time and until this day we did not know if Sheela and her gang were having those meetings seeking informants, or they were actually part of a larger false-flag operation on the part of the government. Had Sheela and her gang been approached by and agreed to conspire with the government, in order to save their necks and ultimately destroy the Ranch? We could not know. But there were reports from people who were lower down on the chain-of-command, about meetings that had occurred between members of Sheela's gang and government agents, before Sheela's departure from the Ranch.

The poisonous atmosphere which had slowly grown around Sheela and her gang, was not only figurative, but literal. People came forth then with astonishing information, how she and her cohorts had poisoned DevaRaj, Vivek, the U.S. attorney Charles Turner, and perhaps others, with the testing for these psychopathic actions having been done on unknowing innocent victims in the very medical center where I had been for 7 weeks.

The experiments had been done by Sheela's private nurse Puja, a shadowy Chinese-American character with a smiling face and a strange dark agenda. She had gained control over Sheela, won her trust, her mind, and eventually influenced her behavior slowly and stealthily, by administering drugs. Sleeping pills, uppers, downers, slowly Sheela had become addicted to these 'helpers' coming from the beckoning hands of this ever-present, ever-helpful 'friend', and in so doing, her mind weakened, deteriorated and was more and more in the grip of the lower, darker aspects of her own character. I now understood the weird feeling I had in the medical center while I was there for all those weeks. The poisoning of Vivek occurred when she had been invited to live in Jesus Grove for a short time, seemingly in a gesture of friendship from Sheela. Vivek was Osho's companion of many years, and his Beloved, a position which Sheela envied and wished to take her place, to be the closest woman to Osho. That wish would never be fulfilled. It remained her fantasy, and perhaps the jealous motivation in her downward spiral into more and more psychopathic actions.

At that time Osho publicly in discourse invited all the law-enforcement agencies to come in and check the whole thing out, and came they did, the very next day, along with the FBI, the CIA, the army, the navy and Air Force, the state police, and probably even the dog-catcher. I remember walking into the ranch that morning, and there were at least 300 government cars parked everywhere, on every inch of open ground available around the downtown of the Ranch. They started digging here, pulling apart there, the Air Force was doing low-level flyovers with huge cargo planes, C-5As that can leave tanks in a hurry just about anywhere, the Navy was diving in the lake, the Swat teams were rumored to be massing at the perimeters of the Ranch. Ronald Reagan's great chance to win this little cold war in the hills of Oregon had come, and they were going for all the marbles.

In spite of and in stark contrast to the presence of the government agents everywhere, those two final months of the Ranch after Sheela's departure were the true flowering of the commune. Suddenly, people could work without some overbearing commissar on top of them with top-down orders telling them what to do. The commune was under new management, from Hasya and 'The Hollywood People', a group of wealthy disciples from Beverly Hills who recently had moved to the Ranch, and were much more 'human' than their predecessors in the halls of power. With this change, there was a huge wave of initiative and self-responsibility taking over. People started living their lives again, not in fear, but in creativity, sharing, and participation, instead of the numbness and contraction which had set in over the past year.

At the time along with editing Osho's discourses, I was writing articles for the magazine, mostly book and music reviews. This gave me a new freedom which I had not had in years, and instead of having to sit or lie in one place and work all day long, I could go where I wanted, find a place that suited me, and read and write. I felt like I was out of jail, and having a life again, creating and enjoying, and watching the drama unfold.

Counteracting the mounting pressure from the U.S. government which was bearing down on us in so many ways and from every possible direction, Osho was giving press conferences in the evening, to various members of the world press. I had the great and good fortune to be able to play music again by that time, because He was enjoying to come in and go out from the press conferences with music. And now with the fascist bosses

Playing for the Master in those days of autumn 1985

no more running the music department, we could actually play MUSIC again. So we accompanied Him, literally. I was there almost every other night, it was a great gift. I would be walking just a step behind Him, as He danced with each person on the way, and dancing with us as we played, both coming and going from his car. He loved danceable music at that time, so there was a few of us playing string instruments for some of those Russian folk songs and gypsy tunes that worked really well for dancing. I had an old viola, whose bow hairs I had snatched from the fences around the horse corral on the Ranch, and it worked well enough. But we had to play so fast and fiercely for the dancing, that sometimes the bow hairs on my fiddle bow would actually burn off, until I was playing with just the wood, and all the hairs flying.

After playing for his entry into the pyramidal salon, we would all sit and Osho would answer questions put to him by members of the world press. These were very interesting interactions, as these people were not in any way at the outset sympathetic to him. And yet, the atmosphere of love and humor which surrounded the Master would often win their hearts, and the discussion would become interesting and at times profound, covering all kinds of topics and pertinent questions. I would sit very close to Osho, in front, and could feel his energy pouring into me, right into my hara, bathing me in light. It was a great gift every time, and made it totally worth it, all what I had gone through. The previous 2 years of pain, exhaustion, and conflict with the Ranch tyrants was washed away in a flood of joy.

At other times, I was playing flute for Him in those press conferences, and when I played the flute, He would often dance very close to me, smiling sweetly, almost dancing cheek-to-cheek. I got it that He really likes the flute. He was so close, just a foot away, I would play looking into his eyes, and could smell that soft and particular blend of sandalwood and camphor which He used. It was a delight to be that close to him, and play to Him looking into his eyes, and he looking into mine. This intimate dancing with the Master was an unbelievable uplift after the suffering and transformation which had preceded it.

And yet another time, there was already the other players there, and they needed a bit of percussion to keep it together, so I grabbed a tambourine, and started banging away to hold the beat, for all I was worth. When Osho stood up to leave after the press conference, He came right up to me and started dancing fast and furiously with me in that distinctive and wonderful way that He would, pumping me with energy, like a hurricane. I was jumping up and down like a wind-up toy monkey you might have had when you were a kid, and after He walked on I just kept going. He then turned around, CAME BACK AND DID IT AGAIN! This was far beyond any Zen dialogue, it was energy transmission 'to the max', just pure energy. I was flying that night. Later, as I was getting my dinner in the cafeteria, Teertha came up to me and said, with some measure of envy in his voice, "Well, YOU sure got some juice tonight!!" And it was true. All I could do was laugh. It was too good of a feeling to talk about it.

The atmosphere of the ever-increasing tension surrounding the commune on a world-level, the greater freedom we all were feeling in the internal life of the commune, the deep love I was experiencing moment to moment in seeing Osho acting in these epic circumstances, and the incredible joy of closely being face-to-face with Him, playing and dancing with Him nearly every night had a surreal effect on me. I felt like Harry Haller must have felt standing before that fateful doorway in Hesse's classic novel 'Steppenwolf'. All possibilities lay before him, even unheard or undreamt of before. On the doorway, these simple words:

THE MAGIC THEATER.
PRICE OF ADMISSION: YOUR MIND

The commune was indeed a magic theater, reflecting to us all possibilities of life, love, and human drama, showing us at each and every moment, who we were.

One night, in the first days of October, there was to be a huge press conference in Buddha Hall. That night I was to be the one to open Osho's car door for him, as he got out of the Rolls and walked into the Hall.

I remember it clearly, the supercharged atmosphere of tension and expectation, the questions of the world press revolving around the immanence of arrest. Osho responded, in words that I wish I had never heard, that he wanted to be taken in chains, to show the world the hypocrisy of the phony American Christian democracy, and that if he was arrested, his sannyasins worldwide would bomb embassies, hijack airplanes, and create all kinds of trouble. At that very moment, I knew we were 'finished'. Saying those words was the equivalent of giving a blank cheque to Ronald Reagan to pay for your own funeral. I knew that with words like that, in America, they can do anything they want to you. I wondered if Osho knew that. I knew he was bluffing, but why he was bluffing, and what was the intention of the bluff was incomprehensible to me, as certainly myself and nobody else I knew had any intention of engaging in violent acts of retribution. We were not terrorists and had never any intention to be such. I had left behind any shred of that possibility years ago, when I started meditating. So what on earth was He talking about? Maybe he was buying time. Maybe setting the ante higher in the poker game, so that the government would think twice before bursting in to the Ranch with guns blazing. But in my knowledge, having lived through the 60s, the brutality of the American police state and the FBI was well known to me. Having faced the clubs and tear gas in Berkeley, I knew very well that with those words, the fate of our commune was sealed, if it had not been already. Either way, we were 'toast'.

As the discourse ended, and Osho brushed past me and got in the car, I closed the door of the Rolls and looked at him. I was speechless, shocked, stunned, and also thrilled by his audacity. Some part of me was silently saying, "What are you DOING??" And some bigger part of me was just stunned into silence, awe and love. He looked at me from two feet away through the car window, and nodded his acknowledgement to me, and the car sped off.

Like a piano wire pulled tighter and tighter until it snapped, so it went with the commune. The forces of destruction gathered momentum around us and grew, the air became thick with expectation of immanent action from the Federal government. Each day Osho came for discourse, each night, for a press conference. One morning, in the discourse there was a spot on his always spotlessly impeccable robe, and it shocked me more than the F-16s buzzing us at treetop level. Deep inside me, the symbolic impact of that spot was ominous: it meant that the forces of chaos and entropy had penetrated that deeply, into the heart of the commune. One day I was walking along the stretch of road by the airport at sunset, and two Leer jets were warming up on the runway, and as I watched, they soon shot into the sky overhead, sounding like the howls of coyotes in the Oregon desert.

I knew it must be Osho leaving, and the long night passed in tense silence. That night inside my townhouse, a big scorpion was found walking on the walls, and it seemed to me another ominous omen. At 5 in the morning, Vairagya, an Indian friend and colleague who was an early disciple of Osho, knocked on the door to tell us that Osho had been arrested in North Carolina, along with Vivek and some others. I knew our lives would never be the same after that.

Osho arrested, in chains and custody of federal marshals,
in Charlotte

CHAPTER 17

The End of Civilization

The sane man accepts life whole, as it is...
without needing by measure or touch, to fathom
the measureless, untouchable source of its images,
the measureless, untouchable source of its messages......

Lao Tzu, from 'The Way of Life', 500 BC

"There is nothing neither good nor bad,
but thinking makes it so"

William Shakespeare.

Osho had been arrested in Charlotte, North Carolina, on the tarmac while his plane was awaiting refueling, along with several others on the plane with him. It was unbelievable, yet terribly true, that the government now had moved to take advantage of the crimes of Sheela, i.e. wiretapping, biological terrorism, attempted murder, and through insinuation and association, they had arrested Osho for that. And it was Osho who had invited the government in to investigate the whole thing! A climate had been created, over the past few months, fomented in the press, that He was the culprit. And yet the government had no charges as such to pin on him. He was arrested on charges of arranging illegal marriages, something which never in the history of the INS (Immigration and Naturalization Service) had ever been prosecuted. On the plane with him there were Vivek, Chetana, Nirupa, DevaRaj, and Jayesh, who was a newcomer on the scene. He had arrived recently as part of 'The Hollywood crowd' who became the new management of the commune when Sheela left, 6 weeks before. He was relatively unknown, but shifted into close proximity to Osho immediately, and was now managing the commune finances.

The plane carrying Osho had travelled across the entire United States, a journey of six hours, to land in Charlotte. While the plane was in flight the Federal agents had enough time to put together an arrest team to be waiting at that airport. It was hastily made up of Tobacco, Alcohol, and Firearms Agents, the same branch of the government that would be involved in the Waco Massacre a few years later. The government had been tipped off about Osho's destination, because the call to the rental company to rent the two jets was made from the house phone at Lao Tzu Grove, Osho's residence at the Ranch, which of course was being tapped by the FBI at that time, as Osho was under intense investigation and facing imminent arrest. The fact that the plane travelled across the whole country to land in Charlotte gave the Government time to organize an arrest team and be there waiting at the airport, far away from the Ranch and the subsequent massacre which would have happened as 'collateral damage' if they had come in there with SWAT teams.

If Osho had actually wanted to escape, then it would have been incredibly easy, just the plane could have instead of going East, headed straight North. Within 30 minutes it would have been in Canadian airspace and free as a bird, so to speak. Curiously enough, Jayesh was released very quickly, soon after the arrest. Vivek and the other women were released a couple of days later. Osho was held, for nearly two weeks, and no-one knew where he was. He was transported on what should have been a 5 hour flight back to Oregon; it took twelve days, during which time he was taken in and out of federal prisons, FBI concentration camps, and holding cells, with no public announcements being made as to his whereabouts.

As the days moved into November, and we waited at the Ranch in stunned and frozen helplessness for news about Osho in jail, certain strange signs became visible in the face of nature all around. In the streams which joined at the crossroads of the Ranch, where the old farm once was, the beavers suddenly began cutting all the trees, obsessively, relentlessly. Metal plates were put around the trunks, in a futile attempt to curb their voracious fore-teeth, but to no avail. Down they went, all the big willow trees all over the Ranch, as the beavers furiously raced to make dams in anticipation of the coming natural calamity, in conjunction with the social calamity now in progress; Osho's incarceration and the collapse of the commune itself.

The night Osho came back from jail to the Ranch, was unforgettable. It was evening, already dark, a frosty night of mid-November. The whole population of the ranch, all 5000 of us, were lining the roads from the airport to Lao Tzu house. I was on the bridge just before the entrance to the Lao Tzu compound where he lived. We were all singing and celebrating, and keeping warm by dancing, deliriously happy that he was out of prison, seemingly safe, and back with us. As his car pulled around the corner I could see him practically jumping out of his seat as he did his particular way of keeping the rhythm of the music, a kind of diagonal conducting with both hands, like karate-chops, very vigorous. Chetana was there in the car with him, a white Rolls, and he seemed to be full of life and energy and power.

The next few days we didn't hear much, there were some rumors about deals with the government, an impending trial, etc. Osho left one day to Portland for a court appearance, a deal was made, and he left the USA there and then for India, without returning back to the Ranch. Although I was sad that I would not see him, I was deeply relieved that he got out of the USA without getting killed. That was all that mattered to me then. His last words to us from the door of the airplane were, "We shared a beautiful dream…and now that dream is over. Go back to your home countries."

There was a meeting called, a day or two later, in which it was explained by Osho's lawyer Niren and the new management, that without Osho's presence there to attract people for the yearly festivals, the commune could not manage to pay its debts, and would be closing. Another stunning bombshell, after so many:that this place which so many thousands of us had worked so long and hard to build was now ending, just when the last few nails had been pounded in to finish it. Such was the irony of it all.

Just after Osho's departure, around Nov. 28, the snow began to fall…and fall, and fall. People were leaving the ranch in cars, on foot, hitchhiking, however they could. There were not enough suitcases for 5000 people to leave with, so anything became a backpack for the enterprising voyager, and many people walked out in the snow with pillowcases stuffed with their clothes, slung over their shoulders. It looked like the end of the world; it WAS the end of our world.

At that time, as Osho would obviously not be giving discourses anymore, and the staff of the magazine were leaving town, my job morphed into delivering necessities to the townhouses, the group of about 120 large two-story residential houses winding through the central valley. Each house had 20 people living in it. As the snow piled up and the roads clogged with ice, it became impossible to use vehicles around the townhouses, so I improvised a little sled out of cardboard boxes, and mushed my way along the snowy paths, with my cargo of bread, milk, coffee, sugar, soap, and toilet paper for each house. On the paths I would often meet friends, walking their way out to the top of the ranch, and we would hug there in the falling snow, and say goodbye for the last time.

After 4 years of living in this island oasis, the 'world' outside was quite far away, culturally, ideologically, and economically. For 4 years those of us living at the Ranch hadn't touched money, we spoke even a different language, more of silence and friendship and laughter than of competition and technology. At that time, as our world collapsed all around, that friendship became a wry kind of ironic humor, laughing at the fate which was making itself apparent all around, the ending of this chapter, this dream. Nobody knew if at any moment the predicted SWAT teams would come in, there had been seen National Guard tanks on the perimeters of the ranch. Buildings in the downtown mall were being chained and locked shut by the Oregon District Attorney, invoking anti-racketeering laws. Rabid Christian preachers were standing on soapboxes in the downtown mall shouting about the devil: it was getting beyond surreal. In our case, the locked doors downtown meant having no more restaurant, cafe, and no way to get our worthless credits out of the Ranch banking system. So, my friends and I would play Satsang in the morning, have a beautiful meditation with music, and have champagne for breakfast, paid for with the now fake virtual credits in our accounts, which could never be redeemed as 'money' but could be spent on what remained still unsold in the now-closed restaurant. It just happened to be champagne...

At night, we would gather and make theatre plays about what was happening all around. It was hilarious, the stories and the creativity that flowered as the walls collapsed all around us. It had been such a touching of hearts, all of us having passed together from hell to heaven and back to hell, and there was no other way to let it go without celebrating it as much as possible;

Saying goodbyes all day long, as this or that beloved would pass by in the snow; most of them, in fact nearly all of them, I would never see again.

As I mushed through the snow from house to house to deliver my supplies, each door that opened was an entry into another aspect of the human mind, another facet of the way that people face their world. In one house, twenty people would be huddling around a small kerosene heater, fearfully commiserating about the unknown fate awaiting them 'out in the world'. In the next house, there would be a great party going on, salsa music, everybody dancing and enjoying, celebrating the end of the long, long work that we had been through. In yet another house, people hugging and playing guitars and enjoying each others company in laughter for the last time. I felt during those days of farewell to the thousands of friends, that I was being given a glimpse of the end of civilization, what it will be like to see the collapse and fall of an age, and all the ways that one can live it, in misery and anguish or joy and love and silence.

It had been, quite simply, the best time of my life, and I wanted to say 'Thanks' somehow…I decided to stay a few months and help clean up the mess left behind.

And so it went, a long good-bye, as the roads and paths slowly emptied. The snow continued to fall. The bushes turned into white mounds, the mounds turned into soft undulations in the endless and deep blanket of whiteness; the 93 Rolls Royces were loaded onto five semi-trailers and trucked slowly out on the icy road. The friends on the roads became less and less, the houses one by one became empty and were closed. One night in January, I walked out into the hills above Magdalena cafeteria, it was about 15 below zero outside, all crystal white under the full moon. In a cloudless sky, the moon was reflected in millions of diamonds in the snow all around. It was utterly beautiful, a beauty that touched me all the more deeply because I knew that soon I would never see that landscape again, a landscape that had seen so many changes happen in me and all of us, with so much joy, sorrow, pain and happiness.

Like the moon,
Come out from behind the clouds!
Shine.
You want nothing.
Your words are still.
You are still.

By your own efforts
Waken yourself, watch yourself.
And live joyfully

Gautama the Buddha, 500 BC

The city that had been full of life and love and 5000 very lively people, now was containing less than a hundred. I had the un-expected experience of extreme wealth of possessions, without possessing anything, as there were many more objects of personal wealth than one could ever use or wish to own. It was a surrealistic scene of an abandoned city, like being the only person left after a nuclear war, with most of the personal items of 5000 people still there. It became my task to organize, categorize, sell, or dispose of whatever remained. One could hop in a pickup truck, drive 100 meters...leave it there, and take another car or a bicycle; change your entire wardrobe 3 times a day, take your pick of any make, model, or size of stereo system, redecorate your room with Indian sculptures and Chinese porcelain, and even smoke Havana cigars if it so pleased you; and then dump it all in the trash tomorrow! Material things, the possessing of them, became simply a river that passed through one's hands, with no fuss about it whatsoever, no stress to obtain or maintain or cling to. It was a bizarre episode in a bizarre movie, a brief moment of comic relief in a film which had contained already far too much pathos.

After nearly two months of constant snow, it suddenly changed into rain. It rained, and rained and rained for two weeks non-stop. The entire snowpack of the 100,000 acre ranch melted almost overnight, and it lived true to its original name of The Big Muddy Ranch. The flash-flood came down the creeks, as they became raging torrents. The bridges we had painstakingly built that once spanned the rivers became piers reaching hardly to the middle of the waters. The check-dams and holding ponds so carefully constructed by hundreds of people to heal the eroding landscape became so much kindling floating downstream in Big Muddy Creek. Every single shred of evidence of 5 years and thousands of hours of intensive human labor to reverse the environmental damage of that battered landscape was washed away in the space of 5 days.

The danger was that the dam we had built three years before which had created the quite large Krishnamurti Lake would not hold the flood. I went to see it in those days, the water had poured over the spillway, carved its way through it, and created a gouge down about 50% of its height. We were all living directly downstream in the path, and were expecting any night that it might give way. We slept with ears cocked for the siren that would signal the dams collapse. In the end, it held. The waters subsided, the creeks became empty gravel gouges in the barren landscape as they had been before we ever arrived. Hundreds of rooms were cleaned and closed, thousands of pairs of shoes were sorted and discarded. Thousands of sleeping bags and sheets and blankets were cleaned and sorted and sold here and there to this or that charity, staircases dismantled, trailers sent away, time flowed in reverse as all the work of 5 years was slowly erased to nothing, In a few months, as the John Day River was in flood with muddy water and ice floes from the

Wallowa mountains, with the coming of the grasses in the spring, it became time for me to move on, and leave Oregon forever.

Before leaving, I sat on the banks of that big river, watching the passing ice floes in the spring thaw, and wondering what it had all been about. That wondering has changed and deepened with each passing year, as the events in the world came to echo and reflect what I had already seen happen, there in our little experiment in the hills of Oregon.

END OF PART I

PART II

CHAPTER 18

Flowers Shower, and Hot Houses

Cease all activity; abandon all desire;
let thoughts rise and fall as they will like the ocean waves.

He who abandons craving and clings not to this or that,
Perceives the real meaning given in the Scriptures. .

Tilopa, Song of Mahamudra

Exactly 4 years after I had arrived, I left the Ranch at the beginning of May 1986, with a beautiful and beloved friend named Jalada, who coincidentally came from my home town. We had been working together much during the last months of the taking down of the Ranch, cleaning and organizing and selling thousands of odds and ends left over from the departure of the entire population there in the desert city. She was Mexican-American and looked like a Kashmiri high-caste Brahmin, with deep-set dark eyes and a wonderful smile, and was simply one of the most beautiful persons, both physically and spiritually, that I have ever known. We were very different in temperament and outlook, but we shared our Californian sense of humor, a good deal of attraction, and the intention to be back with Osho as soon as possible. We helped each other through the difficult time of adjusting to being back in 'America'.

News about Osho was sketchy; we heard through the grapevine of friends around the world that he was on a World Tour, which actually meant he was landing in a country, getting refused a visa, spending a night in a holding cell and having to take off again within a day or so. We had no idea where he would end up. We followed a tip from a mutual friend at the Ranch, and decided to go to Aspen, Colorado, where we had heard there was quick and seasonal jobs available in the summer that paid well. That tip couldn't have been further from the truth.

Jalada had a job for a time as a maid for a wealthy Jewish lady from New York with a very nasty disposition and a few clothing shops in town. I created my work, for a couple of weeks re-designing her shops and building the interiors. I got paid 'zilch', because although by then I was a good carpenter, I had zero experience in estimating jobs; we had not used money for 4 years at the Ranch! Hence, I got fleeced, doing extensive remodeling jobs in which I would make, with cost and time overruns in the painting, about 3 bucks an hour. I learned quickly, the hard way. I took, or created, whatever jobs I could: handyman, cleaner, reorganizing and documenting a warehouse of stained glass windows, cleaning skiing condos, you name it. I would do it, while in the nights I would start working on sketches for an album that was brewing in me, on a piano and a little 4-track tape deck.

We lived a short distance outside of town on the edge of a massive national forest, where bears and elks would come down to the house in the nights. The air was thin and usually cold, as the town was up many thousands of feet on the slope of the Rocky Mountains. They have a saying in Aspen, that, "if you don't like the weather here, just wait 5 minutes". And it was very true. I went to work one day in the blazing heat of August on a motorcycle, wearing shorts and a tee-shirt, and I drove home that evening shivering in a blizzard in sub-zero winds. It snowed every night for the next 8 months. By November the streets were solid blocks of ice, and I had to learn how to snow-drive real quick...and also, how to start a car when it's 40 degrees below zero. In December we got word that Osho was coming back to India, and that clinched it. Within a week, I found a carpentry job that would have unlimited overtime, I was working again 12 hours a day 7 days a week for good pay, and within six weeks I had the 5000 dollars needed to go to India and stay for a very long time.

I sold an instrument that I had made all those late nights at Geetam and the Ranch, a sarod, to an art gallery in Aspen, and we drove out of the snow, followed the Roaring Fork River down to Glenwood Springs, and then down the deep gorge of the Colorado River heading west. One night in Arizona, we were camping just outside of the Hopi land, and Jalada was sobbing deeply all night long. Some ancient sorrow from her Native American Mestizo ancestry seemed to have penetrated into her soul, after passing the Navajo villages in the day and seeing how they were a conquered and subjugated people, an occupied land, like Tibet under Chinese Invasion. And this was America, the land of the free and home of the brave, a Hollywood dream which we had seen unmasked through the destruction of the Ranch. The veil of 'democracy' had dropped, and had been demonstrated all too clearly as hypocrisy, with the arrest of Osho and destruction of a city of whose people of which the great majority of them were only interested in living in peace and joy in their community. It was all too obvious to me now that the American dream of religious tolerance and freedom had nothing to do with reality. We stopped in LA to see our parents and say goodbye to the USA for an indefinite period, selling my car and the rest of our possessions in San Francisco before getting on the plane to India.

We arrived in India on March 21, 1987. It was a day of Celebration in the Ashram, Enlightenment day, commemorating the day when Osho was enlightened at the age of 21. Osho had just gotten back to Poona after staying in Bombay for some time. He was coming out for discourse that morning in Buddha Hall, I believe for the first time, and we arrived at the ashram gates at 7:30 in the morning, time enough to enter before He would come out. Jalada was dying to see Osho, so I took the luggage and went to find a hotel for us to stay, while she could go in for discourse.

I got to the ashram about 9:30 in the morning, and went in to the back of Buddha Hall where Osho was just about to leave. I sat in silent joy, watching; There He stood, He whom I did not know if I would ever be able to see again, and when He left the hall, I burst out in tears. Many friends came to hug me, it was a day of joy, meetings, hugs with old friends, and catching up on news.

It was hard to find housing then, Poona had been emptied out of sannyasins 6 years before, and all the huts and apartments we had occupied in 'Poona 1' were no more there, or not available like in the past. In a couple of days, we found a room in a house in the center of town, in an old Indian bungalow. Our room was the attic, and March being the summertime in India, a summer where it can easily get 120 degrees Fahrenheit, our attic room was a sauna in the night; we would have to throw water on the stone floor to cool it off, and sleep sweating. ...

Jalada and I had different jobs in the ashram, she taking care of Osho's library and myself as a musician and handyman once again, and we became more and more distant, as our lives changed and more and more time was spent apart. It seemed our time was over, as we had crossed the waters together, and were now back in the commune. It was without rancor, and we stayed good friends, but I moved to a tiny apartment closer to the ashram, where I didn't have to travel far to go home and back, and could easily get to the ashram early in the morning for the music rehearsals to play in discourse.

My new home was a small apartment newly built, reeking of new concrete and whitewash, and the occasional smell resembling 'fried chicken' drifting in clouds of smoke from the nearby burning ghats, where the bodies of the Hindu dead were constantly being burned alongside the river.

There were not many people in the ashram yet, especially ones who had experience working around Osho, so immediately I was back in my old role of doing things in his house, and very glad to be so. Soon, it became doing things in his private quarters, and I became his handyman and carpenter. Part of the responsibilities of my job were to be available 24 hours a day, if anything was needed in his apartment, fixing a mosquito screen or a leaky roof or a door that was squeaking, you name it, I did it, whenever it happened. So, within a short time I was given a hut on the roof of one of the ashram buildings, Francis house, which was just 30 feet from Osho's house, so I could easily be found anytime, day or night. This was a great privilege at that time, to have a place to live in the ashram. I loved my job, it was wonderful to be close to Osho again, and to be seeing him and playing for him nearly every day in discourse.

Neelam, a beautiful Punjabi lady who had been with Osho for many years since the beginning of his work in India, was now the manager of the commune and Osho's secretary. One day she gathered us musicians together to talk to us about the music. It seems that Osho was having pain in his arms, and the dancing that he would do with the music we were playing was aggravating the condition. So, it was asked that we play soft meditative music for him to come in and out of discourse. This was totally fine with me, it was what I was made to do.

On that very first morning of the 'new music', I was playing my flute, Milarepa was playing guitar and Nivedano on percussion. We were in the small auditorium called Chuang Tzu, just next to Osho's residence, which was much more intimate than the vast expanse of the Buddha Hall at the Ranch. We musicians were about 20 feet away from Osho's sitting chair. Osho came to the door of Chuang Tzu auditorium, and stood there, saluting with his Namaste, smiling broadly, and …just enjoying the soft and sweet music for a long time. My heart leaped out to him. He was just DIGGING it! And I could feel it, and I played my heart to him. It was a magical communion, and a total delight. And something I felt which I had never noticed before, that the flute is not just a one-way passage; it goes in both directions. As I played to him, and the notes would reach to him, his energy would reach to me. The flute was an open door, a hollow channel that made me completely vulnerable and available. I was drinking Him in and happily drowning in it, and each day after it, again and again. He was obviously loving the music, soft and melodic, with the flute, and when he would sit down, he would respond by talking about music, sometimes for an hour or so. He would talk to us about the REAL music, which takes the listener into silence, not sensuality. That music had sacred origins, in ancient India, and it consisted of a vertical dimension, not just the horizontal, which is all that Western music knows about. He used the analogy of the five fingers of his hand…the notes are the fingers, but the gaps between the fingers are the silences, which is where the real energy transfer is happening, the real happening in the music. That music has to contain silence as well as notes, and the notes give a shape to the silence.

This was a delight each day, to sit there, totally in love with him, in that intimate atmosphere, and be bathed in these remarkable lessons in how to play meditative music. He was filling in the blanks in the message he had given me years before after the first festival at the Ranch.

One day soon afterwards, I had been fixing something in Osho's room, and I was coming out of the glass doors to Osho's apartment, I was surprised to see Vivek. She had just gotten back to

India and arrived at the ashram. Her name had been changed to 'Nirvano'. She smiled sweetly at me, and so many memories were revived inside of my heart. As days went by we often met in passing, and she was the one who would let me into his room for the numerous jobs that I would do there while he was in the dining room, or sometimes, while he was in discourse. One night in music group in Buddha Hall, I was playing and she came to Buddha Hall, a rare event, and danced there just in front of me, with that same wild and dynamic energy she had when she had been dancing with Osho and myself in those last evenings at the Ranch. It was a delight to see, and inside me I smiled, and thought, "Wo, what's this about?".

One day as I was passing by the gate of Lao Tzu, she was there sitting, and she asked me, "Did you ever make anything out of MARBLE?"

I said, "No, I am used to working in wood".

She said, "Osho needs a little table for his questions that he would answer in Buddha Hall, and he would like it to be made out of marble".

I said, "Okay, I'll give it a try!"

These were fateful words, whose implications were unimaginable to me at the time. I found some marble tiles of the same color as the podium in Buddha Hall, so it would blend into the background on the videos, and started working on it. In a couple of weeks the little table was ready. It looked kind of royal, and kind of medieval at the same time, like something that might be in a 12th century European castle. It took its place right next to his chair in Buddha hall, and Osho would pick up his tablet of questions from it after he would sit down to speak.

At that time, there was a German disciple named Niskriya who was doing the video taping of Osho in discourse. He was having problems getting a good sound from the side-stand mike that they had been using up to now to record Osho in His daily discourse, so he got some super microphones from Berlin with the idea to put them in Osho's chair. I was pretty resistant to the idea, as I was a bit skeptical about people who asked for changes in the structures around Osho, especially Germans. They always have great technological ideas how to improve things. But around Osho, everything had to be done so carefully, cleanly, without any smell whatsoever, and of course I would be the one to do it, that it was difficult to manage big changes in the small time slots available each day. But after I argued with him for some time, I saw that he really meant well, so I jumped into it, took apart Osho's chair and installed the hidden mikes, and put it back together in about an hour. He looked me over with his round metal glasses, and scrutinizing me thoroughly, said, in an Einstein voice with a thick Berlin accent, "First, you make ze big fight, and zen you do it like it vas NOZING! You are a most unusual person". From then on we were always friends, and I enjoyed him very much, because he was just as unusual a person, and even more so. He was the one making the videos of Osho's discourses each day, being there a few feet in front of Osho all through the discourse...never wavering, never losing his composure, even while at times the Master joked and prodded and kidded him in front of thousands of people. I have great respect for the depth of his centering in the midst of the storm. It's not easy...

CHAPTER 19

The Table

*"Human beings are creatures of awareness,
involved in an evolutionary journey of awareness,
beings indeed unknown to themselves,
filled to the brim with incredible resources
that are never used.".*

Carlos Castaneda

At that time, I was Osho's carpenter, handyman, sometimes night guard, and flute player. Each day I would be all day in his apartment, in his bedroom, in his bathroom, in his dining room, fixing things, making adjustments to doors, shelves, squeaky hinges, leaking roofs, whatever. Of course, he was in the apartment all day too, so I would manage to work in the room where he wasn't, always. If he was in his bedroom, I would be in the bathroom. If he would go to the dining room, I would go into the bedroom, and so forth all through the day.

On a certain day I needed to go into Nirvano's room, to fix the table in His dining room, which was in fact the balcony of Nirvano's room, as she lived with Him and shared the apartment of two rooms, one being His, and one hers. Her bedroom had a balcony which looked out onto the green of the garden behind Lao Tzu house. On that balcony was the small table where Osho would eat His meals. Although for the public, it appeared that Osho was extravagantly rich with a Rolls Royce, and elaborate robes and watches, in his daily life he was actually very simple, almost Spartan, and was content with the few simple things that were there. It was the table where he would eat lunch, and it was wobbly and to get there to fix it I had to pass by Nirvano's bathroom.

As I passed the doorway, I noticed something strange on the floor of the bathroom, a pile of blankets, which seemed out of place in the orderliness and simplicity that was always there in this apartment. In the balcony I did the work, setting a few screws and some glue in the table, and as I passed by the doorway on the way out, I looked closer into the door of the bathroom, and in the pile of blankets was Nirvano, sleeping in the middle of it. It was strange I thought, that she would be sleeping in a lump of blankets on the bathroom floor with her bed just a few steps away in the next room. As I thought this, she stirred for a moment, and I said softly, "Are you OK?"

She looked at me, and just opened the blankets, and she was lying there, the most beautiful woman I had ever seen in my entire life. I remembered the day of the Rolls Royce, three years before, when I had refused to go with her, and this time, I said nothing, and just got in the blankets, fully clothed. She looked a little startled, like she wanted me to be there, but also wondering, "Who is this guy anyway...can I trust him?". I kissed her very softly, on her cheek, and again, softly on her lips. I didn't think at all about what was happening. We didn't say a word.

We silently hugged each other for a long time. She asked me if there was anything I wanted, and I said, no, but that I was happy this had happened. Then I kissed her again, and got up to leave. She still had that surprised look on her face, but the expression mixed in with it was of happiness.

The next morning I was playing flute in the discourse, and I was interrupted by someone bringing me a note, from her. It said, "It was beautiful. It was magical. Let's meet again."

That night in the evening, after the discourse, She came to

my hut on the roof of Francis house, my little hut on the roof, high above the ashram, made of bamboo and there nestled in the branches of the trees. She came up the ladder and sat on my little bamboo bed, like the glorious princess or queen of which she could be both, and we smiled. Being comically polite in the stark poverty of my simple bamboo hut on the roof, I asked her if she wanted something to drink. I'm not a drinker, but there was a little liquor in a bottle that a friend had given me, and I poured her some in a wooden teacup. She said in a startled voice: "You're trying to get me DRUNK!". Then she gulped the whole bowl down, all at once. It was then that I knew this was a different kind of woman than I had ever known.

It was around midnight, and I asked her, "What was the world tour like?". She took a big breath, and slowly began to unfold the whole story of all the plane flights with Osho, all the rejections in every country, all the imprisonments in airports and holding cells in 50 countries, the take-offs with no flight plans and nowhere to land, the escapes from crummy hotels and CIA agents, all with Osho in HER charge, her responsibility to keep his body alive and intact, her being his slim anchor to this world. As the night unfolded, so did the story, until the first light of dawn, and I felt with each passing hour the tension release from her, as she told me all this.

She was physically very lovely, with a deep and mysterious beauty in her crystal blue eyes. But embracing her as I closed my eyes, that outer beauty was nothing compared to the strong and bright light that burned inside her. Whether it was her, or His energy in her, I'll never really know, but it burned through me as if I was a paper lamp, turning in the wind. In the dawn's light, she climbed down the ladder and went back to Lao Tzu House, and the ashram was stirring, along with the birds in the soft wind of sunrise.

At this time Osho was coming out twice a day, every day,

speaking about 2 hours each time. It was always preceded and ended with music, while he would slowly walk into the Chuang Tzu auditorium and greeting us in his 'Namaste'. It was usually Milarepa on guitar, myself playing flute, Nivedano playing percussion, Sat Gyan on Bass, and Karunesh on keyboards. The atmosphere in Chuang Tzu Hall was full of the deep love and gratitude we were all feeling to be near Him once again in the relative safety of India, after the storm of the breakup of the Ranch and the debacle of the World Tour. Osho would slowly walk in, with his hands joined in Namaste, which in India is a greeting which means "I salute the god within you". Before sitting down, He would stand and look slowly over the whole audience, His eyes shining with love. As He sat, we would stop playing, and he would begin speaking. It was very intimate, as Chuang Tzu could not hold more than 400 people, sitting very closely together, and it was full always. People usually had to come on rotation, and could not come twice in one day. We would do the same, the musicians usually being a morning, or an evening band. I was in the morning. It was very meditative instrumental music, simple, not provoking Osho to dance, as His arms were starting to hurt Him quite a lot, and if we played uptempo, He would start to dance anyway. So we tried to 'cool it'.

When He would speak, it was at that time in answer to disciples questions, about love, relationship, meditation, fear, death, everything. It was a beautiful time, after the destruction of the Commune in Oregon and the long separation of the World Tour, this was a deep and intimate meeting in love, and relief, that we could be with Him again, and He with us. There was in it for me, a joy like having another chance at living, unexpectedly, after all had been seemingly lost.

One morning, we were playing a very sweet tune when he came in, and when he appeared in the doorway, I felt so free

234

and at one with the music, that I could just give him all the love I felt for Him through the flute. And in doing so, I was wide open, and he poured into me. He just stood there, a long time, smiling, and I could feel that He was just loving it! He was delighting in our music, and the love that we all were enveloped in. This was pure magic. I could have died in those days, of beauty and wonder, with no regret whatsoever, I felt that my life with him had now been fulfilled, beyond measure.

Nirvano and I continued meeting and were together nearly every night after that. After we had been together for some weeks, she asked me to move in and live with her there in her room, which was a part of Osho's private apartment separated by a glass door from the rest of the Lao Tzu house. Her room, all marble, next to Osho's, was practically barren of furniture, other than her bed. She had a little pillbox, in which she used to keep Osho's medicine next to her bed. She had no bedside table, so she would set it on the floor next to her pillow, so as to find it when she would get up in the night to give him his medications. His body condition was fragile at that time, and worsening each day. He would often be getting colds, and often needed antibiotics or some other medicine, which required that she wake up once or twice in the night to give it to him.

I had just finished to make some weeks before, that little table out of marble tiles, which was used by Osho in discourse, placed just next to his chair, to set his clipboard which held the questions which he would answer as he spoke in discourse. It was made out of the same green marble as the whole podium, so as to be unobtrusive and in the same style, not attracting attention on the videos. It blended in with the background and disappeared as such on the videos. This being the first thing and only thing I had ever made out of marble, it was not an easy experience for me, it was very slow and hard to work with compared with wood. There were no tools that worked well with it in the ashram at that time, and it made really a LOT of aching arm-muscles and many hours of rubbing to polish it, but I did my best and it came out all right, albeit a little stiff-looking. It had been Osho's wish, to make it out of marble, and that's why I had done so.

Now, seeing she didn't have a bedside table, I used a few of the left-over tiles, and made her a very little bedside stand, for the pillbox of Osho's medicine and her jewelry when she slept. It was so simple, just a marble nightstand. But it looked nice, and fit with the room. And it had all my love in it. She was so pleased, delighted in fact, as she was not someone who put any energy into her own scene, her whole life was devoted to taking care of Osho 24 hours a day. Little did I know what I had done...

So that little table sat by her bed for a couple of days, and that was the route that Osho would take as he walked from his part of the apartment to the dining room: he would pass through her bedroom. And one day, he stopped there and stayed awhile looking at it, even squatting there in front of it, checking it out.

Later in the morning, I was in the bedroom for a moment, and she came out of Osho's room and she told me, excitedly, that he really liked the table. And she added, "He wants you to make him some tables!" I was sitting on her bed, and she was going back and forth from her room to his room about 5 meters away as we spoke, and she would relay what I would say to him, and then she would tell me what he said in his room for me ... I would ask something, she would walk the 5 meters to his room, come back and give me the next answer. I could hear him answering her through the open door, but not make out the words. I asked, like a carpenter: "How big does he want them?" She went in, came back and said: "He wants two long ones next to his chair (indicating with her arms about 2 meters). and two double decker ones by his bed (indicating about one meter) and one for his alarm clock in the bathroom (indicating a height of a half-meter or so and a kind of square shape.) And he wants them about THIS thick (indicating with her fingers about 5 inches). And he wants them out of ABU GREEN."

I was desperately calculating in my mind the amount of time this would take, and it started to approach infinity, and in my smallness of mind and desperation to not be trapped in a single task forever, which seemed like death to me, I frantically started squirming to find a way out, namely, thinking that I would put them together from tiles, as I had done for her little table. And so I asked the fateful question:"Do they have to be ALL marble, or can I put them together?".

She went in to his room, asked, and came right back out in about 5 seconds, looked me straight in the eyes, and with all her intensity and power, said: "He says you have to CARVE THEM FROM A SOLID ROCK!!".

Her words landed in the place between my eyes like a sledge-hammer. With the impact, my mind went completely blank. I walked out of there as if I had just had a lobotomy. Really, this was the gap between the five fingers. I knew my life would change from that moment on. I was a musician, or so I thought. Marble is as far away from music as you can get. Music is instant gratification. Marble..takes...forever...and then some more time. I felt like the floor was falling out from under me. There was no escape. This was straight from Him. Nowhere to run or hide. It had my name on it, and he was right there, watching, 24-7. A voice was saying in me. "Okay, so you want to be close to him, here's what it means, Bozo. You asked for it, you got it.".

CHAPTER 20

Nirvano

Osho and Nirvano on The World Tour in Greece, c. 1986

One day, when we had been living together for a few
months, out of the blue, I asked her about her relationship
with Osho. She said that they had a beautiful love affair for
many years. They met in a meditation camp he had in Mt. Abu
sometime around 1969. She would have been 19 or 20. She
was so afraid to meet him, she hid in the bushes when his car
passed by. One day during the camp as he was passing, he
stopped his car, and opened the door. She shyly got in, and they

spoke for the first time. They slowly got to know each other, and spent more time together, gradually becoming closer and closer. After some time, they spent the night together, and after some time more, became lovers. They never parted after that.

He called her Gudiya, from the name she had in her last lifetime, a lifetime in which they also had been together. This was just before Osho's enlightenment, in this present latest lifetime of his, before he was 21. She had remembered this lifetime of hers, which was now for her a 'past-life', remembering that she had brought him food daily as he meditated for long hours in the temple by the river in Gadarwara. She told me that she remembered clearly there was one day when she was 15, she brought the food for him, and someone was there to stop her, saying, "He needs to not be disturbed". Soon afterwards she died, of Typhoid; and probably, a broken heart.

Osho and Nirvano in the 70's

She told me many intimate details of their relation of many years together in this life, of which there is no need to speak of here. Suffice to say that their love affair and relation as man and woman was beautiful, deep, mysterious, natural and remarkable. After she told me these things, she asked if I felt weird, if I felt different towards Osho. I answered that in fact it made me love him more, because I realized He is also a man, a human man, and that made his enlightenment all the more amazing to me.

After saying these things to me, I asked her if she ever tells these things to other people. She paused and said, "I NEVER TALK about these things to anyone...but one day...I WILL TELL ALL!"

She never got that chance. I could not know it then, but she would leave this world within 2 years; and the fact that she told these things to me, has remained in me like an unresolved koan in my heart. Speak of these things? Carry them with me to my grave? I have never had an answer to that. But the answer has come, when I realize that each day is my last on this earth, we are in the end-times, that mark the ending and the beginning of an age, and there is nothing to remain secret, it is the time when all must be made available to everyone. Those who can hear it, will. Those who cannot, or choose to take offense when their ideas are offended, it couldn't be helped. It is not my intention to offend anyone.

She would wake in the morning, open her eyes, and say, "Oh, I love you!" with such a joy, and we would embrace. In the middle of the night, sometimes Osho would wake her with a little alarm because he needed something, and I could hear them talking as I lay in bed, and He in His bed just about 20 feet away in the next room, so softly and sweetly the voices murmuring in the night. She would come back to bed, in such a beautiful mood like a mother who had cared for her child: I asked her,

"What did he say?" She said, "COULD YOU HEAR US?!"
I said, "Yes, but I couldn't make out the words. What did he say?"

She said, "HE SAID, GUDIYA..I'M HUNGRY!" And she smiled, with such sweetness, innocence and beauty.

Often I would not be able to sleep at night, as His energy presence in the room was so strong. And in the morning, she said to me, "How are you doing, is it too much for you?" I then said, "I couldn't sleep so good". And she said with a smile, "Okay, I'll tell Him to turn it down, sometimes He's a little too much." I asked what she meant, and she replied, "He walks around, you know; without his body. He visits here and there; does things....makes trouble."

One night she had fallen asleep before me. It was about one in the morning, and I got up to lock the outside door to the apartment, which she would always do as the last thing before going to bed. Inside was just Osho, Nirvano, and me, and outside was the rest of the world. I turned the key in the lock, and realized at that moment that for some reason unknown to me, the universe trusted me. At that moment, the inner afflic-tion of worthi-

Osho, Nirvano and myself dancing together...

ness and unworthiness ceased to be a theme inside me. I just accepted that the universe accepts me.

Being there and living with Osho and Nirvano had become

such an intimacy, like being part of the family, with all that is entailed in that. Barriers fall, when you live together. In the morning she would make two cups of tea, one for Him and one for me. Somedays his cook would make a particular dessert called rasmulai which he really liked, a kind of milk and rice pudding with cardamon which was really delicious. They would be in little cups, 5 of them. He would eat two or three, and I would eat the rest. Each day, what I was doing was being discussed by him with Nirvano, fixing this, or making that. I would be almost like his shadow, if he was in the bathroom, I would be fixing something in the bedroom. If he was in the dining room, I would be waiting in the bathroom, and so it would go, all through the day. Sometimes fixing his wobbly dining room table, sometimes filling cracks in the floor, or going into his room while he was outside in Chuang Tzu speaking in discourse, to do longer jobs that needed an hour or more while he was out of the room.

Once, she had forgotten the keys to his room inside in the night, and the door was locked with him sleeping inside. She hated when this happened, because it meant she would have to knock on the door and wake him up, instead of coming into the room to his bed to wake him. This would mean she would be chastised for her forgetfulness, lack of awareness. She would get 'The Zen stick', that symbolic staff of bamboo that Zen Masters would use to hit disciples when they would be falling asleep in their meditations. In this case, it is figurative, not physical. But this stick was always present, ready to fall when any action was not impeccable, when any slip of awareness reflected in the simple actions of daily life would be evident. Living with him was for her, a labor of love and a constant crucifixion, both at the same time. There was no escape, and I was in the same boat now.

One of those times, in the early morning light, in fulfillment of her request, I crept through the garden to silently remove the bars on his bathroom window so she could enter through the bathroom and retrieve the keys. and wake him up in the bed, instead of knocking on the door to let him know it was time to get up. Now, 'waking up' is a fairly ambiguous term in relation to Osho. I don't think sleep as such meant the same for Him as it would for you or I, as his consciousness was quite active and in fact, impressive, in the night hours. But he was not really 'locked into the clock', as we humans generally are. In my understanding, he lived pretty much outside the psychological perception of the passage of time as such, so 'waking him up' in the morning was more like letting him know that a certain hour of the clock had arrived for the rest of us. I think he was basically in 'timeless eternity' all the time, so to fit into human schedules, like, 400 disciples gathering at a certain hour at a certain place to listen to him speak, he would have to be told that it was time to get up and get ready. As for us slipping through the garden to open the window instead of banging on the locked door to retrieve the forgotten keys, I'm fairly sure He knew we were doing that, but I think that he appreciated innovation, improvisation and humor in the solution of problems. It was a kind of game and a dance, this play of living with the Master, not really serious, but fun. If you lost the round, you got the Zen-stick on the head. If you managed to slip around it in total alertness, there was no congratulatory pat on the back: the next round was starting immediately, the next task, the constant reflection of awareness-or-unconsciousness as seen in the results of little actions of daily life.

There was a story Osho would sometimes tell in discourse, about a man in Japan who was a great swordsman, but not a Master yet. He found a great Master, and begged for instruction. The Master agreed to it, and said, "Come to my house". The man came, very arrogant and proud of his skills, with his sword in hand. The master put the sword in the closet, and said,

"Please could you sweep the floor...?" When that was finished, he had to do the dishes, then rake leaves in the garden, then another and another small task. Nothing at all was said about swordsmanship. Days, weeks, then months went by. The man was frustrated, then despondent, he wondered why he had come at all. But he absorbed himself in the tasks of living in this little house with the master and serving him.

One day, when he had forgotten all about swordsmanship, he was doing the dishes, the master silently crept up on him, and with a wooden sword, struck him with a terrific blow from behind. Bruised and shocked, he looked at the master, who said to him, "BE ALERT!"

From then on, anytime, anywhere, the master would silently creep behind him, and he would receive an unexpected blow from the wooden sword. He could be eating, sleeping, doing a job, anything, anytime. He was covered with bruises, but he came to develop a feeling, just before the blow would land, and he would duck. Then he would feel it when the master was entering the room. Then the master said to him. "Now you are ready. The next time I strike you, it will be with the REAL sword!"

Now the game was for life and death! One strike of the masters sword, and a man is dead, there is no second hit at that level of swordsmanship in Japan. So with his life at risk at every moment, the man became a burning flame of alertness, until there was no way for the master to approach. Just the thought would come into the master's mind to pick up his sword, and the man would shout from the other room, "DON'T!"

The Master picked up the man's sword forgotten in the closet, gave it to him, and said, "Now you are ready. An opponent's sword cannot touch you now. You are free to go".

Now, this was my exact situation, living with Osho. I had come there, 10 years before, to learn how to play meditative music. Now, every word, every action, every feeling, every moment of my existence, was subject to the Master's hit. And… the Master's love. It was a double sword, and I can't tell you which one cut more. If I was putting silicon in a crack between the window and the wall in his bedroom, and the line of the silicon wasn't perfect that day, because I was in a hurry to leave the room before He came in, the next day in discourse, he would say, without saying my name, "And when you work, you work, SO unconsciously! You cannot do something perfectly, you cannot stay with something and complete it until it is perfect." I knew he was talking about the silicon on the window in front of His chair, that I had put there that morning, and I felt like a bug that wanted to crawl out from under the mosquito net and escape from Buddha Hall. Sometimes bits of my conversation with Nirvano from the day before would come out, word for word, in Osho's discourse, and I knew that she had been telling him things I had said; or even worse, that he was hearing my thoughts. It was terrible, and wonderful. I had paddled my little canoe out into the middle of the Pacific ocean, and I had no idea in which direction was the shore anymore. I was completely exposed, 24 hours a day, with no exit.

What was being asked of me? Impeccability in action: total awareness, alertness, to every thought, every emotion, every action, every word. I was under a bright, bright spotlight, and there was no room for shadows. I could not hide from myself. I could not cut corners. If I felt jealous, insecure, possessive, grumpy, petty, it was mercilessly exposed to Nirvano, and thus, to Him. And at the same time, the love that I felt for her was provoking me to be totally vulnerable, it brought up my deepest fears, insecurities, shame, self-negation, all the wounds I had ever experienced in love from day 1 of my life, and probably earlier.

Sometimes in the night, in the next room to His, she would ask me to play bamboo flute, about the time when He would be falling asleep. So, I would make a little mini-concert there, from the next room, as He lay in bed listening.

One morning, there was playing on her stereo a new tape from the Ashram, and it was me, playing a very wild opening phrase on the flute in the morning discourse. She shouted out, with a tone of British apprehension, "Pretty spacy character… !" And I replied, "Yep, he sounds a little dangerous…". We laughed.

On the exterior, if you didn't know her, she seemed very English. She could be EXTREMELY critical, and dry. Or worse, depressed, despondent. Her father was English. But her mother was French, and she grew up until the age of 10 in Paris, and this Parisienne side of her was much the stronger when she was in a good mood. Vivacious, gracious, lovely and sweetly delightful, she could be the rarest and most feminine of birds, a queen in her court, or the nastiest adversary you could ever imagine. In short, she was one hell of a woman. If she was happy, it was like the whole universe was shining on you. If she was in a bad mood…just get out of the house, Quick!

She had remembered several other lives she had had before this one. She had been Rani Rasmani, the queen who gave to RamaKrishna the temple in Calcutta where he lived. She had cared for that enlightened man, and protected him; the same occupation she was having in this life.

I asked her about Osho's statement that she had been Mary Magdalene; she neither affirmed nor denied it, but this she answered me: she had remembered a lifetime in which she had been with Jesus. She described the day she met Him, in Galilee. She had seen a light, passing in a valley, and she walked to that light, and met Him at the well.

And then she told me the strangest thing of all, and that was that she had also known Osho in THAT lifetime. That, in fact, Osho had been John the Baptist, and John the Baptist was the real physical father of Jesus.

With that, an earthquake went off inside me, and a chain of

246

associations. Suddenly, something just fell into place inside me, like a piece of the puzzle. Why had Osho gone on a quest, a mission in fact to destroy all the falseness and pretension of Christianity, to unmask its lies and its hypocrisies, time after time, until in the end it would get him crucified by the fundamentalist Christian American government?

It was, if in fact this was true, his responsibility to do so. To leave this world without correcting mistakes, would have been impossible. It was his last lifetime: after Enlightenment, you don't get another body. The account had to be closed. He wasn't coming back into a body again. The birth of Jesus was not an impregnation by a Holy Ghost, the creation of the spin-doctors of the middle ages. It was a conscious impregnation by an Essene Master, to bring a very high soul to the earth, to bring the Teacher, and provide the suitable situation for Him to enter the world.

It was known in ancient mystery schools, the Sacred Ritualized Union to invite a higher being. This is what he had done, literally prepared the way of the Lord, and the first teaching of Real Love on the planet. The baptism at the River Jordan was the initiation rite. Jesus, or Yeshua, as was his real name in Aramaic, was bringing into the world a new Vision of Love, an understanding that had never been before in the Western World of that time. And the centuries to come would twist and disfigure that teaching into myths and fairy tales that would masquerade under the name of religion, used to murder women, control minds, enslave millions, and conquer territories for the next two thousand years.

Now I understood the intent behind the myth given to me in my childhood of the 'Virgin Birth'. I had always wondered why, if the God of the Bible had created sex for every creature in the universe, this universal law would not apply to his own procreation? Of course! Because if the birth of Christ was from a Virgin Woman, she did not participate in the act of procreation, she was passive in the story. It was 'announced' to her after the fact by the angel, so the story goes. But in the real orgasmic union between a male and a female, the woman equally participates; it is the two polarities of energy in Sacred Union which opens the door for the manifestation of a soul at the moment of conception. The myth that we were taught puts the whole power of creation in the hands of the male God the Father, and the male Holy Spirit. So it completely denies the creative power of Woman, which the patriarchal church deeply fears and has constantly tried to destroy. She is demoted from equality as a co-creator. This denial is the basis of the subjugation of women, for the last two thousand years. It sits like a seed in the basic assumptions of the society, unquestionable, 'Holy'; the operating system of the Dream of the Planet.

And now the soul that had acted as the pathway, the progenitor, the physical father of Jesus, had come back, to destroy the falsehood, and prepare the way for the truth, before leaving this earth for the last time.

It's not saying that Yeshua was the 'son' of John the Baptist; Yeshua was a very High Soul that came from the Beyond to the earth through the doorway of a Sacred Union, two people merging in love in deep meditation, which allowed this very high vibration to be manifest here on this planet. In that sense, it was 'virgin', not arising from base sexuality, but from their highest centers, a Sacred Union, and yet through two bodies. There was a physical father, and mother, but of course the soul is not created in the act of love; it simply arrives through that doorway onto the material plane.

So now Osho, in righting something from the ancient past that went wrong, the pseudo-religion that had taken the place of the Real Teaching which he had prepared the ground for, would in the end poison him, and crucify his body. This time, the Caesar was Ronald Reagan, the Pontius Pilate: Ed Meese:

bit players, wearing masks, in an ancient drama...

After several months had passed, we went to Thailand for a week, to get new visas for India. We stayed in a hotel in Bangkok, and had the time to deeply relax and be together 24 hours a day for the first time. Those days were a kind of heaven. If I had died in one of those days, there would have been no regret in me. She melted, and washed me away in that flood. She said to me, in one moment, with a mixture of glee and fatality....THIS IS MY LAST FLING! And somewhere in the flow of love and silence, the friendship deepened as well, as she began to unload all the things on her heart which she had held for so long. She began to cry for the love of the man whom she had been with before me, a long and beautiful relationship that had ended shortly before. She looked at me, as if to say, "IS IT ALRIGHT TO FEEL THIS!?"   And I told her, "Don't worry about that boyfriend and girlfriend stuff between us right now, just let me be your friend". Then, she relaxed and cried deeply, and said, "You are a GOOD person..."

And as she spoke those words, in that simple statement, there was a hidden subtle tone in her voice, which I felt: both appreciation, and the subtle feeling of distance: that 'goodness' was too one-dimensional, was not on a level of equality or depth with her. Because she could be good, she could also be so bad, so beyond both, so powerful and needing a man with the same degree of power. I was just a flute player, not a man with a position or attitude of power in the world, or wealth. All these things were subtly, or telepathically expressed in that moment, not with recrimination, but just the fact. In that moment, I sensed she would soon be going away, and that our time would end.

She left to return to India. She had been constantly getting phone calls from Jayesh saying that Osho was asking when she would come back, and so she got her new visa and was on the plane back to Bombay. I had another week to wait for my visa, on the island, Ko Pipi. It was a time of beautiful aloneness, swimming in the sea sometimes at night, the air and the sea and my body all the same temperature; days spent meditating, watching, sometimes wondering what changes would happen now. When I returned to Poona, she so beautifully welcomed me back, it seemed that nothing had changed, and we were still living in the room next to Him together. I had found for Osho in Bangkok a crystal drinking glass with gold trim that I thought he would like, and a smaller matching one for her, of which she was really pleased.

But a shadow had come over our relation. She told me that Jayesh had been approaching her while I was away, and soon each day she would be talking about him, the things that happened in their meetings, interactions they had, how she didn't trust him. I took note that she was often talking about him, and I said to her: "You have a lot of energy for Jayesh." And she said, "REALLY? But I would NEVER be with him…"

Inside me the bell went off that says a woman is saying something that is not really the case, shall we say, but maybe she doesn't know it. I have heard that bell a few times, and now it was ringing like the bells of the cathedral in Florence on Christmas day.

One morning which I will never forget, she came out of Osho's room with a look of utter despondency and depression on her face, and said solemnly and gravely: "OSHO WILL NEVER BE WELL AGAIN!"

I said. "How can you say that?! You don't know that!"
She said: "I KNOW IT"…

Since that day her mood and character changed. I never saw her happy again. Osho's health had been deteriorating, rapidly, pain coming in his arms. It was said he was losing teeth, and he would get colds more often. Usually, if he got a cold, she would get it too, and then I would get it. Then I would have to stay out of the house for a few days, back in my hut, to get well, in order not to give it back to Him. She used to jokingly call it. 'The trasference of the flem'. Then it got worse. He would sometimes faint, just fall down while walking in His room, it was getting very bad, none of his doctors could understand what was happening, and they were sending tissue samples to laboratories in England to see what was happening with Him. That day that Nirvano became despondent was the very day that the information came back from the laboratories in London, saying that apparently Osho had been poisoned with a heavy metal, Thallium, which leaves the body after a certain time leaving no trace, but its devastating and lethal effects keep on degenerating the body. Apparently, calculating the damage in his body and the time elapsed since he left America, it was in the 12 days of his incarceration in secret jails in the USA that he had been poisoned: a very cruel and silent form of assassination–untraceable, painful, slow, and degenerative until death.

Sometimes, during one of those periods when I had caught Osho's cold and was staying outside in my hut to get well before going back into his house, I remember just lying in my hut, feeling this enormous pain inside me, an enormous love that wanted to go to her and couldn't because I couldn't see her if I was sick, and in a certain moment, that love just melted all boundaries, and started going out to the whole universe, the trees, the bamboos, the sky, everything, with no address. It was the first experience I ever felt of a love without form, without object or condition.

Now it was becoming painfully clear with each passing day as Osho's body grew weaker and older by the minute, that he had been poisoned while in jail in America, and his body was suffering more and more in this unnatural aging. As His illness was getting worse, he was having to take special medications throughout the night, for which Nirvano would have to wake up every hour or so. This would make her much more stressed-out and tense, as she could never get a deep sleep, on top of worrying more and more about his health, trying this or that medication with nothing working. It was her warriors' task, this care for His physical body; it was the thing that motivated and dominated her every moment. One night when we were sleeping together, she relaxed so deeply that the terrible thing happened, she slept through the alarm, and missed one of his medication timings. From that moment, she felt she had to sleep alone, as with me she would relax and sleep too deeply. So, it was back to my hut again.

One late evening, she came briefly to visit me, wearing a white dress, and she seemed like a frail young girl. She looked so beautiful, and fragile, it being obvious that she had not really slept in quite awhile, and she was getting more thin. We held each other closely, but her heart was tucked away somewhere, and she was afraid that she would fall asleep and miss the timing to return to the house, so she left. It was the last time we would be together.

Within a few days I was taken with Dengue fever, a very nasty and high fever which comes in October with the post-monsoon mosquitoes in India. I was in my hut for some weeks, very deeply sick. No message would come from her, no word of any kind, and in my heart I knew what had happened. Slowly, friends would tell me the gossip, that now she was with Jayesh, he lived upstairs from her, and had made his move with her in the meantime while I was out of the house and sick, and they were in love. From stories she had told me about previous relations she had had, I knew that it wasn't her way to make a clean ending, an acknowledged ending, but that's what I wanted, and I figured she probably wanted to say something too, but was worried I would be too angry: so I took the step. I wrote her a little card, saying, "THANKS for everything, it was all a great gift. I am glad you are happy in your new love"... And despite my sorrow, it was my true feeling, that what I really wanted was that she is happy. I didn't matter in the equation, I knew and accepted that; what did matter was that she would be there for Osho totally, she was his lifeline to being in a body on planet Earth, that was utterly clear to me.

That night she came to my hut to see me, and sat on my bed, and told me what had happened, that she had always expected that she and I would be back together, but while I was sick, Jayesh had started coming to her, and one thing led to another. We hugged and parted as friends, in a beautiful way. It was sweet, but bittersweet, as I knew that the tremendous joy I had was now gone. Still, in a moment like that, one can only be glad that it happened at all.

When I had recovered, a couple of months later, there came a cold morning in January, when I was playing in discourse. It had been a wonderful lively music, a high energy kind of bluegrass tune I was playing on the flute, in which Milarepa, with his Virginia finger-picking guitar style was totally at home and we really flew together, the whole band. That day, in the middle of the discourse, Osho suddenly said, "A Buddha doesn't necessary just sit and do nothing... He can be a dancer, or a carpenter, or...a FLUTE player!!" Immediately I cringed, as the bright light was on me, sitting there in front of him. He waited and slowed down a little, and paused, and it felt like he was sensing that I would close up if he loved me too much. Then, out of nowhere, Osho starting talking about the fickleness of women. He said, "And if you choose a man to love, choose a man with some higher quality, an artist, or musician. Not, a BUSINESS-man!" At that, inside me, my inner crowd was jumping up and down in a standing ovation. "Right on, Osho!" I felt, elated, supported, vindicated, released.... He was talking about us, right there in front of her, she was there in the front row. That cleared up all my doubts about whether I was still under his wing. In fact, from that day I was COMPLETELY His! Everything I did was for him, all day, every waking moment. But now there was no woman in between, no distraction. And in the work that I would be doing, grinding away at marble, he would be grinding away at me.

CHAPTER 21

The Road to Rajastan

Alas, all things in this world are meaningless;
they are but sorrow's seeds.
Small teachings lead to acts.
One should only follow teachings that are great.
Transient is this world; like phantoms and dreams,
Substance it has none. Grasp not the world nor your kin;
Cut the strings of lust and hatred;
meditate in woods and mountains.
If without effort you remain loosely in the natural state,
soon Mahamudra you will win and attain
the Non-attainment.

Tilopa, Song of Mahamudra

Here I rewind the clock, to a month before, in December, to pick up a different thread:

I was still in my hut, recovering from Dengue fever, and the separation with Nirvano. I slowly gained strength, and was recovering the ability to do simple things, like sit up in bed, eat food again, etc. As I still lay in my hut, too weak to get up, after some time had passed I had one visitor who started coming to see me, bringing me one day a glass of orange juice, one day some vitamins, another day some good Indian food. Her name was Neelam, and she was Osho's Secretary, the head of the commune. Her footsteps were so soft and silent, I would never hear her coming up the stairs, until she would appear at my hut in her beautiful saris, and big smile. We hadn't known each other much, but I knew she loved my music, and once every so often we had a nice hug in the way that those things happen easily in passing in the ashram.

She began to come to see me every day, and we talked at length of so many things. Sometimes she would make little remarks whispered under her breath, such as "I CAN'T JUST LET HER LET THIS MAN DIE", and such things, which made me realize she was quite aware of the situation of my life at that time and the end of my relationship with Nirvano, and yes, certainly I could have died in that fever as it sometimes happens in India. It was a delight to see Neelam, a 15-minute daily gift, and a respite from the lingering fevers that would grip me still in the nights and leave me drenched in sweat and quite weak. But in the days to come the fevers would slowly pass, and when she would come, we talked of so many things, especially Indian music, and her life with Osho, already at least 20 years on. I was amazed to find out that she and Nirvano had not only the same birthdate, in the same year, but even the same MOMENT, one of them born in England and one of them in India, at the same time. It was a strange coincidence, or rather synchronicity, that these two women who were the clos- est people to him, had in fact arrived on this planet on different continents at the same moment.

She had such a wonderful sense of humor, a very deep un- derstanding of Indian music, and an enormous heart, it was re- ally a great healing force to me at that time. She was beautiful as well. It was during those days, of her visits, and my slow re- covery from the fever, that I first became aware of the meaning of an old word, now quite lost in our modern world. But it is a word of tremendous value, priceless in fact. It is 'courtship'; a slow, harmonic and graceful dance of two people towards each other, never rushing, savoring each moment, each delicate turn of the road which shows another face of the other, and reveals to one another little by little the intentions of the heart. One can see it in birds, in animals, but it is something far beyond the animal. It has something of the great intentions of the Creator, measured out in time, and dance.

This dance enchanted me. It is something which perhaps only India still retains, and that only in hidden streams, not the main anymore. Modern India has been all too impatient to abandon anything old and meaningful in favor of Western-style neurosis and speed, like giving up Sarangis for electric guitars. But this silent dance nourishes the heart and allows it to unfold slowly, gracefully, in a way that is impossible if a couple moves directly into sex.

Slowly, I was able to regain strength and began to work again. Our friendship deepened, and often we would see each other, usually spending a couple of hours just being together and listening to Indian music, of which she had a vast and deep understanding and appreciation, and sometimes eating lunch together just across the garden when Osho would be eating his lunch, a few meters away.

There was a bird of paradise, a beautiful white tropical bird with a long tail, that would come at those hours every day to perch on the tree just nearby Osho while he would eat. I could see its long tail, and each day it would come at the same time, sit while he was there, and leave when Osho had left.

Some days, when Osho was not well enough to eat lunch at his table, the bird would flutter and jump here and there as if crazy, totally disturbed that Osho wasn't there. After some days when He would come back, the bird would settle down again and be at peace with its daily darshan, its few minutes with the Master.

As Neelam and I spent more time together, I came to be accepted into the Indian community of the ashram. I became one of the 'family'. This was a new world to me, and I found them to be wonderful people; many had been with Osho for more than 30 years, since the early days when he was traveling on trains all around India gathering his first disciples. They loved the melodies I would play on the flute before Osho's discourses, and I loved their easiness, friendliness, hospitality, humanness, and so much more. Their love and friendship was a great blessing to me, it made me feel completely at home in the ashram, despite the drastic change of life which had happened to me in the past months.

.

As my strength recovered, I was beginning the work of making those tables that Osho had requested. They were to be of a certain color of green marble, called ABU GREEN, which Osho specifically loved and asked that I make them from only this. I went to Bombay, and visited all the marble dealers in that city, but there was nothing to be found in the needed dimensions. All that existed in Bombay was sheets of marble, already cut to be used for walls of bathrooms or hotel lobbies. Osho had specified that I was to make it from solid rocks, It was clear that the only way to find this marble, would be to go to the source, to the deserts of Rajasthan on the border with Gujarat, in the region of Mt. Abu.

So it was arranged, I would journey there, together with one Indian English-speaking marble dealer whom the ashram had business relations with, who knew various contacts there and could guide me. I set out from Poona on the early morning train to Bombay, the Deccan Queen. It was a pleasant enough beginning, the train winding down the western ghats covered with cool forests filled with monkeys, down the long dusty valley to the thick, humid, and putrid air of Bombay. I had no idea what I would meet on this trip, and in retrospect, it was better that way.

If indeed there is an intelligence directing the flow of this universe, and I suspect there is, then Bombay has always seemed to me to be one of those particular places that this Intelligence has seen fit to use as a testing ground to determine what is the lowest possible conditions in which human life can still flourish.

The situations that pass before one's eyes and unfortunately one's nose, are difficult to imagine. For example: Dadar station... It had been 10 years now since I was wandering there in search of a Sarangi; and now, on this quest, it had only gotten more intense and more crowded. How many millions of sweating and jostling human beings pass through those gates each day, is difficult to say. But it is more like a vision of hell than anything else one can imagine; the hundreds of living bodies sleeping on the pavement wrapped in rags to keep off the mosquitoes, the chai-vendors and samosa-sellers darting here and there with bundles on their heads, screaming out sentences which through endless variations and repetitions have become completely unrecognizable as words, but nonetheless mean something to the purchasers... CHAAAAIIIIIEIEEEEE! at loud volume through the nose; the families of what seem to be dozens of children, goats and chickens, complete with cardboard boxes for suitcases, beggars whose faces have disappeared through some form of degenerative disease, people bathing in dirty pools by the side of the tracks, air reeking of human waste, woodsmoke, diesel, curry and saffron, the sheer pressure of thousands of sweating human bodies all pushing and vying to move through the same narrow passages at the same times; all the passages and tunnels stained red by the spittle of millions of people chewing betel nut and spitting out the red liquid it produces onto the walls; it is a bombardment to the senses which can only be called 'unforgettable'. I take a suburban train to Bombay Central Station, and on the way I am shoved in and out of the car at least 3 times by the sheer flux of human volume, like a tidal wave leaving the car and going back in again at each stop. At one stop a bald-

and-bullet headed fat little man simply lowers his head and takes a flying leap into the packed car, like a fullback into the line in a football game, with his head ending up somewhere between my stomach and ribcage. At last, I arrive at Bombay Central Station, and I alight to meet my fellow traveler on this adventure.

His name is Ashok Kapoor, a slightly-built, impeccably dressed and quiet-spoken little man with a neat mustache, who is to be my guide on this journey. We travel to a restaurant he knows in one of the quieter but upscale parts of the city, to talk over our itinerary. It is then that I am introduced to a peculiar aspect of Ashok's character, which came as quite a surprise to me. While sipping our cups of tea talking about our objectives and purposes, he quietly leaned over to me, pointing to all the customers in the shop, mainly composed of middle-class Indian yuppies and college students, and said: "You see all these people in here? They are here for ...SCREWING!"

Somewhat taken aback by this unexpected and extremely general statement, I questioned him what he meant about this, and he launched into a rather lengthy monologue about all the various places in Bombay where unmarrieds or un-faithfuls go to find partners in sex. Not that this was an interesting topic to me, in fact I was quite surprised, having basically thought that India was a culture that was basically repressed in that regard, at least at that time many years ago. And, I wasn't actually interested in the subject, at all. But, whether I liked it or not, he discoursed on this subject constantly and at length for the next three weeks, nonstop, wherever we were, somehow thinking that I would be interested in this, which I was not. It was to become like listening to a phonograph playing scratchy and irritating music, which I could neither turn off nor turn down, nor unplug. In his imagination, under wagons on the road, in brothels, bathrooms of restaurants, hidden alleys, construction sites, under park benches and in the bushes of by-ways, screwing, screwing, screwing, his discourse would continue, leaving practically no space of emptiness to the imagination! Every square-inch of populated space in the whole of India seemed to be covered with discreetly hidden copulating couples, in his mind. It was simply amazing. I wondered if a similar thought-stream had occupied the minds of the architects and sculptors of Khajuraho, those stunning tantric temples of Northern India covered with erotic sculptures from many centuries ago...

As this discourse continued, the train sped on, and we changed to a bus, the land became more barren dry, sparse. The intermittent green trees which one sees on the Deccan plateau near Poona were replaced by stretches of sand, and dry withered palms, thorny bushes making crude fences between 'fields', or what once were fields, but now seem to be roughly divided stretches of barren sterility. Long lines of women in dirty saris blowing in the hot wind, were carrying buckets of dust on their heads, apparently public-works projects to alleviate the effects of drought which had gripped the area for at least 4 years. There was not a drop of water to be seen, or felt. The women seemed to be moving endless mountains of sand to other endless mountains of sand, one little bucket at a time. A Kafka-esque scene of abstract existential meaninglessness could not have been portrayed more clearly. In my greenhouse condition, a relatively sheltered and pampered existence, the entire scene simply pushed my mind into greater and greater depths of depression. I took it all personally. As if the whole thing was somehow engineered to making me feel worse and worse, that I had actually done something really lousy, which I couldn't really remember what it was. But I had 'blown it', I had made this happen, it was my fault. I had put myself here in this quest which I could neither refuse nor enjoy.

We travelled by train, bus, rickshaw, scooter, and horse-buggy.

As we putted along on the little rented scooter, Ashok driving and me on the back, we were passing hills and fields withered by the sun and devoid of life. In my own inner world, I was still playing the movie in my mind of being left by Nirvano, and now I was basically wallowing in self-pity. My lamentations could be summed up in mental discourses, like: "My life will never be the same!...I was a prince, in the palace of my Lord, with the love of my life, and now I'm just on the back of this crummy scooter with my liver being jolted by each pothole, eating dust and heading off into more oblivion with each moment. It will never be the same!" These were my lengthy mental monologues, beating myself up with each jolt of the potholed road. Finally, we gave up the scooter for a horse-drawn buggy, until we reached a little town in the middle of the Rajasthani desert. In this town, there was our 'hotel'. It was a bare cement block building, whitewashed, with a few rooms, and a 'restaurant', which meant, a room with a table. In the bedroom were two beds. Or rather, there were two metal bed-frames, with two mattresses. No sheets, or blankets, towels, or wash-basin, or other furniture. If you touched the walls, the whitewash would generously come off on the hand, or clothes, and it carried that distinctly pungent smell of uncured concrete and lime and a vaguely acidic perfume of human piss. I don't know why Indian concrete smells like piss. I have the vague suspicion it has to do with the curing process, or the water that goes into it, and the lack of outhouses on construction sites; but it is always there, in every cheap concrete building in India. And this hotel was no exception. In fact, it was a case in point. The 'perfume' was everywhere, in abundance.

It was around midnight when we arrived, dead tired after an all-night bus ride and 16 hours of the bouncing horse-cart on the potted roads, so I climbed into bed. Actually, it was more like 'under' bed, because the only way to stay warm was to lie on the metal bed-frame, and cover myself with the thin mattress, as there are no blankets or sheets to be found anywhere. So, I curled up on the metal springs, covered with the thin mattress, and said goodnight to the world. I fell into deep sleep.

When I opened my eyes, It was still pitch dark outside. I awoke, or rather was awakened, by the most unearthly noise blasting into my consciousness. I thought, "Where am I? Am I waking up on Mars?" There is a temple and bus station next door to the hotel, and at 4 in the morning, the loudspeakers come on at 120 Decibels, playing classical Indian Dhrupad style vocals. To someone who is not used to this, it is weird enough, consisting of long phrases of throat-vibrated and manipulated vocalizations, which at that dark hour and high volume in that small village, were subject to extreme voltage fluctuations of the record player as well, so the whole thing would suddenly slow down to a very low and slow monotone, and suddenly speed up and rise in pitch to a frenetic superhuman squealing which would have made cows give birth out of season, I am sure. Only there weren't any cows, there was just me and Ashok, right next to the loudspeakers outside the window. Needless to say, it didn't increase my feeling of comfort and security and being-at-one-with-the-universe. On the contrary, it served as a kind of shock to my buffer system, that even that last respite of safety, deep sleep, was not at all under control, and anything could happen at anytime.

The shower was a bucket, with a huge electric coil in it. The floor of the shower being wet, if I took the coil out of the bucket, or tried to unplug it, I would get a shock strong enough to knock me off my feet. Food was once a day. It was basically chili pepper soup with a lot of garlic and a little bit of the memories of yesterdays lentils in it.

I had given my sweat-and-grit-stained white shirt to the hotel to be washed on arrival. When I got it back, it had been dyed bright blue: completely–the whole thing! I asked, "WHATS THIS??? This was a WHITE shirt!!!" And the answer they gave me, in that absolutely characteristic Indian-English, with the head rocking side-to-side and a big smile, was, "RE-ALLY white is BLUE!" Now, try to figure that one out: instead of washing the white shirt, it gets died blue, and that means it's really white. The logic is compelling!

The next day, we travel again by horse-cart and scooter, to a marble mine where we will find Abu-Green. The mine is a circular pit, or depression, about half a kilometer in diameter, and about 50 feet deep. The sides are clearly that cool soft aquamarine color of stone, called Abu-green. The bottom of the enormous expanse of the pit, blazing in the naked sun, is strewn with large boulders of marble, each one weighing about 8 tons, a block of stone roughly cut about 6 feet by 6 feet by 8 feet. On the walls of this enormous pit, are men, dressed only in a dhoti, a little kind of underwear consisting of a single wrap of cloth covering the private parts, and a rag on the head. Their dark-skinned bodies are completely covered with white marble dust, so that only the eyes are visible, making them look like white ghosts with eyes. They are barefoot, running jack-hammers, making holes in the marble in which gunpowder will be poured to blast the huge slices of stone away from the hill, which then smashes in boulders as it lands on the ground. These boulders are chipped away at by old men squatting on the stones, with hammers, chip-chip-chip; until the blocks are roughly square and dimensioned.

With a hammer and dull chisel under the burning sun, chipping away a 3 or 4 foot extension on a marble boulder: well, I calculate in my mind that's several months of chips, for each block.... And there are hundreds of these blocks strewn across the pit... The chip-chip-chip is a constant ticking of a clock, ever-present in this otherwise timeless place.

The only other sound in that moonscape is the creaking of a large hand-winch, which stands in the middle of the huge expanse of the pit. There are seven women turning the hand-crank of this enormous winch. They are dressed in dirty saris, brightly colored, and they move as one, hour after hour after hour under the scorching sun. There is a frayed metal cable from the winch which extends about 200 meters to one of these boulders, and wraps around it. As I watch the women turn the crank, after about 10 minutes the boulder has moved about one inch, slowly creeping along the floor of the valley towards the winch, where it will be loaded onto a truck. One inch every 10 minutes...200 meters to go...one block among hundreds, and thousands more to come...Creak, creak, creak goes the sound of the winch, and Chip! chip! chip go the hammers...

The life of those women and men was an unthinkable thing to me. How can one face a life, of each day, all day long under the blazing sun, turning a crank on a winch… day after cloudless day… only to move one nameless block of stone after another, from here to there… until you grow old and die? What force in the universe put them in that role, and me in mine, and we both in the same place at the same time? I was stunned. I did not consider that humans live, in this day, on this earth, in such a way. It's not that I considered myself in a better position than they. But that we live on different planets, at the same moment, in the same place. And I would die if I was in theirs. And maybe they would if they were in mine.

Each block will be put on a truck, and carried to a 'factory', which is basically a stone building in which there is a gang-saw. This is a saw with 50 parallel blades imbedded with diamonds, all arranged in even rows in a rack. The block sits under this multi-blade, and as water is cascading down on top, the saw rakes back and forth across the top of the block. SHOOM-SHOOM-SHOOM-SHOOM... the sound continues day and night, 24-7. There is a gear system, which as the blade moves a few thousand times back and forth, slowly ratchets the block UP into the saw blades a couple of millimeters. After about 5 days of this constant sawing of the diamond blades in the water and stone, the block has moved about 2 meters into the air, and has been sliced like cheese into 50 sheets of marble, ready to be sent to Bombay and installed on the walls and floor of a lobby or bathroom in a new hotel somewhere. Marble was once the sacred material of temples, as it was known since ancient times to 'fix' vibrations which pass through it, amplifying and retaining the echoes of OM chanted in the temples for thousands of years. In the moghul empire days, it became the material of choice for emperors and kings, to beautify their palaces. Now, it serves as the wall paneling for luxury apartments, hotels, restaurants in the booming tourist market of India. And that's where these sheets will end up.

We find a vein of richly colored cool green stone, I agree to it, and the order is given to start the work of blasting it away from the hillside.

I depart from this moon-scape for a few days, to accompany Ashok with his business, until my marble is ready to be taken away.

CHAPTER 22

Abu Green

As I write this, I am sitting in the shade of a great cashew tree, spreading its huge limbs a dozen meters in every direction. The winds from the nearby sea have died down in the stillness of the afternoon, and the sultry mid-day heat sits heavy with expectation of the ending of the summer and the beginning of the rains. I am in a beautiful peaceful meditation garden, called Osheanic, in the northeast of Brazil, waiting a concert I will have.

As I gaze upward, a group of very agitated monkeys have arrived overhead, their faces framed in white fur and their long tails making them look something like squirrels with human faces. They are making a raid on a birds nest in the tree above, and they get away with an egg. The angry birds quickly retaliate, and are harassing them from the air, forcing them to retreat. As they do so, in a fleeting moment while preoccupied with the attack from the birds above, one of the monkeys high in the tree is grabbed by a silent lurking serpent, a boa constrictor, who wraps itself around the monkey and holds it in its coiling and tightening deathgrip, its 'bitter hug of mortality'. The other monkeys chatter and squeal, furious, yet helpless, as they watch the death of their companion from a short distance away. When the monkey becomes still, the boa silently finishes its work, and the lifeless creature disappears slowly into the gaping mouth of the brown reptile, in this drama of the feeding cycle, ever present: the game of life-and-death precariously balanced, ready to be lost in a brief moment of unawareness. Every moment, birth and death, fruition and decay, nature unfolds in its wonderful and terrible dance of constant transformation. It is Kali dancing on the body of her husband with a necklace of skulls, and Shiva in his Cosmic spiraling ecstatic dance, unfolding the worlds and the Divine Music, and Kwan Yin, gently loving all: it is all that and more, each moment...

"We behave as if we were never going to die-an infantile arrogance. But even more injurious than this sense of immortality is what comes with it: the sense that we can engulf this inconceivable universe with our minds.

It makes no difference what complex machines scientists can build. The machines can in no way help anyone face the unavoidable appointment: the appointment with infinity.

Sorcerers, as beings on their way to dying, have someone whispering in their ear that everything is ephemeral. The whisperer is death, the infallible advisor, the only one who won't ever tell you a lie."

Don Juan, as told by Carlos Castaneda.

"Accept your simpleness, humbleness. How can you be an egoist in such a beautiful, immense, vast, infinite universe?

What ego can you have? Your ego may be just a soap bubble. Maybe for a few seconds it will remain, rising higher in the air. Perhaps for a few seconds it may have a rainbow, but it is only for a few seconds.

In this infinite and eternal existence your egos go on bursting every moment. It is better not to have any attachment with soap bubbles. No egoist in the whole history of humanity has said that ego is beautiful, that it has given him great ecstasies. All the egoists have died in frustration, despair, because the ego knows no limits. So you are always frustrated."

Osho

With the marble for my work of making Osho's tables being blasted at the mine, we pursued for a few days the things that Ashok needed to do, which was procuring and shipping the marble to be used for Osho's new 'art porch'. This was to be a balcony off the side of his bed room, which would be used as a temporary bedroom while his room would be remodeled. There was a very particular type of Abu-Green that had been found here for this work, with a very intense and geometrical crystal pattern, bright green and silvery white, and we proceeded to the place where it had been cut into sheets to get it shipped back to Poona.

We had arrived to a factory in the desert, many miles from nowhere. The factory consisted of a large stone building with one side open, and a large gang-saw in the middle of the floor, nothing else. There were two hundred or so workers there, dressed in dhotis and rags on their heads, and they were carrying sheets of marble from the saw to the truck. All outside the ground was littered with broken chunks of marble, and plaster, which was used to hold the marble in place under the saw. We were here for the day, while Ashok's marble was being loaded onto the trucks for transport back to Poona. It would take about 6 hours at least, with nothing for me to do. So, being the fool that I am, I wandered off into the desert to meditate... Or so I thought.

It was about 45 degrees Celsius that day, something like 110 in the shade, in fahrenheit. To cope with the extreme heat of the sun, I had taken a tip from the locals, and tied a large green cloth around my head, like a Rajput turban. But the cloth I had used was a cheaply dyed green cotton that I had found in a shop in the local village, and as I would sweat, the green dye leached out of the cloth and would run down my face and beard, making me look something more like a Pirate of the Caribbean than a budding young sculptor. I had a shoulder bag of cotton, with a water bottle, and sunglasses. I crossed the compound of the factory and the highway next to it, and made my way into the desert looking for a quiet place to close my eyes for a time, for the first time in days. The land was divided into square plots separated by cactus rows, thorny bushes woven into fences. It was sandy, dry, and desolate, with only one tree, a small thorny kind of jacaranda, trying its very best to meagerly and humbly stand up under the withering sun which blasted down like a hammer on an anvil. There were no signs of humans, except for a few goats about a quarter of a mile away, and perhaps there was someone over there near the goats; this I couldn't clearly make out in the shimmering heat waves rising off the desert floor.

I sat under this poor tree, and closed my eyes, and within a couple of minutes, I heard a voice clearly whispering inside my mind:

"Death is nearby...".

This startled me, as I didn't consider myself to be a visionary or clairvoyant by any means, and am not given to receiving whispered messages from spirits habitually, so I opened my eyes to see if something was around. I thought that maybe there was a cobra slithering nearby, or a scorpion or some other monstrosity-of-the-Indian-desert of which I am unaware. I couldn't see anything alarming in the dead expanse of sand all around, only I could make out the figure of a man somewhere around those goats a few hills away.

Time passed, 10 minutes or so, and as could be expected in these kinds of movies, the man in the distance started approaching me, shouting in a loud and angry voice. He was tall, perhaps in his 50s, somewhat skinny, with a large dirty turban and unshaven for the last few days, with a handlebar mustache, which pegged him as a 'Rajput'. The Rajputs were the only people in India who never were conquered by the British, having held them off for 300 years. That maybe gives you, my dear reader, a glimpse into their attitudes about foreigners. They don't like them, period. And he didn't like me. That was obvious. He blustered up to me, shouting and gesturing, in a way that was unmistakably not saying, "Sorry Sir, but you must take your leave..." It was more like, "What the HELL are YOU doing here....!!!????" I stood up, and he was very angry. He was shouting at me in Mirwadi, or Rajput, the local dialects, which were different than the usual Hindi that I was used to hearing. I couldn't understand a word, but the intention was quite clear: challenging, confronting.

A tall man, bony with a big mustache, he reached out to me and grabbed the cotton bag that was on my shoulder. I could smell that he had been drinking. That's an understatement: he smelled like he was completely pickled in straight alcohol. He aggressively looked in my bag, and acted as if he was going to keep the things in it, my cheap sunglasses and a water bottle. "Alright", thought I, "This is ransom for being on his crummy property, big deal, let's get out of here and be done with it". So I gestured and spoke something in Indian English, like, "Ok, baba, no problem, me going..." smiling and acting obsequious and calming. But that didn't placate him. He picked up a rather large red rock and started waving it menacingly at me, and I got the distinct feeling that he wasn't really bluffing, and was on the verge of trashing me out with this rather nasty-looking big red stone.

Well, this had gone a little too far for me. Suddenly, civility evaporated altogether from my personality, and at that moment, something in me caught on fire. BIG fire. There was no way that I was going to let this guy hit me with a rock in the middle of this stupid desert for nothing. I picked up a bigger rock, and I ROARED at him, "Drop it or I'll KILL you!" And, I meant it. And in that batting of an eyelash, a few thousand years of 'civilization' simply evaporated for the both of us, and for a few very pregnant moments, we stood there facing each other in the middle of this desert, two cave-men with our rocks, ready to kill or maim, for the sake of survival, or territory, or who knows what. The silence was deafening, the hot wind was blowing with a dry sound through the jacaranda leaves and thorns, and the blood was pounding in my ears. And I was a lot madder than he at that moment, as I was completely fed up with all the crap I had been putting up with for the past week, and he seemed to realize that I was also younger and stronger, and not the usual tourist, so he did drop his rock. He backed off, and started moving away. I did the same, and started picking my way across those damned rows of thorny hedges, trying to get back to the so-called 'safety' of the factory. It was slow going, my pants would catch and tear on the thorns as I climbed over the hedges, and at the same time, hidden by the rows of cactus, I could hear him running and shouting. I realized that he knew where the paths through the thorns were, and he was reaching the factory compound before me. By the time I crossed the highway and reached the compound, he was there amongst all the workers in their dhotis and marble dust, shouting and pointing at me, and they began dropping their tools and coming to where I was.

I thought to myself, "Oh, shit. Indian mob violence: and I'm the star of the show.." Something started moving, feeling very weird in my stomach, like everything was going off-tilt with horror movie music as the background. They surrounded me, about 200 men at least, and the atmosphere was not friendly, to put it mildly. There were 3 men in white collar shirts, obviously the factory managers, who were trying to hold back this growing mob at this point which was surrounding us, and as they pushed with frantic looks on their faces to hold the crowd of men back physically, they shouted at me, "What have you DONE?".

I shouted back; "I haven't done anything! I just kept this guy from hitting me with a rock!".

They said, "He is telling them that you raped his daughter!"

The feeling in my guts was suddenly something like a galaxy splitting up and spinning out of control into dissolution and entropy. At that point my Rajput 'acquaintance' very dramatically moved towards me in front of the entire mob and hit me in the face. I knew if I did anything in that moment, I was dead. An old and very ugly woman with a very broken nearly toothless mouth started screaming at me from three feet away and waving a large rock in front of my face. Her face was seething with pure hatred. The entire mob started picking up chunks of marble and moving towards me. One of the managers shouted at me to "GET INSIDE, GET INSIDE!!" And I went into the open factory, which was an enclave with 3 walls and one open side. The crowd started to follow me, step by step cornering me with their stones in their hands.

Dear reader, I must tell you that this was not just fear, this was TERROR that I felt. My knees were flapping uncontrollably, like a rabbit trapped by the hounds. There was nowhere to go, just this stone building of 3 walls, with me in it, and the mob converging on me. The horror of the situation was made worse by the feeling in me of utter helplessness, in the face of the absurdity of it all, how quickly, 'unfairly' and without justification it all unfolded. The man nearest to me raised up his rock to throw it at my face, and with crystal clarity as I saw the big, very rough and angular stone in his hand, the last thought that I had flashed very clearly into my mind, saying, "THIS is going to really HURT!"

And at that moment, time stopped for me. What transpired, did so without any way of measuring how long it took. By the clock, it could have only been a split-second, but in my experience, it was absolutely slow, lucid, dreamlike. I didn't see my whole life flashing before my eyes, no. It was more that the sum total of my life experience was felt by me, like a great big nothing. It was just a big soap bubble that had appeared, and now was about to burst, and NOTHING had happened. I could almost see this 'bubble', at its last moment before bursting and disappearing. I had found nothing, I was dying for no reason in this hell-hole in the desert, for no purpose, and my life has been nothing; just a bubble that came, and now is going.

Needless to say, this was a huge shock to me. I had the lifelong belief that I was living purposefully, a 'seeker of truth', on a spiritual path, living meaningfully, but in this ultimate mirror of the last moment of life, it was just my dream. Nothing has happened. I was going as empty-handed as I had come into this world.

At that point, without thought, my body simply started doing things for which I have no explanation or preparation. Instead of cowering and ducking the rocks, I ran straight up to the crowd, opened my arms, and shouted, "Throw your rocks, I've done NOTHING!" They stopped for a moment, as this wasn't really expected, and it's more difficult to throw a rock at somebody who is standing right in front of you with his arms open. In that instant, someone yelled out, in Indian English, "WHAT HAPPENED!?!?" And I VERY dramatically in super fast motion, acted out in pantomime, like a madman, the scene that had transpired between me and the Rajput. I was insane. I had no mind. I was jumping here and there and gesturing in a totally mad and dramatic way. And they were thrown into the 'gap' looking at this madman. The whole crowd started jabbering to each other, and wondering what to do, and in that moment's pause, two of the white-collar guys grabbed me by the armpits, dragged me out a hidden side-door behind the saw, and shoved me into a tiny Maruti car which squealed tires and pulled out of the compound. They took me to a truck and hid me under burlap bags, the truck took me to a scooter in another town, then to another truck, then to a motorcycle, all strangers, one to another, simply passing me hand-to-hand like a sack of contraband and transporting me rapidly and wordlessly out of the district. By some miracle, I got back to the Martian hotel by sunset, and as the last rays of the merciless sun faded behind the brown and distant hills, I pondered my weird life from the rooftop terrace overlooking the twilight on the desert.

Ashok got back to the hotel late at night. He had very conveniently disappeared when all the trouble started, my guide, champion and protector, waiting meekly behind the crowd to see if I would get creamed or not, but making certain that he wouldn't get hit by any errant stones aimed for my cranium. He said that after I left, an old woman appeared at the factory who had witnessed the standoff in the desert between me and the Rajput, and she told it to the mob, that the Rajput was making up the story about rape in order to save face for having lost the showdown. As causing blood to flow from a foreigner is a very serious crime in India, he had put them all in jeopardy, and the crowd didn't appreciate it much. They beat him up instead of me. Rajput justice? Instant karma? Call it what you like, the sun comes up the next day just as bright and hot, in a cloudless sky. And I would still be there, with work yet to do in that place.

CHAPTER 23

Alpha Male

I am already given to the power that rules my fate.
And I cling to nothing, so I will have nothing to defend.
I have no thoughts, so I will see.
I fear nothing so I will remember myself.

(chant of Toltec warriors as told by Carlos Castaneda)

The next few days of my life amongst the marble unfolded in a similar vein. I had accepted the conditioning of being a certain type of man in the West Coast 'spiritual' scene of the 70s and 80s, not macho, vulnerable at times, emotionally self-indulgent, 'sensitive'; at least appearing so, although I couldn't say that I really knew what that meant at that time, other than being sensitive to my own emotional dramas and imagined wounds. I was now in a place which quickly and ever more clearly showed me that in order to survive I would have to totally drop that very limited mode of existence, and BE HERE.. in THIS situation. OR DIE! It meant that every time I would be at a roadside cafe, every glass of tea or chapati that I would try to get to satisfy cravings of thirst or hunger, I would be surrounded by a large group of males who instinctively move against anyone who shows weakness, as a pack. I would have to stand tall, arms crossed and muscles flexed, outwardly projecting the very clear message. "Don't mess with me!" at every moment.

That was what was respected there. On that ground, a dialogue could begin, an exchange could happen. I could buy a chapati, a cup of tea. Without that, I was jostled, pushed aside, laughed at, derided. So, I played the game. I put on the armor, and lived in it. And I got into it. I had to be a man among men, not like in America of the 1980's, but more like the middle ages, everyone with their club and axe, ready to defend themselves. Of course, the clubs were more in the aura or psyche than in the hand, but they were there just the same.

If I was in a chai shop, and wanted less sugar in the tea, it wouldn't work to say, "A little less sugar, please". It only worked to dramatically throw the tea to the ground, smash the glass on the floor in angry disgust and shout, "SACAR NE!" in a loud voice. Then, they would bring me a tea with less sugar. If I was waiting for a man to come with a tractor to haul my marble away, it wouldn't work to wait. I had to ride out on a motorcycle, find him and physically block his tractor on the road and turn him around, make him an offer he couldn't refuse, literally, or else nothing would happen. THAT language was understood: force…the show of power and the willingness to back it up; power games, all day long. This was a different kind of therapy group. This was meditation in action, in a strange way.

Being in the world, and not of it, or so totally in it and one with it, that those separations didn't matter anymore. I stopped thinking about when I would get back to Poona. Forget all about it. I even stopped wondering if I would survive this. There was JUST this.

At that time, 'by chance', I was sitting in a crummy lobby of a crummy hotel one afternoon waiting for Ashok, and there occurred one of those miniscule events which seem so insignificant that they hardly merit notice, but, in truth, it changed my life. I picked up a weathered magazine, some Indian monthly that was there on the coffee table which had never had coffee on it, as there was none in that lobby or nowhere within 50 kilometers of there. And there, on the cover was a smiling somewhat portly face with a thin mustache, radiating jovial warmth, and I read the name: 'Hariprasad Chaurasia…Master of the Indian Flute'. The article was my first introduction to the man, and it struck a chord in my heart, and I knew that I would have to meet him. I didn't know how. I had heard his name years ago. Osho had spoken of him as a childhood friend with whom he had played flutes together. It was a sad story, in which Osho as a boy also played his flute with a friend who played tablas. One day they swam across a river in monsoon when the river was a swollen torrent full of whirlpools, and the friend tragically didn't make it, and drowned. Despondent, Osho threw his flute into the river and never played again. But he loved the flute-playing of Hariprasad, and went at lengths to describe its beauty, its depth, its serenity. I learned years later, from Osho's nurse, that the last night that the Master was alive on planet earth, he chose to spend the whole night listening to Hariji's flute.

I knew then that I HAD to meet this man. I didn't know why. But I would, I resolved, from that dusty little lobby of a hotel in a forgotten town in the middle of the desert of Rajasthan.

As the days passed, my precious green marble was blasted off the hillsides, and transported to a small factory. I thought that things were well on the way, and I would be out of there soon, but, as Gurdjieff used to say, "Don't expect roasted chickens to fly into your mouth."

The factory was a little shack made out of concrete blocks and a tin roof baking under the Rajasthani sun, with a bare light bulb that didn't work. In this little work-shack, there was a different kind of saw, one enormous round diamond blade, on a moving table, that could cut these rough-hewn blocks into rectangular shapes for my tables. There were 4 burly Indian men working there, and the factory owner was there for the first 10 minutes. He had his hair newly washed and oiled after getting paid for my marble. He told his laborers to do what I said, and then he promptly left, not to be seen again.

As soon as he was out of sight, their allegiance to my commands vanished like clouds in the blue and burning sky of Rajasthan. They basically took a holiday, and spent their days laughing and telling jokes, while I wrestled with the 400 kg. blocks of marble, with a crowbar, and wedges and sledgehammers. No amount of angry yelling at them would get them to lift a finger for me. And please remember, dear reader, this was not in these times of mobile phones, internet, capucchinos in the foyer; this was just me and them, in this little work 'shack', a cement box in the middle of the desert smelling vaguely of urine, with one bare light bulb hanging from the ceiling, a lightbulb that of course didn't work, with no way for me to contact another soul; with no food and no water all day long.

At that time, I was smoking in order to ward off the hunger which would often come while working for 12 hours without anything to eat. It would cut the craving for food for a few hours, even with the stomach empty. There wasn't peanut machines in the lobby. There wasn't even a lobby... just a bare building with a saw and a tin roof burning in the sun, my stones, the blazing heat, and my total frustration and inability to make anything happen.

At one point, terribly hungry and tired, I sat down, drenched in sweat, and began to smoke my pipe. The Indian workers, one by one slowly came over, and gathered around me, gesturing that they would like some tobacco. They smoke in a 'chillum', a little crude conical tube of clay, drawing the smoke straight into the lungs, and it is usually a very cheap tobacco which smells more like burning leaves than Marlboro Filters. Pipe tobacco is a different ballgame: it's quite heavy, and you don't inhale it much into the lungs, just drawing it into the mouth and throat. So I offered them a clump and they put it into their chillum. They lit it up and drew it deeply into their lungs, one-by-one. As I watched silently, their faces slowly turned green, and they tried their best without success to suppress the coughs which forced them to expel the smoke. They nearly fainted. They looked at each other, and at me, and it was clear from their gestures that they were thinking something like, "This guy must be SUPERMAN to smoke THIS shit!" And suddenly, without further ado, I became in their eyes ALPHA MALE. They proceeded to bring me a chair, to find me some water, a cup of tea, shade over my head... in short, I became Lord Greystoke, alias Tarzan, and they, my boys. I never could have dreamt a more sudden or unexpected turn-around in fortunes than what had just occurred. They very diligently, quickly and conscientiously did ANYTHING I would ask of them, moving the blocks onto the saw, turning them, lifting them, and cutting them carefully. The work which couldn't move forward in two weeks was completed in less than two days, and my blocks were loaded on the trucks for the journey back to Poona.

CHAPTER 24

The Way Home

I am swimming in deep blue water at the foot of the highest
mountain in the world, Mauna Loa. Its snow-covered peak
rises above the clouds on this morning on the Big Island of
Hawaii, as I tread water, looking all around this turquoise bay.
Actually, it's called the highest mountain, because its measured
from bottom to top, but the bottom is way under the sea, maybe
4 miles or so underneath my treading legs, so, it's all relative.
Anyway, the mountain is HUGE, and its power enters into me,
a silent blue deep feeling of awe, as I wait for the dolphins to
arrive.

At first there is no sign of them, anywhere. All seems to be
a silent deep blue world of emptiness. I am struggling along
with fins and mask, in this deep bay in the shadow of the mountain, occasionally I see a fin, far off in the distance, or the splash
of some precocious youngster spinning by the side of his parents.

They are announced softly by the high sounds, like whistles, or
songs of another world. Faintly I can hear them underwater, and
then from out of the depths, they appear like a mirage, a group
of silvery dolphins emerging towards me, traveling in a pod of
6 or 7. They move effortlessly, making no sign of being disturbed by my nearby passage. Again they disappear into the
depth, again they return, this time a little closer. I swim a little
more quickly, to keep up with them for a moment. There are
two of them very close to me, and I swim up into the middle
space between them. One of them must be very old, with many

circular scars on his flanks, from a type of shark which just bores a hole and then drops off. But right now, there are no sharks, just this beautiful morning in this deep blue world, and we three side by side for this one encounter in this life. We travel together for a few minutes, nearly shoulder to shoulder. I can almost feel them saying to me, "Come on, Come on!..a little faster..." but they slowly gain distance and disappear again into the blue infinity beyond.

Another group swings up from the turquoise depths, and this time there are what seem to be teenagers amongst them. They are a bit smaller, and quite playful: two of them are making love just next to me, in a mode so sensual and playful, anyone can understand what is happening. There is no notice taken by the rest of the 'family', no sideways nasty looks, no frowns or admonitions, no cynical smirks or winks. In fact it seems as normal as breathing and taking a walk together. It makes me wonder what happened to us humans, that we make such a fuss about who is rubbing bodies with whom, and when, and where. For these delightful creatures, all is truly natural, and sheer joy. Along with the family are babies, with their mothers, and from time to time they try to emulate the spinning of their parents, but it takes on the form of a somersault and very ungraceful but comical flop back into the water....

Alas, the morning is nearly finished, and we climb back on the boat for the return to the harbor. A few miles nearer to home, the harbor of Kona, the captain notices something in the distant water, the smallest splash of a silvery fin under the surface, something impossible for me to pick out from the millions of diamond studded waves all around in the brilliant sun. But he sees it, and slowly brings the boat over that way. As we stop, and re-enter the water, I see something which simply makes me gasp in astonishment. There are 7 or 8 manta-rays, enormous, just circling us in the water under the surface, and I jump in and very slowly swim in their direction. They are about 4 meters across, deep purple on top and silvery white on the bottom, shaped like bat-winged extraterrestrials. Their eyes are on extensions, little pods to each side, and their mouths are a huge gaping cavern into which I could easily swim. But they regard me so benignly, in fact, with what seems to be as much curiosity as I have for them; we swim and circle each other in a magnificently graceful dance, in which I feel to be flying above the clouds with them, free of body, free of mind. For a time I am swimming on top of one, about 5 feet above him, and as he flaps his magnificent wings, so gracefully, I find myself flying, caught in his magic waves, as he silently cruises below me.

After the magical swim of the morning, in my ruminations on the veranda of house where I am staying, my mind returns back to the stones and sun of Rajasthan.

With Ashok's marble for the art-porch, and my marble for the tables on trucks bound for Poona, our work was finished there. The only thing left was to go home. But that was not such a simple task. The draught conditions, which had worsened constantly for more than 4 years now in that place, had become so bad that on all the highways out of the district, crowds were rolling boulders onto the roads and robbing the passengers of public taxis with bows and arrows. So, we had to find an alternate plan. Instead of taking the highway to the nearest big city with a rail station, Udaipur, we could bypass on dirt roads the troubled zones and go straight in the direction of Mt. Abu, a journey of about 300 kilometers. So we travelled in an ancient Ambassador, one of those big Indian cars that looks like a black turtle from the 1940s, and rumbled and bounced along dusty dirt bi-ways through lands where there are still hyenas and cheetahs. We came upon ancient temples abandoned long ago in the dusty jungles, without rain for so long. The statues in the temples, Abu Green of course, were still radiating the polish which was lovingly put into those stones hundreds or thousands of years ago. The radiant smile of the Mahaviras, the sensual curves of the Apsaras, all sang of a time when 'time' was not so important, when labor happened with love and intent, and eternity-value: that is, with attention put to that which will endure forever. And in a village near those temples, we came upon a group of marble sculptors slowly and quietly working away at the figured columns of a new temple, the same figures I had seen in the temple in the jungle. There was one little man squatting by a column on the ground, working so concentratedly, with a tiny chisel, bringing out the features of one figure, and he himself radiating a silent joy, a bliss in fact. He was one with himself and his action. I didn't want to leave.

We came upon villages hidden in the hills, where every single person looked exactly the same. The women, vibrantly alive, barefoot with bangles, were radiantly and wildly beautiful, dressed in red Saris. Their faces, all the same face, their bodies, all the same lean and compact shape.. the entire town! With a wild expression, the alertness of foxes or wild animals, which one never sees on the bored and complacent faces of modern and fat western people. It was clear that no person outside of this village had married an outsider here in centuries, every face was identical.

We reached to Mt. Abu, which rises like a vision out of the desert between Rajasthan and Gujarat. If a child were to draw a picture of a mountain, it would look something like that, as it rises up out of the desert floor as if it had been shaped and piled up by two hands, and patted into place. Ashok took me to the temples of Dilwara, which from outside were disguised as mounds of earth, almost invisible as you approach. They had been built about 8 centuries ago, and constructed in such a way as to fit into the hillside. If you didn't know they were there, you would never see them. It was done to hide them from the Mohammedan conquerors, who often in their fanatical interpretation of their narrow idea of Islam, made it a point to destroy images created by other religions. I guess it makes them feel less insecure in their own choices and beliefs, why exactly that is I have never been able to understand. It's an aggressive form of the ostrich-head-in-the-sand formula; first, you destroy the beautiful creations of other belief-systems, and then say: "Well, I don't see any other alternatives, so what I'm doing MUST be right!"

Once inside the temples, the vision that is presented to the mind boggles the imagination. White and green marble, carved in infinite variety of human and divine figures, interlaced with animal figures. Men, women, serpents, elephants and tigers and celestial maidens, interlaced in infinite spirals of creation, whose overall effect would simply stop my mind with the infinite variety of the manifold universe. There were huge marble lotuses floating down from the ceiling, carved with such delicacy that the thousands of petals are transparent. I was told by Ashok that a man would begin one of those lotuses, and perhaps his grandson would be the one who would finish it. A cloth was spread under the carving at the beginning of the day, and at sunset, the dust that was gathered would be weighed out to the sculptor in gold powder. The artisans worked for 300 years. When the temples were completed, the workers went on, and used the scraps of marble to create an entirely other temple, just from their joy of creation. There were temples even dedicated to each of the elephants that carried the marble up from the desert to the top of this mountain.

As I stared into these figures towering overhead, faces of Ghandarvas and Apsaras intertwined in a celestial dance, with large eyes and thin aquiline noses, I turned for a moment and saw the faces of some Indian tourists who were there staring up at the same goddesses. They had the same faces, the thin aquiline noses and prominent inquisitive eyes of the Gujaratis. I was struck with the timelessness of it all, the sculptors carving these reflections of themselves to be viewed by their descendants centuries later.... Perhaps, even viewed by themselves, in other bodies, in other roles.

We arrived to Allahabad several days later, a city much like any other big dirty Indian town, except for the camels walking on the streets. We found a train to Bombay, and boarded it, and it was not without regret that I left behind my days in the desert. I had found something which I had forgotten all about, from another lifetime.

CHAPTER 25

The Gates of Hell, and Heaven

Whoever clings to mind
sees not the truth of what's beyond the mind.
Whoever strives to practice Dharma
finds not the truth of Beyond-practice.
One should cut cleanly through the root of the mind
and stare naked.
One should thus break away from all distinctions
and remain at ease.
One should not give and take but remain natural,
for Mahamudra is beyond all acceptance and rejection.

Tilopa, Song of Mahamudra

One day, a Warlord came to visit Rinzai, the great Zen Master. This Lord was the ruler of an entire domain, a military commander of great fame, with thousands of soldiers and servants. He bowed before Rinzai, and asked:
"Sir, where are the gates of heaven, and of hell?"

Rinzai replied, "How can you ask such an idiotic question?. You must be retarded!"

No-one had ever insulted this Lord in this manner, and lived. Humiliated and enraged, the Lord put his hand on his sword, to teach Rinzai a lesson…

Rinzai then said, "Here opens the gates of hell…"

Realizing the significance of these words, the Lord withdrew his hand from the sword.

Rinzai then said: "Here opens the gates of heaven."

The Lord bowed deeply, and withdrew.

When I got back to Poona, Neelam immediately asked me what had happened, because on the day when I nearly got killed, at least 40 people in the ashram had asked her, "Where is Devakant?" I told the story, it was retold in the way that gossip spreads in the ashram. Later in the afternoon Hasya asked me to tell it to her, later Nirvano and DevaRaj, and by the evening it was being talked about in Osho's room to Him. Apparently he had chuckled when they told him that the mob was after me because of a story 'with a woman'. It couldn't have been farther from the facts, but it's funny how things get turned around as they pass from one person to another. I suppose that happened a lot at the Ranch too. I wasn't expecting to get condolences for my brush with death, and Osho certainly was not the person who would pat me on the back and say, "There, there, Devakant, it's o.k. now.." Somehow without it being said, it was understood by me a long time ago that this game was one in which the stakes are very high. And like the Tibetans say when you close yourself into seclusion in a cave for 3 years of meditation: "If you get sick, you get sick. If you die, you die." It was like that.

I wished to leave behind the incident. As Soon As Possible and get on with what I needed to do now, which was BIG.

Every day, all day, I worked on the tables. The first part of the task was three tables: one, a cube about two feet on every side, carved from a solid rock, into a shape with a thick top, and supporting graceful legs, with a kind of marble knot tying them together. This was for his bathroom. The other two were massive slabs, five feet by 2 feet, and 5 inches thick, on a supporting marble base, to be on either side of his sitting chair, where he spends most of the day. The green marble is hard, brittle, crystalline. The steel chisels which I was using are tipped with carbide, sent from Germany. They are made for European marble, which is softer and has smaller crystals; these tools often shatter against the very hard Indian marble, and it takes months to wait for replacements. I must slowly convince the marble to change, to release its chips one-by-one, painstakingly. My arms grow heavy with the labor; to change the shape of the stone even a little requires a hard labor of a full day, and some days pass where I do not see any change at all, no matter how hard I work.

Not being familiar with the technology of working marble at that time, I constantly came up against the limitations of my knowledge and the available means at hand. The only electric tools I had there were tools meant for carpentry; the rasps and files, of cheap Indian steel, work even badly on teak and rosewood and sal wood, but they become almost instantly dull and useless on the hard crystalline stone. I had a small Japanese electric saw, fitted with a diamond blade to cut grooves into the stone, which then allows me a point of entry into the surface, to chip away pieces from the block. To use this saw, I must have a constant flow of water streaming onto the blade, without which the friction of the diamonds on the marble melts the blade and destroys as well the surface structure of the stone. The saw, having been made for woodwork, is not insulated for use with water.

The place where I work is a slab of concrete under a huge peepal tree, whose branches are so enormous they could easily shade a few hundred people sitting under them. This slab, my 'workshop', was once a pump-house, as far as I can tell, because of the stumps of iron pipes going deep down into the ground still sticking up here and there above the concrete. The stubble of these pipes protrudes a few rusty inches above the surface of the concrete. I come to realize in a 'shocking' way what these rusty stumps are; while I work with the saw, it is perhaps 100 degrees in the shade under the tree, wearing shorts and sandals, and sweat pouring from my face constantly and profusely. The saw in my hand is running on 220 volts of current, with water pouring onto the blade from a little hose in a bucket that I rigged up, hanging over my head, and it flows onto my hand as well, water spraying profusely everywhere as it cuts.

In a certain moment, as I turn to follow the cut along the side of the stone, my bare ankle barely touches the iron pipe stubble in the ground behind me, and the next thing I know I am flat on the ground, feeling as if I had been hit with a telephone pole across my whole body. I tried to understand what had happened, but it didn't occur to me until the 2nd time that I picked myself off the ground, that the rusty iron pipe buried 100 feet in the ground was acting as a potentially lethal ground to the wet electric saw in my hand, the voltage arching across my entire body when my skin would touch the metal of the pipes near my feet. I realize that it is only luck and the weak amperage of the Indian electricity that I was not dead, yet again. "Electricity-water-bare skin-wet metal - earth….hmmm… bad combination!" I thought to myself. I try to find a way to hook up a constant ground wire for the saw, wear rubber sandals, and keep my ankles away from the pipes!

As the days moved on, I was becoming desperate to move forward with this work. In retrospect, there was a compulsion in me to produce, to complete things, be recognized particularly by Him, that I was fulfilling the task, being good and right, doing the thing that was put to me to do, that apparently he was waiting for, and that was constantly getting reminded to me by the women who took care of his personal space. Neelam would ask me every few days, "When will the tables be ready?", or Shunyo would ask me with a huge smile, "Will they be ready by His birthday?" The days disappeared, and the future appeared to me as a vanishing mirage on the desert floor, with no water in sight.

I loved doing things for Him, but mixed in that love was a wish, and hence the tense expectation, to be esteemed and appreciated, to have him say, "Good, Devakant!"... I wanted that so badly.

This was such a big part of my identity then: I WAS what I did. My self worth was completely identified with this in my mind. Failure in the task for me was failure as a person. That was my 'Book of Law'... my own personal judgement system that ruled my life. In short, the task was everything, the judge inside me was sitting in black robes on the high bench, gavel in hand, hanging his decision on failure or success, judged by Osho's reaction, and the rest of my life could be sacrificed for it.

And yet, through this process was happening a 'crystallization' in me. All was becoming concentrated in one unbending intent. My whole being was forced into one channel, one action. I sensed somehow, dimly, that Osho knew this, that he was playing with me, gently, yet firmly, using my own value system to dismantle the programs in my personality. To complete the task was all I wanted, I had no other thought, no other diversion, and the future dissolved for me into a seemingly endless pall of marble dust, which in order to survive I simply had to forget about, and just live each day one moment at a time, with no hope of exit. And although all this was occurring just a few yards from his home, I couldn't see Him anymore! With my allergy to marble dust, I was constantly coughing and sneezing, and I couldn't go to take my seat in the daily discourses, as it was forbidden to cough or sneeze in the discourses. My seat was there waiting, sometimes in the front row and sometimes in the second or third, but there was no way to be there with bronchitis, you couldn't cough in Buddha Hall.

My only consolation, as time, days, weeks, months passed, was that, because of my years of experience as a carpenter, I knew that every task was an accumulation of many small tasks, of finite number. And that if I could just complete each step as it presented itself to me, in time, the task would be accomplished. It was beyond the capacity of my mind to count the days until something would actually be 'finished'. In total, it looked infinite and hopeless, but it was within my grasp to complete small actions in a daily way: taking off the corner of this block… making level and smooth the surface of that one… carving the right shape on one side of a table leg, then another. In this way, the days passed, the hot and dusty and sweaty days under the peepal tree. The life of the commune was far away, although it was just on the other side of the road. But no sannyasins would ever pass by that side of the road, which looked like a dusty and muddy Indian construction site and totally uninviting to the clean-robed and aesthetic westerners visiting the ashram. So, my days were passed in a solitude made more intense by the irony of the invisible walls separating me from the life of the thousands of other disciples just a few steps away. Here I was, and here I would stay, even if it is forever. And I had set it up. 'Gotcha!'.

Do not go to the window for better seeing…
Better abide at the center of your being…
The more you leave it, the less you learn….

Lao Tzu, 500 BC

Grinding the marble was laborious. I had the uncanny feeling as the days and weeks wore on that I was being ground away by the marble. My impatient and restless mind was being filed away moment by moment by this seemingly impossible-to-fulfill task, of which the actions themselves gave me no pleasure. My mind found it to be disgusting, being covered with slimy marble dust all day long. I had rags wrapped around my face to keep from breathing the dust, and goggles on so I could see, and earmuffs

The first table

on to block out the screeching of the marble saw. My arms ached, my fingers became muscular, calloused and stiff; I could not play music, both from the condition of my hands and the lack of time. At sunrise I would be at the marble, and fall into bed late in the night. In the ashram, at mealtimes, the line to get food would begin an hour before lunch and last until the food was nearly gone, at least until all the salads and vegetables and tandoori chapatis were gone. I had no time to spend waiting an hour in line for food with 10,000 German and Japanese visitors in the midst of therapy groups, so I would take off my powdery apron and go to get something at the end of the hour, when the crowd had passed. Except, by then, most of the food had passed too, and I would find a few boiled carrots and some white rice, with the occasional rubbery tofu intended for the terminally ill, it seemed. The food in the ashram was usually

very good, but at that end-of-the-lunch-rush, the only bits left
here and there resembled the kind of food one might get in a
cancer ward of a third-world hospital. This didn't do me too
well, my aching arms were crying out for protein which was
nowhere to be seen, and my pockets had long ago emptied of
any personal cash reserve which might make possible some sup-
plementary visits to a local restaurant. In short, I found myself
at the mercy of the situation, and resigned myself to my fate. I
was losing weight each day, as I was basically working in a sauna
outdoors in the summer months of India. My deep-set tendency to emotionally bewail my fate was exactly offset by the
energy expenditure of the labor… I had very little time to think
about it, just the time and energy to go on.

At this time, there arrived in Poona a little woman whom I had
met at the ranch, 5 years before. In the disco at the ranch, in
the early years, after a very long work day, we would be madly
dancing and always find each other on the dance-floor. She is
an ecstatic being, a crazy Chilean dancer and mystic woman
named Aseema. She would always show up just as the song was
playing; "She's a Maniac, MANIAC…" She loved my music, and
I loved her, from day one. Now, we started running into each
other at teatimes, when I would dash into the ashram to get a
cup of chai in the afternoon. Then when I could no longer
come to the ashram for breaks, she would come and find me
during her tea breaks working in the kitchen, her pockets full
with smuggled cheese sandwiches, a luxury which kept me alive
in those months. Sometimes she would come, at 11 at night
and find me grinding away there under the tree, white powder
and slime covering me head to foot, and streaks of tears running
down my cheeks, caused by my sheer frustration at the limits of
my patience and the impotence of my muscles in the face of
those maddening and unchangeable stones; Polishing, Polishing,
Polishing. Using finer and finer diamonds, rubbing it with water

and a kind of 'toothpaste' made from tin oxide and oxalic acid, until my arms would feel like they were about to fall off; drying off the stone, checking it with my face just against the stone looking sideways at the light, to catch the reflection of a scratch. Finding that scratch again, now smaller, drawing a circle around it with a pencil, going back to a rougher grade of diamonds and starting again, rubbing, rubbing, rubbing... this went on for weeks. I would rub all day, and find at the end of the day that the scratch was still there, and I would have to go back to a coarser grade of diamonds and start again tomorrow. On top of this were coming frequent messages from Neelam, from Shunyo, "When will the tables be ready? Will they be ready for the celebration of Enlightenment Day?" Truly, I reached my physical and mental limits, and it was not in the glory of success, but the agony of defeat.

Just at the apex of that dark time, in the midst of my inner hell projected onto those innocent Abu-green marble blocks, I received a message to come to Lao Tzu gate, the portal of Osho's house. I washed the powder off my face, it was around 5 in the afternoon on a hot April day. As I reached the gate of His house, there was Shunyo waiting for me, with an enormous smile. She handed me a gold 'Rolex' watch, one of those ones from Bangkok that I had seen when I was there with Nirvano, and she said: "Osho said to 'Give this to Devakant, my flute player'."

Suddenly, the heavy and dark clouds of my internal oblivion cleared and revealed a blue, blue sky. Suddenly I realized that He knew all along what was happening, what I was going through. I was not forgotten, he was still hearing my music, even though I was not playing at all, and in a very loving and simple way, he let me know that he was waiting for me to grow up, in total love and acceptance.

In retrospect, it was the genius and insight of the Master to work with me in this way. A Master does not brutally demolish the personality. That would be simply destructive of the whole mechanism, and doesn't work. In the terms used by the shamans of Mexico, to reach the Nagual, the unknown, one must perfect the Tonal, clear off the island of 'the known', the personality, leaving what is essential to function perfectly. This is what he did with me. I was a very egoistic and closed type, a solitary and unsocial bear, keeping myself apart in order to protect the walls of my self, created with fear. Sullen, aloof, a solitary creator, but creating out of struggle and pain rather than overflow and joy. I was a balloon with dark painted faces hidden in its folds, and he pumped it full of air, inflated it to the extreme, so it became huge, larger-than-life, every face exposed and the walls very, very thin, so all it needed was a pinprick to pop the whole bubble.

One day in the discourse I heard him explain it, that his way of working with very egoistic people was to put them in positions where they would have to give him something. That way their ego would feel satisfied, somehow on a level with the master, that. "Look how much I give Him, so of course, I can also receive some wisdom or some energy from Him. It's only fair!" All this works on an unconscious and unspoken level, but somehow it allows this type of person to let down their guard, and let in the energy of the Master, which then works in an alchemical way. His energy was a transformative force: simply being open to it made huge changes take place, in one's inner world, in one's openness to existence, in one's level of day-to-day awareness.

After all, who was I?: just a beggar...and he...an emperor, if not of the universe then at least of the 3 or 4 nearest galaxies. What could I possibly give Him? He didn't need ANYTHING from me, especially 17 marble tables. He would one day just walk away from it all without so much as a look over the shoulder. So, it was a big drama created for my benefit, using my own desires, ambitions, capacities. In short, the master gives you a long rope, and with it, you can either jumprope, or hang yourself, or any combination of things. And then you believe it was Him doing it. That was the story of the Ranch, and now, that was my personal drama unfolding under his direct gaze. This was Zen-in-action, not just chanting mantras or burning incense sticks, but burning your body-mind structure on a funeral pyre with the wood of your own desires, played out in 3-d 'reality', not virtual, while you watch yourself burn, and watch, and watch.

One day, years later, I was in Oaxaca in Mexico, watching artisans painting exquisite little wooden statues. They spoke no Spanish, only Zapateca, and their lives were basically unchanged since centuries before the Spanish conquest. They mixed all their colors from simple natural elements: a bit of resin and bark from the copal tree, lemon juice, ground berries. I watched, fascinated, for hours as they would mix their pigments, in an alchemical process of transformation.

This alchemical energy touch of the Master is like those painters in Oaxaca, dropping a few drops of lemon juice into the cactus-and-copal-bark yellow pigment. Suddenly, the whole thing turns a deep red, which you could never have predicted. As I listened to him reveal this strategy in the lecture one morning, I knew without any doubt that he was talking about me, and I squirmed in my seat, and would have liked to disappear from my own skin. But his love held me there like a magnet, just a few feet in front of him as he spoke, and I, a bug under a microscope, a strange dual feeling of being totally and unconditionally loved whilst one is being dissected without anesthesia. If you choose to relate to it from the standpoint of mind-ego, it was hell. If you choose to look at it from the position of your spirit, that is, essence and true freedom, it was the greatest gift that another human being could ever give to you. I would fluctuate between these two poles, like a note on the flute which jumps back and forth between octaves.

Those days when he would be talking to me or about me in the discourse, and me sitting a few feet in front of him, he was a merciful surgeon. He would cut, and then wait. If it got too much and I would be really crawling in my own skin unable to stand the pain, he would back off, start to walk around the subject, figuratively speaking, and I could physically feel his attention, watching, lovingly observing what I could stand and what I couldn't. The day when I brought the first completed tables in, after months of work, was just such a day. The tables I had completed were three; two big ones, about 5 feet long each, and one smaller one, about two feet cubed, carved with the knot of marble tying the legs together like a figure 8. I had a big wagon which I pulled myself, and I felt like Santa Claus coming through the gates of the ashram, into Lao Tzu house, carefully and attentively placing the tables in the room adjacent to His, so they could be yet again thoroughly cleaned before being brought into his room. The polish was perfect, I felt as if I had given birth to the babies and was walking out of the hospital after 9 months of labor. But I couldn't just leave! I had to leave some kind of signature, like saying, "See! I did this!". Although this was not in my conscious mind, certainly that seed was in me, wrapped in other paper. I wrote a small card, saying, "With love and Gratitude". And signed it with my name, and left it on the table. And it was not dishonest. But it was not the whole truth. I should have signed it, "With love, gratitude, and the wish for recognition..."

The next morning in discourse, I was sitting in the second row in front of Him, and suddenly, out of nowhere, completely non sequitur with what he had been talking about, he suddenly said, in a voice which leapt out of the depths of the universe; "And you know NOTHING about GRATITUDE! Gratitude is not just a WORD. It is a state of being which has nothing to do with the superficial 'Thank you', like Americans are always saying, just as a social formality!"

In that moment I became a squashed bug on my cushion, wishing I could simply crawl under the mosquito net and fly away. The big light was on, my game was exposed, and all my dreams of recognition and appreciation crumbled in that moment. My labor and struggle of months had been literally 'in vain'; a self-reflective game, and I had missed the point completely. Just when I thought I had won the round, I lost the match.

The table and I, in the workshop under the peepal tree...

CHAPTER 26

Eagles and Roller Skates

If one looks for naught when staring into space;
If with the mind one then observes the mind;
One destroys distinctions and reaches Buddhahood.

The clouds that wander through the sky
have no roots, no home,
Nor do the distinctive thoughts floating through the mind.
Once the Self-mind is seen, Discrimination stops.

In space, shapes and colors form
But neither by black nor white is space tinged.
From the Self-mind all things emerge;
The Mind by virtues and by vices is not stained.

Tilopa, Song of Mahamudra

Offshore, the two islands seem to be just a half-mile away. They beckon to me, like a portal to another world. The locals say that's what they are, these two islands side by side off this eastern shore of Oahu. I swim and swim, and it seems I am getting nowhere…the tide is going in, and I am trying to go out, it's like stubbornly fighting the whole universe. After 2 hours, it still seems I have gotten nowhere, I am not even halfway out, and I turn to go back to shore: suddenly I find myself racing along like greased wheels on buttered rails.

And I realize, it's like that with my life. I have choices, I can choose to swim against the direction the whole universe is moving, if I want... That's the small ego, it thinks it has a personal destiny. But the whole universe is moving in another direction. It is INTENT... we are carried along by a great ocean, which is moving in a certain direction in waves. We can swim with that, float, or swim against it. Swimming to an offshore island, in one direction I struggle, each swell brings me to a standstill. Swimming in the other direction, I fly, each swell propels me over great distances, because I am one with the direction of the sea. That is INTENT. When our small desires merge with the great desire of the Universe, the INTENT of the Universal Spirit, then our motion is effortless and a joy. We do have the gift of 'Free Will'. We can fight, struggle, float or swim. It's our choice. We are going to end up in the same place anyway, but our attitude towards that is essential. Merging the small personal intention, desire, with the great INTENT of the universe is what used to be called 'Surrender'. But without the connotation of defeat. The ego defeated lies in wait, for an opportunity for revenge. The ego merged is light, transparent, without a hidden program...

As it is said in the world of Zen: "Let go...or be dragged!"

And so began, the next day after the surgical discourse, the second round, a new set of tables... these ones, by His specific instructions, were to be double-deckers, to be by the side of his bed, one on either side, just next to Him while he sleeps. I had no idea how to do it, so I improvised, and started gaining a bit more confidence in this medium, knowing now that it doesn't actually take FOREVER, it just seems like it. If you forget about time, it goes much easier. Forget about getting it done within a human timeframe! Just do it, carefully: VERY carefully. The marble blocks come without spare parts, and I sure as hell didn't want to go back to Rajasthan to get some more if something breaks!

I started carving the columns, from long rectangles of the marble; 8 columns, one on each corner of the two tables, making them round by hand slowly. Then I began working the 4 slabs, one below and one above for each table, 5 inches thick …one-by-one bringing out the shapes.

By that time Aseema and I were crazy in love. We had very, very little time to spend together, she was full on running the kitchen, and I was full on grinding the marble. I lived then in a small room in the building next to the peepal tree. It was called Mirdad, and on the roof there was a hammock under the vast canopy of the tree. Sometimes we would find a stolen hour at lunch there together in the hammock, and the eagle that lived in the tree would come and watch us from the treetops, screaming. We would throw him a chapati, and he would catch it in midair and be gone. That we had no time made it all the more intense, every moment together was very precious, and passionate. Our love grew much in those days, and deepened into something which would stay with me all through my life. I am deeply grateful for the gift of her love and friendship.

The work on the second set of tables continued. It seemed to flow faster, though it was more complicated. The problem was that, being made from thick marble slabs and columns, they really weighed a great deal. And Nirupa, who cleans Osho's room more thoroughly than a hospital surgical ward, needed to move them every day to clean next to his bed. But they weighed so much, that to move them without picking them up would gouge grooves in the marble floor. But they were too heavy for anyone to pick up. So they had to get wheels. But His design and wish didn't include wheels. I hemmed and hawed, and tried this and that, and finally ordered some kind of chrome art-deco wheels that came from Germany, that would make it easy to move, and yet weren't too obvious or industrial-looking; they were kind of modern and stylish. I added them to the bottom of the columns. After several weeks of polishing, the tables were ready, and they were exquisite, shining, like diamonds...on rollerskates! The polish was like a mirror, and I brought them in, waiting for the axe to fall again, wondering if my head or something else would get cut off this time.

Sure enough, the next day, the message came to go immediately to Lao Tzu House. There I got the message to take the tables back: He felt that the wheels destroyed the look of the tables. Deflated and without a clue what to do next, as it takes months to get some new wheels from Germany, I brought the tables back to my workshop, and pondered my dilemma.

In his room, EVERYTHING had to be taken into account. It can't squeak, it can't smell, it can't leak, it can't break, it's got to be clean, neat, it's got to be moveable, but stable, it's got to be beautiful, but simple...

I looked at the tables honestly with those god-awful German wheels there, and I realized it was true. They looked like hell. What had I been thinking of? I chopped the wheels off. I chopped off the bottom of the columns. I realized that it's not that the tables have to move around all over the place like Russian ice-skaters at the Olympics, No! They just have to be moved away from the bed, and back, every day: the same movement. Like a sliding door. BINGO! I went to all the hardware stores in the dark industrial quarters of Poona, and found the strongest, smallest, simplest and less squeaky wheels for sliding glass doors I could find. The marble of the table was thick enough that I could imbed 6 of them under the table in a groove carved there, so the table just floats off the ground by a quarter of an inch, and the wheels are totally invisible. I did it in three days, and brought them back, and YES! It was accepted, no axe, no Zen-stick, no surgery, no rejection, no raking-my-naked-body-over-the-spiritual-coals in discourse. The tables found their place by the side of his bed, and there they would stay.

Whew! So, it IS possible....it's a real situation, with real solutions. It's not an unsolvable Greek tragedy devised for me personally by the distant and cold gods who govern human suffering. Suddenly, everything inside me moved out of the realm of drama, into the arena of creation and possibility!

As I worked the stone, I slowly came to realize that my internal compulsion to get things done, in a hurry, was just my private movie, and had nothing to do with reality. The stone was a great teacher, in that it moves at its own speed, and it will do so, whether I freak out about it, or relax into the happening and forget about time. This was the dawning in me of something which I had never known before, something called 'patience'. It's not to bite the bullet and impatiently wait and count the minutes and hours and days. It's just to be here 'in the process', totally, with what is, and forget goals and future. And in so doing, you forget about 95% of the internal anguish that the mind likes to generate. Relaxing into the now, even relaxing into the marble dust and slime and sweat, was becoming a great relief to me. After all, there IS no future, there is no 'AFTER' this. When 'after' comes, it comes as 'here and now'.

Now it started to get fun. Next was to be a big cabinet for the radio and CD player, all in white Italian marble. I did it with smooth curves, like a Mercedes, polished to perfection. Then, another cube, matching the cabinet, to serve as a bed-stand next to the stereo cabinet. Then, another Abu green table, something like the first one for the bathroom, but more ornate; I started to get playful and set jewels into the side, carving more patterns into the lines of the legs. I wasn't doing it to be impressive, it was just fun, this game between us now...

Though words are spoken to explain the Void,
the Void as such can never be expressed.

Though we say "the Mind is a bright light",
it is beyond all words and symbols.
Although the Mind is void in essence,
all things it embraces and contains.

Tilopa, Song of Mahamudra

Along with the creations I was making for Osho's personal living space, I was often guarding now at night in the garden outside his window as He slept. This was rotated amongst a group of close disciples. We would take turns at that, and sometimes I would be sitting outside his window for hours, between midnight and 4 in the morning. That was mystical, wonderful. I loved this sitting in His garden in the middle of the night, just outside his window where he was sleeping. It was a very magical time, the big birds in the jungle-like garden would wake up for a minute always around 2 am, and then sleep some more until just before dawn. He would often wake up at 3 in the morning, and put on a little light in the room, while I was just sitting outside. I noticed that the light was really bright, and I thought it was must be kind of tacky for Him, that bright light so abruptly coming on. So I made a lamp out of Abu-Green marble, in the shape of a pyramid, so that the light would softly filter through the marble sides of the pyramid. He really liked that. So the message came next that he wanted me to make him a clock out of marble. It became a kind of dance between us. He would ask for something, and I would make it, or I would come up with something, and that would provoke something else from Him…It was a ping-pong game with the Master, to try to guess what he would like, and see what would come next, always a surprise.

After the clock, I got the message from Him that he wanted me to make a BOOK out of marble, one of His books. I pondered that for some time, and looked at samples of old books in Asian museums, Tibetan box-manuscripts, Egyptian things. I couldn't quite figure how to make something that wouldn't break or be brittle, and yet wouldn't be too heavy to pick up. This would be a challenge.

CHAPTER 27

The Himalayas

The mountains are the body of the Buddha...
and the sound of running water is his Great Speech.

(Zen saying)

Transient is this world; like phantoms and dreams,
Substance it has none. Grasp not the world nor your kin;
Cut the strings of lust and hatred;
meditate in woods and mountains.
If without effort you remain loosely in the natural state,
soon Mahamudra you will win and attain
the Non-attainment.

Tilopa, song of Mahamudra

It was August, 1988. It is the last month of grey and steamy monsoon skies, and my visa was just about finished. As luck would have it, so was Aseema's, and we decided to go together to Nepal by train to get new entry visas to come back into India. The long train ride from Poona took us to Varanasi, where we would spend a couple days before taking a bus over the border to Katmandhu.

Varanasi...the ancient holy city of Shiva, was called 'Kashi' for millenia. It's said that it was contemporaneous with Babylon, and has existed without interruption for more than 7000 years. I believe it. Probably some of those streets weren't cleaned in all that time. The streets are small, some of them hardly big enough for two people to pass by walking side-by-side, and the grime and filth of ages of humanity is everywhere evident.

But as I passed the last few alleyways, and arrived to the river, the sacred Ganges that passes through the city, I was awestruck by a palpable atmosphere, something other-worldly, indescribable, and wonderful. There were many steps leading down to the water, many temples here and there, sadhus, Brahmans (Indian priests), women and children, young and old bathing in the river. But what struck me was the unearthly silence. It had nothing to do with sound. It was an inner feeling of silence, of depth, of mystery. Everywhere there were funeral pyres burning, bodies going up in flames, or already in ashes; some fully burned, some not, a constant departure of souls from that riverbank. It is the city where the Hindus come to die, and be cremated on the banks of the Ganges, and it seemed to me to be a Grand Central Station for soul departures. The atmosphere was charged with a strange and wonderful presence, a doorway to another reality.

We walked along the ghats for a little while, and after a time, I heard a little sweet mumbling voice behind me that was notably and softly persistent. I had already become jaded after years in India to the constant begging that one is subject to, as a Westerner. At that time, we were assumed to be wealthy, but in point of fact, as I had been living penniless in the ashram for quite awhile now, I was making this journey with borrowed rupees, and that, not much of them. It was bottom-budget all the way. But this voice was very sweet, not pathetic, just simply stating, "Want ride my boat? Very nice boat…very nice…Good boat.." He was a little guy with a little rowboat, and the way he talked about his boat, with so much love, and he wanted the equivalent of half a dollar; who could say no? So we got in. He paddled out into the river a little bit, and we sat silently watching all the fires on the banks, all the bodies, bathers, dogs, vultures and monkeys that make up that strange scene. Just by the side of the boat, not 12 inches from my shoulder, a strange creature rose up out of the water and arched the full length of the boat, silently re-entering the water just next to me. It had a long nose, was about 8 feet long and looked like a pink dinosaur. The boatman said it was a kind of dolphin that lives only in the Ganges.

We stayed a few days in the city, and drank in that mystical atmosphere by the river. As Aseema's visa was expiring the next day, we bought two bus tickets for Nepal, and found ourselves in the morning sun standing on the sidewalk on the hot out-skirts of the city waiting for the bus to take us over the border by late afternoon.

That bus never came. We waited for a couple of hours, and slowly realized the tickets had been fake. We had no clue what to do next, as we had no alternative plan, and we had to leave the country that day, to not overstay our visas. Just then, from out of nowhere, a big black rambler Ambassador, like one of those American Turtle-cars from the 40s, pulled up to the side-walk, and out jumped two fat and jolly Indians shouting in thick Indian English with their heads wagging side-to-side, "Come on, Come ON! Get IN! Ve are going to the AIRPORT!"

Well, this was so off-the-wall, and we had nothing to lose, so, we got in! And they drove 40 km. straight to the airport that we didn't know existed, laughing and joking the whole way. When we got there, they refused to accept any money from us. Instead they ran into the office, saying that their cousin-brother is a pilot or something, and they found two tickets, the LAST tickets, for a plane that was going to Katmandhu in 10 minutes. Wo! This was too weird to even think about. We thanked them profusely, and they said, "God Bless You!" And we boarded the plane and left India. As the dry and hot plains below us slowly turned into the green Himalayan foothills, and the snow peaks of the Annapurna and Everest ranges became visible in the distance, we both realized that these two beings must be what is known as 'Angels'...emissaries from another dimension, beings that serve, and exist for that purpose. They came out of nowhere, no-one knew we were there waiting for a bus that didn't exist to get out of India. They were full of joy, although without the customary wings and white complexions that I was accustomed to from the Catholic paintings of my childhood; They wanted nothing from us, and they only did us good. That is a rare event in this world.

Our plan was simple: put in our visa requests in Katmandhu, and wait out the days while they processed them, walking in the mountains...it would be cheaper than staying in hotels in the city. We took a long bus ride to Pokhara, the bumpiest and most grueling bus-ride I could ever imagine, with long views of deep gorges and plunging canyons dropping hundreds of feet to the river below, studded here and there with buses smashed up at the bottom. "Hmmm, not a good sign", I thought to myself. Sometimes on the curves the bus would have to stop and all of us passengers would get out, and wait for it to round the curve with only three wheels touching; we hoped for the best, held on to the seats for the potholes, and watched the stupendous peaks of the Himalayas unfold before us. The river was raging, a boiling caldron swollen with the monsoon rains, and we were betting that at this time of year there wouldn't be many tourists. We would be more right than we ever could have imagined.

We were dreamers, in love and dreaming a beautiful dream. As we stood on the shores of the lake of Pokhara, our hearts were thrilled by the soaring peaks in front of us, the huge expanse of the Annapurna range, several peaks of 8000 meters height. The ashram is a very lovely place, with lots of young, beautiful and lively people meditating there and enjoying life: but I actually wasn't much partaking of that. My life had become a very intense labor, once again, even more than at the Ranch, and there in Poona it was yet more concentrated. The very intense and focused life I had in the ashram with all its petty tyrants, day passes, keys to open locks to open locks, and every one of them had someone protecting his or her territory with the key tightly held in hand, it seemed so far away suddenly. In the vastness of these huge mountains before us, it seemed like we had been plunked down in Paradise. We rented a rowboat for almost nothing, and started rowing out into the lake. It was a glorious sunny day, the Annapurna range was towering majestically in the distance, and the lake was vast, serene and beautiful.

As I rowed happy, calm and relaxed for 10 minutes, clouds began to appear over the mountains, and the wind started to come up. The wavelets got bigger, rapidly bigger, and soon the wind was howling as the storm approached much quicker than I could have imagined. The waves on the lake were becoming 5-foot swells, and I quickly heave-hoed for a little wooded island as the rain started coming down in sheets. We barely made it to this little knoll protruding from the water, with two trees, about 3 square meters of space. As we got out of the boat that was getting swamped by waves, Aseema held onto one tree and I held her arm as I held the boat with my other hand, to keep it from getting swept away, as the rain pelted down on us in the mud. We waited for the squall to pass, and within a few minutes the rain stopped, the wind died down, and the lake returned to calm, as if nothing had happened. Rowing back to shore, the fireflies started to come out like Christmas lights in the trees and grass, and all appeared magical and serene once again. Little did I know this was a great trailer to the movie which was just about to happen to us.

We searched the markets of Pokhara for a couple of sleeping bags and ponchos for the rain, for our trek into the high mountains. In one of the shops, I found a weathered copy of 'The Story of Milarepa, Tibet's Greatest Yogi', and I read it from cover to cover that night. It had been written about 8 centuries ago, and told the story of the Tibetan Yogi Milarepa, and his struggles to fulfill the directives of his master, Marpa. He had begun as an innocent young man, who took to black magic to avenge a wrong-doing as requested by his mother. He ended up killing about 30 people, and thus incurred great amounts of negative karma upon himself. When he sought freedom from his evil-doings, he prostrated himself before the teachings of the great master Marpa, disciple of Naropa, to whom had been given the SONG OF MAHAMUDRA, by Tilopa, the original master in the lineage. Marpa was extremely hard on Milarepa, having him build and rebuild a stone tower 7 times, each time, finding it a little imperfect, or the wrong shape, and ordering Milarepa to tear it down and start again, his back becoming bruised and bloodied and infected by the carrying of countless stones for years. I couldn't help but think of my own story, ongoing, with Osho, and the labor of the stones, the failures, the long hours, months, and years of 'purification' that I was still immersed in…

We had almost nothing, just street clothes and shoes, and in the market we found a couple of sleeping bags for 5 dollars, and decided to see what trekking would be like. The mountains called to us, and after the too-controlled and civilized world of the ashram, it was a call impossible not to follow. A half-hour jeep ride took us to the base of the mountains, and we started walking, up and up and up into the first slopes, of the Ghurka villages on the southern slopes of the Annapurnas.

The feeling of entering those mountains for the first time, where so many enlightened ones had walked before, thrilled my heart. Bodhidharma, Buddha, Tilopa, Padma Sambhava, Shiva and Parvati, all these awakened ones had passed these valleys through the ages, and now we were there; it was a dream come true! The trail quickly changed into stone staircases leading into the clouds, with waterfalls here and there amongst the bamboo forests. We were to follow the gorge of the Kali Gandaki river, the river of Kali, the Hindu goddess often depicted standing on the corpse of her dead husband, drinking blood from a skull. At this time of year, that image couldn't be more fitting, as the river was a raging and violently thundering and surging mass of brown water. As you stood on its banks, the ground would shake with the boulders rolling downriver underwater. It is the deepest gorge in the world, passing between two mountain ranges 8000 meters high, Annapurna and Dhaulagiri. We were traveling in street clothes, with nothing but a topographical map in my pocket; no compass, no provisions, and no guide. We had enough cash on us in small bills to last us two weeks, so we thought. According to the map, there would be villages to stay in, where we could buy simple food, every half-day. We couldn't have dreamt of what was to come, and it was better that it was that way.

It was a hot day, with great masses of billowing clouds, and after several hours of sweaty uphill hiking, we stopped at a waterfall to wash off. The cold water felt so refreshing, and we stood there a few minutes in the sun, standing on the rocks by the stream. Suddenly I heard a 'SMACK!' As I turned, I saw Aseema on the ground. She had slipped on the rock, and landed straight on her tailbone. She was in a lot of pain, and as I helped her stand up after a few minutes, suddenly she gasped, and I looked down to my legs, where there were streams of blood running all the way down my legs. My god, what happened! I didn't feel a thing! But there were small leeches with their heads already buried in the skin of my crotch. Yikes! This was gruesome…these little creatures appearing in the mud, as soon as we would stop to rest, they would feel our heat, silently crawling up our legs to gorge themselves on our blood. You couldn't feel their entry into the skin, and they had some kind of anti-coagulant they injected; it made the blood flow quicker, and made it hard to stop the bleeding. After we got to the next village, Aseema limping and me bleeding, we asked what to do? The locals told us different things, that you have to put salt on the wounds to stop the bleeding, and the best way to get the leeches off without pulling them is to rub chewing tobacco on them. That way they drop off on their own, and take their heads with them. If you pull them off, the head stays in and gets infected. So we bought salt, and chewing tobacco, and rubbed it on our shoes to keep the suckers from getting in through the laces. We found out the safest places to stop were where there were chai shacks where they had chickens. The chickens eat the little leeches as they cross the open ground, so if you got to a tea-shack with chickens in the yard, probably you could rest near the house and there wouldn't be any of those little monsters to harass you.

So there we were, already a day into the mountains, with a dilemma: the mountains would be full of these horrid leeches in this season, something the tourist manuals didn't mention, and now Aseema had possibly a cracked tailbone. But she insisted it was better for her to walk: being the dancer that she is, she knew the sense of her body, and it healed by moving, and we both didn't want to give up the adventure just with this first setback. So on we went...on and on, upwards into the clouds and the bamboo forests, each day back in time, each day the villages different. The Hindu people of the plains whose villages were always dirty and chaotic and literally full of excrement, gave way to Buddhist villages, where every one seemed to be engaged in some kind of creative craft, making carpets, or weavings, or paintings. The whole village would hum with a peaceful silent creativity. Each day, further into the mountains, was another century further back in time. TVs and radios disappeared, electricity too, even wheels were nonexistent, just stone, stone, stone, up and up and up into the sky. Chimneys didn't exist there, they had yet to be invented; the smoke filled the houses, everything above the height of 4 feet was coal-black, faces, walls, pots and pans. Faces would appear in open windows, faces that cannot be seen on a modern city street, innocent eyes looking clearly into your own like a bright and radiant mirror with no thoughts. Pilgrims were passing on the path, Tibetan women and dzos and yaks, traders in turquoise and salt. We would be passed by little Nepalese girls carrying loads of firewood which would have made me stagger, but they would run past me going uphill, laughing and smiling. Up and up we went, for days. In the nights we would find a house where we could sleep and get a meal, for about a dollar. We would stay with Nepalese families, sitting around the fire and eating together.

I was always surprised at the strength of the children in the mountains, how they were not pampered, but were fearless. One night, a little boy was playing, he must have been about 4 years old. As he played, he fell into the fire, backwards. He was immediately pulled out, and dusted off. Without a tear or sign of fear, he turned to the fire and kicked it!

One rainy night, in the darkness of a village, I could hear a ritual going on across the valley, the whole night, as the misty rain fell in the valley and the darkness deepened. It began with drums, softly beating, and women's voices, many of them; a soft rhythmic chanting in the distant fog. As the night went on the chanting became moaning, and wailing, until before the dawn it was clearly screams of ecstasy. I don't know what they were doing, but I'm sure they weren't reading Bibles!

The Nepalese women were beautiful, and earthy, and without shame. They bathed openly in the streams and rivers, and were not self-conscious about having naked breasts. They looked me in the eye, and were not shy to talk, and laugh. One night we were staying in a village house, and the proprietress was very well-endowed to say the least, and she went out of her way to stand in such a position in the room that she was visible to me and not Aseema, and she would take off her shirt and adjust her bra again and again, I suppose making the point to me about her natural gifts, and demonstrate her silk underwear, as if it needed adjustment and re-adjustment. I was surprised by this, and then it occurred to me that in the villages we passed, there were only women, no men to be found anywhere. It seems it was the season where the flocks and herds were up on the high ranges with the men, and the women were constrained to spend those months without male companionship in the villages. They were sometimes quite demonstrative about their natural unfulfilled inclinations, flirtatious without guilt or tension, during our sojourn, and I found them to be kind and friendly hosts, and strong, beautiful people, and very real.

As we walked, most days we were soaking wet all day long. Sometimes we would pass days of nothing but wet and dripping bamboo forests, on and on and up and up, for 12 hours. And some days, high above the clouds, breath-taking glimpses of magnificent snow-mountains, that seemed to get higher and more shining as we climbed. Some days we walked the whole day through forests of marijuana, 12 feet tall, breathing deeply of course. And some days, craggy trails of stone stairs disappearing into foggy infinity, going up and up and down and down all day.

After a week, we climbed through a forest that was hanging with moss from all the trees. We hadn't seen a soul all morning, and the usual hundreds of footprints in the mud were thinning out, considerably. As we entered a clearing, we came face to face with a herd of quite large apes. They were much bigger than monkeys, and had white faces, and black bodies. Their bodies were the size of chimpanzees, or somewhat bigger. There were about 80 of them, about 20 yards from us. The whole herd was quietly grazing, and there was one individual, the 'chief' maybe, who had his eye on us, without stress, with a stick in his mouth, acting very cool. If we moved or made a step in their direction, he would make some little sign, a click or a motion, and all of them would be suddenly alert. We watched for about 20 minutes, until they all moved off, as one, through the forest, like dolphins, in waves. It was incredible to see, how they moved through the branches of the forest as if they were going through water, in wavelike motion, as a group.

As the cloudy and damp morning passed into afternoon and our hunger increased with each passing minute, I kept checking the Topographical map to see when we would get to a village for lunch. We had started walking at 6 am, without anything to eat, it was about 2 by now, and we hadn't seen any sign of a village. According to the map we should have hit a village by 10 a.m. The footprints had disappeared, and the mud was getting deeper and deeper, and the trail thinner. Aseema was starting to get really freaked out by the leeches, as it was deep rainforest here: if you stopped even for a couple of moments they would start wiggling out of the mud, and this really gets on your nerves when you are tired and without food, and need to stop to catch your breath. She got to a place where the mud and span of water was too big for her to cross, and started panicking about the leeches now emerging from the muddy water in her direction. I found a rock and tossed it in the mud for her to step on, but instead it splashed the mud up onto her, and this triggered in her a major recession into 'inner abandoned child', shall we say. She started crying, I started scrambling for more rocks and trying to get her something to step on to get out of there, and we both ended up a couple of muddy, hungry emotional messes.

Finally, at about 4 in the afternoon, with no food since the previous day, we came upon a village, only to get to the first house and find they were all abandoned, with caved-in roofs.

"Funny, it didn't mention that on the Topo map", I thought. Aseema said, "Well, here starts the REAL adventure.." The only village within a days' walk was on the other side of the river, and we had to get to the bridge on the Kali Gandaki to get there. We kept on walking, and walking, and walking, as the fog came in, and we could see less and less. Finally, with our visibility about 10 feet, and our brains and bodies famished, we came to the end of the path, and a precipice, that yawned below us into infinity. Through gaps in the fog and movements of wind, we could see that we were on the edge of a huge chasm, probably up around 4000 meters in elevation, hopelessly lost in the vastness of the mountains, with no food or water and the night coming on, and the river nowhere in sight.

It was then that Aseema said, in the most naggy wife-ish voice I could ever imagine, "I KNEW we were lost, I just KNEW you didn't know where we were!" And I started yelling at her, and she yelling back, and there we were, in desperation, screaming at each other at the top of those mountains in the fog, hungry, exhausted, lost, and scared.

Probably because of our yelling, there and then out of the fog came wandering a surrealistic phantom figure, a little man, barefoot, dirty, wearing ragged shorts, with a broken red umbrella over his head. It was actually the broken web of the wires, with a few small scraps of red cloth still clinging to them here and there. The effect of seeing this apparition somehow comical and surrealistically ghostly, emerging from the grey swirling emptiness in front of us stunned us both into silence. As he got closer, it became apparent he wasn't a ghost, but a real person. Slowly with sign language, he communicated to us that he was a cowherd up there with his cows, and he had heard us yelling. And we let him know that we were lost and needed to find the trail to the river. He 'said', or gestured, he could take us there, for 100 Nepalese rupees, which was an astronomical sum in those mountains, but it was actually about 5 dollars and it was the difference of life or death for us, so we said, "Ok"!

With that, he opened up his broken red umbrella, and started RUNNING straight down the mountainside in the rain. And we, ran, sliding and slipping and skidding behind him in the rain and the mud and the grass. It was long grassy slopes down and down and down. And lots of sliding on your butt in the mud. And all that mud had leeches waiting in it. But we had no time to think of that, he was going full speed and he knew those mountains like a jackrabbit, and all we could do was run, roll, slide and skid to keep up with him.

After about an hour of this, my knees were really killing me, my clothes were soaking wet and covered with mud, and he finally stopped and pointed, to a thin line of a trail visible, about 500 yards below us. We thanked him, paid him the 100 rupees, which was probably one-fourth of our net worth at that time, and we took off running to get to that bridge before dark. We got to the first village of that long day around six in the late afternoon, and with a cup of tea and some glucose biscuits, I unrolled my pant legs to find 25 streams of blood running down, profusely, and my shoes completely full of blood from my little 'friends' on the trail. I packed my legs in salt to stop the bleeding, and we took off for the bridge, nearly running the whole way.

As we rounded the last bend approaching the river at sunset, my heart sank, and I couldn't believe what was there before my eyes. The river was a roaring, raging mass of brown water, spitting and foaming before us, at least 500 feet wide. And the famous steel bridge, built by Swiss engineering, The ONLY bridge across the Kali Gandaki in all these mountains, was now a twisted and broken bunch of metal laying on the riverbank. The only possible crossing was a single rope spanning the raging torrent, about 20 feet above it, with a few knots in it, and a swinging basket, pulled by two guys on either side of the river, creak, creak, creak, all the way. Aseema and I watched this for a minute or two, and it was clear, that either we die crossing the river, or we die of hunger waiting for another option. So we may as well cross. We climbed into that little basket, swinging above that raging torrent, and watched, and swung those very, very long minutes as the basket tipped and dipped above the foaming and spitting black waters, as we swayed and rocked with the knotted cord pulled by those two guys 500 feet away, 'creak-creak-creak'. When we climbed out of the basket on the other side of that river, we didn't say a word. We bowed down and silently touched the earth with our foreheads, We were both grateful to still be alive. It was just about dark and we had two miles or more to go before we would get to the next village to sleep.

In the village that night, we arrived in pitch darkness, and banged on a few doors until we found a guesthouse. They told us, over a plate of potatoes, that in the previous monsoon, one night they had all been awakened by the strong smell of mud. There had been a massive landslide upriver, and for a few minutes the river was blocked. It rapidly built up, like a huge lake within minutes, and the lucky ones, smelling the mud in the wind, climbed the nearby slopes. Within minutes the monstrous river broke free of its temporary dam, and it swept down the banks with a raging force that took away half their village. We saw it the next day, the big curve in the river, and an abrupt gap in the line of stone houses that had been the village. As we walked on, the fury of the river seemed to grow: I watched whole mountainsides falling into it. We walked a trail hundreds or thousands of meters above the raging waters, and suddenly the trail disappeared where the land had fallen away, continuing again across the broken slope about 200 meters away. In between was a slipping and crumbling mass of broken shale, that had to be passed running, before it would disappear under your feet. My bamboo walking stick slipped out of my hand, and I watched for 5 minutes as it slid down down, down and never stopped until it reached the river thousands of feet below. I knew that one false step, and that would be me, not just the stick.

In late afternoon we came to a place where a side stream, about 100 meters wide, had flooded, and we would have to cross it. The water was freezing cold and raging by, so we tied ourselves together with a rope, took off our shoes, and started wading across, up to our waists, yelling all the way. We found out later that night that someone had died in that same place that day, a Nepalese man, who was unlucky with the crossing.

Thus passed our days in those mountains, sunlit peaks, cascading waterfalls, the raging torrent and death whispering in our ears at each moment.

Why do it at all, you may ask? I can only say, that each moment was tinged with life, death, marvels and disasters, and each step deeper into the mountains, I felt more and more enraptured with them. When we would be walking in elevations above 3000 meters, it seemed my thoughts stayed deep in the valleys, as if they had weight, and could not rise up with me. I felt more elated as I walked, higher and higher. And a strange and mysterious thing started happening to me: those tables I had made, that were now with Osho all day and night in his bedroom, were functioning like a psychic cord tying me to Him. Just I would remember making them, and with the thought, instantly I was there with Him, I could feel Him, and see Him. And I saw him not as a physical man, but as a golden Being, luminous, shining, radiant, filled with golden light. This ecstatic vision filled me throughout the days, this vision of his Golden Body gave me great joy, ecstasy in fact and it filled me with energy, even as my own body was straining just to step one foot in front of the other up the long, long stone staircases.

As we climbed and dropped and climbed again, I fell into a rhythm of walking and breathing, in time. Three steps per breath on the level path, two steps on the uphill, and when it was really steep, one breath per step. Thoughts became less and less, and exhaling became a mantra OM mane padme hum… OM mane padme hum…It came naturally that way, without thinking about it…and so we walked, for days upon days.

Basecamp, Annapurna

At the height of our journey, we reached to the base camp of Annapurna, 5000 meters high, on the glaciers. By that time Aseema's shoes were practically rags, and mine weren't much better. In front of us was a wall of ice reaching upward another 3000 meters. The afternoon sky was deep indigo overhead, even at midday as the air was quite thin. Breathing was difficult, I would take 3 steps and have to stop to catch my breath. Traveling without a guide, up at those heights we had counted on following Sherpas who were portering supplies up to the base camp. But on the glaciers, the trails disappeared, and the Sherpas walked too fast for me to keep up with them with the lack of oxygen at that altitude. So there we were in a white world, lost again, and I would put my face against the ice, like I had been doing with the marble polishing, to try to catch the reflection of the shiny places where feet had walked, thus indicating the trail. It worked, and in this manner we found our way to the shelter of the base camp and a place to sleep in that icy vastness. The glacial moraine was enormous, miles and miles long, the mountains thundered with avalanches every few minutes, and in the night sky there were a billion stars, bigger than Van Gogh could ever paint them.

We went on and on, towards Jomson, and the north side of the Himalayas, passing beyond the cultural frontiers of Nepal, into villages that were completely Tibetan, in a land called Mustang. The land became arid plateaus, dry and windswept, between the Himalayas and the Karakoram Range. It reminded me of the Ranch, right down to the juniper trees. The altitude was affecting Aseema, giving her headaches, and we were running out of rupees, so we decided it was enough, and began the long walk back down to Pokhara. Coming down the mountains, I felt like a snow-lion, my strides were effortless and confidant, instead of the arduous struggle of the uphill journey. One could see from that height, through the accordian-like patterns in the mountains and rock formations, how the land of Asia had crumpled up like paper with the Indian subcontinent ramming into it, in some great cataclysm lost in the timeless past. Everywhere the rocks were shining, filled with metals, bronze, silver, gold, quartz. It was dazzling to see. We arrived in Pokhara completely broke, our clothes filthy and in rags, Aseema had tossed away her shoes a few days before and was walking barefoot, and we both were practically starving... But very, very, very happy.

On the Annapurna Trail

324

CHAPTER 28

Stone Books

We re-entered India on a hot slimy day, after a long crossing of the mountains by bus, from a small border station near Pokhara. We had to bribe the Indian guards to let us through, a normal occurrence in India anywhere. It was 'suggested' by them, as they pointed to an ancient stack of brown and filthy books 5 feet high, gathering dust in the corner of the guard house on the border checkpoint. They said they would have to keep us there waiting while they checked to see if our names were in any of those books, being the records of the people who were forbidden to return into India. That looked like it could easily take 3 or 4 months, and it was very hot and there was no place to sit and it was 20 years before computers would arrive, so I asked them, "What's the alternative?" They said, "Bhaksheesh, baba. A bottle of Coca-cola". That was an easy choice. I like that about India: there is no indecisiveness or shame about corruption. It simply is the way that the system works, nothing hidden, just pure and simple. We slept in a very rotten hotel near the station on the edge of Gorakhpur, waiting for the morning train back to the south, and Poona.

Aseema, being Chilean, had not been granted a lengthy new visa, but instead had only some days, to transit, and then figure out what to do from Poona. The situation didn't look good. I got another three months visa, but to spend it there without her was not something I wanted to think about.

When we got back to Poona, the situation was changing: Osho was getting visibly weaker and moving more slowly. I immediately started the work on the marble book for Him, and within a few days Aseema had to leave for Europe. She had gotten work with friends in Italy, a book publishing commune in Florence, and we said a very poignant goodbye, not knowing what would be. I just knew that I loved her madly, and somehow life would take care, I didn't know how.

The work on the Marble Book that Osho had requested went easily now. I knew how to manage the marble by that time, and it was a lovely interlude in what were to be my last days of living in the ashram. This last project of the book was a kind of lifeboat: as it had come as a direct request from Osho, no ashram bureaucrat could pull me off the project and have me doing other things, like carrying marble slabs for the new bedroom/Samadhi, which would have put me back in the hospital with my herniated discs. Because my work was a direct 'request' from Osho, I had a kind of amnesty from the ashram hierarchy, and I was left to do my thing and fulfill His request under the peepal tree in the post-monsoon days of September-October.

At the same time, Osho had asked that a Buddha statue that had arrived from Burma via the long road from Oregon, would be mounted in the front of Buddha hall, "To show my people how to sit for meditation", in His own words. It would be set in a large marble rock, so naturally the task fell to me. Each day Osho would inquire how it would be going, through Shunyo, or Neelam, or Avesh, his chauffeur, and the word would get to me.

One day, as I was guarding, hidden in the bushes next to the doorway of the car-porch of his house, as He was returning from the evening discourse in Buddha Hall, Osho got out of the car and said to Avesh: "And how is the Buddha statue coming along with Devakant?" And Avesh replied what I had told him earlier that day, that, "The Buddha could sit in the rock, but isn't yet comfortable". Osho then said something about how it must be comfortable; I can't explain to you the strange mixture of emotions that passed in me as I overheard unwillingly this conversation from the bushes a few feet away. My heart was pounding to overhear my Master talking about me, and I wanted to disappear and not hear it, and at the same time I wanted to leap out of the bushes and say, "Here I AM!". It was another of those weird events in my life of visible invisibility. I suppose it is my strange destiny.

At that time, this destiny would take another dimensional turn. I had been playing one morning in the Buddha hall for the Sannyas celebration, a ceremony when people take initiation into disciple-hood, and we musicians play throughout the whole event. After the ceremony, I received word from Neelam that Hariprasad Chaurasia was in the ashram, and was going to have lunch at the cafe there, and I was invited to come.

I remembered the magazine I had seen in that Rajasthan desert 2 years before, and I was excited to meet this man who was already something of a legend to me.

At the lunch, when I was seated there, Hariji (as he is called by his students and disciples) turned to me and said, "I heard you playing this morning". I was surprised, and waited to see what he would say next. He turned to me with that remarkable sweet smile of his, and said, "Have you ever tried Bamboo flute?" I said, "I don't know how to play it, and I don't have a teacher." He said with a wink and a shake of his head, "I can teach you!" Well, this is like Einstein offering to give you lessons in arithmetic. Hariji is the best flute player in the world by many accounts, and I gulped and said, "That's great!" He said to get a flute, and come to see him in Bombay.

Now in those days, Osho was speaking about Maitreya, the form that the Buddha had said he would take upon his return, the

Buddha of the Future that the historical Gautama Buddha had talked about 25 centuries before. It was a mysterious time, in which, as usual, one could never be sure if Osho was joking or serious about it, but apparently he had been 'visited' by this entity, and had allowed this presence to enter into him for some days, as it was seeking the proper vehicle, or channel, to give its message to the world. Maitreya means 'The Friend', and this particular incarnation of Buddha was always portrayed in sculptures in centuries past not as an ascetic monk, like other Buddha statues, but rather as a wealthy, worldly, yet enlightened man, with jewels and rich clothing. Osho, being one who did not disdain wealth, but enjoyed everything as a play, seemed the natural choice to be the host of this soul. But after some days, Osho said that he had kicked him out, and was not interested in hosting somebody else's soul!..And that he was perfectly content to just be himself, 'an ordinary man'.

By then I had been moved out of my room in Mirdad, and was living in a smaller hut on the roof of Francis house. This hut was about 4 feet high, and I could not stand up in it. That month, although it was October and long past the usual monsoon time, there were torrential rains, and the bamboo hut was getting very soggy and moldy. There were leaks in the roof, and the rainwater dripped into my bed. I couldn't play my flute at night, as I was now in the middle of the ashram and there would be always some therapist or 'coordinator' to complain if I would play in the night. Ah, life in the ashram….I was having medical problems at the time, those things that westerners get in India, bacterias, infections, parasites, etcetera, all related to getting run down and overheated and over-wet and undernourished by Indian food, for too long. There wasn't a medical center anymore in the ashram, I would have to go to an Indian hospital for tests, and I simply didn't have any money left, and would basically have to beg and borrow to pay for essential medical care. The ashram would not give me the 50 rupees (about 2 dollars) for the exams I needed, it was not approved by the ashram doctor.

The fact that I was working about 14 hours a day seven days a week, of course without payment…that didn't bother me… but the fact of having to beg for something unavoidable yet one more time, just snapped something inside me. I was fed up with all the compressions, contortions, compromises that I had to constantly do to adjust to life 'in the commune'. I knew that Osho's body was dying, I didn't want to spend the short time left that He would be here, struggling with the fact that I never had time to actually sit and close my eyes in peace with Him, but instead was working constantly to maintain my position of having a front seat and a soggy hut and someone always ready to tell me what to do or where to live, as soon as the book was finished. I was finished too. I just wanted to sit in silence with Him, while there was still time…I wanted 'the state of independence': to be Out Of The Structure, standing on my own feet once again, while Osho was still here. My unshakeable connection and love affair with Him was so absolutely clear to me now, and independent of any interim entity, or ashram bureaucracy, that my decision was clear and without hesitation. I finished the book with all the love and creativity I had in me, and borrowed the money for a plane ticket to Italy.

I told Neelam about my decision, that I would be going away for some time. The next day, in discourse, Osho began speaking a set of lectures called 'The Point of Departure'. As soon as I heard the opening phrase, I wanted to just disappear again like a bug under the mosquito net. He spoke about a disciple leaving the master, saying, "Goodbye, Goodbye, I am going here and there…" And the advice of the Master was, "Don't stay where there are no Buddhas, and don't go where there is one!" In short, an unsolvable riddle, with the gist of it being, you cannot go away from your Master. I felt like once again my skin was pealing off, without anesthesia. The minutes crawled by, the words went into me like thunder, I knew every word was aimed straight at me, and yet, this time, I would do it just the same, the decision was mine and I was accepting that responsibility. I knew I was not leaving Him, I was leaving a role in which I could no longer be at peace in a structure in which it was not my nature to continue, and finally I was accepting that.

CHAPTER 29

An American in Florence

As I landed in Rome and set foot in Italy for the first time in my life, Aseema was there to greet me with all her love at Fiumicino airport. I was overjoyed to see her. We took the train from Rome to Florence, and I watched the green hills of Umbria and Toscana pass by the window. It was mid-autumn, late October, and the hills were covered with bare grapevines, and new grass on the ground. I was touched by the beauty that came to me with every passing hill and turn in the way…Green, so green! In India, I had become used to seeing the dusty brown hills and the brown air everywhere, and everything covered with a patina of tiredness and dirt. Here, even the hills looked clean, the vineyards well-kept, and pleasing to the eye.

I arrived in the train station of Florence, and walked into the main hall. It seemed to be a dream. The poverty of India, the dirt and filth and ocean of need that surrounds everything that had become the background scenery of my inner movie for the past several years, it just was not here! Instead, beautiful women dressed like they just stepped out of a Fellini movie were walking here and there, policemen in their spotless uniforms and high white hats strolled by watching the girls, there were capucchino bars and nice things to eat, well-dressed people eating ice cream, everywhere there was light, and color, and beauty, and a sense of fun. My ears perked up as I picked up Italian phrases here and there… I could not understand the words, but my heart could tell what people were saying. I had spent many days as an infant and young child with my Sicilian grandparents as my babysitters, and they spoke to each other in Italian always. I never heard them speak English. So, though the words had not been learned by my rational mind, my unconscious knew what was being said. I felt instantly at home.

We went to the house where we would stay, a big villa on the side of the hills overlooking Florence to the North, in the area of Cercina, above Careggi. The villa was named 'Bel Vedere', which means 'Beautiful View'. And it was! I could see the Duomo (the cathedral) and the whole city of Florence from the big windows, and everywhere were olive groves and sunshine. The villa had once belonged to Enrico Caruso, the great operatic tenor of the last century, and now was being rented by Master's Press, a book-publishing 'commune' of sorts, of about 15 writers and artists that were writing and publishing new-age books. They had given a job to Aseema, and now, me. I arrived as a refugee from India, with one corduroy 3-piece suit that I got in a second-hand shop in Poona, a pair of Sandals, and my flute.

I started life anew again. I began to taste, feel, sense in a different way. I was happy, so happy to be 'out': to be working for hours with a beginning and an end, instead of timeless tasks over which I had no control. I was being paid for my work. I could do what I want with the money. These were simple but great things to me, which I never appreciated before.

Aseema was the cook, and I was the handyman, and driver. The old villa was very run-down. One of my first tasks was to find out why everyone got an electric shock every time they took a bath or used a toilet. I learned Italian by visiting hardware stores and figuring out with a dictionary how to buy nails, wires, tools, gasoline. I made friends with an electrician, who didn't want to do the job of 'earthing' the whole building, but was willing to show me how to do it. It would have cost about $10,000 dollars if he had done it. I did it for about $200. There was a charge of 40 volts of electricity bleeding into the water system from badly insulated water heaters, and it would fry any-body mildly as soon as they put their bare fanny into the bath-tub: not very fun! So I set up ground-wires to every outlet and water heater, and buried a copper stake 6 feet deep into the stony earth outside, running everything to that, and... it worked!

By then winter was coming on, and it was freezing in the old villa. There were fireplaces in every room, but no wood. The painters couldn't paint, the writers couldn't write, the typists couldn't type, everyone was bundled up like polar bears and stamping their feet, so, I found some dusty, decrepit old chairs in the basement, that seemed to be abandoned and forgotten. I made a nice fire in the studio, and everyone went on with their work...until the landlady paid a visit, and started yelling about the strange absence of some of her Renaissance-era chairs that were in the basement. Oops! I had no idea they were THAT old! I decided to try to find another way to heat the house....

There was an ancient little red Renault 5 that I would drive into town to do the shopping with Aseema. It was a great ad-venture, re-learning to drive on the 'Viali' in Florence. The Viali Circondaria circles the historic part of the city; it is 6 or more lanes, never stops, everyone changing lanes here and there like a bumper-car ride at a county fair. Only they aren't bumper cars: they are Alfa Romeos and little Cinque-Centos, a lot of Pandas, Porsches, scooters, and, an occasional Ferrari.

This was a totally new experience, driving in a big speedy Italian city, whose only rules of the road are 'Don't look back!' If you changed lanes while looking in the rear view mirror, you would disturb the flow and fall out of harmony, and dent your fender! Everyone just looks forward, so you better do that too. Lane markers are vague suggestions, red lights and stop signs are recommendations. Basically, Italians do whatever they can get away with, and flow with the traffic. I slowly memorized the city traffic patterns, how to get here and there, where one can find parking, how to get to the veggie market and where are the good buys, and where is a good capucchino bar while Aseema does the shopping. It was fun to re-enter 'normal' life and be in this world. And often, we would disappear for three hours, and go to the Uffizi Museum or the Accademia gallery and sit together in front of masterpieces of Botticelli or Leonardo da Vinci or Michelangelo, and marvel at these wonders, right in our own town. I was like a kid in Disneyland, only this wasn't plastic…it was the real thing!…. I was seeing things I had only dreamed of before, artworks which I had grown up with, looking at them each day in the prayerbooks or schoolbooks or on the walls of my mother's kitchen, and here they were, the originals, bigger than life, and imbued with the living touch of those Masters. I drank it all in, and relished it. Aseema, through her love, was opening wonderful doors for me, that was bridging the mystic in me to this world, through art. I learned to delight in the things of this world, touching beautiful objects made with love and care and patience, spending time with friends laughing about nothing, going for walks in lovely old villages made of stone, seeing sunsets in olive groves, forests filled with fireflies at night…She opened my eyes to a world I had never known, that had always been there, but I had not been ready to see it. Her love had a special quality of lightness and humor, perhaps because she trained as a mime and professional dancer, and lived a great part of her life on the stage, all over the world. She is a mystic woman, but a very unusual one, because she is a marvelous dancer who can never take herself seriously. That is a rare, rare combination.

It was a happy time, and fun to live there. The 'commune' in the old villa was a very heady and yet playful loving atmosphere; the dinners were witty, with constant jokes about the books they were making, the life outside in Florence, Nostradamus, techniques of air-brush, the lack of punctuation marks in someone's writing, Tarot cards and magic, how Ivan-the-Terrible had reincarnated as a book publisher, the Medici and modern-day witches, pregnant robots; it was a constant and delightful banter. I would make bread, or chocolate-chip cookies, keep the gas and water and heat running, while Aseema made her wonderful food scraping it together with the minimal budget she was given, and we made the best of it. Purvodaya was the owner, and he was a great guy, an Englishman with a big body, big heart, very sharp mind with a delightful sense of humor. Madhu, his beautiful wife, was a budding writer; Yatri, an artist and writer with his wonderful drawings and sharp English sense of humor, Padma and her fantastic oil paintings, Siddhena, Sandipa, Diti, many others came and went, it was a rich and creative atmosphere that nourished me very, very much. 'Purvo' would be telling about his teen years in a tai-chi monastery in Tibet, real or fantasy none of us knew, and while he would be worrying about paying the bills to the Chinese printers in Hong Kong, Padma and I would sing songs from West Side Story; 'When you're a jet…you stay a jet!' I was thrilled by the beauty and fun that surrounded me now in Italy, and it called out to me to create beauty.

One weekend Aseema and I took the old car and drove to Pietrasanta, to the marble mountains near Carrara, where Michelangelo had quarried the beautiful white marble for his masterpieces. The mountains dramatically rise above the sea, 2 hours outside of Florence, and they are covered in white…not from snow, but marble dust. These mountains, the Apuan Alps, are all marble, the rivers and waterfalls are beds of pure white stone. I picked up two stones from the riverbed, fascinated by the pure white and tight grain, and brought them back to the villa. There I began carving, with a chisel I bought in a shop behind the Duomo, first a little naked dancing apsara figure, a female deity, from one. From the other, came my first Buddha statue.

One day, when we were downtown, we went to the Duomo, the cathedral of Florence. It was the first time I had ever been there, at least in this lifetime. As I entered the main doors, I was dumbstruck by that vast expanse of light and gracefully arching stone. It is magnificent and simple in its grandeur, high vaults of grey and beige stone, with little decoration to disturb the elegant and majestic lines of the architecture. We walked all around the church, somewhat in a hurry as there were things we had to do before getting home again.

A few days later I returned, and I had it in my mind to go to the left nave of the church, which is laid out like a big cross, because I remembered seeing a reddish-brown 'pieta' of Michelangelo there, which I wanted to see more of, slowly, 'con calma', not in fret.

As I reached the left nave, I was surprised…there was no such statue there! I couldn't figure out what had happened, I could have sworn that I had seen it exactly there just a few days before. I felt somewhat dis-oriented, and left.

A month later, I was in a small museum on the side of the Duomo, where they keep many artworks that had originally been placed in the Duomo, and also many tools that had been used in its construction centuries ago. It's called the 'Museum del'Opera del Duomo. There, I came upon the very statue of Michelangelo's that I had thought I had seen in the Duomo some weeks before. It is quite large, about 9 feet tall, and the main figure is Nicodemus holding the body of the dead Christ, the figure of Nicodemus having been carved as a self-portrait of the artist. I was stunned to read the inscription, that it had been exactly in that left nave of the Duomo, as I had thought I had seen it, for 2 centuries, but was moved out of the church for safe-keeping THREE HUNDRED YEARS AGO!

Now, that was a curveball. I often have had the feeling, walking the streets of Florence in the historic quarter, that I have been there before. The feeling of the alleyways and turnings of the road, and the placement of the buildings seems uncannily familiar. Turning a corner in an alleyway, you pass the house of Dante or the workshop of Ghirlandaio, and I felt completely at home in those stone alleyways, like I knew them already. Aseema and I would often go downtown in the winter evenings, when, in those years in that winter season, there were very few tourists, and we would walk the streets arm in arm for long hours, in the grand manner of the Florentines, who like to take a relaxed stroll in the evenings and see everyone and everything. It was a great delight to partake in this lovely ritual of daily life in Italy.

When I had been in Florence for about two months, there arrived a letter from the ashram. It was from Neelam. She said that she had been in to see Osho that day, to show him the marble book which I had made for him before I left. He loved it. He touched it, and told Nirvano to touch it, and He said that He wanted all his books to be made like that in marble. Then Neelam showed him some photos in which I was playing for a poetry reading in Buddha hall, and she said, "This is Devakant, who made the book.." Osho said, "I know. Give him my love". Neelam said, "I will have to send him your love, he has gone away for now.." Osho raised his eyebrows and asked, "He has gone for his visa?" Neelam said, "No he has gone for a longer period." Osho was silent for a few moments, then said: "He will be back soon".

It was true in my feeling. After two months, I was wanting to be back again. I was saving every penny, to be able to be there, but not dependent on the ashram, but rather just BE there, with him, and meditate. But it was not time yet, there was no money being paid out right now in the book publishing commune, there was a constant 'shortage of funds', especially when it came to paying out salaries, and I had to wait a few more months to get paid and be able to leave.

On the ground floor of the villa there was a beautiful sunny room with glass doors, a kind of solarium. In that light-filled room, was a piano. When I wasn't working, I spent most of my hours there, composing and recording, on a little 4-track tape recorder, 'Eagles Flight', which would be my first solo album. All I had at the time was that piano, my flute, an oboe, and a viola, and the freedom to play what I wished. It was a joy to make that album. Technology was still so simple then, you just plugged in a mike, pushed the 'record' button, and played your heart out. No computer sequences, breakbeats, loops, expansion modules, midimaps or arpeggiators, these torture devices would not be invented yet for several years. It was still just music and very little mind.

At that time Aseema received news that her parents weren't well, and she went to Chile to visit them, for the first time in many years. I finished my tape in the villa, and passed the spring moving the commune to another villa, a lot cheaper, on the far south side of the city, in the hills of Impruneta. It was getting time to go back to India, I felt, and when Aseema returned in June, we made our resolve to be back in India by the first day of August. I did whatever jobs I could on the side to gather extra cash, and we started dispersing and narrowing down our possessions, discarding the winter clothes we had needed there, for the journey that would await us.

CHAPTER 30

An Untimely Death

No man is an island, entire of itself.
Everyman is a part of the whole, a piece of the maine..
If a clod be washed away by the sea, Europe is the less,
as well as if a promontory were,
as well as if a manor of thy friend's or of thine own were:
any man's death diminishes me,
because I am involved in mankind,
and therefore never send to know for whom the bell tolls;
it tolls for thee.

John Donne

As we were ready to board the plane to India in the airport in Zurich and we passed the immigration checkpoint in the airport, we realized that we had done it: we were actually on our way back to India again, and we looked at each other and laughed. Immediately there appeared a very serious man in a dark business suit who emerged from behind a mirrored window and confiscated our passports temporarily while he checked all the computers to see if we were terrorists. Obviously, laughter was linked to terrorism, makes sense, right? We stifled our giggles, and remembered that still the world was as it was, and we were then silently glad to be leaving Europe and going home in a way, to India.

I had been away from the Commune and India for 9 months. I had enjoyed immensely the change of living in Florence, working and making money, and now I was just as glad to be going back in India, once again near to Osho, not being dependent on the commune, and not having to do whatever was thought to be the most important thing by whoever-may-be-running-the-show at the present time. I was on my own, could spend my time meditating for a change, and was filled with new inspiration. Aseema and I arrived to Poona, and found out that for most of the time that we had been in Italy, Osho had not been speaking. He had been staying in His room, but had been in ever-declining health. Just in the days when we came back, I started playing music in Buddha hall again for the evening meditations, and Osho started coming out again to share in a new way. He would come out for about 10 minutes, and be there without speaking, while we would play music, and he would conduct the music in his way. That is, we would start playing, and then he would start moving his hands, in very unpredictable ways, sometimes beating time, sometimes waving one hand while the other rose up high in the air, wiggling the fingers…Never would anything be explained, you just had to intuit what the actual instructions were. It was very difficult to know what he was trying to get us to do with the music, but we had to just respond and DO it without thinking much about it, all of this, live and in front of a microphone with Osho and about 10,000 people listening.

When I arrived to the ashram, on the first or second day, I was in the back part of the compound, at Mirdad, where I had had a room the previous year. Going up the stairs, I suddenly found myself face-to-face with Nirvano. We had a long hug, and spoke a little while. She was happy to see me, and I also was feeling a deep happiness in seeing her. Her hair had started to turn white at the temples, and her body was different, more thin, she seemed more fragile. Her smile was as beautiful as ever, but not as whole-hearted. I gave her the tape I had made in Florence, EAGLES FLIGHT, my first solo recording, and I asked her to give it to Osho, and I showed her the dedication to him on the inside cover. She promised she would give it to Him. I could not know it then, but that was to be the last time I would ever see her face-to-face.

Just after seeing Nirvano, I went around to the back of the building and searched for a little while under the Peepal tree, where had been my workshop for the tables nine months before, and I found, under a pile of leaves, the last block of marble I had gotten in Rajasthan, that I had risked my life for. I cleaned it off, and started working on making a Buddha statue from that last block of Abu-green marble, the ending of the long story that had begun with that little table I made for Nirvano some years before. I carved it each day, slowly, and as the figure took shape, Osho's health became more precarious with each passing moment.

At that time, a play was being produced in the ashram, called 'The Song of Meera'. It was the story of an Indian mystic and singer of many centuries ago, a beautiful woman who gave up being a Rajput queen to dance and sing her love of Krishna in a temple. She had left the palace in disgrace, having left her husband and given up all for Krishna, her mystical love, a being who had lived along before, the Avatar of Vishnu who is always portrayed in Indian statues as playing the flute. He was a mesmerizing being, reputed to have 17,000 gopis, which are something between adoring disciples, and girlfriends, maybe all mixed together, whom he enchanted with his flute and brought them to heights of ecstasy in the play of love between Master and Disciple. Meera's love for Him, centuries after he had died as a physical being, transformed her life, and she is revered as a saint in India. This play was being produced by a sannyasin named

Dwabha, who long ago left her career as an actress in Hollywood and lived in the presence of Osho ever since. She is a wonderful woman, very flamboyant, big-hearted and creative. Aseema was in the role of Meera, and I was the flute of Krishna that she would dance to. Aseema was incredible in the role, her acting was more than acting. In the part of the play where Meera was watching the bodies of her two dead parents, it was all the more poignant as Aseema had just that week received word from Chile that her own parents had just died, within a week of each other, one from illness, and the other in a car accident. Her tears onstage were real, not acting. The play was a huge success.

At the same time, I had started going to Bombay to meet with Hariprasad, and take lessons from him in earnest. Aseema and I were living in a rooftop apartment above Prem's restaurant in the middle of Koregaon park.

Indian music consists of melodies called RAGAS, which is a fixed scale pattern which is practiced and practiced until it becomes engrained in you, like second nature. Each of these patterns of notes has associations with a time of day, a season of the year, an emotional mood. One has to play that particular type of raga at the right time of day, or else it is not harmonious with the moment, and does not produce the healing and soothing effect which it can provoke if it is played rightly and in the right time. One can even get ill playing a raga at the wrong time. So if you want to learn early-morning ragas, you have to play them in the early morning, or the vibration won't be right. I was getting up at 4 in the morning to practice pre-dawn ragas, so I had to have a place where the neighbors wouldn't hear me. There was a little tiled room on the roof that was perfect for this, I could play there at 4 in the morning, for hours, and come outside to see the glorious and golden-red dawn sky over Poona each morning.

The lessons with Hariji were each Sunday, which was the only day when he was sure to be at home, as he had a very busy recording schedule in the film industry of Bollywood, and also was a much-requested concert artist. I would call him up on Saturday to see if he would be at home, and invariably he would tell me, "Yes, yes, you simply come! Don't be worried". I could almost see his head shaking side-to-side in that Indian way, as he would say this on the other end of the telephone.

So I would get to the train station in Poona by 6 am Sunday and get on the Deccan Queen down the ghats to Bombay, a 3-hour journey, then get off in Dadar and take the suburban train out to Khar, where he lived. The suburban trains were always a memorable experience, to say the least, as they carried all manner of people, things, animals, and some objects which were hard to classify. Then I would take a local bus, which was even better. Once I was sitting on the bus next to an old Brahmin, which is a member of the highest priest caste in India, whose dhoti didn't seem to have been washed for weeks. We both looked at each other with the same disdain, me being worried if he had lice, and he being worried that he was being defiled by sitting next to someone of a lower caste.

At Hariji's I never knew what to expect. Sometimes he was there, sometimes there were other masters there with him, like Shivkumar Sharma or Zakir Hussain. Sometimes he was walking out the door as I was coming in, and he would say, "Sorry, Devakant, I have a sudden recording session…you simply wait here!" And sometimes he was just sleeping upstairs after having played a concert all night long.

And I would wait, for hours in his living room. Sometimes he would get back and we would have lunch together. Sometimes he would be there and we would have a lesson all day, together with one or two of his oldest disciples. And sometimes, he wouldn't make it back at all, and I would wait until 5 p.m. when I would have to start the journey back to Victoria Station and get my night train to Poona. I would arrive home after midnight, dead tired. On those days when I had had no lesson, but instead had been waiting for him, while he slept in his room upstairs, I would get home late at night and play my flute a little bit, and was shocked to find out that I was playing completely differently, better, more fluid, with more 'rasa', which is feeling, or depth. I then realized that Hariji was a real Master, and it was not information that he was giving me: it was a transmission of energy, something mystical, that transpired between us. Just by my being there in his home or near him, present, some of his wine would pour into my bottle. And it was very sweet wine, very, very sweet.

Back in Poona, I was playing in the evening meetings when Osho would come out. He was very weak, and seemed to be aging by the day, his movements slower and his walk more wobbly. The evening meditation with Him was about 10 minutes long. He would enter into the hall, Namaste to everyone as He slowly walked to his chair, and then would lovingly and slowly turn to the whole audience and give his blessings. All this while, there was playing a kind of samba music with big Surdo drums from Brazil, and it was very powerful and intense. When he would sit down, that music would stop, and we would play a much softer type of music that was more akin to classical Indian music. Often, usually in fact, I was playing, with Aseema playing tamboura and Maneesh on tablas. He is a very dear friend of mine, who is also a student of Alla Rakha, the father of Zakir Hussain and one of the best tabla players in the world. Maneesh is no slouch either, he could flow with anything, with flair, precision, presence and creativity. It was always a joy to play with him.

Osho would conduct this music every day while we played. We would begin slowly, and he would start a pulse with his hands. We would pick that up, and he would then do any number of things, again with no explanations given to us what to do. Sometimes one hand would be beating softly, while the other would raise over his head and stop...or flutter...or move in waves. We just kept playing, faster and faster with his rhythm, and it would open into more and more dimensions of melody. I can distinctly remember, when we were going extremely fast, that I had the thought, "Geez, I can't play any faster!" And RIGHT then, as if hearing my thoughts, Osho would start pushing ever faster and harder, and push me through whatever barriers I thought I had. Suddenly he would stop, and there would be a profound silence. This would happen 3 times, and then he would get up to Namaste and leave, with the Samba music. Sometimes he would do massive STOPS with the Samba music, and all the drums would follow his beats. The silences in between the stops were very, very intense, as he would hold his look with his eyes wide like a tiger, at whoever he was looking at when the stop happened. It was intense, riveting, stunning.

During the day, I kept on with the Buddha statue, slowly it found its form. Carving the crystalline marble was more familiar to me now, and I could slowly, carefully bring out the form of the body and face. The thing about marble sculpture, is that every step is forever. Every chip taken away, is gone, and there is no turning back. If in one minute, your chisel slips and off comes the nose, then you end up with a much smaller Buddha and a lot of powder. So I worked carefully. There is a moment, when you circumscribe around the marble, like around the neck under the head, that the marble starts pinging with a distinct ringing sound, and that's the sure sign that it's going to break off in the next moment. So, you have to be listening, and watching, and moving without haste. I like it that way, you cannot go fast, and what was once an irritation to me became a pleasure, the slow and eternal quality of the work became something I came to love. As the days moved into December, the polish came up, step by step.

The Buddha Statue, from the last Block of Abu Green

I finished the statue at 5:30 pm on Dec.10, 1989…the day before Osho's birthday. That evening, I was playing flute in an art exhibition in the ashram, and Neelam was there. I told her about the statue, and asked her to give it to Osho as a birthday present the next day, Dec. 11. I asked her if she wanted to see it, and with a strange distant look of sorrow, she said, "Not now…" It was a look she would wear when there were things on her mind that she couldn't talk about. I pondered what was going on.

I brought the statue to Lao Tzu House, on the porch where Osho would come out to get into the Rolls for the evening meditation the next day.

The next morning, Dec. 11, Osho's Birthday, I was in the ashram at 7 in the morning, and my friend Asha, a beautiful Varanasi lady who always kept me well informed with all the latest ashram gossip, came up to me and grabbed my arm, saying, "Hey MAN! Have you HEARD? Nirvano has DIED!!"

I was stunned. Apparently she had died the day before, at 5:30 in the afternoon, exactly the time when I had finished the Buddha from the last block of marble, the story of which had all begun with her request. Neelam had been at the burning of her body in the ghats by the river in the evening, and said nothing to me when I had met her face-to-face at the exhibition an hour later, with just that look of unspoken sorrow. Nothing was being said to anyone about the death, officially. A stonewall of silence... No ceremony, No public funeral.

I was filled with a mixture of shock, dismay, anger, and disgust, about yet another cover-up in the commune, another 'skeleton' pushed into the closet. I went down to the river, to the burning ghats, where Nirvano's funeral pyre was still smoking where her body quickly and without public ceremony had been burned the night before. I sat there a long time...a very long time. I felt her, that she was glad to be dead, to be out of that body, free for now....I could hear her laughter.

Not a word was said to the commune about her death. No statement, and no explanation was given. Only that awful silence that marks the lid being closed on a story, about the life of someone who had meant so very much to so many people. We had become a totally dysfunctional family; nothing said about realities, just a facade to keep up pretenses.

The next day, I was called into the office by Jayesh. He was wearing glasses, which I had never seen him wearing before in all our interactions. On his face was a strange mixture of grief-that-was-not-exactly-grief. It was something more complicated, and I couldn't decipher what it was. I had the feeling that he was showing a seriousness that was appropriate to the occasion, of talking to me, the previous boyfriend of Nirvano, but inside him there was something else, and I couldn't tell what it was. Feigned guilt? Relief disguised as grief? Too much sorrow to allow oneself to feel? I cannot say, but it was not a simple look. He said that Osho had told him not to feel guilty. I wondered why he was telling me that; the desire to placate me and make it all 'o.k.'? The need to share a heavy burden on the heart? I had no idea, and could not catch the unspoken feeling.

He told me that Osho wanted me to carve her funereal marker, which would be a plaque of black granite, set in the side of the new pyramid in the ashram, with her photo, and the words:

"IN LOVING MEMORY OF MA PREM NIRVANO,
WHO DIED AN UNTIMELY DEATH."

I began at once this project, which would take me several months. As I worked on it, slowly carving the memory into granite of the woman whom I had loved more than anyone in this world, as the bits and grains of granite would spit into my eyes, and my eyes would fill with sweat and grit from working under the burning sun of India in summer, there came clearly in my mind the words which Osho spoke 5 years before at the Ranch, one night when he was looking straight into my eyes, as I sat before him in the packed small room in His house, "You are going from this life, and you look back, and see all your pleasures were just written on water, and your pain was carved in granite, and you suffered all that pain for those pleasures, which were just writings on water..."

C H A P T E R   3 1

Never Born, Never Died

Since the consciousness is not born,
no one can obstruct it or soil it;
Staying in the "Unborn" realm,
all appearances will dissolve into the ultimate Dharma.
All self-will and pride will vanish into naught.
The supreme Understanding transcends all this and that.
The supreme Action embraces great resourcefulness
without attachment.
The supreme Accomplishment is to realize immanence
without hope.

Tilopa, Song of Mahamudra

Chala Vahi Des...
I am going to that Sorrowless Land

Meerabhai

As I write, I am in Oaxaca, Mexico, in a large garden of Jacaranda and banana trees. The rain falls on the balcony like a soft rhythmic music, as the ground breathes in relief at the end of the day's heat. Birds call at a distance in the large trees filled with orange flowers... More intensely now comes the rain, and the calls of the birds more sparse now as they settle down. There are banana trees with massive stalks bearing green fruit, resembling huge phalluses of purple; enormous jacaranda trees filled with orange flowers.

After the rain in the morning, the sun returns brilliant, radiant, the sky luminous and pulsating with the cries of tropical birds, never repeating, always changing.

The garden is filled with fruits and flowers...the women at their looms, weaving strands of colors with deft fingers, nimbly separating and rejoining the strands, over and over again, wordlessly. The weaver's body weight maintaining the tension of the woof, while the nimble fingers toss the warp back and forth. Her brother with his paintings, large oils, simple and extravagant colors, forms, innocent bodies calling out for sex, incessant urge of procreation...

In the mango garden, there are bouganvileas hanging, and a simple open-air kitchen, with a stone table, a mortar and pestle, and a fire with a clay dish on top. They need nothing more...

I return to my story: the next day after I finished the Buddha statue on the day of Nirvano's death, I began working again in Osho's house, this time in his library, helping to make the new cabinets for all the books. I did not know it, but it was to be a brief time, and each passing day Osho was growing weaker and weaker. Sometimes after the evening meeting, he would comment to Anando that someone was sending negative energy to him from the public, with the intent to weaken and harm his body. Sometimes he would point in a certain direction in the evening meeting, or another, when he felt it was coming his way. Nobody was ever found. But each night in the sitting with Him, the feeling was more and more strange and intense, as this final chapter in the drama was unfolding. On the day of January 17th, I was given for the first time since I had been back, a seat in the front row, and I waited in silent anticipation for that chance to sit so close to him once again, after more than a year.

That night, he did not come to the discourse, he was apparently too ill.

The next night, January 18th, I was guarding on the road around Buddha Hall as his car came for the meeting, and from a few meters away, I watched him walk in and out of the hall, from his car. As he was leaving, and he got into the car, something inside me wordlessly knew that it was the last time I would ever see Him.

The following day, January 19th, I had been working in His house all day with a strange feeling inside me. Passing a corridor, I saw a large silver multi-tiered flower-stand being cleaned in the kitchen, the kind that are used in funerals in India. I had never seen that in the house before. I asked Jalada, who worked in another part of the library, "How is Osho?" She couldn't answer me, it seemed we both were having the same strange feeling.

That night, I was to play for Him in the evening meeting, with Amit, Osho's brother, on tablas. We began the music in Buddha hall as the auditorium filled with 10,000 disciples all dressed in white. We were playing a raga which goes on for about 20 minutes before the samba music begins. After a few minutes, Divya, Amit's wife, Osho's sister-in-law, ran into the hall crying hysterically and fell into Amit's arms. The music stopped, and we all knew what had happened. There were 10,000 or more people gathered in Buddha Hall, a great wave of shock started to spread, as voices cried out, "Osho! Osho!" in despair. I looked at Milarepa, and Nivedano, we all three looked at each other and there was just love between us, after all the battles in the rehearsals, struggles, celebrations, and good and bad moments of all those years playing together, now there was just love, and we started the music to give a proper sendoff to this man who had touched our lives more deeply than anyone else ever would or could. The music started, the energy changed into a deep feeling too profound for words, but if I had to describe with the poverty of words it could only be called gratitude and love. DevaRaj, Osho's doctor came in to read the statement that Osho had died 2 hours before, and his body was carried into Buddha Hall for the celebration.

As His body was being carried out of the hall, the crowd was following it to the burning ghats, about a half mile away at the river. Jayesh was one of the pallbearers in the front, and he kept gesturing to me to come there, and walk with the body. I did, and walked the whole way to the ghats just next to Osho's head, playing my flute the whole way. I knew he was still there listening. All were singing, some were too shocked to feel anything, some were trying hard not to collapse into sorrow, and some were simply in the 'gap', that space where feeling is so deep, the mind stops to function, the deepest gap that could ever happen to someone, outside of one's own death.

The walk to the ghats was slow, achingly slow, a walk that one wishes would never happen, to walk to the funeral pyre with the body of your Master. It was unthinkable, and yet it was happening. But, it was not sorrow I felt. It was too big for that. It was a disassociation, it was beyond emotion: I felt I was staring into the face of something which until that moment had been totally unthinkable to me, and yet here it was, and yet, nothing had happened. What is, IS! We arrived to the burning place by the river, and the white-robed sannyasins came and came and came, thousands upon thousands. We musicians played, all night, as everyone sang, in a deep shock, or stayed in a deep silence, as each in their own way responded to that love within them, a love beyond love, for a being who had helped us all in a way we could never have imagined before we met Him. I watched the flames of his burning body climb into the night sky, and I knew deep within me that it was not sorrow I was watching, it was a deep and vast joy, His joy, pouring into the universe. He was really free now, from that body which had been such a burden, from the whole long, long line of bodies which that vast soul had inhabited over all the course of the evolution of that great and beautiful Being, now he was FREE, He was the sky itself, He was joy itself released into infinity.

As the dawn arrived, Aseema and I left the ghats by the river and walked back to our apartment, silently, deeply grateful to be with each other, paradoxically in our aloneness, in that day which would mark forever our lives, as a 'Before' and an 'After'.

CHAPTER 32

Dorje Chupta: Rightful Action

It was now January 21, 1990. Osho had departed, or 'left his body', 2 days before. At the burning ghats by the river under the ancient banyan trees, the fire where his body had burned had turned to ashes, and cooled and became a memory. His ashes, this day, were being carried into the ashram. The ashram itself was packed with people, singing, dancing, celebrating. There was not one square inch of space in the road that led from the main gate to Lao Tzu House, the principal 'street' of the commune. It was one throbbing mass of energy, thousands of people from all over the world, singing their hearts out.

As the ashes, being carried by Osho's elder brother, were being taken into the gate of Lao Tzu House, I was at the other end of the road, at the main gate, playing my flute, a few hundred meters away. Suddenly, the whole crowd started calling my name. "DEVAKANT!!!" It was, like a call from the Master, to go in with him back to his house. I couldn't believe it. The whole cortege stopped, and waited, as I struggled to move through the packed crowd to get to the gate where his ashes were waiting to go in, holding my flute over my head as I squirmed through the thousands of people. Somebody yelled out, "Play your flute, man!" and as I got to the gate, I started playing, and went in, with the ashes, into Chuang Tzu auditorium, which had been made as a kind of mausoleum-temple for the ashes of Osho. It was extravagantly beautiful, all marble and glass, and I started playing there as the whole commune slowly passed in file to pay their respects to the ashes of the Master. It was a remarkable, other-worldly atmosphere, deep, silent, sacred, beyond words. I played there for 3 months, every day. That became my life for a while.

At that time, in the days just after Osho left his body, there was a tangible change, in almost everyone. It was in some small way, as if we all were 'enlightened' for a brief time. Everybody was telling the truth to each other, transparent, no masks. Love was there, in everyone, like a tangible presence, far more important than sex or power or position or anything. I found myself saying things to people, spontaneously, which I had long held in my heart, without any inhibition, anger, or shame. It was magical. I simply didn't have many thoughts, for weeks. The wave of Osho's energy which had passed into and through us all was a transforming force; we all were lifted to a different dimension of being.

I had been living and working for 10 years near to his physical presence, almost every day. And yet I was almost always out of sight of him, just around the corner, or in another room, feeling where he was but not putting myself in the same physical space with him, so as not to intrude on his privacy. I had to feel always where he was in the apartment... So the FEELING of his presence was very familiar, tangible, and had nothing to do with my eyes or faculty of sight.

On that day, and for a very long time after that, I once again had that very well-known feeling, of His nearby presence, which I always had while working around Him. It was not like He was in one place, but a Presence. And the question would come into my mind, "But WHERE is He?". I realized in my heart that He had done the very thing He had spoken of; He had transcended death, in a very real way; not like a ghost, but a dissolving into existence itself. This feeling remained in me for a long time, even months, and years, and still returns when there are gathered a group of people in celebration of love for him.

The 2nd day that I played, which meant it was 3 days after Osho left the body, there began for me a strange tail to the story, of the life-changing events which had just transpired: when I began to play inside the marble hall of Osho's Samadhi, I heard a loud banging on the glass outside, just to my left, at the top of the large plate-glass window. There, hanging on a branch of a tree outside, was a big black crow, or Raven, intensely staring into the window and banging its head against the glass when I would play. Bam-bam-bam! It had an intention to it, it was distressed, and it was making some kind of signal. "Perhaps sometimes birds do that when they see their reflection in the glass, and they feel their territory is violated", I thought to myself. Looking again at the bird, my fleeting impression was how much its curved beak resembled Nirvano's nose, and its intention resembled hers when she was pissed off. It kept banging its head against the window when I would start to play...bam-bam-bam!! Each day it would come back. Sometimes the gardeners would shoo it away, but it specifically wanted to return to THAT window at THAT time and bang its head on the glass when I would play the flute. As the weeks passed, it would return every day, and it seemed like a vignette from an Edgar Allen Poe novel, a dark bird like an omen of evil, banging its head insistently against a window repeatedly, in the silent marble and glass temple. It was unnerving.

A hundred days passed. Each day I played flute in the samadhi with Aseema on tamboura. Each day, the Raven came and banged on the glass. The ashram slowly moved out of its shocked and numbed state, and a kind of new 'normalcy' started to set in. The 'Inner Circle', a group of 21 disciples whom Osho had chosen to continue his work after his death, met regularly as a governing body, and there was a general atmosphere of helpfulness, pulling together, getting through and continuing his vision.

My time of playing for the people who came to meditate in Osho's temple, which had deep meaning and beauty for me, slowly changed into a very different 'job', as other musicians were slowly integrated into playing there, and it was up to me to see that the timings were filled and all was going harmoniously. Only, that meant that if someone neglected, or 'spaced-out' their appointment and didn't show up to play, I would run to get a tamboura player and my correct robes on and white socks and everything else that was needed to be there to play instead. And if someone in the Inner Circle didn't like a certain player of Japanese flute, then generically Japanese flutists couldn't play there, by heavy-handed decree 'from above', and I had to communicate that to the deeply despondent flutists, and incur all the deep resentments that it generated, as if it was my arbitrary dictum. It wasn't. I very much disliked doing that. I don't care if someone is playing a hurdy-gurdy or a harmonica, if they do it beautifully and with heart, great. I do dislike dictums from 'above', by people who have no taste or feeling for music, and are simply lording it over on someone with their petty tyrant likes and dislikes, and I have had plenty of that in the ashram over the years.... By the bucketfuls! Yes, it has been great for my 'growth'. And a point comes, when something inside just says, "Finished". This time, I simply felt that it's enough, and I decided to take a break from life-in-the-commune, and take a look at myself and all what happened inside me, and go back to the Himalayas.

Aseema and I left Poona, and travelled by train across the vast hot and arid plateau of India towards Delhi. India, in April, bakes in the sun. It is the last month of the long dry spell, when the heat is the worst and the promise of rains is not yet on the horizon. As we crossed the Ganges, the whole train compartment fell silent, out of deep respect for the sacredness of the river. A silent vibe touched my heart, as we watched that great expanse of water all around us. We arrived in Delhi, another of the points of the universe where 'The Great Magician' experiments on what are the worst possible conditions that humans can exist in. That is Delhi. At one point we were in a riksha, a small 3-wheeled motor-taxi usually with two stroke engines like a lawnmower running at full tilt and drivers that are in a kind of fixed-stare trance, like kamikaze pilots heading hellbent for their final 'destinaton'. We were crossing the city to get to another station, and in the impossible snarl of traffic we were trapped in a tunnel, with hundreds of rikshas, trucks, cars, camels, buses and scooters. There was no air to breathe, just that particular heavy and humid exhaust of badly burned Diesel and carbon monoxide that one always encounters on the roads in India. There was literally no air, and no way out. We just looked at each other, eyes watering, choking on the fumes, and waited it out.

Delhi station was a zoo, literally. The platform was filled with rotting vegetables, numberless crowds of people standing, milling, sleeping, or dead, on the ground wrapped in sheets, with bundles and goats and chickens and patient Tibetan refugees and endless queues leading nowhere. I can still see the sadistic twisted smile on the face of the platform manager as he told us with only half-hidden delight, "Sorry, there are no tickets… There is nothing I can do." We jostled our way through the living and the dead, and found our way to the bus station, where we managed to get onto a bus which was going to Manali. The bus ride was 12 hours of bumpy road, endless curves winding into the mountains, abysmal drop-offs into the river below where again we could see more buses wrecked down at the bottom…and spectacular views of the Himalayas, which grow in height as you approach them. There is one particular seat on the bus which was always empty, and I asked why. It seems it is the death-seat, which is where the impact would be if the bus driver misjudges his passing of another vehicle as another bus or truck is oncoming. The collision always happens at that point in the bus, so people have learned, in the way of Indian Wisdom, to not sit there.

Arriving in Manali was like arriving in paradise. It truly is the valley of the gods. The valley is lined by peaks of more than 6,000 meters, and at the far end, bordering Tibet, Ladakh, and Zanskar, the Rotang-La pass rises up and up, with its Deodar pines majestically disappearing into snow and mists. We found the house of a friend of Dwabha, named Ageha, who lived on the side of the valley in the wooded hillsides overlooking the pass, the Rotang-la, and a Tibetan monastery (gompa) in the valley below.

Ageha is a wonderful woman, German, who lived at that time with her 5 year old daughter Sara in that magical place. She loved horses, the mountains, and decided to make her stand there, and do her life. I occupied myself with meditating on all what had passed, and reading the Tibetan Book of the Dead, and going for walks in those wonderful valleys and canyons where Shiva and Parvati left their names and their legacies.

Meditating in those deep valleys covered with pines and cliffs carved with Buddhas, I delved deeper into the Tibetan Book of The Dead, a treatise meant to be read or whispered into the ears of a person dying, or recently dead, which serves as a guide-book to the soul, beginning its new journey towards another incarnation. According to this scripture, the human soul passes a period of 42 days after the death of the body in a kind of limbo, called the Bardo, where not having the roots of a body to keep it tethered, it is blown about by the winds of its own desires and unfulfilled experiences, like tempests in a nightmare. The Book of the Dead serves as an aid to such a soul, wandering in the jungles of thought-forms created by its own mind, hal-lucinations, in this in-between-body state. A major focus of the book is, if total liberation (enlightenment) has not been accomplished by such a soul, at least it can be helped to gain a more auspicious birth in a realm which will enable it to evolve spiritually. In this part of the book, one paragraph was dedicated to admonishing the soul to see, if it was coming upon a land which was crisscrossed with black roads, and having hot brown air and houses all in rows the same, to move on, it is a hell-realm and not a place to take a birth.

"That's a perfect description of Riverside!", I thought, and I realized that the place of my birth in this lifetime, having been conditioned into me by all the commentators on radio and television at the time of my childhood that it was a kind of heaven desired by all, was in fact spoken of in an ancient Tibetan scripture 8 centuries before as being a Hell-realm, and not at all a good choice of places to land when searching for a new womb to enter! Needless to say, this caused a major re-evaluation in me of the state of my spiritual evolution at the time of my last death; "No wonder I've had to go through so much crap in this lifetime!", I thought. Osho was helping me pay Karma, in big installments: I remembered the story of the Tibetan yogi Milarepa, having to carry thousands of stones up the hill in old Tibet to make a tower, over and over again 7 times, each time his master Marpa deciding that it wasn't quite the right shape, and he would have to tear it down and start over…

After about 2 weeks of being there, in that little house on the pine-covered mountain with Aseema, Ageha and Sara, in conversations with Ageha about what had happened in the last months at the ashram, the death of Osho and Nirvano, I came to know that in the previous year she had passed a deep and powerful meeting with death, as 7 of the people whom she had been closest to had passed away in the last 12 months. She said that the only thing that really helped her get through it was a Tibetan Rinpoche in the monastery in the valley below, who does a special work of finding souls in the Bardo, the intermediary state after death, and before the soul moves on to a new incarnation.

I said immediately that I wanted to meet him, and I knew I had to do this. So she agreed to take me.

When we arrived at the monastery, there on a scaffold outside the building was a Tibetan monk, making sculptures in relief, out of concrete, on the walls of the monastery, slowly and carefully scraping away the wet concrete in a way which brought out the figures. He would make the Wheel of Dharma and the 'Sermon to the Deers', and other symbols from the Buddhist iconography. I watched him for a long time, and asked him questions about how he did it, and he told me all about it, taking care to mention many things to be careful of in the doing of it, all in a very joyful and simple way, which was his basic character. I felt deeply moved by meeting him, as if I was meeting a part of my destiny that day. He makes Thangka paintings, and does sculptures of Buddha and Tara and such things, and travels from monastery to monastery in the mountains, getting what he needs to survive, and moving on. I knew that was to be my fate as well, although in different clothing, much the same thing. This was truly 'right livelihood', doing his art for the Dharma, the Eternal Law, and receiving what he needed, and moving on.

I met first the new Rinpoche, a young Tibetan Lama in his 30s, dressed in jeans and a cowboy shirt and levi jacket. He spoke English, and would be the translator for his father. This man, the old Rinpoche, never sleeps, but remains sitting in a kind of wooden box all night long in meditation. He searches for souls in the Bardo, guided in his meditations by ancient scriptures stored on scrolls which lined the walls of that room in which he sat. I told the old lama that a friend of mine had died recently, and that I wanted to know if she had 'gotten free'. I said it exactly in those words. He asked me for a picture of her. I had a picture of Nirvano, with her back to the camera, as she was hugging Osho. I gave it to him, and he said to come back in three days time.

The photo given to the lama...Osho and Nirvano

The Rinpoche went into meditation.

After 3 days I received a message from his son to come back to the monastery. There, I sat in front of the lama, and his son translated as he spoke. He said, "Your friend at this time is either a bird or a monkey".

I was stunned. I immediately thought of the Raven banging its head every day on the glass of Chuang Tzu auditorium.

I asked him, "Why would a human being come back in the form of a bird?"

He answered that it indicates there has been a suicide. When one takes one's own life, one is killing a potential buddha, and that is a great crime. The soul then takes birth in an animal form, as the descent to animal form is like a rest, to look at what happened, before getting another chance as a human.

I was silent. As I felt very clearly that the Raven had been trying to communicate with me, a kind of insistent demand for help, I felt I had to inquire more. Then I asked him, "Is there anything I can do to help her come back to human form?"

He said; "You can make a Buddha Statue; and recite the Dorje Chutpa sutra (which means.'The Sutra of Rightful Action')."

I was taken aback. The 'coincidence' of the bird, and the fact that I had made a Buddha statue from the marble which all began through Nirvano, and the statue being finished at the moment of her death, was a bit much to let in at that moment, not to mention that the old lama knew nothing about me, or what I do, not even my name.

I thanked him, bowed, and went outside. I asked the young Rinpoche to write out the Dorje Chutpa sutra for me in Tibetan script, and gave him a large sum of money (large for me at that time. In rupees, up there in the poverty of the mountains, it looked like a fortune. It was about 50 dollars.) I asked him to have the monks recite the sutra in the monastery for 21 days. I went back to Ageha's house up the hill, and immediately began making my 3rd Buddha statue, which took one week, in concrete. I made a stone altar there for it, on that hillside in Kulu-Manali, where I imagine it is to this day. The day after I finished it, Aseema and l left for the long trip back to Poona.

When I arrived in Poona, I immediately went to find some Tibetan friends of mine who spoke English. They sold religious artifacts on the road outside the ashram. They agreed to write out a rough translation of the Tibetan script of the sutra, and I began to prepare it to set it in place behind the photo of Nirvano in the memorial that I was making for her in the ashram. The first day I was back, I was again called in to the office by Jayesh, and given the task of making in the new Nala park behind the ashram, a series of Buddha statues, large heads mostly, which was Osho's express wish before he left, to be made there and placed in the surroundings of nature, 'to help my people to meditate', in His words. This chain of events could not in any way be explained by 'coincidences', and could only now be called 'synchronicity', to quote a term coined by C.G. Jung to explain simultaneous events mysteriously connected one to the other.

After two more days, I was again playing in Osho's Samadhi, and, as before, the Raven showed up, banging feebly on the window. But, its leg was broken, and it was very weak. It would fall to the ground and hop around, and didn't have the same energy as before. After 3 days, it disappeared, and I never saw or heard it again.

At this time of my life, I neither believe nor disbelieve, nor place any judgement whatsoever, on Nirvano's actions. I can truthfully and without a shadow of a doubt say that she was a higher being than me: higher in the sense of more crystallized in her energy, in the evolution of her consciousness, her being. She lived on a different level energetically. I could feel her look at my back, from 100 feet away. My body involuntarily shivered when I first saw her smile. She had a power inside her, which made me only love her, and not in any way feel myself to be her equal. She knew something, and had been somewhere inside that I had never been. And as such, she is subject to different laws than me. I don't know what they are, as "The lower cannot judge the higher". I don't know what happened to her or why she died. I do know it was covered up, whether out of embarrassment or guilt or awkward fear by the people who surrounded her and ran the ashram, I cannot say.

Suicide is not such a simple subject, painted in black and white. A person maybe as a last act, takes too many sleeping pills and falls asleep forever, thus ending the life in this body. But the road to get there, if that road is paved with seeming 'friends' who envy that persons power and position, and in her moment of weakness. push her further and further into a dark corner, who is really 'responsible' for the suicide? Is it really so clear? Are we all really so separate? Nirvano, although a very crystallized energy as a Being, had a personality in THIS LIFE with a tendency to 'genetic depression' as she herself called it, and she lived very apart from the entire rest of the ashram. Her emotional state was very much affected by stress, and she lived under the great stress of feeling personally responsible for Osho's survival in his body. For the 21 years that she was there, her entire adult life, while all of us were meditating, doing therapy groups, working in the commune, she was in a world apart, taking care of Osho 24 hours a day was her one and only task. In the two years she was with Jayesh, she stopped doing that work, and was isolated in the relationship, never entering really the commune. Although people loved her and admired her, it was mostly distant admiration and in some part envy. Although she had a few close friendships, as she was living in such a rarefied different world than the rest of the community, it was not easy for her to be social. That had never been a part of her life, she had one and only one reason for living, and that was to keep Osho in his body. She told me that personally. As Osho's health deteriorated and it became clear he was dying, her reason for living was disappearing with Him. Her depression grew, and her dependent relation on Jayesh, like a lifeboat, started leaking.

At the same time his power and position and money dominated more and more the forming of the Inner Circle of 21 which was to be the governing body of the commune after Osho's departure. Being the controller of the ashram finances, and the fact that no-one else was really able to keep track of where the money was going and coming from, gave him an unshakeable advantage and position of leverage over the whole movement at that time. I state this as neither good nor bad, it is just a fact of the jungle of money-power-and-politics of this world of duality we live in, a 'reality' already made very clear to me through the experience of the Ranch.

As Nirvano's depression deepened, Dhiraj, the 'founder' of the Tibetan Healing movement in the ashram who had 'miraculously' helped my back injury years before, had offered to treat her, and the offer was not accepted by her doctor, She was having a hard time in the relationship with Jayesh, and no longer living with or caring for Osho. Her mood shifts became more extreme, as she lost balance.

There was no autopsy performed on her body, she was already burning on her funeral pyre an hour after declared dead. There was no public ceremony, no recognition of the death given in any way, except for the funerary marker being given to me to do. Many questions...no answers.

I wish that Nirvano could have had the chance to 'tell all' as she said she would. I do not know what happened to her or how she died. I do know that through her passing away, I was given a very direct and existential lesson about suicide, and as far as I know, the lesson was for me. I have close friends from my adolescence and many relatives who have committed suicide. It has never been something I have thought about doing, but after that experience with the Raven and the Rinpoche, I would rather walk barefoot on burning coals in a hellish life, and find my way out of it rightfully, than end my own life prematurely. I thank the Rinpoche for that, ...and the Raven.

END OF PART II

PART III

C H A P T E R   3 3

Rites of Passage

After the tidal wave of life-changing events that had transpired in the early months of 1990, Aseema and I got back to Poona from the Himalayas in June of that year, at the start of another rainy season. Again, as with every approaching monsoon, the clouds arriving from the western seas piled high in magnificent columns of pink and orange and white. The rains came, and with them the relief from the heat, and a new beginning to the cycle of life. So too it was for us, and life went on in the ashram, and in fact thrived. At first I was working on the memorial for Nirvano, setting it in place with the Dorje Chutpa sutra behind the photo of her, in the black pyramid by the side of Lao Tzu House. When that was done, I began the work on the Buddha Statues which Osho had wanted in the Nala Park behind the ashram.

As I was now living outside the ashram, I began doing this project on the roof of our apartment above Prem's Restaurant, a landmark watering-hole which had grown from a little bamboo hut out in on the edges of 'civilization' in early days of Poona 1, to now a full-fledged MUST visit on the itinerary of any tourist seriously wanting to get to know the scene in Koregaon Park, fast becoming the hottest real estate in the entire Indian subcontinent. The roof of the building was a large open terrace, and it meant that I had no problems with the ashram bureaucracy, to grant me a space to work. There was always a lack of space in the ashram, it being about 6 acres in all, and many thousands of people involved in many activities all day long, so usually putting your workbench somewhere meant stepping on someone else's toes, literally and figuratively. There on my roof I could work whenever I wished, and also experiment without many eyes passing by all day long, a much needed respite from the 'tours' which would pass when I was working in the ashram on the Buddha statue. It always seemed just when I was trying desperately to carve forth a smile-less smile on the face, I would be there in the midst of a 'welcome tour' with dozens of pairs of eyes staring at my every movement, and I would not like to answer questions. It's something about carving a face in stone...once you start on the mouth, it seems like one is hallucinating...one moment you see one expression, benign or benevolent, another moment it becomes snide or twisted or sad. That determining moment clarifying the expression on the face needs utter solitude, and relaxed concentration. It would be better just to do it on my roof, at least the first one.

The problem was, it was a new medium for me, forming the face in concrete instead of carving it. Concrete is a strange material: when you want it to stick, it slips. When you want it to flow, it sticks. When you want it to set up and stiffen, it absorbs humidity from the air and falls to the floor. When you want to mold it, the humidity pushes out of it and it sets up and stiffens. I had a lot of learning to do, especially figuring out how to work with gravity and not fight the downward flow of the concrete. Once again, I could not 'expect roasted chickens to fly into my mouth'. With the coming of the monsoon on my roof, it was getting complicated, the air was getting wetter and wetter, and I would have to improvise tents and awnings to keep everything dry, but not too dry, keep it damp, but not too wet. Once the face was there, it would have to be perfected within 18 hours before the concrete would set; so that meant a marathon long into the night. I was working with black charcoal powder in the concrete, and my face, hands, and the rooftop terrace were all turning black.

The first Buddha came out just 'allright'... I wouldn't send postcards of it to the Dalai Lama for his birthday, if you know what I mean. It was just a beginning, and not a profound work of art, by any means. I had tried to capture the feeling of the androgenous face of Buddha, neither clearly male nor female, but it ended up looking like a young boy, rather innocent, and I can't imagine the Buddha as innocent. Osho is a Buddha, and he was anything but innocent. He was powerful and male, and yet he had a woman's grace, in the gestures of his hands and the nuances of his expressions.

I tried again....The second one was twice the size, and easier to work the larger features on the face. It ended up being about 2 meters high, and it weighed at least 600 pounds. I enlisted 12 Indian porters from a construction site to help me carry it down from the roof, on a kind of sled made of giant bamboos. It looked like a scene from the Ten Commandments when the Hebrews were building the pyramids, but we got it to the Nala park and set in place, and it looked good there, kind of spiffy and other-worldly. So, I got encouraged and my next one was more ambitious. This time, the head was 3 feet tall, but I made the whole Buddha! More than 12 feet tall, with the hands big enough that you could sit in them. It took two months, and probably 300 buckets of concrete, and weighed many tons. The body was a brick-and-steel-bar monolith, like a building, and the black concrete was smeared onto that, bucket by bucket, as the features took shape. The head was made separately, and lifted onto the body with a crane, and fixed in place as the neck was formed. It was dramatically fun. My workshop was in the park now, a large bamboo hut which was an ironic echo to the place I used to live in Koregaon park years before, which was about 100 yards away from that same spot, but by now was an apartment block in the trendy booming real estate market of Koregaon Park.

The 3rd Buddha, in Nala Park

During the 6 months of making these statues, and by now about a year after the departure of Osho, the relations between us (the sannyasin population surrounding the ashram) and the local municipal government, had significantly deteriorated. It had never been very good, but now it was getting rapidly much worse. Nobody quite knew why exactly. Perhaps some bribes had not been paid or some police commissioner was feeling offended for lack of a vacation fund, but the police were stopping people on the street to check visas and were banging on the doors of apartments in the night, looking for over-stayed visitors. Aseema and I decided to take a vacation, to Thailand, and we stayed a month there, exploring ruins of ancient Buddhist temples, statues lost in the jungle, 50-feet tall, wrapped with vines and creepers. We visited a strange place, called Phra-Nang, a primitive beach resort on a peninsula in a remote part of Thailand, where there was a cave dedicated to a goddess of that name. In front of the cave there were enormous wooden phalluses erected as offerings to the goddess, ostensibly to have better luck while fishing. I felt very fine there, welcomed in fact by the nature, and the tangible female presence of the deity in the cave, which was not just the imagination of the locals. Aseema, on the other hand, felt nearly pushed away from the place, and we decided to leave. We found another place, a beautiful bay with an island about 200 yards offshore. I decided to try my hand at being a real tourist, and rented a snorkel, and started to swim and snorkel around the island.

Swimming out into the warm bay was easy, there was no strong current or wind and I could make good time heading for the island. I crossed the brief stretch of water separating the beach from the island, about 200 yards, and when I reached the island and was swimming around the far side towards the open sea, a voice inside me yelled out, "GO BACK! GO BACK!". This alarm going off inside me was unusual, intense, and insistent, and I remembered the similar voice in those dusty hills of Rajasthan years before, so I listened to it, and started swimming back straight towards the shore, I was in about 4 meters deep of water, 100 yards offshore, when there appeared in my mask just below my face, the body of a huge great white shark passing just underneath me. I could not see the whole shark, it was too large to be in my field of vision, I could only see from the dorsal fin to the tail, which was about 3 meters. It means the whole shark was probably 5 meters long, or 16 feet. It cruised by, about two feet underneath me. I could have easily touched it as it passed, I could see the texture of its skin.

Adrenalin was pumping into my blood and I started swimming like a toy motorboat, thrashing the water…I was telling myself, "Don't be scared, they react to fear!!!" But that was useless, as I was scared shitless. The thing moved so effortlessly in the water, and I felt like a sitting duck, literally. I swam as fast as I could, reaching the shore, and I guess the shark had already had its lunch and wasn't interested in me, but I kept swimming up onto the shore like a Popeye cartoon. I took that snorkel back to the rental shop straight away and decided to just play my flute on the beach next time I get the urge to have a long swim. It seemed to be the right time to leave the beach behind and get back to the statues in Poona.

By this time, about one year after Osho's departure from his body, signs were arising of changes in the ashram. Positions of power were starting to solidify, messages of 'Osho's guidance' were being handed down from 'above', apparently from The Inner Circle. This governing body of 21 people whom Osho had specifically chosen to act as the administration of the ashram and his work after his demise was now having growing rumors of friction amongst the members. They were a very diverse group of strong individuals, and word spread about power blocks and divisions forming. Jayesh was now the chairman of the Inner Circle. There apparently was a struggle going on within the Inner Circle, although it was never openly talked about; and those who were against the directions and wishes of Jayesh were not-so-subtly pressured to leave. Among those were Kaveesha, Prasad, and Hasya, who had been Osho's secretary in the tumultuous post-Sheela Ranch days. Although the membership of the Inner Circle had been intended by the Master to be for life, some members left, some died, others took their places; notably one of which was Jayesh's brother–notable because it seemed the reason he was there in that position of power was because he was Jayesh's brother, not because of any inherent merit or understanding of Osho's vision on his part. "Sounds like a corporate decision made in Siclly", I thought. A smaller subdivision of a governing body was formed, called the 'Praesidium', which was 3 or 5 people, we never were told how many. They would make a lot of decisions, and then bring them to the larger group for approval. It's easy to envision what was starting to happen; namely, rubber-stamping, a dis-equilibrium of power was forming, heavily weighed on the side of Jayesh, and those who agreed with him, with tacit agreement from the other members.

As time would go by, as managerial power over the physical ashram became consolidated in fewer and fewer hands, the ashram would reflect more and more the particular predilections of the few who now held power; i.e. less and less emphasis on devotion, no Osho pictures in the ashram itself, no wearing of malas, the marble podium where Osho sat and gave discourse for 14 years destroyed and dismantled one night, no songs of devotion to the Master allowed to be sung, etc. These are 'personal' choices, that is, reflecting those personalities, and is not particularly the Master's directive; Osho's guidance gave freedom and leeway for each person to relate to the Master in his own unique way. That was the beauty of it all while the Master was here, a garden of wildflowers, each growing in the sunlight, not a monoculture of roses or tulips. Some connect to the Master's energy through devotion, the heart, a flower-strewn path through a lush garden, like Sufi poets. Some prefer the simple, pristine clarity of Zen, and some prefer the dry austerity of a rocky path straight to the mountaintop under the burning sun, like Jaina monks. Each human on the inward journey has his or her own predilections, and the right to express their Union with the Divine in their own unique way. Osho gave space and freedom to that, he did not force everyone into a certain mindset.

At the same time of the reinforcing of managerial control in the hands of a few, another current in the overall situation of the ashram was becoming apparent. This was the emergence outside the ashram but in the general energy field of all the thousands of sannyasins who still were in Poona, of new 'mini-gurus', people who had been disciples of Osho, content to keep their heads bowed reverently while Osho was in the body, but now that he had gone from the physical plane, their desire and predisposition to gather disciples themselves started to become apparent. Up they quickly sprung here and there, having sittings and satsangs outside of the ashram, or in Goa, and word was spreading amongst people hungry to sit 'in the presence of an enlightened one' and not simply listen to the videotaped discourses of Osho in the ashram at night.

Whether or not some of these people were enlightened is not my position to judge, as I never visited any of these budding new gurus. I had no hunger inside me to continue to seek out enlightenment from the outside as such, having had a relationship with Osho that showered me with all that was possible for me to receive from outside. What I did with it now was my concern and responsibility, and I didn't want to stuff myself with more 'energy' and seek new sources. For the purposes of this discussion, I mention it simply to indicate that this new trend was definitely perceived by the managers of the ashram as a threat to the ashram itself, and stricter and more heavy-handed measures were beginning to be taken to try to curb the exodus of people, and money, from the ranks of the disciples there in Poona.

I do not find this hard to understand, business is business, as they say. And the people in charge of the ashram, not particularly in a position of abnormally high spiritual wisdom or evolution themselves, were definitely taking more and more the position of running a corporation instead of an energy field for human transformation. So cutting out the competition is par for the course. Privileges were being withdrawn to those residents who would begin to visit these mini-gurus, and eventually people were banned from the ashram who openly took part in following or listening to someone other than Osho.

So, in this way, religious orthodoxy started on the part of the ashram rulers. This was never Osho's teaching. In fact, when J. Krishnamurti was alive and speaking in Bombay in the years of Poona 1, Osho would urge his sannyasins to go and hear him, and sit in the front row, dressed in bright orange. Apparently this would irritate Krishnamurti very much, and he would launch into tirades about followers and Masters. It was all part of Osho's delight in stirring up the pot and creating controversy, as he deeply respected Krishnamurti as an enlightened being, and often spoke about this. But Osho was playful, even with other Masters.

Moreover, the last 6 months that Osho was still speaking, he was specifically talking about how to know if a master is enlightened or not. The reason he gave for doing this is that he would not be here long, and we will need to sit in front of other enlightened beings and learn from them. I heard Him say on several occasions: "When the musician is gone, the music is finished!"

So, polarization started to set in. Many people began to visit other gurus, notably a teacher known as 'Poonja-ji' in Lucknow, or Tiohar in Poona and others in Goa. Many other people felt this was some kind of betrayal of Osho, an opinion which I don't particularly share. But the root behind this judgement was in great part the wish to keep the ashram rolling, and not lose numbers. The motivation behind that is perhaps a 'loyalty' to his vision, the wish to see his work continue, and I shared that feeling at that time. I very much wanted it to continue and flourish, and was working for the better part of 12 years constantly for that very thing.

But in some individuals certainly there was vested interest in keeping the business rolling, particularly those whose pockets were at the end of the chain of the ashram's sources of revenue, in the form of subsidiary corporations profiting from OIF (Osho international Foundation). This is an entity founded in Switzerland dedicated as a 'non-profit corporation' to preserve Osho's work, but whose legal right to do so would be the subject of litigation and investigation for the next 25 years, as of this writing. It is not in the scope of this book to explore all the aspects of that story. I would like to simply relate how that corporate interface of Osho's Spiritual Teachings, OIF, affected my life.

When I had brought EAGLES FLIGHT to the ashram and handed it to Nirvano to give to Osho, at the end of 1989, Osho's response, and message to me was that it should be sold in the bookstore at the ashram. I found that to be something of an honor, as it was the first time that an individual's music was going to be a part of the ashram offering of music-for-sale. I was called into a meeting with Anando to sign the papers giving the ashram the legal right to publish the music, and she said, "Of course, you will get a fee for this". I said to her, "I don't want to receive money from the ashram, that's not my relationship with Osho". She was surprised, but was fine with that, and all proceeded smoothly. This was a few months before Osho left his body.

About a year after He had left his body, the ashram attitude towards music rights was greatly changing. The person who at the time was in charge of ashram finances, a fellow named Chiten, suddenly without warning and any consultation on the part of all of us musicians who had been playing music for years for Osho and the Ashram recordings, decided to give all the rights of the music to another disciple who was now starting a record company and would promote and publish the meditations of Osho, as well as music by other non-sannyasin, musicians, including Hariprasad. Having done that, Chiten promptly resigned all responsibilities in the ashram and left for Lucknow to be with Poonjaji. So, there we were, musicians who had been giving all our music for years to the ashram out of love, no money involved, and now someone was set up to make quite a lot of money from it, but from our side we would get, of course, nothing. That's o.k. so far, but it gets more complicated...

An early western sannyasin of Osho, Chaitanya Hari, had beautifully made the meditation music for Osho's meditations, such as Dynamic and Kundalini, among others, under the guidance of Osho years before, in Poona 1. This music was a great inspiration to me as a new sannyasin, and it became almost 'iconic', a sound that would mark every dawn and sunset in the ashram. Now, 15 years later, after many thousands of copies of this music had been sold by the Osho Foundation International in Germany and elsewhere in the world, the ashram was 'legalizing' its music sales through the fore-mentioned publisher, who was given en masse the rights and the responsibilities to publish all the music of the meditations, and all the music we had made in the ashram up to that time. Of course, nobody asked any of us musicians about this, nor were any steps taken to give any kind of real acknowledgement about composing or performers rights or even our names, which we had implicitly forsaken when we made the music for the ashram. It was understood. From my side, what I had given, I had given, and I didn't expect to make money off it.

It seems that a lawyer working for Chaitanya had gotten wind of the amount of Euros going unclaimed by the state-level copyright protection agency called the GEMA. As time went by, the GEMA in Germany, which is a mafia-like agency which controls and oversees musicians rights and as well limits them, with nearly governmental powers, presented a bill of about 60,000 Euros to the Ashram, for the back-rights to Kundalini meditation over all those years.

This made a kind of tsunami in the ashram economic bureaucracy, and soon we musicians were all being required, in order to play in the Buddha Hall for the meditators there, to sign statements not only forfeiting all future financial claims to the actual recordings of us made in Buddha Hall, but of the 'composing rights' to the compositions as well. The small-print and implications in this legal jargon means, if I take a tune which I have written, say, in Siena, Italy, and play it once in Buddha Hall in Poona, India, for the meditators there, then for the rest of the duration of my life on earth, the ashram would have the right to charge me a fee every time I play that tune anywhere else in the world....Because I played it once in Poona! The logic of that just seemed to escape me then, and it still does to this day. Most tunes don't just spontaneously pop out while you are playing in Buddha Hall for meditators. They get composed, they get reworked, refined, polished wherever you are and whenever they appear, and they usually first appear in your own brain, wherever that apparatus may physically be located at the time. It's something like fishing in the astral ocean of music. You catch a fish one day, and you bring it in, it has nothing to do with WHERE or on what property you happened to be when the tune swam into your head. I had no problem sharing my music for everyone in Buddha Hall, I loved doing it and did it almost daily for years, all recorded and for sale by the ashram, and I don't asked to be paid for it, but I don't want to be penalized or fined for that, either. I was called in to the office, and in a rather explicit way, threatened to be banned if I did not agree to the new rules. I argued at length and high volume about this with the ashram bureaucrats, telling them exactly what I thought, that they were 'screwing musicians', nothing less and nothing more.

Some months before, the afore-mentioned music publisher and his new company had published my 'Eagles Flight', and was waiting for my next offering. He at that time presented me with an offer which I literally couldn't refuse: that I would have to sign an exclusive contract with his company, forbidding me to publish anything with anyone else, forever. As there was absolutely no mention in the contract of any obligation on the part of the record company to publish my recordings or remunerate me for this forfeiture of my means to a livelihood, I refused, and told him that if he wants to represent all sannyas music, he has to have more concern for the rights and welfare of the musicians. I was answered by him with a few, shall we say, 'insults and recriminations', and I then wrote to him that I no more wished to publish my music with him. He then replied that if I don't publish my new album with him he would sue me for the 'costs incurred to date'. I couldn't imagine what those were, as I had paid the recording costs, but I was struggling at the time to keep alive on the rupees which I had gotten from the sale of Eagle's Flight to Sony Music India, and having to pay this aforementioned publisher a few thousand dollars to 'free' my album from his hands, I was being made an offer I couldn't refuse, and neither could I accept it. It seemed to me to be very much policies which 'could have been written in Sicily', and I resolved to finish the contract with this person and as such, the ashram, as quickly as possible and have nothing more to do or say with him, his record company, or Ashram lawyers. May they go wherever they wish on their journey crossing the sea of Eternity, I wish them well and may they learn what they need to learn, but we are not in the same boat or apparently with the same goals in mind, and I bade them farewell.

At that time I was composing, directing and performing the music for the Gurdjieff Sacred Dances, a once-annual performance of ancient dances from the Near East brought to the West by George Gurdjieff in the early part of the twentieth century. I would make original music for these, composed in the apartment where I lived with Aseema overlooking the river in Poona, and work with the dancers in the ashram to get them to 'work' as a ballet. There was to be a large performance in Buddha Hall with about 50 dancers and 8 musicians, the dances being taught and led by Amiyo, a french dancer and teacher who was a very dear friend of mine. The performance included a group of about 6 very talented Japanese dancers, of whom the principle was a Butoh dancer from Osaka named Neesha, a very powerful and electrifying performer. As well as being innovative and electrifying on stage, she was frightening too. She did things which were not expected by 'New Age' audiences; she was shocking, intense, and wild. The company called itself 'Wild at Heart', and it was truly that, and the performance was a mixture between the solemnity and depth of the Gurdjieff dances and the brilliant and outrageous contrapuntal flights of fantasy of Wild at Heart. The performance was a huge success, and shocking as well, as many people in the audience of 10,000 had been expecting the usual offering of the solemn, deep and traditional dances of Gurdjieff.

Many members of the Inner Circle and Praesidium were there in the front row of the performance on that night. As the last dance finished, the audience rose as one in a standing ovation and these people came up to us to congratulate us at that moment, big beaming smiles on their faces in front of the whole crowd. The next morning, we were given an equal amount of scorn, criticism and judgement by the SAME PEOPLE, privately in the office. It was wild. I loved it. That they were shocked was fine with me this time, and I have no regrets. If a politician wants to live with two faces, one of them is bound to have a frown on it, and their need to criticize in order to exercise power has nothing to do with real intelligence. If the music opened someone's eyes out of bureaucratic slumber for a brief moment and made him or her feel a bit of the life within, albeit expressed in disapproval, its purpose was served, and the real Power which rules this universe was pleased, I am sure.

The rights to the music which I made for the performance, were demanded by the ashram, and I refused to sign over the composing rights. I had composed it, in my apartment, paid for by me, on instruments paid for by me, and if they want to sell the recording they made in Buddha Hall, fine with me, no royalties expected from my side. But the compositions by right are mine and I told them very clearly I do not agree with their policy, even if they wish to ban me for that.

In this transitional time of the ashram taking on its 'new phase', it came to light that dozens, if not all, of the original paintings that Osho had made in his own books in his personal library had been cut out of the books in his personal library and sent away illegally to New York, by the management. This was one of the many issues provoking a fracture in the governing body of the Ashram, the inner circle of 21. Neelam, who had served for years as Osho's personal secretary and head of the ashram in Poona, left the Inner Circle and consequently, left also the ashram as a result of this break, and she in turn was 'banned' from even entering the premises. An advertisement was taken out by the management of the ashram, defaming her in a brutal way on the entire back page of the Times of India. This advertisement alone, an ugly exercise in character assassination, cost the ashram at least one million rupees. It was ironic to think that all the constantly rising entrance fees to the ashram were paying for this hatchet-job, more along the lines of Richard Nixon's Dirty Tricks than the commune of my beloved Master.

The ashram was rapidly changing with the passing year. Aseema was working in the mystery school, and beginning the first groups of women's liberation in the ashram, and I was working as a musician and artist. I made a few more statues for the park, including a female Buddha, and a life-size group of a male-female Shiva-Shakti for the Tantra Room. But with each passing year coming back to Poona, I felt less and less at home there, the friends I had known through the years were coming back less and less, some being banned from entering into the ashram, the prices were going up radically, making it much more difficult to stay for months at a time, and the ashram which once had been a place of deep heart, explosive transformation, and wildflowers was becoming more and more a place of passes, rules, regulations, and 'Osho's guidance' as chosen by the powers-that-were at that time. Being banned became almost a sign of respect, a kind of medal of honor in the struggle for freedom against the growing pall of bureaucratic control and dogma settling like a fog over what once had been a place of rebellion and the search for real freedom.

I had known, from sitting in front of Osho for 12 years and listening to Him deep in my heart, that His guidance was in every possible direction and dimension and always self-cancelling. Osho's way of speaking was entirely paradoxical and seemingly contradictory. He could one day speak of the beauty of Jesus' message, and the next day completely demolish those same teachings. And both statements would be completely logical and believable. He would speak in a way that was mysteriously tuned to the audience, as if playing upon the very prejudices and predispositions of those seated there that day, but not playing upon them politically in a way to gain followers; on the contrary, He would specifically shock and disturb the assumptions latent in the minds of the listeners; not only the listeners at the moment of speaking, but those to come, those who would read or listen to those words years later.

In the years that followed his departure physically, those acting 'in his name', instead of publishing the original discourses as they had been spoken, began to publish his words in shorter systematic collections or compilations: they choose his words revolving around a certain topic, like 'Love' or 'Sex' or 'Freedom', or 'Relationship', and those choices are made by human minds, not the no-mind which was the channel for the words in the first place. It is useful for the sale of the books, and as such it makes his words available to many people who otherwise would not have them. Small excerpts from various discourses would be gathered together around that topic, presenting the 'teachings of Osho' in a more 'rational' format, more easily packaged, marketed, and understood by a public which exists somewhere out there in the minds of book publishers.

That is just what it is, neither good nor bad. But curiously enough, many of Osho's clear statements regarding the essential spiritual necessity of rebellion, have been edited out of those compilations.

Although I can see the 'functionality' and practicality for the book market of presenting Osho's teachings in that way, as it probably opened up a much wider worldwide audience for his teachings, yet Osho never spoke that way. In the same discourse, or in the next days, he could contradict himself again and again. He spoke paradoxically; affirming and negating both; It was logical, illogical, and beyond logical at one and the same time. It was impossible to create a set of doctrines from his words. You could never make a pattern out of it. He did this purposefully, and expressly stated that. It was impossible to form a fixed 'teaching' around it. By making compilations, this way of teaching was watered down and diluted, made palatable so that the mind who is reading it can remain in its logical format, no threat, no paradox, and hence, no de-structuring.

As it was impossible to put your finger on 'What is Osho's guidance', one had to listen to the voice in your own heart, and 'be yourself'. That was his message to me, clearly and literally hammered in through living experiences and long years. There was no way to live or learn through outer directives, but through the hard path of accepting and living the energy and contradictions within you, with awareness, And then making your decisions, and your mistakes, until wisdom came to you through the life experiences themselves. Osho's guidance was not something that could be printed out and stapled to a bulletin board: it was something that came on the wind that morning, you heard a passing phrase, something came to you in a dream, or you opened a book of His at random and there the paragraph was staring you in the face, exactly what you needed to hear that moment. And it was always changing, alive, pertinent. It could not be generalized, given or controlled by a third party.

There is no way to form a priesthood around Osho's teaching, and if it formed, it could only be a falsehood. Osho's words were and are always so alive in themselves, I continually hear new things in them every day, which I never heard before, 40 years after he spoke them. And yet, ironically and unbelievably, that's what was happening, a priesthood was forming, people were coming into positions of power and using that position to give Osho's guidance, as if they themselves had attained some kind of insight, simply because of their position in a bureaucratic hierarchy. They had attained the illusion of knowledge by being in a position of relative social power, and they would believe in their own authority to hand out guidance. I was surprised to see this happening, growing day by day, as if a social position, a job in the ashram, suddenly gives you spiritual authority, insight, wisdom. It was a great trick of self-delusion, and perhaps it is an unavoidable weakness of human nature.

At the same time that my relationship with the changing ashram was becoming more distant, my relationship with Hariji was constantly growing, and he was often voicing the same feelings as I had about the situation in the ashram. One day after our lesson at his house in Khar in the suburbs of Bombay, we were having lunch together, and he began talking to me about my relationship to music. He knew that I was also a sculptor and artist, and always my time was split in the two pursuits. He told me: "You have to realize that everything is for music. Everything IS music. When you are shaping the marble, it is also music. And you as a Western and Eastern musician are in a very particular position, because you are the only flute player who can really understand the two systems, East and West, together. And you have to treat them both as equals. You have two wives, one is Indian, and one is Western. And you have to have the strength and the power to hold the two wives, and make each of them feel that, 'You are the only one, my darling'... When you are playing Western Music, the audience must never feel that you are an Indian musician, and when you are playing Indian music, the audience must feel that you are truly Indian. And the reason why I never ask money from you, is that when you become the greatest flutist in the world, THAT will be my remuneration."

I left his house, and wanted to remember every word he had said. I stopped in a chai shop, and on some pieces of a napkin, I wrote all that I could remember, word for word. I was filled with gratitude and love to him as I took the train from Victoria Station back to Poona that night.

A few weeks later, he asked that I come to Bombay to help with the organization of a concert he was putting on in a large park in Bombay. Aseema came with me this time, as she loves Indian music very much. It would be a chance to hear all the great masters in India, who are Hariji's friends and colleagues. We took the Deccan Queen at 6 in the morning, and got to Hariji's house by 11. Always when meeting him, I would touch his feet, this is customary in India between guru and disciple. We asked him how we could help out, and he said, "Please help to make the place more beautiful, and Devakant, please take care that no disturbances happen in the crowd!"

After my experiences in Rajasthan I had a twinge of anxiety in my guts with that one, I knew how totally unpredictable can be crowds in India, situations which seem at first 'manageable' can rapidly deteriorate into bad scenes. But I said, "O.K., I'll do my best"

When Aseema and I arrived to the park, it looked like a disaster area. Everything was dirty, old, decrepit, covered with leaves and dust and the dirt of ages. We took one look at the toilet, and I knew I had landed once again in hell. We found a bazaar and bought buckets and mops and soaps, and we started recruiting people on the street to work for a few hours cleaning. Eventually we put together a 'crew', and started to work, sweeping, mopping, cleaning, cleaning, cleaning...

As the day went on the crews arrived with sheets and sofas and towers for the sound system and lights and colored lanterns everywhere, by the nightime it looked like the scene of a huge Indian wedding. As darkness fell, the crowd started pouring in, by the thousands, 15,000 in all, and it was up to me to make sure that people could get a look at the stage and not start a riot.

The great Masters of Indian music were gathering backstage, Pandit Jasraj, Shivkumar Sharma, Zakir Hussain with his father the legendary Allah Rakha, a long list of stellar names which would go on all through the night. The rows just in front of the stage were filled with Queens and Kings of Bollywood, the stars of the Bombay film world, and all was set for an unforgettable night.

Zakir Hussain is the enfant-terrible of Indian Music. He was a child prodigy who on the tablas was like Mozart on the Piano, and more...He took the instrument from the hands of his im-

mortal father Allah Rakha, and brought it into dimensions unheard of. Now, as an adult he is a mature and electrifying performer. Listening to him is literally like getting electrocuted on
some other dimension. You find yourself sitting on the edge of
your chair, pressing forward as much as you can, and eventually
jumping up and down and screaming. Around midnight, when
Zakir came on to play, the crowd went wild. All of a sudden
about 3000 people started rushing and moving their chairs
nearer to the stage, and another 3000 started complaining that
their view was blocked now. And those complaints were not in
an English style, like, "I say old boy, would you mind moving
your chair a bit to the left?", but more like furious people yelling
at each other, on the edge of fistfights. I was real busy there for
awhile, trying to keep things cool. The fact of me being a westerner didn't help sort out the conflicts, but as soon as Zakir
started playing, the crowd became mesmerized and things settled a little bit.

Zakir has an uncanny gift to 'turn on' a crowd with his cap-
tivating rhythms and fat tabla sound. He is a spellbinding, enchanting and powerful performer, and a glorious rebellious spirit
with the joy and spontaneity of a precocious child at the same
time. That winning combination thrills the audience, and they
were going crazy that night. I was running around like a rabbit
trying to calm down conflicts and disturbances, everyone pushing and shoving to get closer to him, and it wasn't until he was
off the stage that I could breathe easy. That night he was having
a constant argument during the performance through the microphone with the sound man, and at one point it was getting
menacing, the crowd showing its impatience with the sound
technician with boos and catcalls when he would respond
through his microphone. I myself have had so many conflicts
with so many sound technicians, I could understand Zakir's intention to get the sound he wanted, but it made for an electri-
cally tense crowd situation.

After Zakir left the stage, the crowd calmed down to deeper and more tranquil music spaces; Jasraj and his unbelievable vocal acrobatics, Hariji's grandeur and grace as a performer and host, the night progressed in wave after wave of magic, until the dawn came on with Hariji playing an early-morning raga, greeting the birds and the reddening sky with the glowing ball of the sun in the new day.

I often have the feeling when Hariji is playing that it's not him that is playing. He is just a doorway, and Krishna himself, the very soul of India, is singing through him. There are moments when his melodies become so sweet and joyful, it is surely the divine flute-player singing through him.

It was then late February, and in March, Aseema and I decided to leave India definitively, and make a new life. I decided that I would do my music and live solely from that from now on, come what may.

CHAPTER 34

A New Life

At the beginning of April 1991, Aseema and I arrived in Italy as refugees once again, from India, and began our new life in the West. We landed in Rome, and travelled by train to Venice to stay in an apartment of Chilean friends of Aseema, where I could practice and prepare for two scheduled concerts in Germany with Hariprasad. He was giving those concerts, and he asked me to accompany him. That was a major leap out of my comfort zone, as far as I was concerned, and I had no idea why he wanted me to do that, as I felt I was in no way ready for it. While still in India, I had said to him, "Hariji, I know nothing yet...How can I play with you on stage??" He said, wagging his head side-to-side in Indian English, "Don't be worried, you just follow the tune, I won't have you play solo, it will be alright."

So within 10 days, there I was, on stage with Hariprasad in Koln, in front of about a thousand people in a big disco, and again in Munich in a huge theatre, the Gasteig. He was playing his bamboo flute, and I was accompanying him with my silver flute. It all started out well enough, he introduced the raga, playing slowly, and myself echoing his phrasing. When the tabla entered, he began playing the tune and I would pick it up and repeat it while he would play variations, with the tabla. Then he looked at me, and gestured with his head, as if to say, "Jump!" And he waited. I felt like a little bird who didn't know to fly, that was getting booted out of the nest in a high tree: can't stay there, and can't say 'no'. I jumped, and started flapping my wings....I just started jamming, in the raga, and he joined me, and we flew together like two birds. It was a gas! Just like playing ping-pong with a master player, suddenly you play a hundred times better. He was delighted afterwards.

When the concerts ended, Aseema and I travelled by train to Toscana, to stay at a small commune in the mountains near Siena. It is called 'Miasto'. I had played there a couple of times when we had been in Italy three years before, and they had liked my music. One of the residents there in Miasto was a wonderful friend we had met in Master's Press, named Prasuna. She is the best Italian cook in the world. She was interested to produce a series of concerts for me in Italy, in various cities, Milano, Siena, Verona, Modena, etc. and with that in mind as a starting base, I made the jump into 'life in Europe' as a concert artist, living by just doing my music, come what may. I started out forming a band, with Prem Joshua, Ravi, Miten, and his young girlfriend Deva Premal, and although we had some good times, we found that as a group we didn't coalesce, our various personalities and approaches to music being very, very different. Soon we all went our separate ways. There was some good times, and some hard times, which only made it more clear the calling of destiny. Such is life... It could be said, that the universe was playing a different song on my radio, and I had to listen to that one. I remained good friends with Miten and Premal, and we toured sometimes together in Germany, at that time when they were just beginning to find their way as mantra singers. Premal was only about 20 and was just starting to sing at that time, I liked her voice and recorded her on my album 'Sacred Dances' in 1995.

I often played in Miasto, for the community there, and Aseema and I were traveling all around Italy doing groups of meditation and dance, as well as my concerts, in which she would often dance. With money that I got from selling my viola, I bought a tiny Renault 5 that we would load up with all my gear, including a full size electric piano, and we would be scrunched up against the windshield for the long drives on the hot Italian freeways, which by the way are by no means 'free': they cost a lot of lira, the money in Italy at that time. We made the best of it, making just enough to survive and save a little to go back to India each year in the winter months.

We were living on a mountaintop in the forested hills of Siena, in a 500-year old stone house with wood heat that had been the servant's quarters of a large villa-estate owned by an aging Florentine Master artist and sculptor, Emilio Ambron. He was 85, very wealthy from his father's family, and had lived his life as an artist throughout all the turmoil and war of the 30s and 40s , in Bali, China, Cambodia and Viet Nam. He was a wonderful friend, a gifted artist and mentor, and I learned much from him in those years, and am extremely grateful to him and his wife Carla, for the gift of living as their guests for years on top of that forested mountain in the middle of the Siena hills. We lived simply, on what we would earn from giving our meditation groups and my concerts around Italy. Aseema would make chapatis in the little kitchen and I would create my music upstairs, in that little Tuscan house in the midst of the deers and the Cinghiales, the wild boars which live in the forest there. It was a magical time: Aseema and I meditated together first thing every morning with our chai, and the day passed with me in my simple recording studio, or making clay and marble statues outdoors. In the golden glow of the Toscana afternoon filtering through the cypresses, the maestro Ambron would often come over to see what I was doing, as he was happy to be reminded of his years in Asia by my statues and flute playing. He would invite us over to the villa, and I would learn much through his conversations, drawings, and statues, about the processes of Italian classical art, figure drawing, bronze casting, anatomy, and much, much more. Through him and his tutelage, I moved from creating imaginary figures of idealized Buddhas, to real figures of real people.

I had been enchanted by the faces of the people meditating in Osho's Samadhi in Poona, the temple where his ashes were, where I played hundreds of times, And it was those faces which I tried to capture in my statues and drawings. It is neither joy nor sorrow on those faces, nor thought nor contemplation, nor elation nor passion nor worry, but something different, a subtle feeling which emerges from inside, a joy which has no counterpart of sadness, a deep contentment without thought or causation, welling up from within.

During my recent visits to India, I had gotten to know in the ashram a drummer, a very great drummer, music producer and colleague, who would become a mentor, brother and friend to me over the next 15 years. His name, RajRishi, means 'The Great King', and it's very appropriate, as in Vi-king, as he comes from Scandinavia and is a giant of a guy with a huge heart and even more huge intelligence. Over the next 15 years, he would gently and lovingly collaborate with me in the production of every recording I would make, patiently answering thousands of my questions from all over the globe, about the abyss of technological change yawning before me, the arrival of digital music, like a dark impassable swamp full of virtual crocodiles and piranhas. He has been the guide through this morass, shining a light of intelligence, candor, and wit into the deep caverns and long hours of learning to cope with operating systems, hardware, software, interfaces, and eternity value, somehow never losing sight of the original intent, to simply share beauty with more people. I thank this brother from the deepest recesses of my heart, as I couldn't have done a thing without him. I salute you, great soul, for the gifts you constantly give humanity, while asking relatively nothing in return. Such a being is a rare and beautiful gift on this earth.

CHAPTER 35

First Concerts in Japan

I take up now a different thread of my story, having to back-track and retrace a few steps in doing so. Threads in a tapestry often run parallel, and so do parts of this story, as life is not a train on one track or timeline, but a multi-colored tapestry of rivers running simultaneously together with their own color and light. And yet, speech and thought being a limited mech-anism, of Bytes of sound passing one at a time, we are com-pelled to scrunch our perceptions into that narrow matrix, in order to communicate. It is a pale reflection of the real picture....

We returned to India, in November, 1992, and once back in India I started composing for the coming performance of The Gurdjieff Sacred Dances in the Poona Ashram. The performance was to be in January, 1993, This was the aforementioned per-formance of contrasts, between the solemn dances of Gurdjieff and the fantasy flight of the troupe of young dancers called Wild at Heart. The lead dancer of the troupe, Neesha, was a very dy-namic Japanese Butoh-dancer . At that time I had no idea what was Butoh dance, and in fact Japan to me was a distant place of which I was curious and pretty much completely ignorant.

Neesha and I found that we worked well together, even with the language barrier, she did not speak English, and I didn't speak Japanese. She was planning a series of dance concerts throughout the length of Japan, and she invited me to come and join her for that. Little did I know what was to unfold, and it would be a life-changing event for me.

I arrived in Narita airport outside Tokyo one rainy day in

May, 1993, and was greeted by Neesha and a friend of hers, who then drove us for a few hours, to a small meditation center on the flanks of Mt. Fuji, where we would begin. Things started off well enough, and after the concert and group there, we caught a plane to Hokkaido, the northern island where we would begin our North-South tour.

Our tour would cover the 3 largest islands of Japan; Hokkaido to the north, Honshu, where is Tokyo, Osaka, Kyoto, and the largest cities, and curving away to the west and south is Kyushu, the southern island of warmer climate, bamboos and volcanoes.

The concerts were in all kinds of venues; Buddhist temples, Shinto shrines, public theaters, lobbies of luxury hotels, tiny natural-food cafes where the people would be packed in like sardines. We wandered from place to place with our backpacks and my flutes, making the stage setting and concert with each new situation. As Neesha spoke very rudimentary, telegraphic English, and never spoke in the future verb tense, I would never know what was going to happen next. She would buy a train or bus ticket, I would get on the bus, and off we would go. It was a constant mystery, and exercise in 'Trust'. Sometimes we would be in a 1000-year-old Buddhist temple where everyone was speaking in hushed voices and deeply reverent, sometimes we would be in a hot-springs spa where everyone was pretty much smashed on beer and Sake and waist deep in hot water, and sometimes we would be in perfectly pristine surroundings of Zen gardens and tea ceremonies and utterly refined beauty. I never could know what was coming next.

Neesha opened my eyes to many wonderful and astounding things in Japan; the beauty of Zen Spirit, which manifests itself in every aspect of Japanese life; the economy of form, sense of balance, the deep connection to nature which remains in all Japanese, although obscured by the dazzling distraction in technology. The directness and intensity of art forms there grows

394

out of the deep experience of meditation, and in direct contrast to that is the indirectness and complexity of social intercourse, evident in every social interaction and discussion. It was a fascinating new world in which I was immersed each day. We travelled south, to Morioka, Sendai, Kamakura, Tokyo, Nagoya, Hamammatsu, Osaka, and Kyoto, and each place was a new world, of impressions of huge bustling modern cities punctuated here and there with ancient temples and shrines and gardens.

One day, after a concert in the ancient capital of Nara, we went for a walk in the old part of the town, which 13 centuries ago had been the capital of Japan. Neesha, having seen my statues in Poona, wanted me to see the 'Daibutsu', which in my rudimentary knowledge of Japanese at that time, meant 'Big Buddha'.

In that town, in the ancient streets leading up to the historical center, there are parks where roam herds of deer, small and quite tame. It was in honor of the fact that the historical Buddha Shakyamuni Gautama, immediately after his enlightenment in Bodha Gaya 25 centuries ago, gave his first sermon in a Park in Sarnath, near Varanasi, where there were many deers roaming wild, and they listened to him. This event was known as 'the turning of the wheel of dharma', where the Buddha first outlined his concept of the 4 Noble Truths, and the 8-fold path, the principle framework of Buddhist teachings. 'The turning of the wheel of dharma' alludes to the ancient scriptures of India, in which it is stated that the wheel of the law, the Dharma, the Way or the Great teachings which serve as the basis of spiritual life on Earth, has a cycle of 25 centuries. An enlightened being, known in Buddhism as a 'Buddha' or in Hinduism as an 'Avatar', an incarnation of the divine in a human form, comes every 25 centuries to turn this Wheel of Dharma, to set in motion once again the cycle. The deer park in Nara is an allusion to that sermon of the Buddha which set in motion once again the turning of the wheel of dharma, when the deer came to listen to his first words, in Sarnath. Now, 25 centuries later, that cycle has wound down and a new cycle is being set in motion.

We crossed the deer park, the paths converging from many directions, to a vast temple complex surrounded by a great wall. As we entered the gates of this enormous temple complex, there were two huge guardian figures on either side of the gate, carved in wood. They are incredibly expressive and dramatically fierce warrior figures, the guardians of the Dharma, about 15 feet tall, each one... I stood watching them for a few moments. As I turned to enter the gates, suddenly my body reacted by having goose bumps all over, and the hairs on my neck stood up. Entering that courtyard, this 'first' time in Japan, I knew, beyond any doubt, that I had been there before, in that temple complex, walking up to that enormous ancient building. But when? It was built 1300 years ago, as the protective housing for the biggest bronze statue in the world, an enormous Buddha. The building itself is the biggest wooden building in the world, supported by massive pillars of great cedar trees. I was told that there were 250,000 carpenters working on that building alone. I believe it; just to carve one beam of those enormous rafters probably would have taken all 5000 of us at the Ranch...

The bronze statue itself rises in its dark shadows like an apparition when one enters the doors of the building. It is stupefying and awesome in its size. It had taken 70,000 metal-workers to cast it, and had used up all the bronze in Japan, for the next several centuries.

I had been struggling in Poona with problems relating to making a Buddha 12-feet tall, thinking it was a big deal, and here was the Mother-of-all-Buddhas, from more than 1000 years ago, bigger than a mountain, beautiful, profoundly proportionate, in silent witness to the participation of an entire nation in its creation.

Many times in Japan I was moved to tears, for reasons that I could not explain. Sometimes walking along an ancient street in Kyoto covered in cherry blossoms, or a pine-covered island in Iwate, or a forest of giant bamboos eternally creaking with the winds, my heart would be overwhelmed by the beauty that surrounded me, the Zen Spirit, the whispers of ancient teachings fading away on stones by the side of exquisite gardens...

We had a concert in Hiroshima, in a shrine that had been destroyed in the atomic bombing, and rebuilt. I went to the Peace Park and atomic museum the day after the concert, and as I wandered in the museum, I felt deep in my soul an unspeakable horror at the atrocity that is nuclear war. The museum is an eloquent reminder of just how far humans have lost the thread of balance, of understanding, of sanity, in modern war.

It deeply shocked me to see what happened to the city and people of Hiroshima at 8:15 in the morning on August 6th 1945, simply because a politician thousands of miles away in Washington signed a paper on his desk, and the clouds on that morning were thick over Kokura, and the skies clear over Hiroshima. The consequences of those actions seemed nonexistent in the minds of those politicians and generals who make such decisions, actions which dragged the human collective so much further into the chasm of darkness, truly signaling the stopping of the wheel of dharma. As I walked in the Peace Park outside, I had the uncanny feeling of hearing the silent screams of 150,000 souls who perished in agony that morning, some turned into walking ghouls, some into instantaneous carbon-statues, and some just vaporized.

I wept for 3 days after being there at ground zero and going to the museum. I felt ashamed to be American. I realized deep in my soul that the atomic bombing was a disgraceful act of terror, on a massive scale, beneath the dignity of human beings. It was a lie that the bomb had to be dropped. The people who died in Hiroshima that day were not soldiers, but, overwhelmingly, they were women, children, and old people. Murder does not end war. That gross violation of human decency started a chain of fear and bondage which to this day holds the human collective in its grip. The thousands of bombs which today sit on top of fully fueled missiles in silos and submarines now waiting just the push of a button to be launched, at the whim of any madman politician, make the bomb that annihilated Hiroshima look like a firecracker, some of them being 1000 times more powerful than that first one. Technology is never perfect. Entropy, that 2nd law of Newton, states when translated into the words of Murphy's Law, that whatever can go wrong, eventually will go wrong. This tendency for random chaos multiplies in complicated systems. The smallest thing can go wrong and cause the worst scenario imaginable from which there is no turning back. There have been documented and covered-up instances of computer chips worth less than one dollar giving erroneous information to worldwide radar systems, nearly provoking the launching of hundreds of missiles which would bring an end to all life on the planet. We live now poised for destruction in a precarious teetering on the brink of annihilation, maintained only by the perfect functioning of all the technology involved, every day. Any fool can recognize that sometimes technology fails. Sometimes Titanics sink. Sometimes airplanes fall. If only one missile erroneously launches on its trajectory and completes its course, nothing will stop the ensuing Armageddon. When will humanity realize collectively that these politicians hiding in their underground bunkers with the worlds' most devastating weaponry at their fingertips are simply insane, drunk with their own power?

We continued on, to the far west and East of Japan, to Okayama, Shiraishijima, Kokura, and Hakata. As we got into the south, the faces and attitudes changed, the people of Kyushu and especially Fukuoka being more like the people of the South in Italy or Spain, expressive, smiling, more likely to look you in the eyes and say, "Who are you?" The warmer air, friendly faces and nearby sea everywhere I went in Kyushu was a welcome gift, and I delighted in it.

One day, while preparing for a large concert with many dancers in the city of Kumamoto, we went to visit a master of the Japanese flute, Koku Nishimura. His house was in a little back alley a few hundred feet from the ancient Castle of Kumamoto, a samurai castle where had lived the greatest Japanese swordsman, Musashi Shinjo, centuries ago. Koku's little house was surrounded by his vegetable gardens, and wooden statues in various stages of completion. He was a little man with a huge presence, a long white beard, and a deep heart. He was the real 'last samurai', being a Kung Fu master, master swordsman, and a calligraphy master recognized by Japan and China, and a great sculptor and painter. On all the walls of his house were many sumie-paintings, china ink on rice paper, of Buddhas, dragons, bodhisattvas, and deities. Every nook and corner of his house had wooden carvings, figures real and fantastic, all of which were his creations. His flutes were quite famous all over Japan at that time. They are made from a long bamboo usually with the end being roots. It is a very hard and thick bamboo, which grows in the snowy mountains near the slopes of the huge dormant volcano Mt. Aso. It is the biggest volcano in the world, the cone of which is basically the entire island of Kyushu, where I was at that time.

These flutes have a rich and deep sound, and were used for centuries, by a sect of Zen called 'Fukui Zen'. It means 'Blowing Zen'; the only meditation practice of these monks was to wander the streets playing these flutes all day long. The breathing, long and slow, eventually puts you into an altered state of mind, the state of meditation. This sect of monks began 1000 years ago in China, and spread to Japan. It was their practice to wear a wooden sign on their chest, on which was written the characters. 'FU SHO, FU METTSU', which means, 'Never born, Never died'. These are the words of the Prajnaparamita sutra of the Buddha, which was used as the epitaph on the marble samadhi of Osho, where now resides his ashes.

We had a beautiful and heartful meeting, Koku and I, for several hours. He spoke a little bit in halting English, and his son was there to translate more for me. In that meeting he gave me a flute he had just made, and told me emphatically , holding up one finger, "ECH ON JO BUTTSU!!" Which means: "With one sound, FIND THE

Koku Nishimura

BUDDHA!" I left very fulfilled and delighted for what had passed between us... 'With one sound...find the Buddha' can be translated as, "in the tone of the flute, a single note of presence and totality, find your being within!"

This flute, and this quest, to find the Buddha with one sound, would stay with me for my whole life. My relation with Koku continued, for the next 10 years, often going to see him whenever I would be in Kyushu. He would give me little tips about sumie painting, holding the brushes, or carving Buddhas out of wood, or playing the Kyotaku, the long flutes he would make. Sometimes he was even giving me some Kung-fu training exercises to keep the energy flowing when I would be feeling drained on a tour. He made it a point to come to my concerts when they were within driving distance of Kumamoto. I could feel it when he would arrive, and quietly enter and sit in the back of a temple where I would be playing, sitting like a samurai-lord, his hands poised on his walking stick which was actually a very long flute.

He was just about 90 when his health took a turn for the worse. I would go to see him often then, and every day he was trying to paint a dragon, one of his favorite subjects. 'Koku' means emptiness, but it also means 'dragon' in Japanese, and his dragons in black ink were very remarkable masterpieces of drama, shade, and light.

One night I had a concert about 50 miles from his home, in a big buddhist temple, and I thought that he had come during the concert, about the time when there was a brilliant and loud burst of lightning and thunder. After the concert, I didn't see him, and the electric storm continued for the whole drive home, about 2 hours.

The next day I got a call from his son, who told me that Koku had passed away that night. I went as soon as I could to see him and Koku's wife, Tai-san, at their home. His son told me that that evening (of my concert) Koku had again been trying to paint a dragon, from his hospital bed, but not being able to do it, he lay down and was quiet. After a few minutes, the son noticed that he, in fact, had departed. His son pulled the sheet over Koku's face, and closed the window, and at that very moment there was a huge bolt of lightning and a thunderclap. The son looked out the window, and there was a cloud across the sky in the unmistakable shape of a long dragon...

In our concerts together during the tour, Neesha would usually wear a white flowing kimono and dance in a very expressive and touching way to my music. But sometimes, her roots as a Butoh dancer would penetrate the performance, regardless of what I was doing.

Butoh is an art form which grew out of the horrendous experiences of the Atomic Bombings in Japan at the end of the War. It was a way to express the inexpressibile horror and grotesqueness of mutilation by atomic fire and exposure to radiation, which people had experienced en masse, 60 years ago there in South Japan. It was a release and necessary purgation of that unspeakable trauma experienced by an entire population, seeing themselves, their family, friends, relatives mutilated beyond recognition. The dancers sometimes, shake, quiver, move like worms or insects, take weird distorted positions and angles with their bodies and faces. I wasn't mentally or psychically very prepared for that, and sometimes my music and Neesha's dance were really happening on different planets. Neesha herself had lived through great trauma in her life, having suffered severe burns as a young child, and dance was the way that she regained control of her body, and psyche. She was a master of her body, she moved with great power, presence, and emotion. When her dance was positive, it was really delightful. When it turned negative, it was quite intense for the audience.

Down in the far south of Kyushu, we had our final concert of the tour in a public park sponsored by the city of Kagoshima, a community festival, under the smoking shadow of Mt. Sakurajima, the live volcano which dominates the skyline of the city. There were lots of families with kids, and pretty girls in hotpants giving away beer to everybody. Something about the situation had ticked off Neesha, sometimes she was very infuriated by the complacency and control of the 'normal' Japanese, or perhaps there had been an argument between her and the organizers about the payment, or maybe it was the girls in hot-pants handing out free beer, I wasn't really sure. But suddenly her dance became a kind of street-theatre protest to 'normality'; the smiles and bows and hypocrisy: she started to dance more and more furiously, ripping down the bamboos around the scenario and thrashing the walls and floors with them, snarling and basically acting like the WHO in the midst of their instrumental demolitions onstage at the end of the '60's. Most of the three hundred people in the audience gathered up their kids and ran away, the few who remained sat in frozen awe with their mouths open. I was there trying to keep it a little bit Shanti-Shanti on my flute, but, the battle was lost and so was our tour. We parted soon after, having had a very intense and full two months, 22 concerts in 20 different Japanese cities. I was very grateful to her for the experience, although very glad that the tour was over.

Back in Italy, with the relief of having enough money in my pockets after the Japan tour to pass the winter months, I began working on a Buddha statue in black marble, there in the forest of Cotorniano near the house where I lived. I found the stone in the lot of a sculpture workshop in Pietrasanta. It practically yelled out to me as I was passing by. It was just the size and weight that it could still fit in my little Renault 5, without the wheels rubbing against the metal. I drove it back to Siena, and found a place to carve it under some cypresses in the forest near the villa.

As the face slowly took shape with each stroke of the chisel, and the pile of chips and powder grew slowly at my feet, I recalled often the faces I had seen in Japan, particularly one very powerfully Shinto priest, a kind of shaman, who was the keeper of the Shrine of Tenkawa, and a very deep, powerful and openhearted character. His deep smile which was neither joy nor desire nor derision, but rather a massive self-contentment and peace which can only be seen on the face when a person is deeply in harmony with his destiny, his self-nature: this was the look which slowly emerged on the face of the Black Buddha. It was a very, very hard stone, smelling of carbon and sulfur as I worked it, and polishing the face took all the winter months, working under those cypress trees in the forests of Siena.

In the spring I was invited to have a few concerts in Germany with Premal and Miten, who were beginning their careers as Mantra-singers at that time, and I would be their flute and keyboard player. We had great fun traveling together, always laughing , but it was clear to me that my destiny was not to continue to play with them in Germany. As their careers were beginning to really blossom on their path of mantras, and my fate was calling me to imbibe Zen Spirit in Japan, we said goodbye and went on our divergent ways.

I was wishing to go back to Japan and see what happens next, in that land which was so fulfilling to me on an esthetic and psychic level, nourishing parts of my being which I did not know existed until that time as they began to blossom in the very particular and deeply touching atmosphere of hidden and ancient Japan.

What is Zen Spirit? It is not a philosophy, or an intellectual construction. It's not even anything that I can say. It's a finger pointing at the moon. It's a frog jumping into a silent pond: "Plop!" It's not a complicated system of spiritual discipline, dietary rigors, purification, chakras, lights in the head, past-life experiences; none of that. It can be summed up in the statement of one Zen Master: "Hungry, I eat. Tired, I sleep". It's not "Hungry, I do a lemon purification drink and do yoga", or, "Tired, I drink coffee and stay up all night on Facebook."

It's just seeing things as they are, and living in that. And out of that simplicity, that esthetic that cuts things down to their essentials, a tremendous space is revealed inside. The ordinary IS sacred. And from there, arises expression, creativity, spontaneity;

With one sound, Find the Buddha

Not as the signature of an ego, a personal identity, But a reflection of consciousness, individuality, being. Many, many Zen Masters were great artists, and none of them studied art, nor practiced it. They studied themselves. They practiced, by sitting in Za-zen, observing their self-nature; and sitting, and sitting, in constant meditation. They worked on their inner realization, and by the way, pulled out a piece of paper and a brush, and in a few moments created reflections of those crystal clear moments of consciousness. These artifacts remain, like footprints of those eagles flying in the empty sky.

C H A P T E R   3 6

The Circulation of the Light

At the beginning of autumn, in 1995, I returned to Japan for my third tour. Soon after arriving in Japan, I took the Shinkansen bullet train from Tokyo to Kyoto, and from there a small local train up into the mountains of Yoshino, in the province of Nara, and then by car up the long winding valley that leads to the very sacred Shinto shrine of Tenkawa in the 'Hara' of Japan. Japan has the form of a dragon, with Kyushu and Okinawa the long tail, and Hokkaido the head, facing East. Under the turn of the belly, in the mountains near Nara, is where the Hara would be, that center point of energy in the body, which is the real center of Japanese life. The Japanese move and feel and act from there, it is that which gives the Samurai his power, the centering, the unwavering presence and fearlessness. It is also there, where life is taken away, in the act of Hara-Kiri (literally, 'to kill the Hara')

In this area of Japan is a special place, on the river called 'Ama-No-Uzume'; 'The River of Heaven', or, in English words, 'The Milky Way'. It is a deep valley high in the mountains near Yoshino, and it is said it was formed from the impact of a meteor in the center of the valley, long ago, and that the meteor remains buried underground, underneath the shrine of Tenkawa. Who can say if this is legend or fact? But I can say for a fact that there is a very strong energy presence in the shrine. People come there from all over Japan to feel it, to be healed, inspired, nourished and consecrated by it. There is a Noh stage in the shrine, a perfectly polished large wooden platform, where artists of all kinds come to perform their art, and dedicate themselves to the goddess of Music and Art, Benzai-Ten. She is one of the eight most revered Shinto deities, one of the eight Chinese immortals, and is revered in India as Saraswati-Devi. This shrine is dedicated to Her, and rituals and performances happen there constantly as a way of artists offering themselves to this divine beneficent power.

I had been in Tenkawa two years before, in my first Japan tour, to perform a joint concert with Neesha. I was so deeply moved by the energy 'presence' there that I wept after the concert, neither with joy nor sorrow, it was simply an overwhelming feeling of being showered with something unnameable, indescribable, that moved me to the depths of my soul. It's not necessarily that there was an 'entity' of some kind or a deity, perhaps yes and perhaps no, it depends on one's beliefs how the reality is interpreted. But for me it was the undefinable unnameable presence of the Sacred. As soon as one walks into the shrine, one's vibration is heightened, everything becomes more brilliant, more intense, more deep, more alive. One can't say what is generating that feeling, but it is so.

The head priest there, who is called Guji-san, is a big bear of a man with a big heart, who administers the temple in a powerful and unique way. At that time, two-years before, under the shrine, in a special room, a meeting place, we sat together, he smoking slowly, and speaking with deep silences and pauses. He gazed at me, and in an old, slow and almost archaic style of Japanese, asked me, "What is outstanding in your mind, of all the impressions you are receiving of Japanese culture".

I replied, choosing carefully my words, "What impresses me most is the concept of space …'ma'… and the way it manifests in Japanese art".

"Ah, so, ka….Ma…hmmmmmmm…" he said in his deep baritone hara voice, as the smoke from his Camel Light slowly pervaded the room...

And thus began his fascinating discourse for about an hour, on the mysterious and profound sense of space which pervades all aspects of human behavior and action in Japan. 'Ma' was there, in all relationships, business, everything. It worked like a key, his words, slowly opening my mind to a way of looking at the indecipherable actions and events I had been witnessing in my interactions with Japanese for the past 2 months. All was ruled by a sense of the right 'ma'...the proper space, between people, things, sounds, words, musical notes, events...it pertained to everything. Not too close, not too far. When the 'ma' is violated, all disturbances arise, between people as well as things. That's the difference between music which simply entertains, and that which touches the soul. It is 'Ma'. In the absence of it, there is only noise.

Guji-san's wisdom in his deep harmonious voice remained with me, as did the expressions of his powerful face, sometimes like a smiling Buddha, sometimes like a bear. I remembered it when I returned to Italy after that first Japanese tour, and it was his face that appeared as I carved the face of the Buddha in Black Marble, that I was making in the woods near my home. The same smile which is not smiling nor frowning, but radiating a deep energy and power.

As I returned to Japan for the second time, and again was in Tenkawa, I brought a picture of this statue I had made in his likeness to show him. I thought it was cool that it really did look like him, and I gave him this photo when we met again, in the downstairs room under the shrine. The statue was made of Porta d'Oro, a black Italian marble with streaks of gold and white. It was 5 months of work, under the Tuscan sun and the winds in the cypress trees. When I polished the statue, these streaks of white and gold came out dramatically, like lightning zigzagging across the statue, and particularly the face. When

Guji-san looked at the statue, some words were passed between him and the translator, he smiled and bowed, and was deeply happy, saying that his name meant 'Lightning', and he accepted the gift, saying that a special place would be prepared for the statue there. I was surprised, to say the least, as I had no intention of giving the statue to him, but just the photo! There had been some mistranslation, and he now believed I was giving the statue to the shrine. To correct the mistake then would have been a huge loss of face for the translator, and this being a very highly placed mistake, to the head priest of one of the most important shrines in Japan, and the translator being a lower level Buddhist monk, he probably would have had to commit suicide. I didn't want to provoke that, and found myself suddenly stuck between a rock and a hard place, in a very real way. So I smiled, and said, "Yes, Great!" And so it went.

Now, a year later, I was coming back with the statue from Italy; I had picked it up from the air-cargo depot in Tokyo, and personally dragged the 100-pound trunk on some little wheels, through the subways of Tokyo, up and down the hundreds of stairs to the Bullet train bound for Kyoto, and then onto the local train to Yoshino, before the taxi ride of the last 40 miles up into the mountains.

When I got to the shrine, there were hundreds of people there waiting, dressed in white, and clouds of smoke rising into the autumn sky from all the incense burning. The statue was carried on a kind of bier, by 6 people, the Miko-sans were accompanying it (they are young female attendants dressed in red skirts and white kimonos, who act as attendant-priestesses in the shrine); there was a huge Taiko drum being beaten, it was two meters in diameter and had a sound like thunder; conches were blown, echoing all across the deep valley; Yama-bushi mountain warrior-monks were shaking their staffs with bells on them, and the whole crowd of about 500 people dressed in white robes were chanting and accompanying the statue up the

The Black Marble Buddha, in the shrine of Tenkawa

stairs of the shrine, chanting the Heart Sutra of the Buddha:
'Ga-te Ga-te Hara Gate Boji So Wa Ka!' It would have been a
good scene from the life of Moses in Egypt or some such Cecil
B. Demille Bible movie. The Buddha was placed in the center
of the shrine, shining with a radiant natural light, a light I had
never seen on it in Italy, and it was dutifully worshipped by all
present. Well, I couldn't exactly complain about its fate, who
could ask for a better placement of one's work of art, an en-
shrinement in a sacred place, showered with divine light? And
the fact that no money came or went for it, who actually cares?
As money soon disappears anyway, and the statue is going to be

there centuries after I am gone. I fulfilled my task, a task which was ordered and ordained for me by powers which I know not of, and I can only dimly grasp their designs and intentions.

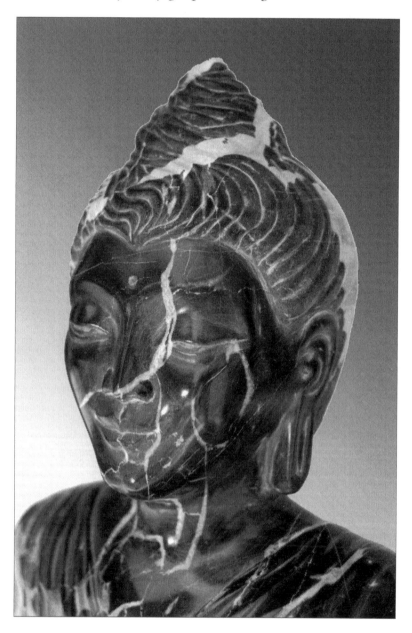

Later in the afternoon of that same day, I played another concert in the shrine. It was a cloudless and calm September day in the middle of the Crysanthemum Festival, the day of the harvest full moon, without a breath of wind. When I played the opening notes of the concert on my flute, a huge wind suddenly echoed and answered the first two notes of the flute, blowing across the shrine, actually strong enough that it blew my flutes across the stage and I had to scramble to get them back. I blew three more notes, and…another 3 gusts of wind answered. The whole crowd of 300 people fell to their knees, and bowed their heads to the ground, whispering something about 'Kami Kaze', which actually means 'Divine Wind'…The Wind of God. The wind blew a few more times throughout the 40 minutes or so which I played, always in apparent answer to the sounds I was making, and when the concert ended, the wind disappeared, as mysteriously as it had come, and there was not a breath of it for the rest of the day. I felt clearly then, the deep intimacy of the relation of the gods, or powers, of nature with the people. It answers them, it interacts with them, in a way which has been forgotten for centuries in the West. In a land where people still worship the forces of nature, those forces manifest, and respond.

After that concert of the Divine Wind, I would visit the shrine many more times over the next 12 years. Each and every time I was there I was treated with deep respect by the people in the village. I would often sit in the sacred enclosure of the shrine, facing the 'abode of the deity' for wont of another name to call it. One can go there anytime, day or night, there are no gates or fences or ticket-takers, and I would wrap myself in a few blankets and sit meditating there in the silent shrine long hours in the cold depths of night in that mountain place. I felt to be in the very heart of the mountain, in the great embrace of the ineffable. Sometimes Guji-san would call the whole village to the shrine, and I would play my flute for them, acoustic, in the

413

evening. They all knew me and would remember me, and in a way that small village in the depths of the mountains of Yoshino came to feel like my home.

There I was invited to play in many Shinto ceremonies, in early spring the cherry blossoms, and late spring the rice-planting, the fire-ceremony in the nights, where a powerful ritual is carried out utilizing the forces of fire and water, with incantations. In the darkest cold of winter, in mid-January, I played for a night-time ceremony in the heart of the shrine, where a symbolic bed was prepared, for the deity, the divine force of nature, to sleep in the depth of winter. That night, the full moon in January, it was snowing, and the silence of the shrine under the falling blanket of snow and the appearing and disappearing full moon was breathtaking. There is a huge Gingko tree there, the biggest tree I have ever seen in my entire life, and it towers over a good third of the village near the shrine. It has a mysterious power, and people worship it. It certainly is a fountain of life, and I often spent much time under it, drinking in its silent power.

Concert in Tenkawa

After this dramatic arrival in Tenkawa, and the mysterious concert dedicating my statue and music to the goddess, I was invited by a famous Okinawan Rock Singer, Kino Shokichi, alias 'Up-

414

anishad', to play with his band for a couple of gigs, and record an album together. We had met in Poona sometime before, when they had come to play at the ashram.

I flew down to Naha, the capital of Okinawa, to meet him and his band at their nightclub there, and we started in the studio the next day. Okinawa is very different from the rest of Japan, the people are very strong, straightforward, and they all know Karate. On the streets of Naha, every bush and tree is nailed or chained down. That gives you the idea of what it is like there in typhoon season, and the strength of the people is a reflection of that fact, living on an island where howl the biggest storms in the world, and which has also seen the biggest and last battle of the 2nd World War, which wiped out a third of the civilian population.

The band was quite an interesting bunch, Upanishad being the son of a famous Okinawan folk-singer. Upanishad had taken that art form of singing the traditional folk-songs of Okinawa, and given it about 5000 watts of power, backing it up with a massive rock band while he sang and played Shamisen. His two gorgeous sisters, Taru and Bayu, were the 'doo-dah' chorus. They looked Polynesian, and when they sang, they emanated a wonderful mixture of Kwan-Yin compassion and primal animal magnetism. In the band there were taiko drummers, dancers, a massive drum kit, keyboards, bass. Their sound was sometimes very interesting Okinawan themes that would get everybody in the audience up and dancing within two seconds, and epic, heroic percussion compositions that could have come straight out of a Kurosawa samurai movie; and sometimes heavy-metal-ish tracks that devolved into Japa-noise, as it's called.

My task would be to sort things out somewhat on this new album, and create a new sound for them. It was a challenge, to say the least. Okinawan folk music is not 1-2-3-4: it's more like 1-2-3-3-3-4-3-7-1-2-3-5-...I could never figure out what kind of bar would be coming next, because they would throw in occasional bars of 7 or 5 or something else, without any rhyme or reason that I could figure out. But it all made sense to them. I asked "How do you know when the rhythm will change?" and the bass player would stop for a minute, like when you ask a centipede how does it walk, and he said, in broken English, "Just don't think about it too much...Go with the frow! It's O.K.!"

I very much enjoyed playing with Upanishad when he would sing, he has a very powerful and emotional voice that contrasted beautifully with the bamboo flutes I play. Sometimes when the whole band would be blasting away at full throttle, I couldn't hear a thing, and it rather limited my creative expression, shall we say. But the album, called 'Hinu-kan' (the sun-god) turned out well, and we immediately went off to Hiroshima to play in the closing ceremony for the All-Asian games, the Asiatic Olympics. The concert had about 20,000 people watching, and once the band got really hopping, athletes from Pakistan or Malaysia or Mongolia would spontaneously jump up on stage and start dancing ecstatically. It was wild.

Around that time, I got a phone call from a friend in Tokyo, asking me to come up there as soon as possible for a meeting with a director of a program at NHK-TV. One of my CDs that I had sold in the concerts of the previous year had ended up in the library of NHK-TV, the number one television network, equivalent in prestige in Japan to the BBC in England. This director of programming had listened to it and liked it, and he wanted to meet me. The meeting was arranged by the person who was the importer of my CDs into Japan, Anupa. It was her who had put the CD in the library. It was her who made the contact between me and this program director, Hatano-san, and Upanishad. She would be a major player in the next two years of my life in Japan.

I met with Hatano-san one evening in a small sushi-bar in Tokyo. In Japanese, 'san' is the title of respect, like 'Mr.' or 'Ms.'

in English. It comes after the name, instead of before it. The meeting was late November in 1995. He was a small man, 50-ish, longish hair in the manner that intellectuals and artists wear it in Japan, and he had a strange and inscrutable smile. That is, I could not know what he was feeling just because he was smiling. He was curious about me, as he liked my music, and my character—as a kind of modern wandering monk, playing concerts in Buddhist temples and Shinto shrines all over Japan—intrigued him. As we talked, the Sake flowed, and the conversation went on long into the night. He was an artistic director for NHK with his own regular program, and as it turns out, he was interested to make a program on TV about ancient Noh drama, and the places where these legendary stories took place in Japan.

Noh drama is a mysterious art form, which as legend has it, was started in the community of Gautam the Buddha 25 centuries ago. One day Buddha was under attack by his cousin Devadatta, and to distract the multitudes present and change the energy, a play was performed, which was the first of this kind. The art form continued, passing to China, and eventually, with the entry of Buddhism in Japan around the year 700, this art form began to be uniquely developed in characteristic Japanese fashion.

To modern people, even the Japanese, it seems very weird at first, incomprehensible. The actors move slowly and speak in an ancient form of Japanese, very stylized, wearing elaborate costumes and sometimes grotesque masks. They are accompanied by a constant music from a choir of several voices, chanting incomprehensible things, and a wailing flute, and two drummers, who make gulping overtone sounds and shocking strikes and rhythms on their little hand-drums, such as: 'WOOOU-UOOP! WHACK! Oup, oup…Whack, WHACK!..' The piercing flute wails away, and every time I hear this music, I almost immediately fall into a state in between waking and sleeping,

quasi-hypnotized. I have been to 5-hour-long Noh performances, in which the time passed like one minute, I was not sleeping, I was seated on the edge of my chair the whole time, but
also I was not in the dimension of 'time' as such.

All of the Noh dramas take place on a highly polished consecrated wooden stage that serves as an interface between this
world and the 'World of Spirits'. Usually, a principal character
will come on stage, say a few lines, and lay down and symbolically fall asleep there. He dreams, and his dream becomes the
subject of the drama, and through dreaming he becomes a
medium for a message from the spirit world. In the dream usually there appears a spirit of the place, dressed as such, sometimes
it's an ancient willow tree, or a Samurai General who died in
battle, killed by the now-adult soldier whom he had raised as a
child, or an old woman abandoned in the forest with a strange
story to tell. All these spirits have some kind of unfinished an-
guish-laden tale, of betrayal, or schizophrenia, or remorse, all
filled with heart-wrenching twists and turns that only can happen in real life.

Thus, the performance serves as a kind of psychodrama, more
than a thousand years old in Japan, which allows a release and
healing in the psyche of the audience. The actors themselves
are masters of energetic projection. I have watched great Noh
actors who hardly move or say a word on stage, but simply
standing there immobile wearing a mask, the entire audience is
moved to tears and cry out almost as one at the same moment.
The actors seem to have the uncanny ability to project their
psychic states outward, so that others feel it and live it as their
own.

So with Hatano-san's idea of this Noh documentary, and my
persona as a wandering monk flute player, aided by a great deal
of sake, we hit upon the idea of doing a journey, following the
ancient pilgrimage of the Zen-poet Basho, who exactly 300
years before, travelled all over the hinterlands of ancient Japan,

searching for the roots of these Noh-dramas and legends of classical Japanese literature and poetry.

I had first heard about Basho in India, when Osho had talked about him, often quoting some of his best loved poems, from this very journey that Basho had taken. Basho had chronicled his journey in the ancient classic work of Haiku and travel-diary: Oku-no-Hosomichi. This can translate as, 'The Narrow Road to a distant place', or, 'The Narrow Road to the Far North'. We would use this as the structure of the journey, being in the same day of the year in the same place that Basho had been, to see the same changes in the nature that he saw and alluded to constantly in his poetry. As much as possible, I would travel as he did, on foot, on horseback, by rowboat or sailboat, dressed as a monk of the 16th century, playing my music where he wrote his poems, and the whole thing would be filmed and broadcast one hour a month during the 4 or 5 months of the journey.

It was agreed upon, and the huge machinery to make this happen was put in motion. I was brought to NHK headquarters in Tokyo to meet other executives, taken to the Issey Miyake design studio where my robes would be personally made and fitted. I was loaded with ancient books of Japanese literature and writings of Zen Masters in order to understand what Basho was alluding to in his poems and to understand a little better the Japanese Psyche, as there would be about 20 million poetry fans in Japan watching each program.

There were ancient samurai wars and court romances, notably 'The Tale of Genji', the first novel ever written in the world, about a court official and all the intrigues of his women, sensitively and insightfully written by a woman in the court of the Emperor 1000 years ago, and the Tale of the Heike, which is an 800 year old Homer-esque epic about the civil wars which established the Shogunate and changed Japan forever; also poetry, films and essays… I had to rapidly absorb all of this material and more, to get my brain up-to-speed to be able to talk to some of the literary people I would meet on TV while on the journey.

When I was first in Tokyo, it was an unnerving place to me. None of the signs were in English, and where I was staying, out in the 'suburbs' of Setagaya-ku, every street seemed a jumble of houses, neon and intersections of which I could never recognize anything twice. It all looked to be the same, with those chicken-scratch characters for signs, and the architecture so jumbled up that the chaos of it became a sameness in my eyes. If I left the house and I was walking to buy a loaf of bread and I turned a corner and forget that I had done so, I was screwed. I could never find my way back. Every street I turned would look the same, on and on and on. Sometimes after several hours of this futile and desperate searching for my house, because I had left the house with just enough money to buy the bread, I would have to find a policeman, and beg him to take me somewhere, anywhere recognizable, and I could find someone who spoke English to help me get back to the address where I had been. Quickly I learned that to leave the house with less that $100 in your pocket in Tokyo is courting disaster...

With the time, this first impression passed, and I started to get a feeling for different neighborhoods and wards of the city. As the time for the journey drew nearer, I would be spending more and more time in Tokyo, and oddly enough, I began to fall in a kind of love with that unthinkably enormous mass gathering of humanity. I had always been attracted to oceans, forests, starry skies: now, I was in a forest of humans, an ocean of humanity, and galaxies of numberless black-haired humans passing in the subway stations. With 35 million people in one place, it was mind boggling.

The remarkable thing about that city, is the ingenious way that the population has learned to have its 'personal space'. I have been traveling on crowded subways in Tokyo, with a feeling of great silence and stillness. Everyone knows how to keep their 'space' intact. It's a real challenge, when its rush hour and the car is packed, and there are two guys standing by the doors with white gloves to force the body parts in that are sticking out when the doors need to close. I've been in cars where there were so many people, some of them were not touching the ground, just held up by the human pressure, as the train moved side to side around curves and everyone groans. And yet, I had such a feeling of space.

Tokyo doesn't have one 'downtown'. It has about 20 of them. They all exist in a circular chain, concentrations of several million people each, each one with skyscrapers and entertainment districts, traversed by the Yamanote subway line, which goes around and around this sea of humanity, and never stops. Shinjuku station: it could be called. 'The Mother-of-All-Train-Stations'. Dozens of public and private rail lines converge here, in the midst of department stores, office buildings and hostess bars. It was about 3 months of going there often before I could actually intentionally end up in the same place twice. It was a kind of twilight zone for me, a cosmic black-hole that seemed to warp gravity and bend light each time I went. The train would stop, and you get off, sometimes in front of the cosmetic section of a department store, or the fish market, or electronic shops, or a huge pedestrian underground tunnel. I could never understand where I was, or how to get to where I wanted, it was like swimming by chance in a huge river of millions of spawning salmon, hoping, praying somehow to end up at a ticket counter. I would try to orient myself by seeing where the sun was, where was the 'ground level'. But that's just the thing that didn't work! There were at least 3 different 'ground levels', with city streets on each one, one stacked above the other. The holes that let in the sunlight were so big that it seemed to be the sky, and the real 'ground level'.

Suddenly, one day, the whole gestalt of that enormous vortex of energy that is Shinjuku station suddenly clicked in my mind, and I could figure out how to get where I needed to go! Now the key was in my hand: I was ecstatic, it was a revelation, and I felt thoroughly empowered to embark on my new life in Tokyo.

Two months before the start of the pilgrimage, in March of 1996, I was in Tokyo for some of these pre-program meetings with NHK executives, and a strange thing occurred. I woke up in the morning in the suburb of Setagayaku with ambulance sirens going off everywhere, and people being taken to hospitals by the thousands. As the day went on and news reports filtered in, it became apparent that a 'terrorist' attack of some kind had been carried on the crowded subway lines, especially in Ginza, where I had just been the evening before. Sarin gas, a nerve-gas only available to the CIA and KGB, had been left in many train cars, and about 10 people were dead and 5000 hospitalized.

It was believed, or at least intensely promoted by the mass media, that the perpetrators of the attack was a cult named 'Om Shinrikyu', whose guru would appear now and again in a white Rolls Royce, and was adored by his disciples and hated by the media and government. Oops, I didn't like the thread of this story, it sounded a little too familiar; each day the story filled the news…each day the plot thickened, as disciples were arrested in flight, jailed, and the centers of the cult were dispersed. 'Meditation' and 'Spirituality' became synonymous with evil in the news media at that time in Japan, and a hysterical fear of cults gripped the minds of the masses.

What an ironic moment to begin my journey of meditation pilgrimage on Japanese nationwide TV! It looked like I would be swimming upstream, and it appeared poignantly crucial at that time, in some small way, to change the image of meditation in the minds of the Japanese, using their own history to do so. A terrorist cult, or somebody posing as them, the actions of about 20 people had inflicted grave damage on the psyche and spiritual openness of the population of Japan, and now I would be in the pivotal role of showing Zen Spirit to the Japanese, allowing them to see, through the eyes of a foreigner, their own beautiful culture, now covered over in fear and judgement of anything having to do with 'meditation'.

The poetic justice of the event did not escape my mind, the parallel of the situation of the Ranch and Sheela's gang in the USA 11 years before, where the egoistic and pathological actions of a few people would remain as a black mark forever in the minds of the American population, completely at odds with the intentions and actions of the great mass of the rank-and-file living in the commune itself, who actually were there to meditate.

In a concert I had in the month before the beginning of the journey, I was playing in an important Buddhist temple in Kyushu, and after the concert, I got to talking with the Head Priest there. He was emphatically making it clear to me about the importance of this television program at this time. His point was that 'Om' is a sacred word, for thousands of years of spiritual life on planet earth. It is a fundamental sacred seed sound, and used in every Buddhist practice, every yogic discipline. It had now been degraded and equated with a cult that has nothing to do with real meditation, almost becoming a dirty word in Japan, equated with terrorism. For the sake of all the thousands of practicing monks, nuns, and the whole tradition of 2000 years of spiritual practice in Japan, for the sake of the Dharma, in his words, it was in my hands to change the tide, to bring back the sense of the Sacred in the ancient practice of meditation in Japan.

The impact of his words slowly filtered like the light of a foggy dawn into my consciousness...

C H A P T E R   3 7

The Narrow Road

On May 15, 1996, Anupa, acting as my manager for the TV project, drove me to Asakusa in the old heart of Tokyo, and together with Hatano-san and the 15 people of the camera-light-and-staging crew, we boarded a motorboat and set out on the journey, from the 'Rainbow Bridge', just across the Sumida River from where Basho's house had been. My costumes were arranged just right to catch the wind on the front of the boat upriver, the cameras were in place, and off we went against the current on the massive river. I was nervous, because I am not an actor, I would just have to be myself, and see what happened in the various situations I would be entering into. I would be talking my 'inner dialogue', with no real planned

Starting out on the Sumida river

script. We were to film 'the Happening', and eventually, show it to the entire nation.

Before we got 300 yards on the turbulent river, Anupa and my translator Yumiko were pretty much incapacitated, moaning and groaning, sprawled face-down on the cushions of the boat with sea sickness. The first shots took several hours, the boat going back and forth to the Rainbow Bridge and upriver about a mile, my white skin in the first shots was tomato red in the hot May sunshine by the late afternoon shots, and there was no drinking water on the boat, and no-one to translate the requests and commands of the camera crew to me. An auspicious beginning!

Anupa got off the boat a couple of miles upriver from the Rainbow Bridge, and we said good-bye, as the crew and I, just like Basho, chugged our way upriver, to Kita-senju at the end of the urban sprawl of Tokyo. I disembarked and started walking. I felt pretty cool, with my clean white Issey Miyake kimono and my walking stick, my flutes on my back. The plan was to walk where he walked, but often times it meant walking a special scenic strip of highway while they filmed, and re-filmed, and then catching up on the NHK bus with the rest of the crew, to the next place. Basho walked 15-20 miles a day, so we had to stay in that framework, in order to see the same seasonal changes on the same day which he mentioned often in his brief and telegraphic poems. As his poetry was rooted in appreciation and observation of nature in all its dimensions, it was crucial to stay within the structure and time frame of his journey, in order to observe the exact same seasonal changes which were part and parcel of his poetic imagery. Three centuries of Civil Wars, Earthquakes, Tsunamis, urbanization, industrialization, and eventually carpet bombing by B-29s had definitely changed a lot of the landmarks of Basho's route. But, amazingly there was much that was still intact from the distant past. Sometimes instead of a temple there were just the foundations and stone steps of the temple, but many remarkable places still held the mystery and depth of the ancient legends.

Within a few days I was in rice fields being newly planted, in the area near Fukushima. I passed a farmer planting rice in his paddy, and I tried out a little Japanese in the hopes of communicating. I said, "Tah weh, desu ka?". (Are you planting rice?) and he answered, standing knee-deep in the muddy water: "Set-sue desu ka, terubi-no?" (Are you shooting for television?) A true Zen dialogue, and auspicious beginning....

On that first two weeks of shooting, we went to remarkable places, the shrine of Nikko, where the Tokugawa shoguns are buried (and practically deified). It is a stupendous complex of temples and huge cypress trees, stone staircases disappearing up and up and up into the fog of the mountains.

We came upon a huge waterfall, which was just as it had been when Basho was there, and I played in the deep gorge, with the echoes all around. There was a Temple from which came a Noh legend of a woman who had leapt onto a fire and returned unburned to prove the truth of her love, and another of a Willow Spirit who came to speak to a sleeping monk. This character was played by Hideo Kanze, a master Noh player, who at the time was 86, and danced with a remarkable power, presence, and mastery.

We came to the place of a sulfurous rock that emitted poisonous fumes for a thousand years, and was said to contain the spirit of a courtesan who was the lover and downfall of three different emperors. She was called Lady Tamamo, the fox-spirit. To be a 'Foxy-lady' is not a bad thing in California, but for the ancient Japanese it was the epitome of evil embodied in human form. I didn't know if all the bad hype she had gotten was true, I felt maybe she had gotten a bad rap, a kind of character-assasination by the rewriters of ancient history. Anyone who could snuggle up to the emperors of China, Japan, and India had to have some good points, after all, and I imagine that human nature being now as it was then, probably all the monks and concubines in the court of the emperor would have been pretty jealous about such a knockout, and a foreigner to boot. So the music I played there and things I said were definitely on the side of giving her 'the benefit of a doubt'.

Then I was joined for a performance by the great Hitetsu Ayashi, one of the greatest Taiko drummers in Japan, under an ancient and huge tree on the side of an enormous ancient earthwork, which had once been the limits of Japan, called 'The Barrier of Shirakawa'. Here was the limit of Japanese Culture, empire, language, and customs. Outside of this ancient wall was the tribal territories of the Ainu, the aboriginal peoples of the northern islands who were more Siberian in aspect and culture. The deep forests there breathed a mysterious power, and evoked in us both a sense of awe. His massive drum weighed a thousand pounds, and was carried by ten people up into that forest. He played like thunder, and me with my little flute must have appeared like little flashes of lightning in big thunderstorms.

On and on it went for weeks, every day a new setting, and totally new experiences. One day we came to the Zen monastery where Basho had taken his apprenticeship. This monastery was simple, a few wooden buildings, elegantly made, unpainted and faded grey with the weather. This is in keeping with the esthetic which the Japanese love and appreciate, which is known as WABI-SABI. It is an esthetic sense which at first is elusive to understand for foreigners: like many things in Japan, one can only point at it from various directions, and say, "It's like this…" but without pinning down an exact meaning. Even the Japanese language is that way, it is not like a logical train that moves on tracks in a certain direction, like an English or Italian sentence. It's more like, three cloud-pictures in the sky, piff-poooof-Pofff! Then one steps back and looks at the whole sky silently, and the meaning is realized within. It's more poetic, in-

At Sesshosheki, the Stone of Lady Tamamo…playing Sarangi

direct, and not so mechanical and nailed down. So it is with 'WABI-SABI'.

It is for example the appreciation of a color red, but a red that is not a newly shiny bright painted red, but the red of a leaf in autumn which is lying in a rain puddle on the ground. THAT red has a deeper feeling, it has lived, and fulfilled its life in all its glories and shadows, and now is the expression of the brilliant dying colors of nature in autumn. ALL that is in that red, and they see and appreciate that. So, a Zen temple, is not painted grey. It is faded slowly with the sun and the rain to that shade, over many seasons passing, many monks coming and going, meditating inside day-in-day-out for centuries, many storms and bright sunny days and winds howling and fogs passing. All that is in that color of grey. This is WABI-SABI, but it

428

is not all that can be said about this elusive and multi-dimensional subject…

The Master who was living there in this simple country monastery was a very surprising character indeed. Hatano-san, myself, the translator and a couple guys of the camera crew went together with him into an inner room in the temple. It was very rare that a person of his stature in the world of Zen in Japan would give an interview on television. They normally disdain mass media, preferring to work one-to-one with small groups of disciples, and never with the masses. So this was a great event. We sat at a big simple table, and Hatano asked him, "Could you say something about the relationship between poetry, and meditation?"

The Master was smiling with his teeth, like the Cheshire cat in Alice-In-Wonderland, while his eyes remained as alert as a tiger's. He said slowly, in a soft voice, while looking at each one of us one-by-one, "Well, I..don't…know...much...about…poetry;…but…I…do…know…something...about…..MEDITATION!!!!!".

As he screamed this last word at full volume, he leapt forward in the face of Hatano-san, practically coming nose to nose with him across the table, with his eyes as wide as saucers.

Everybody was shocked, the NHK cameramen got very nervous, and it became apparent to all of us that this man can do ANYTHING at ANYTIME, with total unpredictability. It's an unnerving feeling, to meet a totally de-conditioned being. He regained immediately his 'composure', although really he had never lost it, and he continued in a similar way for several minutes, alternating between soft, nearly whispered monologues that would almost lull you into tranquillity and trust, and then scream something out as if he was enraged a few inches from your face. By the time he was finished everyone was pretty much unglued, and didn't know whether they were coming or

429

going. As we left, the Master said to me softly, like the purring of a panther, "When you play your music tomorrow, play the sound AFTER the sound of one hand clapping..."

This was a take-off on the famous koan that Zen masters give to students, asking them, 'What is the sound of one hand clapping?' It is a riddle for which there is no answer, and students rack their brains coming up with this or that reply, only to be slapped or rebuffed by the master each time and sent back to their meditation cushions for many more long hours of introspection. Now, that koan being a kind of cliche, the Master was giving me another step to take: 'What kind of music is AFTER the soundless sound?'...

I didn't sleep that night, knowing that he would be there glaring at me at five in the morning as I was to play in front of the monastery in the dawn light.

What would I do? I had no idea.

After this sleepless night, which was mercifully short because I had to get up at four to get ready, I realized inside me that there is nothing I can do with forethought or preparation which will be 'right'. So, all I can do is be there, and see what happens. As the sun began to rise and the mists rose in the canyon, I stood on the curved bridge at the entrance of the temple, and the Master stood at the top of the stairs, in his black robe. With my biggest flute in my hands...and a LOT of 'MA', I just let go and let the sound do what it wished, a deep resonant flute sound. With long gaps between phrases, the silence echoing deeper and deeper. My notes were not the music, but just a finger pointing to the moon, of the silence in between... This silence was the real music after the sound of one hand clapping...

After three weeks of shooting everyday all day, we had enough material for the first program. Thirty hours of films would be edited down to one hour. While the NHK crew was taking a week to edit in Tokyo, I had some time to prepare new music, in Kamakura where I was staying in a tiny one-room apartment. Kamakura is a small town on the sea, about two hours from central Tokyo by train, although the city never stops for all that distance. It's a beautiful beach city, having been the ancient capital around 700 years ago, as a result of that Civil War in the Tale of the Heike. There were two brothers that were the

At Basho's Monastery

generals of that war, one named Yoshinaga, who rose to total power and became the Shogun, establishing his government in Kamakura, leaving the emperor as a kind of figurehead pope in Kyoto, with no real power. His brother, Yoshitsune was a figure much loved by the people, who was also a war hero, young, beautiful, and charismatic, and of very pure heart, who rose in

431

the hearts of the Japanese to be an almost Divine figure. Yoshinaga out of jealousy accused his brother of betrayal, and eventually hunted him down in the northern provinces. This story would figure deeply in the second episode of our journey, as it was a central theme of pathos and impermanence in Basho's diaries.

Kamakura intrigued me, it is full of temples, bamboo forests, and ancient little streets that are impossible to figure out. I once started walking in an absolute straight line from my house, never turning a corner, wanting to see where I would end up. After two hours, walking 'straight ahead' the whole time, I was standing in front of my house again. That's how it is.

There is a big Buddha in Kamakura, about thirty feet tall, in bronze, made several centuries ago. It is perhaps the most beautifully proportionate Buddha statue in the world. It had a temple built around it, which burned down in a war. They rebuilt the temple, and a tsunami washed it away, leaving the statue behind and intact. After that, nobody rebuilt the temple, thinking that the Buddha liked it that way. I came to know, after visiting and seeing hundreds of ancient Buddha statues in Japan, all of exquisite beauty and some more than a thousand years old, that for the Japanese, the statue is not just a symbolic figure. It is charged with intention, prayers, sutras and mantras, special vibrations which unlock keys in the mind. After this 'charging' ceremony when the statue is installed in a temple, it is considered to be the Buddha himself, and treated as such. I have often slept in Buddhist temples in the night after having concerts there, as it is traditional in Japan that the temples are open to offer lodging to wandering pilgrims. In the deep and silent atmosphere in these temples, the ancient Buddha statues flickering amongst the shadows of the many candle flames, I cannot say that this belief of the living quality in those statues is not true. It is a mysterious world, and where much psychic energy is directed towards an object through sound, through chanting sutras for hundreds of years, from thousands of worshippers for centuries, that object no longer partakes of the 'ordinary' and has a magnetism of its own.

At this point, drinking, absorbing and living in Basho's haikus, after the first month of filming and encountering many situations on the first program which had been important keys in the beginning of his book 'The Narrow Road', I began to understand Haiku in a different way. On the surface they are straightforward little vignettes, a few syllables, clear images, that bring you into the present moment. Just under the surface, like an iceberg under the sea, is a vast pyramid of meaning, word-plays, allusions to ancient poems and legends from Japanese and Chinese classical literature. They were distilled, crystallized and intense little seeds which would have a resonating impact that continued in the minds and hearts of those who could appreciate them. They were actually the forerunners of modern artistic cinematography; symbolic images with great impact on the unconscious, telling an emotionally charged story while saying very few words, only with the images of nature and extreme economy of form, these are some of the hidden qualities in Basho's haiku...

As we began filming the second part, the crew was spending the night in Sendai, and that night there would be the broadcast of the first program on TV. In the hotel I was extremely nervous to see this, as I had no idea how I would come across on camera. I felt over-exposed and was quite shy in fact. The program was on channel 1, prime-time, just in-between the Japanese Prime Minister's speech to the nation, and a performance by Pavarotti, the great Italian operatic tenor. In the middle, 'Devakant Travels the Narrow Road'. YIKES! I squirmed, I didn't want to look, I was sure it would be a disaster. But no, the program unfolded gently and easily, I liked it, the message of the show came across well in the direction we were trying for, and the music performances were filmed in a sensitive and beautiful way. What a relief!

So on we went, to Matsushima, that legendary place of beauty and romance, a bay filled with hundreds of pine-covered islands, then to Chuzon-Ji, where Yoshitsune had been cornered by the army sent to assassinate him by his brother, and he committed suicide while his trusted servant-monk Benkei protected him, absorbing the arrows of the oncoming soldiers. On we went up the great river Mogami, where there was waiting for us a team of Taiko drummers thundering on the banks.

I played with them in the deep forest of Haguro-san, while

At Matsushima

a monstrous Noh character wearing a monk's costume emerged from the woods and brandished his staff like a challenge and invitation.. This legendary figure, called 'Tengu', is actually representing an extra-terrestrial entity dressed as a monk. According to Japanese traditions and folk-tales of the area for a thousand years, these figures have appeared to people again and again in those deep forests, dressed as monks, and they take people up into ships in the sky, where after some time they would be returned unharmed, and in fact show signs of greater intelligence and evolution after their return. Remembering my experience at the Ranch, I found it curious, these Abduction-tales from ancient X-files, with a happy ending....

By this point in the journey, through the daily meetings and interactions and intensity of living, working, and traveling all together on a bus, I had become aware of some aspects of Hatano's character that had slipped my attention in the rosy glow of the first meeting in Tokyo steeped in sake. Aside from the fact that we were almost always at odds about the basic intent of the program; he was constantly wanting to emphasize the glory of the military past of Japan, the Samurai spirit, the great battles that had happened along the way, while I was wishing to emphasize the love of nature and inner experience which was a hallmark of Basho's poetry. But there was something else: it had become apparent to me that Hatano-san had a very unique way of directing. Long before 'reality TV' would become a fad, he was an accomplished practicing exponent of this dubious art-form, without informing his actors about what he was doing, Alfred Hitchcock-style! For example, if he wished to show 'hardship' on the program, he would not tell me that, but rather, create hardship for me and then film me in that situation. Such as, leave me walking in the rain, in the sun, not have any water, or food often-times, or secretly instruct everyone on the crew to not talk to me for several days so I would feel lonely, have me walk up into the snow and wind and glaciers with just a thin cotton kimono, little things like that; then he would try to catch my reactions on camera. Nice.

By the middle of the third program, I was getting a little fed up with this, to put it mildly, and was sensing that this attitude on his part was not simply his artistic integrity, but was in fact driven by a deeper hidden source. The fact that he had grown up as a very hungry young child in bombed-out and conquered Tokyo, resenting the American occupiers, and the fact that I was 'American', didn't help the situation, but rather exacerbated it. The way that NHK worked as a company was remarkably like the Japanese Army, and sacrifices were expected, without question, in order to obtain the results for the greater good, that is, the success of the program. We weren't shouting 'Banzai!' together and flying off in our Zeros, but that spirit was definitely present, in all the expectations of all the fifteen people on the journey with me, whose lives and identities were intimately and irrevocably tied together with NHK.

So, a normal day would be getting up at four or five, filming a music performance in the early morning when the light is the best, and there are no tourists around, then shooting throughout the day, walking, shooting more all day long, until arriving at a hotel in the night. In the hotel, the crew would eat their sumptuous meals of raw fish, meat, and lots of alcohol, none of which I would partake of, as I don't eat meat, can't digest raw fish, and it made my job impossible if I would drink. I had to keep my mind utterly clear to do the tasks at hand. So, I would get a bit of white rice and supplement it with some soya milk or salad bought in a 7-11, and retire to my room or the NHK bus to prepare the music in the night that I would need to play early the next morning. On this rather sparse diet I was getting thinner and weaker as the time progressed, and also a lot more tired and stressed out with the relentless pace of the program, and the fact of never knowing what was coming next or what to prepare for. It was one of Hatano's sweet twists of character to maintain all the pertinent information secret, and not divulge to anyone what was around the bend.

Along with this, he had an attitude towards any women who came on the program, of something which I can only call 'Adoration-rejection-control'. That is, he would be happy to have on the program classic dancers, supermodels, shamisen players, very talented and famous female artists from the highest echelons of the modern Japanese cultural scene, but only if they were wearing masks. Sometimes the masks were a spitting-image copy of their own face, but actually a mask, very finely made like a wooden Noh mask. I argued at length with dear Mr. Hatano about his strange custom of his, but to no avail.

The only exception to this unspoken mask-rule, was one very unique Taiko player from Okinawa, named Kimiko Kawata. She played a huge taiko drum, so big that she could actually dance on the drum as she played, and she would be dressed in flowing white robes like an Okinawan Shaman. Every movement of hers was poetry, and music. Her dance, and the music, were one, effortless, feminine, sacred, powerful. We played on opposite sides of a deep gorge, her with her drum and me with my flute, hence it was impossible for her to see me across the canyon if she had a mask on, so, she became the only female on the program who could actually show her real face, the music echoing into the vast and foggy distance.

Her sense of timing was impeccable, she would be 'Drumming the Silence'. I came to realize this when we continued working together on big concerts in Tokyo for two years after the Basho program was over. Her sense of 'The Right Moment' is so uncanny and profound, she can actually be playing in a room with no visual contact with her students, they all simply wait and psychically sense the right moment from different rooms in the same building. Then she and her twelve students all come down on the first beat at the same instant, like one person. I have seen this for myself, on numerous occasions.

After the meeting with the Taiko team and the ET Tengu in the forest, we then began climbing the three Sacred Mountains of the far north, the Dewa-Sanzen. From Haguro, we went to Gassan, "Moon Mountain", a glacier covered peak that shone under the full moon with a mysterious light. Up into the clouds we climbed, the camera guys with their big TV cameras on their shoulders, each one costing about a half million dollars, and everyone else carrying spare batteries and film, and me with my

Kimiko Kawata

flutes, as we would be a few days in those mountains far from any roads.

The freezing winds howled on Gassan, the rain came and went, and the crew, following their secret psychological torture instructions to the letter, left me totally alone, treating me as if I was the left-over fish from four days ago wrapped in a greasy newspaper. I made it to the top of the mountain, where in the foggy shroud of mists, there was a little temple, just big enough for one person to enter. This temple represents the height of the spiritual aspirations of the Japanese, at the top of this most sacred mountain. Inside the temple was no deity, no statue, only…a mirror! The message is: that the real god is within, and you only need to look there, deeper and more clearly, to find it.

So it was with me on my journey. I slowly came to realize that I had nothing to find, nothing to say. Only to be present, in each place, and express my non-being in music. I left the temple on the top of that high snow-mountain, and standing in a freezing wind, watched the clouds part and the mists blow away, revealing almost the entire territory of the Oku-no-ho-somichi in the vastness disappearing below. Mountains, rivers, forests and seas all receded in the distance, and with it, my sense of identity. What do I have to say? Who am I to say it? The wind and the clouds and the mountains are speaking, and in some small way I can only reflect that great song and silence.

Walking down the mountain on the other side, we came to a waterfall of crystal clear water from the glacier. The torrent cascaded into a pool about four or five feet deep, and flowed on. Hatano had the idea for me to stand under this waterfall, in the manner that Japanese Yogis stand in stone grottos where they have ice-water dripping on their head, an ancient ascetic practice, standing nearly naked; but they do it with years of training, starting with drips; this was a falling river… and ice-cold.

I said jokingly that if he wanted me to do that, he would have to do it too. Unfortunately and unexpectedly, he took the challenge, and we both walked up there to the waterfall in little white loin-cloths and straw sandals, like ancient Japanese Yogis. He jumped in, and being less than 5 feet tall he couldn't really keep his nose above the freezing water, and started drowning. The cameramen all had to hurriedly pull him out. As he panted on the banks of the river, looking kind of green and really not well, all fifteen sets of eyes turned to me, with the challenge of

On the Glaciers of Gassan

offended honor and destiny and Japanese national pride, as if to say, "Look what YOU have done to our director!".

So, there was no way out at this point, and the buck passed to me. In I went, standing there under the waterfall of that freezing torrential river of water, with my hands in a mudra that the Shinto-monks use. They took about 10 minutes to shoot the scene, during which time I was completely numb with the torrent of ice-cold water coming straight off the glacier. Drying off on the bank, the cameramen said, "So Solly! Battery finished! Do Again!" So in I went for the second time, same scene, same frozen water. Drying off again, they said, "Gomen-Ne! (Sorry..) cassette finished! Do again, Prease, new film!.." And in I went for the third time, after which they shouted, "No close-up! Mo-Ikai onegeishimasu!" (Once more, please).

So, four times I had to stand under that freezing waterfall, for a total of about forty minutes, at the end I started to feel very weird, and asked to go back to the hotel. At the hotel I put myself in a hot bath, for about an hour, but still could not urinate. They eventually took me to a hospital, and found out that my kidneys had gone into shock and I would have to be under medication, of which I had no idea what it was. I was to find out later that it was basically pain killers so that I could continue the job and finish the filming of the rest of the episode, but nothing at all for the illness.

Leaving the mountains behind, we reached to the Sea of Japan, the long coast on the nearly forgotten backside of Japan. It was a long, hot and humid walk, into the setting sun, for days and days. Basho had been ill there, and so was I. We came upon a story in Basho's diary of two prostitutes, who asked to travel with him to reach to Niigata, as a protection, rather than traveling alone, two women on a deep forest road fraught with dangers of bandits and wild animals. Basho, being a monk, refused them, and in the night alone, bitterly regretted his unkind and selfish act. On the show the courtesans were played by two masters of the art of puppets in a heart-wrenching way. We reached the place where Basho had come to visit a long-time student, only to find out he had died in the meantime. This whole passage down the grey and somber sea of Japan took on a kind of greyness, a feeling of sorrow and melancholy, difficult to shake off.

Finally we reached to Eihei-ji, the largest Zen monastery in

Japan. The head teaching monk who came to greet us was named Shinkai-Osho. It is not a coincidence that my Master took the name at the last stage of his life of 'Osho' which is a name shared by every single Buddhist priest or monk in Japan. In Japan, it is the equivalent of 'Reverend' in the USA or England, that is, a simple term of respect, but not particularly a proper nominative or identity.

Shinkai Osho took me to the upper floors of the main gate, where there was his special rooms for meditation and contemplation. We sat in silence together and alone for about an hour, and then he proceeded to tell me about Eihei-ji, and the life of the monks there. He was particularly happy that I was there, knowing about my relation with Osho, because at Eihei-Ji, the most traditional and strict Soto Zen monastery in the country, they actually use the books of Osho to teach Zen Spirit to the novice monks.

The new monks who wish to be admitted to the monastery have to kneel outside the main gate in silence, awaiting to be let in. It can take up to two weeks, and they remain kneeling there, in the sun, in the rain, in the snow. It is an act of humility, and it helps to prepare them for the work ahead, a work whose sole objective is the systematic destruction of the ego.

The monastery was spotless, huge, with polished wooden floors and staircases leading to this incredible garden or that magnificent temple or sitting hall. The monks run in-between their tasks, and are under a very strict discipline and guidance. They sit in silent Za-Zen at four in the morning in the unheated meditation hall, winter or summer, and up there in those mountains it gets well below zero in the winter. I thought of my experiences at the Ranch, and I realized that I did not have it so bad, it was the same kind of training, you always have to pay with your effort in some way for admission in these kinds of places.

I played my music there in the cemetery in front of the grave of Dogen, the founder of Soto-Zen, of which Eihei-ji is the main monastery in the world. As I was leaving, the successor of Dogen, the very old abbott of the monastery, gave me a fan on which he had written the characters that mean: "See the Buddha in the four directions", which means ultimately, to see the Buddha in everyone and everywhere. I thought to myself, "Ah, so...this is the true discipline, to see the Buddha even in Hatano!" There was great insight in this old abbott's simple gift...

In the last days of the long, long journey, we arrived at sunset to a beautiful old shrine with a large courtyard. There we set up for a night performance, under the full moon. I would be joined by Sayako Yamaguchi, a very famous super-model in Japan and the world, whose charisma and beauty had changed the lives of millions of Japanese women. When she became the 'Shiseido-girl', she drastically changed for Japanese women their image of themselves and the acceptance of their own Asian features, and to not be striving always to look like a Western woman. Just before we were to play together, I met Sayako. She is a tall, elegantly beautiful and gracious being of great heart and presence. Everywhere she moves, all eyes are on her.

As I began playing, the darkness enveloped us and the moon rose... a lightning storm came upon us, and flashes of light would illuminate the courtyard. She danced in a long white kimono, of course with a mask, and she appeared like a great white bird, in the mysterious light of the moon. She held a crystal ball in her hand, and it would catch and reflect the moonlight, and shine with the flashes of lightning, as she moved in slow motion to the sound of the flute. It was a wonderful last performance, and a mysterious end to this long and mystical journey.

The next day, I travelled by small sailboat as did Basho, to a small beach by a little town on the sea of Japan, called Tsuruga. I was to play on that beach, the last point on the pilgrimage where

Basho had written a haiku. And yet, something was very wrong. I could not play my music. In front of me across the bay was a huge building, that captured my attention in a negative way. I felt a bad vibration radiating from it. The NHK cameras were turned slightly to block it from being seen in the film, a trick of television to show things as they are not, because this large and ominous building was a nuclear reactor, dominating the landscape. I could feel the radiation, as a negative feeling in my heart, which only made me want to leave as quickly as possible, and no music would come forth from me. As I found out by speaking to the locals, this nuclear power plant was slowly and surely killing the life of the town, which once had been a fishing village. The fish were now inedible, containing high levels of mercury, and the people of the town were leaving. I felt the vibe of the reactor, and I wondered what stupidity could have caused this to be built, in a land of so many earthquakes, this huge intrusion of technology on what had once been a tranquil and peacefully beautiful scene. Little did I know what was in store in the future, as this very technology of the nuclear industry would explode twenty years later in the worst disaster scenario ever envisioned on the planet, in a huge earthquake, tsunami, and reactor explosion and multiple core meltdown in Fukushima where I began my NARROW ROAD, some months before. It is a terrible testament to the short-sightedness of our present system of social organization, that greed for profits far outweighs intelligence, that return-on-investment is all that is thought about, and not the life of the planet itself and the welfare of its people and other creatures, for now and all future generations. What good does profit do you, if the Pacific Ocean dies and humanity itself becomes extinct? As a very wise Indian Chief named Seattle once said: "Only when the last fish is dead and the last river polluted and there is no more air to breathe or water to drink, will you realize that you cannot eat money".

I am sure that the gods of Japan now weep at the fate of this extraordinarily beautiful country, and with it, the entire planet.

On the very day that my Oku-No-Hosomichi ended, the original hand-written manuscript of the Oku-No-Hosomichi that Basho had carried himself, with all of his pasted-in corrections, was discovered in an old book shop in Osaka. It had been there, and elsewhere, waiting, for 300 years. It's a mysterious world.

On the Narrow Road

There is a saying in the world of Zen; "Ichi go, Ichi e'. It means, "One life, one meeting". Or in other words, "In this life, you will only meet each person one time. That meeting can be for a moment, or for many years, but it will only be once, and once it is over, it is over. Therefore, every moment, every meeting, is unique and precious".

So too it was on my Oku-No-Hosomichi. With the exception of Kimiko Kawata, I never met any of those hundreds of people again that I had come to know on my Narrow Road. The 'meeting' with Kimiko continued for a few more years, she invited me to play many concerts with her Okinawan Miyarabi Taiko team in Tokyo and elsewhere. This Taiko team is twelve women, each dressed as shamans of Okinawa, and each playing huge Taiko drums in perfect unison. The thunder of these drums would awaken every nerve and cell in every member of the audiences in those Tokyo concerts. Every one of those experiences was a great enrichment and mystical moment for me, and I am very grateful, as I am to each and every person I met on my Narrow Road, including Hatano-san. And yet, one day, that too was over, and a chapter of my life ended with it. Ichi go, ichi e.

The ancient pond..
Frog jumps in..
Plop!

After the end of the Narrow Road, for a brief time I was living in Waseda, an old neighborhood in Tokyo where curiously enough, Basho had once lived, with a view of a lovely canal outside the window, an old waterway lined with cherry trees. I came to know that this canal had been partly built by Basho when he was working as a civil engineer before he left on his pilgrimage, and the 'ancient pond' where the famous frog had jumped in to the sound of 'plop!' ("Mizu no oto"), in the most famous of his haikus, was actually across the street from my house. It's a small world…

And one other saying, that came from the world of Zen Archery, came into play now in my life. That statement, is :"E SHA JO RI", it is said by the Zen archer as the string is released from the hand and the arrow flies from the bow; it means, simply: "Every meeting ends in separation".

E Sha Jo Ri…

Thus there is no cause for grief, it is the natural and inevitable nature of events. All meetings end in separation...

Basho's canal lined with cherry-blossoms,
in Waseda, Tokyo, where I lived after the Oku-No-Hosomichi

CHAPTER 38

Embrace Tiger, Return to Mountain

After the end of THE NARROW ROAD, I continued to
spend about five months a year in Japan, playing concerts,
concerts, concerts. The impact of the program was such that I
would be invited to play in all kinds of places all over Japan, for
the next ten years. In that time it is possible that I had at least
300 concerts all over the country. Many Zen temples, shinto
shrines, Noh theatres, hospitals, you name it, I probably played
there. I played for all kinds of people, poor Zen monks and
nuns, young people in search of something, thousands upon
thousands of middle-aged housewives, lots of businessmen, and
sometimes a whole golf-clubhouse full of the presidents and
CEOs of corporations like Toyota, Honda and Kawasaki. When
I would travel from Tokyo to Fukuoka on the Shinkansen bul-
let-train the length of Japan, I could look out the window and
see almost every five minutes some place in the passing landscape where I had played some sort of concert. Japan was my
home. For a time I lived in Kyushu, the southern island of the
four main islands of Japan, on a long beach near a small fishing
village. My house was next to a Kwan Yin temple, and for that
time, I would only paint and carve images of Kwan Yin, I was
flooded with her loving, mystical, and benevolent presence. She
is the goddess of compassion, called 'Kannon' in Japan. Her radiant and smiling face is everywhere present in Japan, China,
and Eastern Asia. India, and Tibet know her as 'Tara'. South
America knows her as 'Pacha Mamma', the goddess of the Earth
itself.

448

A beautiful aspect of all the concerts I had in Japan all those years was the great intimacy which occurred with the Japanese public. I was not on a large stage far away with a huge audience, but often in the midst of the public, who were sitting all around on tatami's in the main hall of a temple, or a shrine. After nearly every concert, there was a recurring ritual, of a collective dinner with 60 to 100 of the people who had attended the event. After eating and drinking around a large improvised table in the middle of the floor, and usually around midnight, people would stand up one by one and recount their inner feelings and experiences during the event to the whole body of people present. The collective is so strong in Japan, it is the reflection and the base of every occurrence, event, happening. All is reflected in the mirror of the 'community' in Japan. So it was after my concerts, people would share their innermost perceptions and feelings with everyone present, and all would respectfully and silently listen one by one. This would sometimes take three or four hours, and go on until early in the morning. No one ever spoke about doing this or not doing it, it was simply something that always happened.

As everything with a good side has also its bad, so it was with the impact of THE NARROW ROAD. Many people came forward and sought me out, offering to help me by promoting my music in Japan. Some were very good-hearted and sincere, and actually understood what I was trying to do. Many others saw opportunity in the situation, to use my popularity for their own profit, regardless of the content of the music and message I was trying to give. Some would try to force me into contracts under threat of blackmail, extortion, harassment to my friends. It was the dark side of the music industry. Japan being an ancient country, corruption is deep and systemic, and I was too naive to see what was happening most of the time. In such a world, success always has its price. After a time I became weary of paying it. There came a day when I just had no more feeling to keep trying, and in autumn of 2005, as the leaves turned a brilliant red in all the temples of Kyoto, I said goodbye and left Japan forever.

In the meantime, my concerts in Europe were becoming more frequent, and I found myself traveling to new lands, playing concerts all over the continent, all the way from Copenhagen to Granada, from Amsterdam to the borders of the Ukraine. It happened gradually, but steadily. My audiences were in all kinds of places, from farmhouses in Sweden to enormous concert halls in Germany to meditation domes on the side of Sicilian Volcanos. It was a beautiful time, and a hard time as well, thousands upon thousands of kilometers driven on European highways, usually alone, in all kinds of weather and situations, only to play a concert, pack up the instruments in the car and drive on to the next one. Basho once remarked that the clouds that wander in the sky have no homes and time itself is a traveller. And just as it did for him, so it became for me an endless pilgrimage, and I embraced that as my Dharma and my fate. It is a great joy to share joy, silence and peace through music with many people, and the hardships encountered on the way are a small price to pay for the great joy that I have had and continue to have in my life.

In ironic contrast to the real beauty of playing for people 'live', is the 'controlled folly' of recording music. It is the evolution of digital sound and its technological interface with me, that has been more than any other single aspect of my life the clearest representation of 'samsara'... the illusion of life, the bondage, as a springboard which constantly pushes one to seek moksha, the liberation and the real. From very simple one-track tape recorders which I started using 50 years ago, on through multi-tracking reel tapes, then digital tape/hybrid concoctions with mixing boards that resemble third-world airports, then computer-driven hard disc recording, audio samples and endless other software configurations; it was a constant game of dog-chasing-its-tail, never quite getting it, but running faster and faster. A certain technology would come into vogue, then just as I would get a handle on it and spend a lot of money on it, it

Farewell to Kyoto

would become obsolete and newer technology would take its place. Then just as the technology got to a level where it starts to become actually 'easy' to record with beautiful pristine sound, at the same time digital copying and streaming has made a situation where it becomes nearly impossible to sell the recorded and produced music anywhere. Everybody can download it for free or nearly so, without giving a penny or a thought to the musicians, who just spent thousands of Euros and thousands of hours to produce it. What a joke! It seems technology has devoured itself, at least in the world of music, and the genie is not showing signs of returning into its bottle.

As my concerts in Europe slowly gained momentum, my

wandering life started to gain a foothold of balance on another continent, a surprising and delightful one. Around the year 2000, Aseema and I parted company with tears in our eyes, realizing that our lives had become very different, yet our love had not disappeared but moved upwards into our souls. So we remained as such, friends in the deepest sense, yet not together in a relationship. She had decided to move to Chile, her homeland which she had left 40 years before, and buy some land in the far south, above a big beautiful lake, in the shadow of a snow-covered active volcano. That place is called Pucon. After her house was built, she invited me to come take a look. The first day I was there, a day in January 2001, early summer, there arrived a hurricane, and we spent the sunset holding the plate-glass windows from caving in under the 120 km/h winds blasting off the lake. "What a place!" I thought; "an auspicious beginning...". When the storm calmed down, I took a look outside. The construction workers had left a disaster area, and I set to work cleaning up the mess, finishing the meditation temple, and a million other things. The nature is such in the south of Chile, so abundant and thriving and powerful and intense, that by the time you clear the fallen trees and cut the grass, there are more trees fallen and the grass has regrown double, so it was, and is, and always has been a great deal of work to be there. But, something of the place touched my soul, somehow being there on the slopes of the southern Andes, an occasional condor passing overhead, magnificent sunsets and rainbows and the volcano erupting every once in a while in the backyard, life is never dull.

I started coming back a couple of months each year, helping in the building of what would become a meditation center there on that quietly alive volcano. The name the conquerors gave it is 'Villarica', but the Mapuches, the native people of that part of Patagonia, gave it the name since antiquity, 'RUCA PILLAN'; 'The Abode of the Spirits'. And that name is far more true, as it is a mysterious and alive mountain which rules over the entire

The Volcano Ruca Pillan

area with grandeur and majesty. When the construction was to begin on the meditation hall, a beautiful wooden octagon, on the full moon night we placed in the earth in the very center of the building a stone and a crystal from Mt. Kailash in Tibet, thus completing symbolically the circle of our connection with the Himalayas, and now, the Andes. Each year, I make a few more statues, more people come, for the meditations, and the music, and the silence and the garden, and each year the trees get bigger, and the lake, a bit more blue.

In the night there are several billion stars, when it's not raining, and in the day the air is as blue as my memories have of the sky when I was young enough to be bewitched by it in California. I still am bewitched by that color of blue, even more now, and I am grateful it still exists somewhere on our long-suffering planet. The water comes from the mountain, the heat comes from the wood, and the food, is what we grow in the

"Gratitude"...In Sammasati, Pucon, Chile

garden. It's a simpler life, a great antidote to the time I still spend with a microphone in front of a computer recording music, or behind the steering wheel of a car on European highways. If ever I have felt the loving touch of the Mother Goddess, the Sacred Earth, it is there where I have felt wrapped in her arms, surrounded by her great works.

CHAPTER 39

THE BIG ONE

Earthquake in Chile

In Mahamudra all one's sins are burned;
In Mahamudra one is released from
the prison of this world.
This is the Dharma's supreme torch.
Those who disbelieve it are fools
who ever wallow in misery and sorrow. ....

Tilopa-Song of Mahamudra

As I write this it is February, in Santiago, Chile. I had spent the month here, having had concerts in the city and in the south of Chile. It had been a hot summer. I was staying in a neighborhood called El Arayan, on the edge of the city nestled against the mountains, the first slopes of the Andes which ring the town to the East.

Santiago is a big and smoggy city of 7 million, in a bowl of hills at the foot of one the highest regions of the Andes. The peaks that tower above the city are eternally covered in snow. In those peaks fly condors, the largest and highest flying birds in the world, and with them, the memories and spirits of Incan priests, who left their temples and mummies there thousands of years ago in stone caves amongst the glaciers.

The apartment I am staying is on the 5th floor of a moderately old building, whose back is lodged into the hillside, and whose frontside rests on high pillars, to accomodate the steep slope. Dusty trees line the streets, and occasional cactuses poke their spiny arms out from little rock walls with sleepy dogs dozing here and there under canopies of bougainvillea. From the large plate-glass window, pine trees and oaks hide the many houses, and the brown slopes climb almost vertically behind, giving way to tall snow mountains in the distance, disappearing into the blue vastness. The Cordillera, as The Andes are called here, is immensely impressive from Santiago, 6,000 meters high. The snow-peaks are within close view, and the mountains seem to recede into infinity. On the other side, the city lays under its brown and heavy air, disappearing into the grey flat sea of buildings stretching away beyond sight, where live the 7 million or so inhabitants of this intensely alive city. I would not say that it is a pretty town, not compared to other world capitals, like Kyoto or Paris. But it is certainly an extremely fun city that constantly surprises me with the inventiveness and friendliness of its people. On any day in hundreds of street corners, you will get live shows at the stoplights, acrobats, jugglers on insanely tall stilts, bands, fire-breathers, mimes and clowns doing things you never even thought were possible, for a few pesos from passing motorists. At this time of the year, it is relatively deserted, the population is all at the beaches or the lakes to the south, and the city streets are empty of their constant river of traffic. It was a hot day of late summer, a warm dry wind blowing the air away from the hills and down into the town. It was the night of the full moon, Friday, February 28. I had been painting today, the painting of the dream in Teotihuacan, in the studio of a friend a block away, surrounded by a bamboo forest. It had been a good day. I fell asleep around 2:30 am, and all was well.

I awoke at 3:30. I had that strange feeling that something was about to happen, a feeling I often get just before an earthquake starts. Maybe the Earth emits some low sound which some part of me hears, other than my ears. I don't know why, but it always wakes me up first before the trembling starts. I have been in many, many earthquakes, from those days of being born and raised literally straddling the San Andreas fault in California. I had been in one which toppled a couple of freeways and a hospital, and I had also been in many big shakes in Japan, where strong temblors were almost a daily event. But something was starting to happen that I had never experienced.

The house began to rattle and started shaking sideways, and I could hear a deep rumble. The shaking increased, and the rumbling got stronger, kept going, growing, getting stronger, and bigger. The sideways movement became up and down, like waves and shaking at the same time. The whole building was shaking sideways, rattling, and jumping up and down all at the same time. It didn't stop, but just kept getting bigger, as the rumbling of the earth got louder and became a deep roaring from the bowels of the earth. I was up and out of the bed, with nothing on. I got out of the room quickly and stood on the balcony of the 5th floor, wanting to have nothing over my head. I could hear the sounds of glass breaking, things falling...the shaking got bigger and bigger, and the thought crossed my mind: "Well, this is it. This is the BIG ONE!", having always felt that one day I would be in just such a happening. And I realized I will probably die in this, as it very much seemed the building was about to collapse. The windows were all breaking, and the chimney on the roof in front of me made of bricks was flapping back and forth with an incredible sound of cracking and popping. I looked at myself, at my feelings, and was surprised that I was not 'afraid'. What I felt was too strong for that; it was an intense alertness and urge to survive, my whole body was trembling with adrenalin. I moved to the edge of the swaying balcony, ready to jump onto the adjacent building and 'surf' the roofs down below if the house started pancaking, collapsing floors. The shaking went on for about 5 minutes but it seemed like it was eternity. I have never felt the earth move that way, it was an unbelievable sensation of the power of the earth itself and my own helplessness in the face of a cosmic force. It was far bigger than anything I have ever felt before. But eventually, after seemingly endless minutes, it became less, and quieter, although it went on softly for much longer. The electricity was gone. In the black streets below, all the alarms of all the cars in the whole city were going off. It was a weird moment: I had no shoes on, and the floor was covered with broken glass, so I could not move around. It was very dark, but I could see the bed. I lay on it, and waited. My body kept trembling with adrenalin. After half an hour, another quake came. This aftershock, seemed puny compared to the one before it, but it was easily bigger than 7.0 on the Richter scale, I thought. Every half hour or so, another quake. All night it continued; there were about 10 quakes until the morning. It is a strange adjustment mechanism we have within, that makes all things relative; after a couple of hours, quakes that normally would have me jumping out of bed now seemed not even worth it to poke my head out from the sheets. I opened one eye, and seeing that the walls aren't moving much and the bed is staying in one place, I went back to sleep.

The neighbors across the hall knocked on the door in the darkness, to see if I was o.k. It was very sweet, their voices calling out from the dark hallway, "Todo bien? Estas Bien?" "Si..si..no te preocupes...Estoy Bien!". ("Are you o.k.?" "Yes, I'm o.k, don't worry") The elevators of course did not work, and the stairs were pitch black. So nobody moved up or down. After about an hour, the car alarms petered out, and the sounds changed into dogs barking, babies crying, people rummaging around in the darkness, an occasional car passing on the road.

When the light of day came on, around 6 in the morning, I could see enough to walk around. The plate glass window in the front room was broken, many things had fallen from shelves, but the walls were intact, though cracked, I was surprised. No cell phones or electricity would work all the day. After the morning, I started to get the news, from people in the street, in front of the grocery store....9.0 quake... 5th biggest in recorded human history... Massive devastation at the epicenter.... the Earth's axis shifted... City shut down for two days... No street lights, no phones, no services.

Later in the day, you wouldn't know that it had happened. People were out watering their lawns, playing with their kids. Sunday was much the same. On Monday morning, the picture changed drastically. As

Highway I-5, The morning after...

the big city tried to reopen for business, it was found that computer main-drives were damaged in the banks, nobody could get money. All the highways going in and out of the city were massively damaged and closed, so there were no trucks coming in or out. People started panic buying in the supermarkets, the shelves became empty, it was an unsettling feeling. Reports got worse, that 40-foot tidal waves had hit at the coast, some towns had disappeared, crowds were looting in the devastated areas, and there were no international flights due to heavy damage at the airport.

I knew Aseema was safe in Buenos Aires, as she was giving a group there at the time, but I decided to leave Santiago and go down to the south to see if Sammasati, (the meditation center we were creating) was alright, to see what had happened. I found a bus company that was still selling tickets, and got one for the next night, at 9 p.m. I waited for the bus, until midnight, when finally one of the other stranded passengers, through making various phone calls to government transit agencies further south, found out that all buses had stopped running that night because they were being held up and robbed by looting crowds, and the army was only patrolling the roads in the day, but that the ticket would be good for the next morning.

In the morning I got on the bus, and began what was usually a 10-hour trip, which ended up taking 22. In Santiago itself, I could only see brick facades which had fallen to the street, a lot of rubble on the sidewalks, but the buildings were basically intact. Just outside of Santiago, the first bridges down were the opening signs. The bus would detour off the highway and pass through little villages, which looked like they had been smashed with big fists; Shattered! Any building of adobe was devastated. As we got closer to Talca, and Concepcion, 400 km south, the highway, which was I-5, the Pan-American highway going from Alaska to Tierra del Fuego, was in some stretches ground into powder where it crossed fault lines. There were sections of 100 meters which had simply dissolved into sand. Huge bridges collapsed into rivers, 4-lane freeways dropped 20 meters into gulches, churches split in two, huge grain elevators looking like crumpled tin cans, walls and whole villages gone down like dominoes. I could not count the number of times we left the highway, because of impassable damage. After a few hours, I stopped taking pictures, it was absurd. After a certain point, you just can't take it in anymore. A numbness came over me.

I arrived to Pucon around 5 the next morning, shocked and glad to be alive. I spoke by phone to friends who had very different experiences than mine, much more intense. Two friends had been vacationing that weekend at a beach just near the epicenter. They awoke with their hotel collapsing around them, and they ran down the stairs nude, as bathtubs and toilets fell through the opening cracks in the walls. They passed the night with no clothes, in the public plaza of the town, shivering and waiting until dawn to get their car keys from the devastated hotel.

And worse: one friend was in the town at the beach near the epicenter. She felt the beginning of the earthquake, and with quick thinking, got her kids and her mother in the car and started driving away from the beach. There was a car in front of her, which was going slowly because the road was buckling and jumping. She honked to pass, and overtook the car. A couple of minutes later, one of her children looked out the back window and said, "Mommy, the ocean is coming!!" And behind them came racing the tidal wave, with the car they had overtaken rolling IN the wave!

She turned up another street, and the sea was approaching there too. She turned another, and it was the same. Finally she found a road which led straight up hill, and they narrowly escaped the passing tidal wave, which in some places went 5 miles inland, taking whole villages away in its path. Others who saw the wave coming and ran to high ground, said it was so high that it blocked out the full moon in the sky. It was 40 feet high, taller than a 4-story building, according to official reports. My experience was so mild, compared to those who lost homes, children, parents, beloveds, everything in their lives gone in a single moment.

After a week of bad news and fear, something changed deep inside everyone, a different spirit took hold. Suddenly in Pucon, and all the towns and villages there were rallies for the people who had lost all, collections of clothes and food and money; Many, many people pitched in to help, millions of dollars in aid came out of the pockets of everyone. It was beautiful to see; Chile taking care of its own, not waiting like a beggar for the indifference of the United States, who couldn't even send a single helicopter, they were too busy conquering oilfields in Iraq.

From these words and recollections, suddenly I am jolted back to this moment, as the subway I am riding arrives to my stop. I stop scribbling on my notes, and climb the stairs to the street above. I am inundated by a flood of perceptions, smells, sensations. A familiar and delightful fragrance releases a wave of pleasant feeling in my solar plexus. I turn my head and see the enormous sycamore tree which has released this wave of pleasant memories in me. Associations beneath my conscious mind, of nights spent camping under just such a sycamore on a windy beach as a teenager in California, finding the first few moments of my freedom, as I escaped from high school for a few days. But now, I am on the corner of Avenida Providencia and Ricardo Lyon, at midday in March, in downtown Santiago. The hot breeze of afternoon moves the trees with passion and grace, as the crowd waits for the lights to change. An old trumpet player standing in the shade, his face as creased as the old clothes he wears, wraps himself around his horn like he is embracing his lover, his child, his bottle, his crucifix, and his god. He blows the sweet melancholy sounds of 'The Shadow of your Smile', and it floats over the heads of the mass of bodies that begin to move across the street with the changing of the light from red to green, and the trumpeter's soul drifts far above it, free from time and space.

CHAPTER 40

Farewell

At first a yogi feels his mind is tumbling like a waterfall;
In mid-course, like the Ganges, it flows on slow and gentle;
In the end, it is a great vast ocean,
Where the lights of Child and Mother merge in one.

Tilopa-Song of Mahamudra

I found myself one day, in Chile as the rubble from the streets of Santiago was being cleared away after the massive quake, and I was returning from Pucon. The airport in Santiago was still closed and being repaired, and I received a phone call, from California, that my mother, 89 years old, was now in the throes of heart failure, and was getting worse. I got the first plane I could out of the newly opened Santiago airport, actually the check-in for the flight had to be done in tents, as the buildings were still being repaired. When I landed in LA, I rented a car and drove the hour and a half to the hospital in Riverside, and was there for the last day in which she would speak. We had been seeing each other much over the last few years, as her health declined, I would come and stay with her there in Riverside whenever I could. We laughed much together. She loved Osho's jokes which I would constantly tell her, as many of them as I could remember. She especially laughed at the ones about sex. We became great friends, and I loved spending time with her.

As I entered into the hospital room where she lay dying, I

was silently shocked at the change that had happened in her since the last time I was there, two months before. She was much more gaunt, much, much older, and with much less energy. She opened her eyes, recognized me and smiled, and told me, "This is the end of a journey...I've already been here too long, it's time to go". She spoke to me for an hour or so, and fell asleep, and slept long and deep. The next day she didn't wake up really, and the day after that, only opening her eyes for a few moments to greet me and then closing them again. The doctors, worried about this sudden change in her normally energetic state, took her in for a CAT scan, and found out that in the night she had had a massive stroke. The thinking side of her brain was basically dead, no language function or thought was possible. But her feeling side was still alive and functioning. I would hold her hand, tell her I loved her when her eyes would open, and a tear would run down her cheek and a soft smile play about the corners of her mouth. After many tests, the doctors came to tell me that the stroke was irreversible, and they said that they felt there was no recovery possible. She had made it clear to us a year before that it was her wish to not have life-prolonging measures when it was clearly not necessary anymore. We, that is, myself, my sisters, and brother, all agreed that it was time to let nature take its course. With the doctor, my sister and me in the room, we told her that we felt it was better to take out the intravenous tubes and go home, and asked her if she understood. It was clear by the determined look in her eyes that she had understood, and after a moment's hesitation, she nodded her head firmly in agreement. It was the most courageous gesture I had ever seen, that final irrevocable decision to accept one's death and no more fight or prolong the struggle. It must be the loneliest moment of one's life.

I brought her home from the hospital, so she could be in her bed, and see her beloved garden out the window. In the evenings, I would play some music for her, on the flute, or Ti-

The Angel of Transformation, who cuts away all what is unessential before we can pass beyond....

betan bowls while singing to her softly. This went on for two days, and at one point she opened her eyes wide, and clearly focused on three positions behind me in the room, as if she was seeing three different people, behind me...BIG people. Her mouth was wide open in astonishment, and her eyes awestruck, and she seemed to scan 'Them' up and down. I didn't see anything, but I felt a strange and remarkable presence for which I could only bow in respect, as I felt some kind of entities were there, the 'Guardians' or 'Emissaries' were there, to take her soul. I never believed or disbelieved, in those stories of ministering spirits who take the souls on their journey out of this life, but here they were, and I was a witness to it, albeit an unseeing one.

That night and the next day her breath came slower and slower. We took turns being with her, all the time, my sister Maria and I. Sometimes Maria would read things, poetry, Psalms from the Bible, beautiful things from Buddhist Masters about the journey of the soul, sometimes I would play a little music or sing.

As the sun was setting and the full moon of March was rising, her breath came slower and slower, and I held her hands in mine and we were looking into each other's eyes. Then her breath went out, and didn't come back. She looked at us for a moment, with a question in her eyes, and my sister said, "Yes, mom, this is it. We love you. Have a beautiful journey". Then she stayed looking into my eyes, and simply the light faded out in hers, and she was gone, so softly, so easily.

I closed her eyes softly, and kissed her on the forehead, and it was over.

Within a few moments after her soul departed, I distinctly felt that the body there was simply a wax mannequin, it was not her. The 'her' that I knew was now gone. I remembered those fateful words of the Zen archers as the arrow leaves the bow: "E Sha Jo Ri"...All meetings end in separation...

My mother had seen many hardships in her life: hunger, psychological abuse, poverty, war, overwork, loneliness; but I imagine the hardest crucible of transformation which she had to pass was being the constant companion and nurse for my father in his terrible decline into dementia which was the later stages of Parkinson's disease, and it burned away everything in her which was not real. They were together for 50 years of marriage..and when he died, she remade her life, enjoyed her last 10 years peacefully in her garden, spent much time with her friends, left the Catholic Church and became a Unitarian, and searched for real answers to her real questions, not content with doctrines and dead words that have nothing to do with people's actual lives. She was a mother that had the courage to support this son of hers to become a musician, and a composer, and follow his strange dreams all the way to India, when there was absolutely no sign of any way to make a living at that profession, even Mozart having starved to death at it. She let him follow his dreams as he saw fit to do, even came to see him twice, at that crazy Ranch up in Oregon, and when Osho drove by in his car, she waved at the Master, and did a little dance. She was always full of surprises...

I salute you on your way, dear and courageous soul...Thank you for everything...

CHAPTER 41

Reflections (Epilogue)

The Path to salvation is narrow, and difficult to walk,
as the edge of a razor

from the Kena Upanishad

To my fellow swimmers;
Here is a river flowing now very fast.
It is so great and swift,
that there are those who will be afraid,
who will try to hold on to the shore
they are being torn apart and will suffer greatly.

Know that the river has its destination.
The elders say we must let go of the shore,
push off into the middle of the river,
and keep our heads above water.
And I say: see who is there with you and celebrate.

At this time in history we are to take nothing personally,
least of all ourselves, for the moment we do,
our spiritual growth and journey come to a halt.

The time of the lone wolf is over.
Gather yourselves.
Banish the word struggle from your attitude and vocabulary.

All that we do now must be done
in a sacred manner and in celebration.
FOR WE ARE THE ONES WE HAVE BEEN
WAITING FOR.

from the Hopi Prophecy

A s I write this, my relation with Osho as a disciple has now been for 40 years. As far as my participation in Rajneesh-puram, that famous and infamous episode in Osho's work which left such a deep impression for better or worse on the human collective, I have no regrets whatsoever about being there. It was a great gift, and a crucible of transformation for me. Some-times I rode the waves, and sometimes I got lost in them. But I grew up there in those years.

Looking 'back' upon the days of living in the commune, I have more questions than answers, about who was directing what, and why certain things happened the way they did. To conjec-ture about 'why' something happened as it did is an exercise in futility. And yet, one wonders...it is human. It is true that some courses of action which unfolded in the commune both in the USA and India were born out of Osho's directions. It is equally true that many directions were taken by Sheela which were op-posed by and publicly denounced by Osho, and it was he who invited the law enforcement agencies to come in and investigate after she left.

Of all the events which transpired in the communes which grew up around Osho, every one of those events took on the color of the people acting within it: Osho would say one thing, and Sheela, or others in positions of power after her would sometimes change it partially or totally in the communicating of it to 'us'. I saw this happen personally at times. It is not necessarily evil intention on the part of those persons with managerial 'power' on their hands. Often they were doing this with the best of intentions, believing it to be 'good' and 'right', or 'more practical'. Sometimes it was done with clearly egoistic intentions. As it says in the Mahabarata, "A good man is not completely good, a bad man is not completely bad ". In our human weakness we tend to filter experience, and only see that which fits into our mindset. And hence, we tend to 'change reality', or at least change what we see of it. The decisions might have been His, but the information on which the decisions were based was presented and controlled by the few people surrounding him, and as for the decisions themselves, if they didn't fit with the wishes of those in power, those decisions were sometimes disregarded, distorted, postponed, even denied.

It is often debated as to 'What was Osho's responsibility in all that?' Certainly he was not in the role that we, his disciples projected upon him, like the Christian/Jewish god-the-father managing everything from above. Certainly he knew about many things, probably some things he didn't know, certainly he poked and provoked and pushed disciples on both sides of the imaginary fences to act out and expose whatever neurotic tendencies were there in their unconscious minds.

I don't resent that. In my humble opinion, that's his work, to expose what is hidden within, to unmask and bring what is in the darkness of the unconscious into the light. The process of unmasking is a process of healing that is often shocking, irritating, affrontive. It's not 'nice'. He is not your uncle.

Eastern Spiritual Masters often use methods which are shocking and unbelievable to modern Westerners ensconced and barricaded in their ego-territory with psychological barbed-wire electronic fences up and running, and lawsuits as their weapon of revenge. Many Zen Masters slap disciples, one even cut off a disciple's finger. One in particular, Ma Tzu, had an unusually large number of enlightened disciples. He would walk around on all fours, and was utterly unpredictable, sometimes jumping out of windows to land on unsuspecting disciples walking by outside! As they lay stunned on the ground, he would shout in their faces, "Do you GET it??!" George Gurdjieff would shout out "STOP!" at unforeseen moments in his commune, and all would have to freeze exactly in the position they were in, whatever they were doing, come what may. In his 'Stop' exercise, one disciple of his narrowly missed death, as the trench the disciple was digging filled in with water as he remained frozen in the attitude of 'Stop' until he was nearly drowned.

Tilopa, the Tibetan Master who spoke the Song of Mahamudra quoted in this book, would put his disciple Naropa to extreme tests of faith and trust before delivering that historic message, even to the point of walking on the back of Naropa , who was face down in the mud while the Master crossed a stream. And in a similar way, Marpa, the disciple of Naropa, had his own disciple Milarepa labor for years; building, destroying and rebuilding a tall stone tower 7 times, until Milarepa was covered with bruises and infected, bleeding cuts from carrying the rocks on his back incessantly.

In a similar way, Osho would constantly create situations to shock the ego and stop the mind. He could do that with individuals, he could do that with the whole commune, he could do that with the whole country. Just the fact of having 93 Rolls Royces was enough to shock the religious beliefs of at least every Christian in America, and while their mouths popped open and they were paying attention, he would 'toss in a few pills of truth', in his own words, and talk about the Politicians and Priests being the Mafia of the Soul. People in America were expecting a spiritual master to act like Gandhi or Jesus Christ, living in poverty and half-starvation, and Osho was not at all about to fulfill those fantasies. It is not in the nature of a Master's job to be liked. Historical examples of the social reaction to the unpleasant irritation to the status quo, both personal and collective, done by living Masters has been brutal throughout history: Socrates and Buddha were poisoned, Jesus was crucified, Mansoor beheaded, Jan Hus burned at the stake, to name a few.

It was a big assumption and projection on my part, to think that He knew everything about everything, and just what He said to do was all that we needed to know and all we needed to do. He was not in any way here to fulfill the projection of an omnipotent god or prophet or pope. He himself made that very clear, many times, in his discourses. But why were so many people projecting that role onto him? Because there was a very real energetic presence surrounding him, which could be described and felt by many as 'Divine'. There was a constant energy flowing from him, a constant vibration, that something in me interprets as 'Divine'. But that has nothing to do with an omniscient old guy up in the sky who knows everything and keeps track of everybody. That is a corrupted data bank from childhood fairy tales about 'God the Father' in Christianity and Judaism. Osho was and is a channel for Source Energy, life force; something that when one is in his presence, it naturally evokes in me and in many people a feeling of veneration, of adoration, and deep respect. But he was also a person, with a personality. A very amazing personality, very charismatic, super-intelligent and multi-dimensional, but with his own propensities, likes, dislikes, and all that goes with being in this bio-computer spacesuit that we call 'A human body'. He always called himself 'Just an ordinary man'. This became very evident, when in the last two months of the commune in the USA much information came forth that put light on the situation we had all been in, in a new and shocking way, revealing that many courses of action taken by Sheela and her government were in fact not within Osho's knowledge nor sanction, and in fact were directed against him, including plans to kill him.

In a certain way, during the first 3 years of the Ranch, I was in a kind of dream that he knew about everything that was going on, and therefore I was trusting and believing that somehow it must be playing out in the way he intends. It wasn't until very late in the game during the last year of the Ranch that I realized it was not so. It became slowly and painfully apparent that a collection of people, money and energy so large as the commune in the USA came to be, is a very complicated situation, and no matter how well-intentioned, any outcome is possible. A charismatic being like Osho is a magnet for every type of personality from the angelic to the demonic, a kind of hospital where people come to be healed from their spiritual afflictions. The people who are attracted to wealth and power in their 'normal' lives, in such situations as the commune made possible, gravitate to those positions in the hierarchy, and thrive in them, and exploit them. The situation was set up in such a way, as a centralized organization of a dictatorial format, in my opinion because Osho trusted greatly in the people around him, perhaps more than those individuals merited. That was the nature of his trust and love, which tended to pull one upwards: it gave you the feeling to be the best you can be, to live up to that trust. But not always, and not everyone followed that impulse to rise. That trust which he gave implicitly left much of the decision-making in their hands, which in hindsight, became a self-destructive force for the commune. But nothing is made to last forever, and this was especially true about the commune of the Master.

Most of my time spent living in the commune was beautiful, deep, and transformative. Some of it was incredibly painful, irritating, and frictional. But that pain I felt was in direct proportion to the attachment I had to certain aspects of my personality which in fact were very limiting to me. My mind was being peeled away like the layers of an onion. Often, that hurts. The situations were what they were, neither good nor bad. They were, simply neutral. The way that I reacted or responded to them was the source of my pain and my happiness.

Our situation in the commune was curiously parallel to the situation of whole populations being lived out right here and right now in our world, in 2018. 'We', as the rank and file in the commune, had as little knowledge about what our 'employers' and 'governors' were doing, as the rank and file American has little or no knowledge of the hidden and dark doings of the corporate military-industrial complex of America in 2018.

The 'government' as it was for us at the Ranch, the gang of 20 that was in positions of power in our city of 5000 at the time, was using the situation of the energy-field of a living Master, fueled and paid for by the devotion of thousands of sincere people, to fulfill its own ends. Those ends grew increasing egoistic and political and irrational, as the nature of power is to reveal more and more the corruption hidden in the unconscious of the person wielding the power. And in Rajneeshpuram, the power of the administrators being very nearly total, so too was the corruption.

That was evident in Sheela's bugging of Osho's room and her plans to poison him, and eliminate or neutralize the people closest to him. Our 'society' began as an idealistic attempt at a new way of living, in a way like America at the time of its revolution, and then that society so idealistically created and conceived devolved through the accumulation of power and wealth by those who are not the participants in that idealism, but are merely the administrators on the material plane, having a different private agenda themselves. They have in their hands the means to control and use the energy and economic resources of the population. At the Ranch, the whole society living in a kind of bubble of its own, one could catch glimpses from beginning to end of this shadow-play in its entirety, this reflection of the human collective. The whole picture was hidden from our eyes by layers of mis-information, with each person playing his tiny role in the puzzle and no-one having the whole picture until the curtain fell at nearly the end of the drama.

In our case, it was our collective dream as a community that we were creating a new utopia. I don't think that was Osho's intention in the least. It is an impossible assumption for me to say what WAS his intention, but in my limited perception and understanding of his work, I believe his purpose in having the commune was to mirror to us who we really are, in all our glory and disgrace, the full inheritance of our collective past hidden in our unconscious, brought forth in 3-d into the light of day. That is the process of transformation and healing, to unveil and see clearly what is. And that it did, brilliantly.

The commune was not an escape from the ills of society, nor a utopian solution to world problems, but rather a reflection, of our collective interior state of affairs, projected onto exterior events, our own personal creation as a group of human beings on this Planet Earth in this day and age, with all the inheritances of the full past of humanity.

It is hypocritical to label Rajneeshpuram as a 'bed of terrorism', as the inept attempts at harmful actions by the fascist gang in power were largely failures. What harm they did or tried to do to the outside world, they also did to us in the community, the poisonings, the attempts to kill, the lies and manipulations and illegal wiretapping. Almost the entire population of the commune was AGAINST those people, and victimized by them, and extremely happy that they left. In comparison, every day of the week there are people murdered by drones, secret prisons, and clandestine assassinations masked as 'suicides' by the state of terror that maintains the powers that be at this time, through the work of the CIA, the NSA, Homeland Security, economic hit-men, all arms and legs of the same Deep State apparatus which poses as a democracy. In a similar way, and yet greatly multiplied, these actions are not known or condoned by the general population, and yet they are happening constantly.

The structure of the world governments we now live under is a real 'terrorist cult', exponentially bigger by leaps and bounds. The society in which we live, the human population of the earth in 2018, is a Pathocracy, just as it was at the Ranch, in a much smaller way. What we saw there in a miniature format is a huge 'reality' blanketing the entire earth. It is a society largely unconscious and blind to the fact that it is being ruled by an elite group of psychopaths who have no qualms whatsoever about acting only in their own interests, without regard for the collective life of all the rest of humanity, or the continuation of the planet, for that matter.

A considerable percentage of the people we meet on the street are people who are empty inside, that is, they are actually already dead. It is fortunate for us that we do not see and do not know it. If we knew what a number of people are actually dead and what a number of these dead people govern our lives, we should go mad with horror."

G.I. Gurdjieff

George Gurdjieff on arrival in New York, c. 1927

Of the 'collective past' that we inherit, and that which was the basis of the drama in Rajneeshpuram: one of the principal aspects of that collective past is abdication of responsibility, decision-making power, into the hands of 'rulers'. It's never worked, and it didn't work then. The Ranch was a great example of that for me. We as a body of individuals were certainly letting others do our thinking and choosing for us, in the guise of Sheela and her people. And the results were predictable. I personally did not go there to find a paradise that would last forever, or that would change the world. I went there to be close to a person, Osho, whom I knew was on a level of being, Spirit, awareness, and reality, much higher than me. And I accepted that the price of being near him was to watch and participate in the whole show, the whole commune affair, with all the joys, irritations, expansions, mutations and insults entailed in that. Most of the time, it was incredibly fun, meaningful and transformative, taking me to a state of expanded love, compassion, and joy. Sometimes, it was oppressive and heavy. But I got to see it, the whole process of it, face to face, from beautiful dreamy beginning to tearful bittersweet end. I consider that to be a great gift, a crash course in LIFE as it were, which put me in touch with tremendous resources and possibilities of transformation which I never knew I had. For that, I can only feel gratitude. In my years in the commune, in those magic moments of Darshan with Him, many, many times He took us, existentially speaking, to states of being where our perceptions changed to an unimaginable new level. We experienced altered states of heightened awareness, unconditional love, oneness; what William James called 'The Oceanic Experience', without drugs of any kind.

We as modern human beings, have within us the collective dream in our psyche that we normally call 'love'. It appears to us as the highest reality, the biggest desire. But what we actually experience as 'love' is mostly a set of expectations, possessiveness, jealousy, obsession, and desire, all emotions rooted in fear. We think this is the 'heart' because it seems so real, convincing, and powerful. But rather than being the 'love' that we dream it is, it is memories from our past experiences, triggered by present events, supported by a few hundred years of romantic plays, books, movies and fairy-tales. All these 'dreams' of love surround us like a shell, a suit of armor, a body of emotions rooted in memories, beliefs and attitudes formed when very young, by all we have heard, and watched, and experienced, before we had conscious minds. When this 'heart' is broken, many times, the shell crumbles, and we can experience the real 'heart', which is silent, present, immutable, open, and capable of true unconditional love. In the commune, my heart was broken thousands of times, all the dreams of romantic love, all the likes, dislikes, cravings and loathings which I would project on the thousands of people surrounding me, all the millions of ways that my self-image was created and maintained, slowly ground away by the Master's love and the thousands of beautiful and irritating reflections all around me; the hall-of-mirrors that is the energy field of a living Buddha. And more than anything else, that energy-field in his presence was an experiment and an opportunity to experience a deeper dimension of love, a love that flows from the being, not dependent on an object or a relationship outside.

If I look back on it with 20/20 hindsight, in the 4 years at the ranch instead of doing carpentry 12-16 hours a day 7 days a week until my body simply fell apart; if I had spent that time doing silent meditation, I perhaps would be a different person now, but that is empty conjecture and impossible to know. The fact is, it was those years of working in the commune that prepared me for the real search, and the real journey within. It gave me a ground of being to begin from. One can say perhaps that much of what happened in the commune or around Osho created more and more dependence on Him, but that was a subjective and individual experience, it wasn't necessarily so. If you wanted to be dependent, you could certainly focus that on him, and eventually when he left his body, when his body died, one can be left with a great emptiness. One can try to fill that with dependence on the commune, but the 'commune' just becomes another kind of religion, a fixed structure that limits perception. The real alternative is relying on your own being more and more and freeing yourself from your own past, your 'self', the description of our world and our beliefs which we identify with. Abandoning this description is what the path to freedom is all about. That is a choice that each person makes for themselves. Osho's emphasis, in my understanding from everything he ever said to me, was to take responsibility for my own life, and that emphasis was paradoxically there even in the midst of apparent total control, during the worst days of the Sheela totalitarianism.

When He left his body behind, for me the emptiness wasn't an emptiness, it was a dimension change. It was no more being inundated with his energy visibly in front of me in one physical place emanating from a single human entity, but it was still available. But to experience it, I have to take a step in that direction, make myself available to it.

But the strange paradox is, without having DONE all that, without having been with Him all those years and having had my buffer systems ground away, in difficult and extreme situations of daily life, in the rain and snow and heat and beauty, slowly, arduously, I wouldn't KNOW the way to Zen, Toltec, Tantra, or shamanism, I wouldn't know how to see the truth or falsehood in it, and experiment with it, and learn from it. I wouldn't have had the courage and emptiness to be ready to learn. So for that, I can only be grateful for all those years, all those nails and sweat and insults and marble dust, all those days and nights and petty tyrants and impossible situations and joys and lovers and friends, which gave me a place in this world which I never had before, a foundation in my own being, which enabled me to go on searching after the Master's physical departure, and the mutation of the commune as such.

The ashram that for years grew up around Osho was changed beyond recognition in Poona after the death of his body. It became rather than a 'spiritual ashram', a kind of 'resort': more and more functioning like any other corporation, and that which was Osho's wild flame of rebellion expanded outward with the departing people who loved him all over the world, like seeds spreading in the wind. I personally wished that the ashram could have stayed a place where his energy would have been pooled, concentrated, and deepened, something like the ancient Buddhist University of Nalanda, where the energy field of the Buddha continued to flourish and deepen for several centuries after his departure. This was my hope. But that is just my personal idea, of which the universe is under no obligation whatsoever to fulfill. In the larger wisdom of existence, whose designs are unfathomable, that didn't happen, and the life of the ashram took a different direction. The people in positions of administrative power in the Poona ashram did to a large extent push away those who had been with Osho for years and represented conflicting opinions or trends, and this served to change the atmosphere into one more apparently manageable and 'palatable' to Western tourists. It became a place with much less Indians, more homogenized and less devotional; taking down Osho's pictures everywhere, building swimming pools and tennis courts, and making a lot more money for themselves, as all corporations do. There has been lots of 'beautification' of the physical premises, apparently making the whole package all the more 'acceptable' to newcomers from the West with lots of cash in their pockets coming for a two-week holiday, who can pay the very high entrance fees and the rent and the ever-higher group prices, and not ask a lot of questions about things changing. And those people who go there in large part enjoy greatly being there, it suits them and their expectations, and it still serves as a center of transformation, although less explosively and intensely than before. The love and devotion was a tangible quality when Osho was there in His body, and for some years after. That quality did change, and is no more the way it was at that time, as the management has made many efforts to limit expressions of devotion for the Master now in the physical premises of the ashram. The why and wherefore of this is a great mystery to those of us who did live with Him for many years. It seems paradoxical to forbid devotion to a Being in the very place where people come from all over the world exactly to feel that very presence of that Sacred Being and drink that vibration which was engrained into the very stones surrounding Him for many years, as He made very clear to all of us when He spoke of the mystical qualities of marble and the energy field of a Buddha, in discourses, many times. Mysteriously as well, probably the people who changed the commune as such, see themselves as right and good and sincere, following what they believe to be Osho's 'Vision', with of course no input from the thousands upon thousands of other devotees who risked everything to be with Him in the years he was in a body.

So, in this, what is right and what is wrong? Things are just what they are, and our interpretations color them in darkness or light: perhaps it is an unavoidable aspect of human mind, as the living flame of the Master after his physical departure is structured and established into an organized religion. Perhaps it was the compassion of the Master to set it all up that way, although He was never in favor of high entry fees, knowing how it would limit the participation of those of his devotees and seekers who are not wealthy. His express wish was that the commune would be a place where all would be welcome to share and participate with their creativity. As such, given the restrictions put in place in the ashram, the rest of us spread all over the world, without the nearby dominance and limitations of those 'in positions of power', although they have extensively tried to put up roadblocks and hindrances to the use of His name and words, through copyright lawsuits.

I personally don't believe a Master's legacy can be copyrighted. It is the inheritance of humanity, more precious than any ancient monuments or cultural patrimony, and should be open-sourced, given the crisis of understanding and direction that humanity now finds itself in. Ownership is limitation. I do not choose to engage in that battle over who owns Osho's work. In truth, The Universe owns it. When He himself very tangibly spread into all his people and the existence itself and expressly stated he would do that, how can that Wind be owned and trademarked? That is an insult to his intention.

As for myself, I learned from Him rather than trying to fight the darkness, it's better to light a small candle. And so, I keep singing, playing my flute, and making statues for temples on various continents, and exploring ancient pyramids from pre-history. I sometimes wonder if things could have been different for His work, if He had had more time, and there had not been his crucifixion in the USA. I do not know why he embraced that drama. Perhaps the time ran out sooner than he envisioned, perhaps other forces intervened, or perhaps he knew and was flowing with the will of the WHOLE all along. Perhaps the crucifixion/poisoning of his body was a fait accompli, written in destiny, in front of which he put himself in a position to meet it head-on in a warrior's attitude, as he never was one to take a victim's role in anything. He masterfully managed the end of the Ranch in such a way that none of us were killed. That was a miracle, in every sense of the word. Just a look at what happened to the Branch Dravidians in Waco, or the MOVE Family in Philadelphia, a couple of years later, will underline that fact. An alternative religious community in Waco, Texas, was burned to the ground by the FBI as live news carried the feed, and more than 70 people died. In Philadelphia, the MOVE Family was cordoned off by the police and firebombed, destroying several city blocks: more bodies, many of them children. Both of these were situations where a small alternative community with different religious views than the mainstream presented itself as unwilling to be trampled under the threat of violent lethal force that the state holds as its trump card, always. Thumb your nose at that, and you will be crushed, in America. And if there is a body count, it's just 'collateral damage'. We escaped that fate, by a masterful playing of the cards in Osho's hands. When he left on the plane to be arrested that night, it was drawing the heat away from the commune, and letting himself be taken, instead of having a shoot-out at the Ranch which would have been just another of Ronald Reagan's bloodbaths.

I accept now that I will never know the answers to these questions, the 'why and wherefore' of it all; the universe is an unfathomable mystery, and we, small grains of sand that we are, are just as mysterious.

In his presence I found out what is trust, and that life is much, much more than what I grew up believing it to be: that the mind is not truth, that the 'divine' is not just a word, but a Reality, it is the REALLY REAL. It is available here and now, inside one's own being. I could never thank him enough for showing me the heaven and hell of life-on-earth, and giving me the opportunity to live many, many lives in the space of this one. He did not take me with him, of course, even figuratively speaking. My problems are my problems, to face and resolve or not. I could not steal his enlightenment, nor could he give it to me. But whatever could be given, he showered it on me. And, what happens to me now is my responsibility. And that's right and good that it is that way.

In the atmosphere of the commune, there was a great emphasis put on 'enlightenment'. It became the ultimate desire, an obsession for some. After Osho's demise, many therapists, teachers, and disciples, began to claim enlightenment for altered consciousness experiences that they have and they assume that it is 'enlightenment', and that now they have reached it and they can relax. And coincidentally, now they can get a lot more people into their therapy groups and satsangs!

In the world of Zen, there is an understanding born of centuries of experience that has not yet come to the West, and that is that there are stages, confirmatory signs on the 'path'. There are experiences which come to the meditator which seem like 'enlightenment': no-mind. They last for a brief time, and go away. These are called 'mini-satoris'. Other more deep happenings occur, states of no-mind, unconditional love which remain longer, and reflect a more deeper understanding on the part of the seeker. These are called 'satori'. But even those are not 'Enlightenment' as such. That is something which is known since ancient times in India as 'Samadhi'; a state which does not go away. It is 'Nirvana'; the blowing out of the candle.

The 'I' never gets enlightened, because enlightenment, Samadhi, means the cessation of the 'I'. So how can someone claim to be enlightened? The 'I' that makes the claim is the very barrier to the happening.

Even in enlightenment, Life, and learning never stops. There isn't a 'payoff'. There is just life, awareness, a constant growing. In this universe, that which is not growing or transforming is dying. There is no steady-state. Yes, Enlightenment is a qualitatively different state of consciousness, it does happen. But Enlightened people make mistakes, and learn from them. They are not omnipotent Jehovahs, or popes, handing down decrees to be blindly accepted. They are people, helping other people, from a different perspective, a lot more clarity, a lot more love, but also with a hardness of compassion which can appear as ruthlessness if you happen to be holding on tightly to your petty territory of the ego.

But, although they are 'beyond the mind', to communicate

they use the mind. It's an operating system of a computer that they speak through. It's the interface for a consciousness to communicate with other humans. A Master revises it, upgrades it, changes things from time to time. He is working in a 'laboratory' of consciousness. He takes in information, processes it, sees its effect, and sometimes changes his position. Sometimes information given to Him is distorted, corrupted, or withheld by others. Hence, sometimes decisions and actions of Enlightened beings don't work out like we might expect. That's not something to resent, like a child feeling, "Daddy let me down". That's just part of the game of life on earth, manifestations of divine oneness in a universe based in duality.

Human beings are travelers of the dark sea of awareness, and this Earth is but a station on their journey; for extraneous reasons the travelers had interrupted their voyage. Human beings are caught in a sort of eddy, a current that goes in circles, giving them the impression of moving while they are, in essence, stationary. Sorcerers are the only opponents of whatever force keeps human beings prisoners, and that by means of their discipline sorcerers break loose from its grip and continue their journey of awareness.

Don Juan as quoted by Carlos Castaneda

There is a way of working with the mind to approach Spirit, from ancient Mexico, Peru, ancient India, Tibet, ancient Hawaii, from the 'People of the One' all over the world, long before the Spanish Conquistadors or Aztecs, or Romans or Greeks, Egyptians or even Sumerians. It's a practical way of understanding and experiencing non-ordinary reality and freedom, through silent knowledge rather than analyses and linear thought. It is the core of many real spiritual paths all over the world. In this teaching the only freedom actually possible is to free yourself from the structure of beliefs and ideas that we have, that we call

485

'the mind'. It is that which surrounds us like a cage, determining all our perceptions and behavior. This mind is not a natural emanation of our evolution. It is a planted mechanism in us which limits us and keeps us enslaved. It was downloaded into us, it is not part of our being. It is not part of our nature. In my understanding, this was Osho's real teaching as well.

We humans, inside or outside the community of seekers of truth, although we are at times caught in and identified with the waves of political games and struggles over 'ownership', are not merely the subjects and victims of corporate intrigues and power struggles. Although these things affect us in the mundane sense and seem to create suffering, they are not the source of our happiness or unhappiness. Events are neutral; we interpret them according to our filter systems, and react to our own dramatic interpretations. We, in fact, are limitless magical entities full of unknown possibilities, and actually exist apart from it all. Freedom is within, in leaving behind all 'this and that', and dwelling in the eternal. The Master's guidance at times was to shake us loose from all this and that, have a good laugh at it, and rest in the silence within; AND to live the Lion's Roar of Truth, and if need be, rebellion to the status quo. He was never one to turn away from exposing hypocrisy on this third dimension, and pointing out the absurd lies fostered by those who wear the clothes of authority, religious or political, no matter who they were or what the consequences would be for speaking the truth in the face of those lies.

Regardless of my feelings about the structures of communes as such, the actions taken by Osho are not a subject of judgement for me. I learned a long time ago that the lower cannot judge the higher, and Osho is a Being of freedom who flies on such a high route, we here walking or crawling on the earth can only interpret his actions in the light of our own very limited ideas. In a time on this earth where the great mass of humans are mentally controlled and enslaved through intentional misinformation, and life for misfits is wrought with isolation, misunderstanding and danger, He took me to a place within myself where I could have never gotten on my own, at least not in one lifetime, or even several. It is a place where I became ready to open my eyes and look at things in a different way. The fact was, he was working with a great mass and variety of people, and in his own words, the raw material was of very poor quality. Humanity has become very degraded in the sense of commitment to the spiritual search. Now, even to get someone to not pay attention to their smart phone for 5 minutes is a great achievement, and to get thousands of people to wake up, to come out of their mind dreams and sleep even in a little way was a monumental effort, like breaking rocks with jackhammers. The situations of the commune and the encounter groups and all the petty tyrants and upheavals and physical labor and power games was a jackhammer, and it served its purpose, it broke through the asphalt of my conditionings and left me in a far more neutral position, more open, more vulnerable. And then? Hold the jackhammer in the hand for the remainder of one's life, blessing it or cursing the fact that you once were hammered? That's an individual choice, and it seems to me a loss of energy; and it has very little to do with the events that transpired.

"What is Osho's teaching?, you might ask" He could speak about any spiritual path, and when he spoke on it, it seemed like he WAS that, it was his totality and deep understanding. Zen, Vedanta, Tao, Yoga, Bhakta, Sufi, Mystic Christianity, Hassidism, all the various mystic traditions in human consciousness, he seemed to be that when he was talking about that subject. In his personality, he appeared to me as the personification of Krishna, the beautiful and playful avatar and trickster of the Mahabharata and the Gita, who was willing to use any device, any situation, to save a light in the world and help it grow.

But, through all the years of being with Him, if I must call him one thing, I would call him a Tantric Master, because that was the way he worked. Not Tantra as it is understood today in the pop-spiritual culture, a kind of super-enjoyment of sexuality; but the real roots of Tantra, which is a very ancient teaching, of acceptance and embrace of duality, and through acceptance, transcendence. The lotus doesn't avoid the mud; it grows upwards through it, with awareness. You don't avoid experiences of life; you live them, totally, fully, and in so doing, grow beyond them. You don't avoid or 'spiritualize' emotions, denying them by covering them up with 'positive thoughts'. You feel them, and learn what lessons they reveal. Nothing is rejected. All is absorbed, the good and the bad as well, and in the end, it is an enrichment and fulfillment which ultimately flowers as 'enlightenment'.

Tantra is not a path for the faint-hearted. It has its dangers. It is not just good, not just bad. It is everything. All the joys, pains, sorrows and ecstasies of life are included in it. It was not a path where you could say, "Please, Osho, give me your bliss and save me from my own mind", it was not that at all. Osho's teaching was to know, understand and accept the mind, the emotions, the feelings, the passions, the whole nature, all the inner conflicts and turmoils and contradictory desires that we find ourselves with as modern humans, avoiding NOTHING. With awareness, one can understand and absorb the energy locked up in every behavior pattern, every attachment and game and strategy that maintains the mind as it is.

One of the dangers and pitfalls of this path is indulgence. Many traditions have taught seekers to avoid sex, because of this. To avoid the danger, they avoid the temptation. Thus has grown a lopsided spirituality, which denies a huge part of human experience and the most natural doorway to no-mind, which is the orgasmic experience itself. From that denial has arisen all kinds of perversions: suppression of the natural inevitably becomes a twisted energy. The signs of this are everywhere now;

the pedophilia of Catholic priests being one example, pornography is another; fetishism, sado-masochism, sexual abuse, violence towards women, even the abuse of nature itself, the rape and destruction of the environment, all come from a denial of the natural in the futile hope of rising beyond by avoiding the downward. The perverse and greedy quest for money far beyond need which is the root cause of the suicidal destruction of our beautiful planet at the present time, is in itself an expression of this suppression of orgasmic experience. Lacking the possibility of true union with the cosmos, the mind seeks control instead through accumulation of money. It is a false value supplanting the real possibility of happiness and union.

But in truth, that suppression of natural sexuality was a handle to control people. The strategy is simple; block the natural energy of sex, make people weak and guilty, put them in conflict with their own bodies, and they easily can be enslaved. It worked very well for the powers that have been, for a long time. Just look at the mess humanity is in right now, the separation between body and spirit, material and spiritual, man and woman, thinking and feeling; sex as mutual use/abuse. Human beings are split in every dimension of their lives.

Osho was introducing to a world which had very little interest in hearing it, a new/old teaching: don't avoid or deny who you are. Celebrate it! Experience fully: without guilt, but with awareness. Be all that you are; like a child playing with toys, and in the playing, the child outgrows the toy. It's the same with sex, anger, greed, lust for power: they are toys that humans play with. The danger is of getting stuck there, and in so doing, forgetting the real onward journey, and taking the toy as being the goal. Awareness is the essential key: witnessing every act, every thought, every emotion, every feeling: Just being a watcher, neutrally observing whatever passes in the river of attention, not a doer. Even in the MIDST OF ACTION, one can 'break the yoke', as Tilopa said so long ago. It's not the yoke of an egg; it's the yoke of a plough that he referred to, a plough that every human is dragging, like an ox plodding face down through the thick mud. That is human mind.

An ancient source of these teachings is the Vigyana Bhairava Tantra, sutras spoken by Shiva to his consort Parvati, describing 108 methods of meditation. It is thousands of years old, and as new as the dew on the morning grass. Because it is directly addressing the real nature of human mind, it does not become old.

One of the simplest and most beautiful of these sutras is: 'Devotion *frees*'. That is one of the crucial sutras of Shiva. And what is devotion? Surrender of the mind, will, ego, private destiny, to the ALL. First, you surrender to the Master, as an embodiment of truth. That's just the beginning practice, the first stage, the first step. It's easier that way, because his being and energy is so beautiful, you open a little bit the steel suit of ego armor surrounding you, and you let in a little sunshine. But that's not the end: that opens the door to the real surrender, to the existence, to every moment of your life as being the guru, as LIFE itself is the Master.

My years at the Ranch were a kind of boot-camp in surrender. I 'did' it, but I kept my will as my own. I accepted the situation, like a necessary but unwanted bargain that I had to agree to in order to be near Him.

I couldn't really embrace the idea of 'surrender' to all the petty tyrants and power trippers and power games that went on in the commune. But I wanted to be near Him, this I accepted, I let myself do it, but 'I' was still there, biding my time.

When I was with Osho back in India after the demise of the Ranch in Oregon and the 'World Tour', there was no more commune between me and Him. I was near Him, in fact I couldn't have been nearer physically, and this time my reasons for resistance dissolved. I was a hard rock to break, but he was very persistent. Sometimes he used marble rocks, and sometimes he just melted me in the music of his love. The real surrender happened when my own will melted, and I gave up any ideas about spiritual search, attainment, private destiny. Paradoxically, that's when I became open to Him, in a new way, and the journey began on a deeper level. The journey goes on. It was through his beneficence to me, and the HUGE LOVE that poured from him, that I came to realize Osho is a door, and a mirror. It's not that one has to find HIM. He is that finger pointing to the moon, and the moon that I was looking for, ultimately, was my own Being, my connection to the Infinite, the Divinity, that silent shining void within. Seeking outward for the Master is also seeking outward. The real search is for that silent being, deep inside, that every one of us is, in reality.

I left the commune, now translocated back to India, in 1991. Although I continued to visit for 2-4 months a year until 1997, I never felt again that it was my home. The feeling to go back to India, that inner call which once was so strong within me, faded with the changes in the ashram structure and attitude, and its way of disseminating Osho's work.

That in no way means that I feel Osho's work has stopped, or that I have stopped participating in that. On the contrary, it is growing regardless of the limitations that the 'management' has tried to put on it, and his message is spreading, as well as his meditations. His insights find their way into the mainstream of collective wisdom, and he is often quoted, although usually without mention of his name, in places as diverse and varied as Oprah Winfrey, Deepak Chopra, Sting, Lady GaGa and many others, and his energetic presence in the field of human transformation is constant and visible. He is constantly present in every note of music I have ever played in public, and I acknowledge that with neither shame nor pride, it is simply a fact. I was digging blindly in mud, deep mud, and He showed me where to look to find diamonds. The diamonds I found are in me, and I am utterly grateful to him for that.

In the 28 years that have passed since Osho left his body behind, my life became a constant journey. I have played solo concerts on 4 continents, in Berlin, Milan, Prague, Amsterdam, Tokyo, Kyoto, and nameless numberless other cities. Those concerts had audiences from 20 people to 3000 people, and everything in between. I played many times in front of the cold vacant staring eye of television cameras, and sometimes there was many millions of people watching my 'controlled folly', albeit they were far and distant and unknown to me. It wasn't my fate or particular desire to be famous, and at times I wondered if that was a curse or a blessing. I am glad if my music and art has given some joy and peace to a few other human beings, even if it is relatively just a few, to help pass our brief sojourn on this mysterious spinning ball of molten iron and stardust which we call planet Earth.

There is one aspect of playing concerts which always amazes me. That is, once the concert is finished, and the crowd disperses, and the instruments are packed away, and the music has faded away like echoes in the distance, it all seems like it was just a beautiful dream, and nothing more. So it is too, with the life. Now, at this date, 57 years after my 'search' began at age 6, it appears to me that the entire course of my life is a dream which I dreamed, and nothing more. But, what a dream it has been!

CHAPTER 42

Teotihuacan

Sorcery is a journey of return.
We return victorious to the spirit,
having descended into hell.
And from hell we bring trophies.
Understanding is one of our trophies.

Don Juan

"There are a thousand things which prevent a man from awakening, which keep him in the power of his dreams. In order to act consciously with the intention of awakening, it is necessary to know the nature of the forces which keep man in a state of sleep. First of all it must be realized that the sleep in which man exists is not normal but hypnotic sleep. Man is hypnotized and this hypnotic state is continually maintained and strengthened in him. One would think that there are forces for whom it is useful and profitable to keep man in a hypnotic state and prevent him from seeing the truth and understanding his position."

G. I. Gurdjieff

As I write this, I am in Teotihuacan, an ancient city of pyramids 50 km. outside of Mexico City. It is a mysterious and stupendous place of ancient pyramids, set in a semi-arid plateau of Jacaranda and Pepper trees and Nopal cactus. I spend my days, from sunrise to sunset, at the Plaza of the Moon, at the northern end of the Avenue of the Dead. It is a broad avenue more than a mile long, lined with pyramids and temples. Some of the pyramids are as big as those on the Giza plateau in Egypt, some of them are still half-covered in dust and vegetation which has veiled them in mystery and hidden them for centuries...or millennia.

The air is filled with the strange other-worldly sounds of clay flutes, playing melodies from a different time, in front of the temples and pyramids. The archeologists say these pyramids are 2,000 years old. The local inhabitants say they are more than 7,000 years old. The secret teachings of the Toltecs put them at more than 12,000 years. If that is true, it means they were functioning, practicing mystery schools co-existent with saber-tooth tigers and woolly mammoths. The teachings of this place were hidden and kept alive in several lineages of Toltec warriors stretching from that time until this day, an unbroken chain, stretching back 120 centuries. Those who lived here and once walked these streets had an understanding that freedom is 'freedom from the conditioned mind', and they experimented with powerful techniques that made that understanding a reality, for a whole population.

The entire population of the city disappeared en masse eons ago, and the Aztecs found the city empty when they arrived many centuries before the Spanish conquest. The Aztecs named the empty city 'Teotihuacan'; 'the place where men become gods'. The end of the plaza is filled with the Pyramid of the Moon, a colossal structure of volcanic stone rising in tiers hundreds of feet upward, millions of tons of stone. To each side of it there stands smaller pyramids, of equal size and height, 6 in all. In the center of the plaza is a plinth, where there was a 15-ton stone statue of the 'Mother Goddess'. It has been moved from the site, and now sits in the museum of anthropology in Mexico City, and its plinth remains empty in front of the Plaza of the Moon. In front of this plinth is a far more ancient stone, with rain and wind-worn markings of a statue of the Goddess of Water, imbued with an energy so tangible, palpable, vibrating with knowledge placed there by scientists of the soul, from a different time and age. It is a time capsule, with coded knowledge within. It can tell stories. It can open doors. As I touch it, I feel a mysterious connection with other times, other worlds...

On the sides of the pyramids still remain the vestiges of the white stucco that was frescoed in symbolic figures, brilliant colored serpents and jaguars and eagles, depictions of different states of consciousness, different stages on the path of awakening. The geometry of this plaza has an uncanny effect on me. I sit here all day long, sunrise to sunset, for a week. Each day I am filled with a silent knowing, a wordless teaching comes to me. An unspeakable joy fills me, as a door opens inside me to a higher place of light, and my questions are answered as they arise in my mind, wordlessly, in silence.

In the night, in the hotel a mile away, I DREAM. It is a state between sleeping and awake. I am present, but my mind is not, at least not the part of the mind that speaks words. I can see, I can remember, I can even interact with the dream, but I am not thinking, I am watching. I silently ask. I ask for the answers to my questions. I ask from my deepest heart's core.

As I dream inside the dream, I see the world before me at twilight: the desert, the pyramids, the town in the distance; Then, suddenly, there opens a crack between the 'worlds': a rift that splits the scene I am watching in two, like a veil parting in my inner vision, and there appears to me a dark-skinned woman wearing a simple white robe. Her eyes are deep black pools of light, her face is filled with wisdom and compassion, yet remains young and alive.

She says to me: "You may ask your question."

I ask her, "What happened? What happened here, that made

this tremendous school, this deep pool of knowledge, this ancient and sacred city of artists and mystics disappear?"

She spoke to me, wordlessly, I understood without hearing a sound. She said: "Long ago there was a great destruction on the earth, that reduced humanity to an almost animal state. This place was the new beginning of the world as you know it, the initial phase of a new age of humanity, the 5th age, called 'The 5th Sun', which has continued to this day. A new humanity was born, and developed, and the wisdom of how to live as a god in freedom was known, and practiced here. It was a happy time. But alongside with the knowledge, there grew a dark side: Those who, rather than seeking freedom, used their power to control others, to manipulate and dominate. Instead of mastering themselves, they sought through magic power to be the masters of slaves. A time came when the forces of light and the forces of darkness battled here. The Masters of Light saw it necessary to disappear, transport as a population into another dimension, where they still exist, and are available to help, if you know how to call them. The forces of darkness remained visible in the world, and became all those who manipulate through power, and live through the control of others: the Pharaohs, the Romans, the Greeks, the Aztecs, the Spanish Conquistadores, the Royal Families, the Holy Inquisition, the Nazis, the Robber Barons, the World Bank, The Illuminati, the Communist Party, the CIA, all the institutions of power and manipulation and control throughout history, originated from that split.

IT'S THE SAME PEOPLE, the same forces, with different faces, different masks. They are the Masters of Darkness. They live in illusion, which is maintained through the slavery and domination of others.

The Masters of Light, are the Masters of themselves. They live in freedom, and share love. They are here, and everywhere, but in a different dimension, available, for those who truly seek freedom.

Now is the beginning of a new time, the 6th Sun, a new cycle of humanity. You have the great fortune to be alive in this time, in this world, to see this great change take place, in your lifetime."

. With those words, she disappeared, and I awoke to the dawn of the new day.

The Dream in Teotihuacan

THE END

Appendix

Osho and the 16th Lama Karmapa.
The Preservation of the Tibetan Occult Sciences

In 1972, Swami Govind Siddharth, an Osho sannyasin, visited the Tibetan Lama Karmapa, who had fled from Tibet and who then lived in Darjeeling. When Siddharth arrived, accompanied by his wife and two young daughters, Karmapa's place was completely closed. He told, in an interview at the time, of his initial disappointment at not meeting the Karmapa. Then all of a sudden, one monk came running out to tell him that he was immediately wanted inside by His Holiness. He went in and was greeted by Karmapa as if he was expected there. Karmapa never even knew anything about him beforehand, as he had never made any appointment... he never knew anything about him except that he was dressed in the faded orange of early neo-sannyas.

(Of Larma Karmapa, it was said he was a 'Divine Incarnation', a Boddhisatva. In Tibet, they believe that whosoever attains to Buddhahood, and then by their own wishes are born again to help people in the world, they are divine incarnations — boddhisatvas. His Holiness was said to be the sixteenth incarnation of Dsum Khyenpa, the first Karmapa, who was born about 1110 AD.)

When Swami Siddharth first entered, the Karmapa immediately told him that he knew where he was from. He said, "I am seeing that you have somewhere some photograph or something which is printed on two sides, of your Master." Siddharth answered that he had nothing like that which is printed on two sides. He had completely forgotten about the locket hanging from his mala of Osho's photograph on both sides! There was an English woman who was acting as an interpreter, since the Lama Karmapa did not know English. She immediately saw his mala and said, "What is this?" He then remembered that the locket was printed on two sides and he said, "This is the photograph of my Master." She was curious to see it, so Siddharth took it off and showed it to her. "That is it." He took the locket of Osho in his hand and he touched it to his forehead and then said:"He is the greatest incarnation since Buddha in India — he is a living Buddha!" Karmapa went on to say, "You may be feeling that he is speaking for you, but it is not only for you that he speaks. Osho speaks for the Akashic records also, the records of events and words recorded on the astral planes. Whatever is spoken is not forgotten. That is why you will find that he goes on repeating things and you will feel that he is doing this for you, but, as a matter of fact, he speaks only for a few people. Only a few people realize who Osho is. His words will remain there in the Akashic records, so that they will also be helpful to people in the future."

Karmapa went on to say that Osho had been with Siddharth in past lives. "If you want to see one of Osho's previous incarnations — who he was in Tibet — you can go to Tibet and see his golden statue there which is preserved in the Hall of Incarnations." He continued to chat about Osho and his work, "My blessings are always there, and I know that whatever we are not going to be able to do to help others, Osho will do." He explained that one of the main aim of the Lamas in coming to India was to preserve their occult sciences. Osho from his side also confirmed this in his Kashmir lectures given in 1969. He said then, "The Dalai Lama has not escaped only to save himself, but to save the Tibetan religion, the meditation secrets and the occult sciences."

Karmapa carried on to explain, "We have gotten these things from India in the past, and now we want to return them back. Now we have come to know that here is an incarnation, Osho, who is doing our job in India and the world, and we are very happy about it. The world will know him, but only a few people will realise what he actually is. He will be the only person who can guide properly, who can be a World Teacher in this age, and he had taken birth only for this purpose."

All this still rings true today much as it did thirty years ago. (Reprinted from Sannyasnews.com)

35403837R00296

Printed in Poland
by Amazon Fulfillment
Poland Sp. z o.o., Wrocław